THE SOVIET POLITICAL MIND

Books by Robert C. Tucker

Philosophy and Myth in Karl Marx
The Soviet Political Mind, *Revised*
The Marxian Revolutionary Idea
    (*Edited*)
The Marx-Engels Reader

ROBERT C. TUCKER

THE SOVIET POLITICAL MIND

Stalinism and Post-Stalin Change

REVISED EDITION

W · W · NORTON & COMPANY · INC ·

NEW YORK

TO THE MEMORY OF MY FATHER

CONTENTS

PREFACE
TO THE REVISED EDITION

One of the fronts on which scholarship in Soviet studies advances is the analysis of social and political reality in the contemporary U.S.S.R. Another, which has received less attention perhaps than it deserves, is the reopening of older questions, and reconsideration of older answers, in the larger perspective that time brings and in the light of the new information that has come from Soviet sources, both official and unofficial, in the years since Stalin's death. In preparing the new edition of *The Soviet Political Mind,* I have added to it three studies that seek in their different ways to advance scholarship on this second front.

"The Dictator and Totalitarianism" inquires about the dictator as a personality type on the basis of what is now known of Stalin, Hitler, and others, and reexamines in this light the theoretical problem of the nature of totalitarianism. "Stalin, Bukharin, and History as Conspiracy" approaches this same problem from another angle; it reopens the case of the Moscow trials of the later 1930's, Bukharin's in particular, and the related larger issue of the meaning and motivations of Stalin's Great Purge. "Several Stalins" presents a critique of the literature of Stalin biography—primarily the images of Stalin in Trotsky, Carr, and Khrushchev—in terms of present knowledge. All three studies argue for revision of some widely held views on a number of topics, such as the dynamics of totalitarianism, the ability of aberrant personalities to gain power, the role of foreign policy in the Soviet purges of the 1930's, Bukharin's behavior in court, and Stalin's intellectuality.

Apart from the deletion of a chapter describing "Field Observations" on a trip to Russia in 1958, no other substantial alterations have been made in the book for this edition. I have pruned here and there, changed some tenses from present to past, and inserted a few references to later events. Since the original book was not a history of Soviet politics but rather a set of interpretations of Stalinism and the transition to the post-Stalin era, no narrative account of more recent political developments has been added.

One must of course recognize that political change has slowed its pace and in some respects gone into reverse in the time of Brezhnev and Kosygin. Nothing in this period, however, seems to me to have invalidated the underlying basic contention of these interpretations that the change caused by Stalin's death in Soviet politics and the whole Russian scene was not only real but critically significant. In 1971 as much as in 1963, that event looms as the watershed of recent Russian experience.

In closing the Introduction to the first edition, I quoted Yevtushenko's question—"But who will carry Stalin out of the heirs of Stalin?"—and suggested that the issue of Stalinism and the problem of overcoming Stalin's heritage remained a central one in Soviet Russia. Now, nearly eight years later, one could still say the same. But the extent to which Yevtushenko's may ultimately prove a generational question has become more apparent than it was then. No one, it seems, will "carry Stalin" out of those of his heirs who remain in power now; the hope for a fuller and far-reaching expunging of Stalinism from Russian life and Soviet politics awaits, among other things, the arrival in ascendancy of men who did not grow to maturity in Stalin's school of political life. The era of Brezhnev and Kosygin may, then, be a kind of hiatus in Soviet history between the dynamic reform leadership that Khrushchev tried in his uneven way to offer and the fresh affirmative momentum that Soviet political life takes on during the 1970's as new, younger, and more liberal political minds come at last to power. Let this, at any rate, be the hope that a Western well-wisher of the Russian people shares with members of its own critically thinking intelligentsia.

I am deeply indebted to my colleague Professor Stephen Cohen for generous help and advice in the preparation of this edition, and to Mr. James Mairs and Miss Emily Garlin of W. W. Norton & Company, Inc., for their valuable editorial assistance. My thanks go to Grosset and Dunlap Publishers for permission to reprint "Stalin, Bukharin, and History as Conspiracy," which originally appeared as the Introduction to *The Great Purge Trial* (ed. Robert Tucker and Stephen Cohen, New York, 1965); and to the editors of *World Politics* for permission to reprint "The Dictator and Totalitarianism" from the issue for July, 1965. Both studies were products of a year as a fellow of the Center for Advanced Study in the Behavioral Sciences at Stanford, of which I cherish a grateful memory.

Robert C. Tucker

Princeton, N.J.
April, 1971

PREFACE

These ten essays, which examine various aspects of government and politics in Russia, have a common purpose: the exploration of the mental world of Soviet politics—the patterns of thought, ways of perceiving the world, psychological attitudes, ideological premises, and working theories that in their entirety constitute the Soviet "political mind."

Some of the studies analyze the Soviet political mind as expressed in internal politics, some deal with the mind of Soviet foreign policy, and some range over both these fields and their interrelationship. Soviet political institutions also receive attention insofar as they, and the changes that have taken place within them, are expressions of the ruling philosophy of government. In the middle group of essays, the emphasis shifts to popular political attitudes and the state's endeavors to shape or reshape them by indoctrination and propaganda. The existence of a persistent and significant discrepancy between the political outlooks of the state and the citizen—of "official Russia" and "popular Russia"—is shown from various points of view.

The Soviet political mind as it appears here is not simply Soviet; in many ways it is a Russian political mind. The continuity amid change is apparent in the survival or revival of certain traditional Russian attitudes toward the state. Another line of continuity across the great divide of 1917 is the contribution made by Russian revolutionary Populism of the nineteenth century to Lenin's political thought, and hence to Bolshevism. Finally, considerable attention is given in this volume to a relatively less explored link with the Russian past: the resurrection during the Stalin period, in large part under the influence of Stalin himself, of some patterns of thought and policy, political values, and even institutional forms that were characteristic of Russian Czarism at certain times.

But notwithstanding its debts to the Russian past, the mind of the Soviet regime has been and remains a Communist political mind. That Communist ideology bulks large in the official outlook is not so much an argument of this book as a presupposition and recurring theme. The Communist system in all its varieties is an "ideological system of politics" in the sense that the ruling elite claims to be guided in all its policies and actions by the principles of Marxism-Leninism. So strong is this "theory bias" that even in the contemporary period, when men of essentially post-Revolutionary and practical mental stamp are gaining ascendancy in Soviet political life, words like "practicalism" and "pragmatism" remain epithets that a politician at whom they are aimed (Khrushchev, for example) must reject as inapplicable to himself.

But when all this has been acknowledged, we are still faced with the complex and delicate problem of the precise relationship between ideology and policy under the Soviet Communist system. This is one of the problems with which many of the essays in the present volume are concerned. Implicit in their treatment of the question is a warning against an uncritical "ideological determinism." By this I mean the view—which reproduces the official view just stated above—that Soviet policy is simply applied Marxism-Leninism. Such a view is a most unfortunate oversimplification. For if ideology influences Soviet policy via the minds of the policy-makers, it is also demonstrably true that policy influences ideology, that official interpretations of Marxism-Leninism develop and change in response to policy needs, political interests, and changes in the policy mind. This being so, we can view the ideological process in the Soviet system as a kind of "language of politics." We can study doctrinal evolution as an expression of the evolution of policy—and doctrinal controversy as a mirror, albeit a dark one, of conflict over policy. The methodology employed at many points in these essays rests on those assumptions.

A further general theme of this book, in many ways its major theme, is that the Soviet political mind is subject to change and evolution. It is true that one can trace lines of ideological continuity in Soviet Communism from Lenin to Khrushchev. There exists a Soviet political tradition that displays, as does any established political tradition, certain enduring patterns of thought, politics, and organization. Yet within the continuity, we find the inexorable law of change at work. Between the Soviet political mind in its Leninist phase and what may be called the Stalinist political mind there lies a gulf that is no less real for the fact that

Stalin never admitted its existence or even countenanced the use of the word "Stalinism." And despite the claim of the de-Stalinizing Soviet regime of Khrushchev that it is returning "to the path of Lenin," the dominant spirit in the present-day Soviet ruling elite is no ·longer that of Leninist revolutionism. On this count one must grant a certain validity to the Chinese Communist critique of Khrushchevian "revisionism."

The studies in this volume are thus directly concerned with what has been a principal concern of all Soviet studies in the West in the past decade: the problem of Soviet change. In broadest terms, their position may be described as one of affirmation of the reality and serious significance of change in Soviet policy since the death of Stalin. However, my main motive has not been to prove that this change is real, or to document its many manifestations, but rather to find and apply an explanation. The strategy of analysis has been to approach the problem of post-Stalin change through a study of Stalinism itself as a phenomenon of post-Lenin change. The result is a scheme of Soviet political development in which the concept "de-Stalinization" is defined by reference to its historical correlative, "Stalinization." Stalinism is viewed in this context as a special political formation and autocratic system of rule in which the psychopathological personality of Stalin was a powerful driving force. Accordingly, the death of Stalin is seen as a necessary prerequisite of post-Stalin change and, indeed, as the essential first act of "de-Stalinization."

In the essay on "The Stalin Heritage in Soviet Policy," I have attempted to put this thesis to the test through an analysis of the currents and crosscurrents in Soviet policy from 1945 to Stalin's death. In this final period of his reign, the dynamics of Stalinism turned conservative. Denying his nation the "new period" for which it had waited during World War II, Stalin in the aftermath of victory reimposed the pattern of Stalinism as usual—prewar austerity at home and cold war in foreign relations. It is true, as some Western scholars have suggested, that, especially from 1949 on, there were certain indications from Soviet quarters and elsewhere of a possible impending shift in or softening of the foreign-policy line. But it does not follow that the policy changes that began on the morrow of Stalin's death were the fruition of a new trend of policy that began under his own auspices toward the close of his life. Evidence adduced in the above-mentioned essay shows that in his final years, months, and even weeks, he fought against such a trend. He was engaged in a determined and desperate struggle against change, against forces within his own regime that were pressing for an international *détente* and realignment of policy. His last published work was in part a polemic against these forces. And his concluding policy act—the abortive case of the Kremlin doctors—was, as I have attempted to show, a calculated effort to demonstrate and dramatize the impossibility of *détente*, the necessity of steadfastly persevering in his cold war against the West.

In the concluding essay in this volume, "Dialectics of Coexistence," I have attempted a systematic exposition of the new Soviet doctrine of foreign policy that has evolved in the decade since Stalin's death. It is the thesis of this essay, as of others in the book, that a difference not simply of tactics and strategy but of mental outlook separates the Stalinist philosophy of cold war from the new Soviet philosophy of competitive coexistence. Two distinct Communist images of the coexistence process are involved. One of them sees coexistence as a "protracted conflict" only. The other proclaims the possibility and desirability of an East-West relationship in which competitive struggle for world predominance would be combined with a modicum of cooperation between the adversaries to preserve world peace. One sign of the depth of the division between the two positions lies in the intensity of the controversy that has arisen in the Communist world over this issue. It must be emphasized that the Communist coexistence controversy that has come into the open in the early 1960's is not simply a dispute across space between, say, Moscow and Peking. It is also a dispute across time between the post-Stalinist and the Stalinist orientations in the Communist mind.

Thus the Stalinist political mind did not die with Stalin. How could it in a movement whose membership had been schooled for a generation in the Stalinist view of things? Stalinism has had many Communist defenders—"heirs of Stalin" as they were called by the Soviet poet Yevtushenko in a remarkable political poem published in *Pravda* on October 21, 1962—and not only in foreign Communist parties but in the Soviet Party as well. "We carried him out of the Mausoleum," wrote Yevtushenko, "But who will carry Stalin out of the heirs of Stalin?" At the end of the first post-Stalin decade, this was still one of the important questions in Soviet Russia, and the Soviet political mind was in many ways a divided one.

Two of the studies in this volume, "The Stalin Heritage in Soviet Policy" and "Dialectics of Coexistence," and the bulk of a third, "Field Observations in Post-Stalin Russia," appear in print for the first time. The others have been published earlier and are here reprinted with minor changes. In one or two instances, I have introduced some new material to take account of ˙recent developments in the processes under analysis.

"On Revolutionary Mass-Movement Regimes" was first published in *The American Political Science Review* (June, 1961) under the title "Towards a Comparative Politics of Movement-Regimes." "Stalinism and Cold War" was published in *Problems of Communism* (May–June, 1957) under the title "The Psychology of Soviet Foreign Policy." "Stalin and the Uses of Psychology," "The Politics of Soviet De-Stalinization" and "Russia, the West, and World Order" were published in *World Politics* (July, 1956; July, 1957; and October, 1959, respectively). "The Image of Dual Russia" appeared as a chapter in a collective volume edited by C. E. Black, *The Transformation of Russian Society* (Cambridge, Mass.: Harvard University Press, 1960). "Ruling Personalities in Russian Foreign Policy" appeared as a chapter in a collective volume edited by Iwo J. Lederer, *Russian Foreign Policy: Essays in Historical Perspective* (New Haven: Yale University Press, 1962). And a portion of "Field Observations in Post-Stalin Russia" appeared in *The Russian Review* (October, 1959) under the title "Party and Church in the Soviet Union." The remainder of this chapter has been drawn from a report issued by The RAND Corporation under the title "Impressions of Russia in 1958: A Trip Report." Prior to their publication in journals, "Stalin and the Uses of Psychology," "The Politics of Soviet De-Stalinization," "Stalinism and Cold War" and "The Image of Dual Russia" were issued as research memoranda or reports by The RAND Corporation. I am grateful to the editors, publishers, and copyright holders of the above for permission to publish the essays here.

I would like to express my appreciation to those who have assisted me by their encouragement and suggestions, in particular Robert W. Adamson and John A. Armstrong. To the Center of International Studies of Princeton University go my thanks for its support.

ROBERT C. TUCKER

Princeton, N.J.
July, 1963

PART ONE

Theory

1 ON REVOLUTIONARY MASS-MOVEMENT REGIMES

Those who specialize in the study of Soviet government and politics are beginning to feel and acknowledge the need for a more effective theoretical apparatus. The postwar years of expanded research in this field have been fruitful in empirical studies of Soviet political history and institutions, but the theoretical development has not kept pace; and now the lag may be starting to inhibit the further fruitful progress of empirical research itself. Instead of a gradually developing body of theory, we still have a mélange of "ten theories in search of reality," as one writer has recently summed it up.[1]

It is not my purpose here to propound an eleventh theory. What follows in this chapter is no more than an exploratory effort, a consideration of a somewhat different approach to the problem than has been customary in the field of Soviet studies. In presenting it, I shall try to shed the blinkers of a Russian specialist and take a look at the whole political galaxy in which Soviet Russia is only the biggest star and probably no longer the brightest one.

I

The best way out of the theoretical difficulty may lie in making the study of Soviet government and politics more comparative than it has generally been so far, thus bringing it into much closer working relations with political science as a whole.* As this statement

* Gordon Skilling has advocated this view in his useful article "Soviet and Communist Politics: A Comparative Approach," *Journal of Politics,* XXII, 1960. Skilling is primarily concerned with the comparative politics of different Communist political systems, whereas I shall concern myself with the comparative politics of Communist and non-Communist systems of the authoritarian type.

3

implies, our work on Soviet politics has been characterized by a certain theoretical isolationism. The underlying assumption of a great deal of it is that Soviet politics constitutes a unique subject matter, a political world apart that can only be understood in terms of its own queer if not inimitable laws or motivations. Among the ten approaches surveyed by Bell we encounter, for example, "diaperology," or the view that Soviet politics is what it is largely because the leading participants may have been swaddled in babyhood. Another illustration is the theory of Nathan Leites, who finds at the bottom of Bolshevism and all its works "a reaction-formation to fears of death and latent homosexual impulses."[2]

It would not be accurate, however, to say that no one has studied the Soviet political system in a comparative political way. Indeed, much of the work done on this subject in the past fifteen years or so has been built around a kind of comparative concept—"totalitarianism." This term, it may be noted, was not originated by political scientists, but by totalitarians. It appears to have been put into currency by Mussolini or members of his circle.* Beginning in the late 1930's, however, Western students of dictatorship began to use this term. The phenomenon of the totalitarian or all-embracing state was conceived as a distinctively new, twentieth-century development in the theory and practice of despotism. The Soviet Russian state, as reshaped under Stalin in the 1930's, was coupled with the Nazi-Fascist type of system under the general heading of "totalitarianism." They represented respectively the totalitarianism of the "Left" and the totalitarianism of the "Right"—two different species of one and the same new political genus. Though the political symbolisms differed, in all essentials the two types of system were identical. They shared the *Führerprinzip,* the mass party brooking no opposition and extending its tentacles into all other organizations, the aggressive ideology and dynamism of external expansion, the use of the mass-communications media to keep the controlled population always keyed up, the development of terror by concen-

---

* Mussolini wrote the following in his article on the doctrine of Fascism in the *Enciclopedia Italiana* in 1932: "The Fascist conception of the State is all-embracing; outside of it no human or spiritual values may exist, much less have any value. Thus understood, Fascism is totalitarian, and the Fascist State, as a synthesis and a unit which includes all values, interprets, develops, and lends additional power to the whole life of a people."

tration camp into a system of power, the penetration of the total state into every pore of the "atomized" society, and so on.*

There was an obvious basis for this trend of thought. The fact is that Stalinism was essentially identical with Hitlerism and the other expressions of fascism. Unfortunately, however, the concept of the twin totalitarianisms of the Left and the Right did not clearly fix and delimit this fact. The theory of totalitarianism has tended to equate not Stalinism and fascism, but communism and fascism, and this is a mistake. The two phenomena have a great deal in common, but they also differ significantly. The difference is visible and traceable within the political history of the Soviet Union itself. That is, communism differs from fascism as Leninism (or Bolshevism) differs from Stalinism. And a clear recognition of this is an essential prerequisite for the advancement of theory in comparative politics as it affects Russia and numerous other countries.

It must be said, too, that the theorists of totalitarianism are conscious of this difference. They show it by suggesting in various ways that Soviet totalitarianism is pre-eminently a phenomenon of the Stalin era. According to Bertram Wolfe, "the Soviet government had been established for more than a decade before Stalin, late in the twenties and into the early thirties, began to impose totalitarian controls upon it."[3] Hannah Arendt writes in the same general vein that: "To change Lenin's revolutionary dictatorship into full totalitarian rule, Stalin had first to create artificially that atomized society which had been prepared for the Nazis in Germany by historical circumstances."[4] Friedrich and Brzezinski observe, for their part, that the emergence of totalitarian government in the Soviet Union "is marked by Stalin's liquidation of his erstwhile colleagues in the U.S.S.R's leadership and more particularly by his epochal struggle with Trotsky."[5]

The implication of these statements is that something in the nature of a change of political configuration, a transformation of regime, occurred in Soviet Russia between Lenin's time and Stalin's —and this is quite true. Lenin's system—a "revolutionary dictator-

* The most effective and influential presentation of this point of view is Hannah Arendt's *Origins of Totalitarianism* (New York: Harcourt, Brace & Co., 1951). A notable attempt to elaborate the approach systematically has been made by Carl J. Friedrich and Zbigniew K. Brzezinski in *Totalitarian Dictatorship and Autocracy* (Cambridge, Mass.: Harvard University Press, 1956).

ship"—was revolutionized by Stalin in a process that involved, among other things, the repression of Lenin's Bolshevik Party, and was supplanted by a Stalinist totalitarian autocracy. This process of transformation is accurately describable as a political revolution, although Stalin, for psychological and political reasons of his own, never admitted that fact. He never permitted his own new political order to be officially described as "Stalinism," and maintained to the end the myth of complete continuity between the regime created in the October Revolution and the new regime created in and through his own political revolution from above.

The theorists of totalitarianism, as has been indicated, recognize that a virtual change of regime occurred, but their theory does not. In effect, it says that the Communist political system, established by Lenin and the Bolshevik Party, *is what it became* after Stalin revolutionized it and transformed it into a Stalinist political system. This is a questionable procedure from an analytical point of view. That Lenin's revolutionary dictatorship of the Bolshevik Party paved the way for Stalinism, and that the later system had much in common with the one it supplanted, is true. But if, on this account, we ignore the significant differences between them and view Stalinism as the effective reality of communism, we deprive ourselves of the theoretical basis for a comparative politics of the Soviet Union over time as well as a comparative politics of communism and fascism as two significantly different species of one genus.

A good comparative concept should perform a dual discriminating function: It should direct attention to the ways in which similar phenomena differ, and simultaneously to the ways in which differing phenomena resemble each other. I have suggested that the concept of totalitarianism is deficient in the former respect since it fails to direct attention to significant differences between the closely resembling political phenomena of communism and fascism. I must now extend the argument by suggesting that it also fails to direct attention to significant resemblances between *both* these phenomena and a further class of phenomena belonging to the same genus: single-party systems of the nationalist species.

This century has seen the rise of a large and still growing number of revolutionary nationalist regimes under single-party auspices. Turkey under Kemal Atatürk, Nationalist China under Sun Yat-sen and Chiang Kai-shek, Tunisia under Bourguiba, Egypt under Nasser, and Ghana under Nkrumah are among the many examples that might be cited. If we disregard all considerations of international relations and look at these regimes simply as regimes, we see a political phenomenon that calls for comparison with communist and fascist regimes. We see the need for a comparative-political framework within which communist, fascist, and nationalist single-party regimes may be analyzed in terms of their significant similarities as well as their significant differences, or as three species of a single political genus.

The definition of the political genus presents obvious difficulties. Ideally this definition should fix upon (1) that which is common to all phenomena of the class and specific to none of the three postulated subclasses, and (2) that which differentiates this whole class of phenomena from others that may be more or less closely related to it. As a rough attempt, I would propose the following formula: *the revolutionary mass-movement regime under single-party auspices.* For brevity I shall refer to it as the "movement-regime."

In advocating this category as a tool of comparative analysis, it is not my object to suggest that the notion of totalitarianism is useless or ought to be discarded from political science. The frequency with which we employ it in political discourse strongly indicates that it answers to a genuine need of intellectual communication. My thesis is simply that the concept of totalitarianism has not adequately stimulated the progress of research in the comparative study of the novel forms of authoritarianism that have arisen in profusion in this century, and that it will have its scientific uses *within* a comparative politics of movement-regimes. Expressing it differently, the totalitarian dictatorship as such is not the novel political phenomenon of the present century, but at most one of the forms that this phenomenon takes. The distinctively new type of political formation that needs to be studied as a general form and in its specific varieties is the revolutionary mass-movement regime under single-party auspices.

II

The first element of the formula—"revolutionary"—establishes that we are dealing with regimes born in revolutionary struggle and that once in being, they strive to maintain revolutionary momentum. The movement to displace the pre-existing system of order then becomes a revolutionary movement for national renovation, or a movement to carry the revolution beyond the national borders, or both. This could be called the "postrevolutionary revolution." In its internal aspect, it is—or is conceived as—a *constructive* process of far-reaching change and reform.

In the case of the nationalist movement-regimes, especially in more recent times, the original revolutionary struggle is typically directed against a foreign colonial regime or regime of foreign dependency. With communist and fascist regimes, the typical— though not necessary or invariable—pattern is one of revolutionary struggle against an indigenous order that is treated *as though* it were foreign. So Lenin in 1902 conceived the Russian revolutionary movement as a nationwide resistance movement against an essentially alien Czarist monarchy and its supporters, and for Hitler the Weimar Republic was an un-German phenomenon. Stalin's was a marginal case, in which the revolution against the pre-existing (Bolshevik) system of order was conducted from above. It is notable, however, that the purged Old Bolshevik leadership was condemned as a treasonable, anti-national element.

The reader may have wondered why "ideology" was not included as an independent element of the formula. It might have been, but for simplicity's sake it seems preferable to consider this extremely important factor under the "revolutionary" heading. The ideology is, in its core, a philosophy of the revolution and program of the revolutionary struggle. As such, it not only provides political orientation, but serves as a powerful organizing instrument in the hands of the leadership. As Lenin said, "Without a revolutionary theory there can be no revolutionary movement."[6] Every movement-regime is associated with an ideology. As will be suggested later in this paper, comparative analysis of the ideologies may be useful in differentiating communist, fascist, and nationalist forms of the movement-regime.

Revolutionary regimes are not at all new in history, but the revolutionary *mass-movement* regime is a relatively novel phenomenon. The idea is traceable at least as far back as Mazzini, and earlier intimations of it are to be found in eighteenth-century France, or even in Cromwellian England.* Thus, Mazzini's contemplated revolution of national liberation and unification of Italy was to bring into being a third and greater Rome, "the Rome of the People," which in turn would provide leadership for all of Europe in creating a Europe of the people. The revolution was to be accomplished,

---

* J. A. Talmon discusses the eighteenth-century background in his *Origins of Totalitarian Democracy* (New York: Frederick A. Praeger, 1960).

moreover, with the active participation of masses of the people under the guidance and energetic leadership of an elite organization, Young Italy.

The history of politics in the twentieth century could be written in terms of the realization of the dreams of the nineteenth—and the discrepancy between dream and reality. The contemporary world contains a multitude of regimes, born in revolution, that rest upon and represent—or claim to—mass movements of a national or transnational scope. In the typical case, the mass movement is organized during the revolutionary struggle for power and as a means of waging this struggle. Once the regime is in being, the mass movement is enlarged and given new tasks of various kinds in the continuing revolution of national renewal. In some instances (present-day Egypt, for example) the development of the mass movement occurs after the conquest of power. In some instances, too, it remains largely a political artifact or pretense of a mass movement. Some of the East European Communist regimes might be cases in point.

The third common element is the militant, centralized, revolutionary party, or "vanguard" party as we may call it, which takes power in the name of the movement and the nation and then assumes the new function of governing the country single-handedly. Mazzini's phrase "party of action" foreshadowed the nature of this new type of party. Its character is largely determined by the circumstances of its origin. Since it arises outside of, and in opposition to, an existing system of law and order, electioneering is not its métier. Though it may take part in a given election for tactical purposes, it exists to overthrow a political order rather than to come to power within it. In the typical case it develops as a disciplined elite connected with a mass following through party "cells" in the enemy-order, and usually has a single dominating personality as its top leader and organizer. It is in essence a political-warfare organization, and as such tends toward conspiratorial habits and a quasi-military, authoritarian concept of its internal organization and relation to the mass following. Since its revolutionary ends transcend the destruction of the old order, the destruction is simply a new beginning. The party becomes the staff headquarters of the new revolutionary movement-regime, the territorial committees and cells become units of rule, and the single-party state is born.

The concept of the revolutionary vanguard party, with its "cellular structure" penetrating the pores of the old society, was already rather well developed in the nineteenth century, particularly among the Russian Populists. But it found its most influential exponent early in the twentieth century in Lenin. Unlike Marx, who tended to think that history itself would make the revolution, Lenin based all his thinking on the premise that revolutions have to be organized. His theory and practice of revolutionary "party construction" not only shaped the organization of Communist movements everywhere, it also radiated far and wide into nationalist and fascist movements. A well-known instance of this diffusion occurred in the early 1920's, when Sun Yat-sen decided to remodel the Chinese National Revolutionary Party (Kuomintang) in accordance with the Leninist concept, and the Russian Bolshevik Mikhail Borodin was sent to supervise the overhauling. A little later, Chiang Kai-shek gave the Russians a lesson in what might be called "anti-Communist communism" by turning the assimilated Bolshevik-type organizational forms against the Chinese Bolsheviks and their Muscovite mentors. The lesson was not lost on Stalin, who, in the 1930's, made use of Bolshevik organizational forms in destroying the *Russian* Bolsheviks, save for those whom he permitted to survive as Stalinists.

An instructive present-day example of a nationalist movement-regime with a ruling party shaped in the Leninist image may be found in Tunisia. President Bourguiba's Liberal Constitutional (Neo-Destour) Party "has covered the whole country with a network of a thousand cells," which "replace the 'infrastructure' of the modern state." "The party members who are organized in cells form the party Congress, which elects an executive, the Political Bureau. The Political Bureau is the main instrument of government. . . . The Political Bureau exercises tight control over the party machine, in which it has established a kind of 'democratic centralism.' . . . The Liberal Constitutional party has established a large network of organizations which embrace practically the whole population."[7] The exquisite irony of the situation is that the Communist Party of Tunisia is the sole opponent of President Bourguiba's regime.

One further generalization may be offered regarding the movement-regimes as a class. Since the militant centralized revolutionary party becomes the new foundation of political authority, and its cellular structure the "infrastructure" of the new state, the movement-regime takes on the authoritarian character of the founding organization. In certain instances (about which more later), it subsequently grows much more authoritarian, and the adjective "totalitarian" may become applicable. However, the leadership of the authoritarian movement-regime insists that it is also democratic in a "new way" (i.e., not in the liberal Western way.) This mode of thought, in which the dichotomy of "dictatorship—democracy" is rejected, is an outgrowth of the original concept of the revolutionary struggle as a mass movement for national or supranational objectives under guidance of a disciplined political elite organization. The result is one or another version of the doctrine of "guided democracy," of which, again, Lenin was the pre-eminent exponent.

The notion should not be dismissed as simple hypocrisy, although it may be that in any given instance. If "democracy" here loses the connotation of effective popular control over the regime (which is, by self-definition, the group that knows best what is in the interests of the people), it simultaneously acquires the connotation of mass popular participation in the continuing revolution of national renewal. In practice this means the enlisting of masses of people in the activities of trade unions, youth, professional, and other organizations that are formally nonparty in character but operated under party guidance and supervision via directorates from top to bottom in which disciplined party members predominate (the so-called "transmission belts" of Leninist theory). A large proportion of the population is thus drawn into the whirlpool of guided public life, and many may derive an experience of political participation that was denied them under the old regime. In Russia, the foremost non-Party organs of controlled participation are the soviets or local councils, which arose before the October Revolution and independently of Communism, but were later reshaped into components of the Bolshevik movement-regime. Today they form a pyramidal network of thousands of Party-guided bodies at village, town, district, and province levels, with deliberative and administrative functions in which several millions of deputies and subcommittee members take part. Very many of these people have no direct Communist Party affiliation.

This brings us again to the principle of transferability of organizational forms among movement-regimes of different types. Recently, for example, a pyramidal system of "councils," quite comparable in concept, if not in all details, to the one just described, has been introduced under the auspices of President Nasser's National Union regime in Egypt, and President Mohammed Ayub Khan's regime in Pakistan is introducing a similar setup there under the slogan of "basic democracy." A close associate of President Nasser's has explained to a Western journalist that the purpose of the Egyptian councils is to enlist mass participation at the village level in the revolution of national renewal: "The real revolution must come in the villages. . . . Every village has elected a council, replacing the old appointed Mayor. The council constitutes itself a cooperative and works with the Government's agricultural experts." The journalist reports that Nasser aides are not insulted if this system is described as "guided democracy," and he quotes the close associate further as saying: "We have a concept of democracy, it differs from yours. . . . We need something more dynamic, more realistic. . . . If we use your system the Communists will succeed, because they can speak to the masses."[8] Thus, there can be anti-Soviet sovietism in the field of guided democracy, as well as the previously mentioned phenomenon of anti-Communist communism in the field of party organization.*

A final observation about the movement-regime is that it has no restricted habitat in the world. A comparative politics of movement-regimes is not a regional affair and defies the classifications of political systems according to geographic zone. There is a rough correlation between antecedent colonialism and the rise of nationalist movement-regimes, or alternatively of Communist movement-regimes that ride to power on a wave of nationalist revolution. There is a related and still rougher correlation between the movement-regime and the conditions of economic and cultural backwardness, feudalism, stagnation, etc., that lend a special cogency to the revolutionary call for renovation of the nation. All this might suggest the thought that the specific habitat of the movement-regime is the "East" or, more broadly, the "underdeveloped areas." Yet such regimes, in one form or another, have appeared not only in Russia, Asia, the Middle East, Africa, Latin America, and Eastern Europe, but also in parts of Western Europe (Germany, Italy, Spain, Portugal); and Hitler's Germany was hardly an underdeveloped area. Moreover, movements bearing within themselves

* In this connection, it may be worth noting that a group of anti-Communist Russian émigrés has put forward a program, under the heading of "Kronstadt Thesis" whose slogan is: "Down with the Party, all power to free soviets!" The program takes its name from the Kronstadt rising of 1921, when sailors and workers called for the organization of soviets not dominated by the Bolsheviks. A partial text appears in Novy Zhurnal, No. 59, 1960.

the germs of potential movement-regimes have arisen in many other countries, including Great Britain and the United States. The movement-regime is a political phenomenon to which no nation and no part of the world is immune.

III

The differentiation of the species of movement-regime presents a much more difficult and complex problem than the definition of the genus. There are many avenues of approach to it, variously emphasizing social, economic, historical, religious, and psychological factors, etc. The most that can be attempted here is to present a few general thoughts on the problem.

First, it must be said that we are dealing with classes of phenomena that may be distinguishable but are not fully distinct. Thus, elements of nationalism are to be found in both communist and fascist movement-regimes, and any formulas for the latter that excluded this fact would be useless. It therefore appears inadvisable to segregate the species under conceptually pure "ideal types." Allowance must be made for complexity of character and even for the possibility of genuine hybrids. In short, nationalist, fascist, and communist movement-regimes are best differentiated according to their characteristic *prevailing tendencies*.

What has been said above about the transferability of organizational forms among movement-regimes of different types argues against any attempt to differentiate the types primarily in organizational terms. A more promising basis of differentiation, it seems to me, lies in the motivation of revolutionary politics, or what is often called the "revolutionary dynamism." All the movement-regimes originally have a revolutionary dynamism. They come into being by the revolutionary displacement of a pre-existing order, and seek to maintain revolutionary momentum after they come to power. They may, of course, fail to do so. They may lose revolutionary momentum eventually. When this happens, they become what I shall call "extinct" movement-regimes. Like a star that has ceased to give off light, an extinct movement-regime may go on existing for a long while without a revolutionary *raison d'etre*. We may say of such a regime what Herzen in 1853 said of the contemporary Russian monarchy, that it "exercises power in order to exercise power." The Franco regime in present-day Spain might be a case in point.

The revolutionary dynamism of the nationalist movement-regime is relatively restricted in scope and easy to define. Here the goal of the revolutionary movement is, first, national independence—the creation of a sovereign nation-state. Second, the revolutionary movement is aimed at the modernization of the newly independent state, and this typically involves many elements of an internal social revolution. Old class relations in society, old patterns of land tenure, old customs, old traditions of thought, and generally old ways of conducting the business of life are assailed in an internal revolution of national renewal. However, purely nationalist revolutionary movement-regimes show a definite tendency to spend their revolutionary force rather early. In some cases this happens soon after the achievement of the original revolutionary goals and prior to the completion of the revolutionizing of the old society. Thus, the nationalist movement-regime is peculiarly the prey of the phenomenon of "extinction."

In the best of cases, of which the Kemalist movement in Turkey might be an example, the revolution of national renewal is carried through far enough under the auspices of the movement-regime to make possible an orderly further development in a new and more democratic direction. More typical, however, may be the case of the Chinese Kuomintang, where the early subsiding of revolutionary dynamism paved the way for the displacement of the nationalist movement-regime by a Communist movement-regime that came to power under the slogan of carrying through the "betrayed" revolution of national renewal. In general, Communist movement-regimes, where not installed by direct action of a foreign power (as in most of Eastern Europe, North Korea, etc., after World War II), tend to arise as the penalty for either the absence of an effective national revolutionary movement where conditions call for it, or the inability of nationalist movement-regimes, once in being, to maintain their initial revolutionary momentum.

The relatively low revolutionary dynamism of the nationalist movement-regime is correlated with a relatively restricted revolutionary "constituency." The ideology of the national revolution is itself national. The sovereign independence and renovation of the nation are the objectives. Once installed in power, the nationalist movement-regime may develop an active foreign policy within what is likely to be a neutralist orientation in world affairs. But this will not be a policy of active export of the revolution to other lands. Such revolutionary expansionism is, on the other hand, a distinctive characteristic of *both* communist and fascist movement-regimes. Here the sphere of outlet for revolutionary energy is not confined to the national homeland. The politics of revolution embrace not only the revolutionary capture of power and subsequent internal revolution, but also, in varying manner and degree, the turning of the revolutionary dynamism out upon the world. Thus when a new movement-regime embarks upon a course of active export of the revolution to other countries, this may be taken as a fairly strong indication that it belongs not to the nationalist species but to one of the other two.

Communism and fascism are often contrasted on the ground that the one has an international "class appeal," while the other has a "national appeal" and is nationalist in essence. There is something in this idea, but it is also misleading. The dichotomy of communist internationalism versus fascist nationalism overlooks the fact that national and international elements commingle in both phenomena. On the one hand, the communist movement-regime is committed to a form of the national revolution as well as to the goal of world Communism. It appropriates not only the appeals of the revolution of national renewal, but also the task of carrying it through (in its own special way) when the movement comes to power.

On the other hand, the fascist revolutionary dynamism shares with the communist a supranational scope. Both give ideological expression to this by proclaiming a supranational revolutionary constituency and also an international *enemy* of the revolution. In the classic Bolshevik conception, the revolutionary constituency begins with the working classes of the revolutionary homeland and embraces the working classes of all countries, and the international bourgeoisie (or "international imperialism") is the enemy. Fascist regimes differ in their ideologies, but these regularly show a dualism that is comparable in kind if less comprehensive in scope. They take the *nation* as the nucleus of a larger whole, a supranational revolutionary constituency or sphere of revolution. Thus, for Hitler, the German *Volk* was the nucleus of the "Nordic race," and international Jewry or international imperialism was the enemy of the National-Socialist revolution. For Mussolini, "Romanism" was the key word, and the larger sphere of revolution was reflected in the slogan: "Italy today, tomorrow the Roman Empire!" Many more examples could be cited. The dual symbolism of President Nasser's movement-regime, which views Egypt as the nucleus of a vast "Arab nation" embracing all the separate Arabic nations and Arabs wherever they are, belongs to the pattern in question. Taken in conjunction with Nasserist activity in the export of the revolution to neighboring countries, this suggests that it would be a mistake to construe Nasserism as nationalist in essence, although it does display various features of a nationalist-revolutionary movement.*

In certain instances, typically occurring in smaller countries, we see the phenomenon of "national communism" or, alternatively, "national fascism" (of which Francoist Spain might be a good example). This development may be, and in the latter case no doubt is, indicative of a general loss of revolutionary momentum and the tendency to grow "extinct." On the other hand, it may, as in the case of Titoist Yugoslavia, be accompanied by something in the nature of an internal political "reformation" in which the movement develops with new vigor but in different directions.

One further consideration should be noted in connection with the fascist form of movement-regime. Although its sphere of revolution is not confined to the national homeland, it does indulge in strident national self-glorification. It proclaims its nation to be supreme in all the recognized national virtues and declares that the good of the nation is the highest goal of the regime. This has led some scholars to see in fascism "an inflammation of nationalism."[9] It seems, however, that this inflamed nationalism is essentially a pseudo nationalism, and that fascists must be distinguished from authentic nationalists as being, at best, the pharisees of nationalism. Thus, when Hitler saw that all was lost, he desired the destruction of the German nation as punishment for its unworthiness. Germany had not been worthy of its *Führer*. Obviously, the supreme value was not the German nation but the Hitlerite self, and the official glorification of the nation had been a cover and vehicle of the leader's self-glorification.

I take this to be indicative of a critically important general fact about the fascist type of movement-regime, viz., that here the psychology, or more accurately the psychopathology, of the leader becomes the driving force of the political mechanism. The regime is shaped into a highly complicated instrumentality for acting out the needs of the paranoid leader-personality, whose psychodynamics are politicalized, i.e., expressed in political action. Thus, the Nazi

---

* For a discussion of various considerations relevant to a judgment on this question, see P. J. Vatikiotis, *The Egyptian Army in Politics* (Bloomington, Ind.: Indiana University Press, 1961), esp. chap. vii.

regime started World War II in 1939 at a time when it was militarily not yet fully prepared, and to the chagrin of many of its highest officials, military and civilian. It was propelled into this action not by a cold calculation of relative forces and risks, but by the compulsive need of Hitler for revenge against his enemies. When his advisers warned him against it on the ground of the enemies' strength, he replied: "Then I will build U-boats! U-boats! U-boats! . . . I will build airplanes! airplanes! airplanes!—*and I will exterminate my enemies.*"* Comparable in character (though not in consequence) was the statement reportedly made by a furious Stalin on the eve of his public assault on Tito in 1948: "I will shake my little finger—and there will be no more Tito. He will fall."[10]

In order to shape the regime into a means of expression of his personal needs, the leader must reduce the ruling party to the role of an important cog in the apparatus of the state. It was pointed out earlier that movement-regimes tend to be headed by a dominating individual personality. This, however, does not imply that they are absolute autocracies. In fact, the broad tendency is oligarchical rule by the top leadership of the ruling party under the over-all direction of the dominant personality. The fascist movement-regimes deviate from this pattern and show a pronounced tendency to absolute autocracy, which involves the subordination of the party to the state as embodied in the leader. He emancipates himself from the control of the party oligarchy, and relies heavily upon the secret police and permanent pervasive terror through this organization to ensure unquestioning compliance with his least wishes on the part of everyone, from the lowliest man in the street to the highest dignitaries of the regime. Consequently, fascist regimes tend to become statist in orientation, and the state as personified in the leader may displace the party as the supreme symbol and object of official adoration. For these reasons, the most accurate general term

---

* G. M. Gilbert, *The Psychology of Dictatorship, Based on an Examination of the Leaders of Nazi Germany* (New York: The Ronald Press Company, 1950), p. 301. Gilbert concludes: "Our study of Hitler's lieutenants strongly suggested that if any one of them had replaced Hitler before 1939 (even aggressive Hermann Goering, the heir apparent), or if a slight change in circumstances (such as a little less appeasement) had replaced the Nazis with leaders more responsive to the will of the people, then there probably would have been no World War II and there certainly would have been no systematic 'extermination of my enemies.' " (*Ibid.*, pp. 302–3)

for the various fascist movement-regimes would be "führerism," and the most accurate title in each individual instance would be the one formed from the leader's name (e.g., "Hitlerism" rather than "Nazism").

It was said above that movement-regimes may undergo "extinction" when the revolutionary dynamism subsides. Another possible process is "metamorphosis" as a result of the *alteration* of the dynamism. A movement-regime of one species turns into one of another species as a consequence of a qualitative change in the motivation of revolutionary politics. Such a change is determined in its turn by a change or changes in the leadership situation within the regime. For various reasons it may not be possible for the leadership of the metamorphosed movement-regime to admit (even to itself) that the metamorphosis has occurred. The evidence of it must therefore be sought not in the regime's official self-definition, but rather in changes in the observable complex of ideological and behavioral patterns.

In conclusion I suggest that the political history of Soviet Russia probably offers the best laboratory for the study of the phenomenon of metamorphosis of movement-regimes. From the standpoint of a comparative politics of movement-regimes, this history is one of different *movements* and of different Soviet *regimes* within a framework of continuity of organizational forms and official nomenclature. The rise of Stalinism between 1928 and 1938 involved a process of change far more deep and pervasive than is generally realized. It was the metamorphosis of the original Communist or Bolshevik movement-regime into a new movement-regime of the führerist type. As indicated earlier, the metamorphosis was not accompanied by any change in the regime's official self-definition. But as will be shown in the next chapters, it was reflected in a whole system of changes in the political process, the ideological pattern, the organization of supreme power, and official patterns of behavior. Partly because of the inadequacy of our theoretical apparatus, and partly, too, because of the unduly large influence of the Soviet regime's self-image upon our conceptions, Western thinking has not, on the whole, assessed the full significance of the change from the Bolshevik to the Stalinist political system. A basic continuity of the Bolshevik movement-regime has been postulated, as is implicit, for example, in following statement by Bertram Wolfe: "When Stalin died in 1953, Bolshevism was fifty years old."[11]

Very important issues affecting the understanding and interpretation of the political changes in Russia since Stalin's death are involved in what may seem to be a problem of merely historical interest. On the postulate of continuity of the Bolshevik movement-regime from 1917 to 1953, "significant change" will logically mean change *away* from Bolshevism or Communism. This assumption results in a tendency to deprecate the significance of the post-Stalinist changes in Soviet political processes and policies. If, on the other hand, we take the view that Stalin's political revolution from above transformed the original Bolshevik movement-regime into a new one that was führerist in its inner dynamism and political tendency, we shall reason that in 1953, when Stalin died, Bolshevism had been moribund in Russia for fifteen years, and that the main issue was whether it would revive and, if so, to what extent. This opens the way to a recognition that a whole complex of quite significant political changes have occurred in post-Stalinist Russia within the broad framework of a movement to reconstitute the political system of Bolshevism.

2 THE DICTATOR AND
TOTALITARIANISM*

I

Significantly, we have few if any studies of the totalitarian dictator as a personality type. It may be that we are little closer to a working psychological model of him than Plato took us with his brilliant sketch of the ideal type of the "tyrant" in *The Republic*. The contemporary literature on totalitarianism does, of course, contain materials that are relevant to the problem of characterization of the totalitarian dictator.[1] Yet no frontal attack appears to have been made upon the problem. The purpose of the present chapter is to argue the need for one, and to do this in the context of a critical reexamination of the theory of totalitarianism. In the course of it I shall put forward some ideas of possible use in developing a conception of the dictator as a personality type.

First, a word on the use of the term "totalitarianism." Starting in the late 1930's and 1940's, a number of thinkers, mostly of European origin, evolved a theory of "totalitarianism" or the "total state" in an effort to account for the new type of dictatorship that had made its appearance in Germany under Hitler, Russia under Stalin, and perhaps also in Italy under Mussolini.[2] Hitler's Germany and Stalin's Russia were viewed as the two principal and indubitable manifestations of the novel political phenomenon. While the difficulty of precisely defining or describing this phenomenon was recognized, moreover, these writers felt that they were dealing with something qualitatively quite specific. It

* I am much indebted to Professor Fred I. Greenstein for critical comments on the original draft of this chapter.

20

was not so much a form of political organization as a form of outlook and action, a peculiar mode of political life. Thus Hannah Arendt, whose *Origins of Totalitarianism* was in many ways a culminating synthesis of this entire trend of theory in the first stage, did not treat Lenin's Russia as genuinely totalitarian. She saw the original Bolshevik system as a "revolutionary dictatorship" rather than a totalitarian one, and 1929, the year of Stalin's advent to supreme power and the start of the great collectivization campaign, as "the first year of clear-cut totalitarian dictatorship in Russia."[3] Accordingly, Soviet totalitarianism was treated as preeminently a phenomenon of the Stalin era. Again, Mussolini's Italy was considered by some to be a totalitarian state. But others, including Arendt, did not feel that it fully merited this designation even though Mussolini himself had been the first, or among the first, to use the term "totalitarian" and had applied it to the Fascist conception of the state. The treatment of Hitler's Germany and Stalin's Russia as the prime representative expressions of totalitarian dictatorship has remained characteristic of this school of thought, at any rate until recently. I intend to follow this usage here, meaning by "totalitarianism" the special kind of dictatorship or political phenomenon that existed in Germany under Hitler, in Russia under Stalin and, though perhaps only marginally, in Italy under Mussolini. The possibility that this special political phenomenon may have existed or may yet come into existence elsewhere is not, however, meant to be excluded.

There is a large biographical literature on the totalitarian dictators. These works are typically political biographies that tell the story of the subject's life and career against the background of his time and the politics of his country. The biographies of Stalin by Souvarine, Deutscher, and Trotsky are representative examples. Although they contain frequently very penetrating passages of psychological characterization, these biographies and others like them generally avoid any attempt at a systematic analysis of the personality of the dictator under consideration. A notable exception to this rule is Alan Bullock's *Hitler: A Study in Tyranny,* which essays, in its well-known chapter on "The Dictator," an extended character portrait of the mature Hitler. Bullock depicts Hitler's obsessive hatred of the Jews, his craving to dominate, his need for adulation, his grandiose fantasies, and his extraordinary capacity for self-dramatization and self-deception (his *Wahnsystem,* as the British Ambassador, Sir Nevile Henderson, called it). But he also sees Hitler as an astute practical politician of very great ability, and suggests that the defining characteristic of his political personality lay in the "mixture of calculation and fanaticism."[4] Some elements of this characterization of Hitler may be of use in defining the totalitarian dictator as a personality type. But it is notable that the biographer does not view his subject in comparative perspective or note the broader implications of his analysis of Hitler's personality.

We should not underestimate either the difficulty of "typing" the totalitarian dictator or the resources available to us for dealing with this task. On the first point, it is clear that the dictators significantly differ from one another. Thus Hitler lacked Stalin's administrative talent and associated psychological traits, whereas Stalin was lacking in Hitler's remarkable oratorical powers and the qualities of personality that went along with them. A conception of the totalitarian dictator as a personality type would have to be sufficiently broad to transcend these differences and embrace only those decisively important characteristics that were shared. On the other hand, it would have to be sufficiently specific to enable us, in principle, to discriminate between the authentic totalitarian dictator on the order of Hitler or Stalin, and others, such as Lenin, Tito, Franco, and Perón, who may belong to different dictatorial classifications. The requisite combination of breadth and specificity will obviously not be easy to achieve. On the other hand, the present-day social scientist has impressive resources of data and ideas to draw upon in dealing with this problem. A rich store of factual information on the totalitarian dictators and others is available to us now. And work done in recent decades on personality and politics has yielded general concepts that may serve as useful tools of analysis. In his classic study of *Psychopathology and Politics,* to take the most important example, Harold Lasswell laid the groundwork for a "functional" politics that would focus prime attention not on political office as such but on political personality types, such as the "agitator," "theorist," and "administrator." Lasswell did not include the "dictator" among the original group of types, nor has he, to my knowledge, undertaken in later writings to define the totalitarian dictator as a personality type. But he has enunciated concepts and propositions that may be of great help in this enterprise. Notable among them is the proposition that "Political movements derive their vitality from the displacement of private affects upon public objects," and the closely related thesis that such displacement involves certain "processes of symbolization" whereby collective symbols are made proxy for self-symbols.[5] We shall have occasion in what follows to apply these ideas.

Also noteworthy in the present context is the literature that has developed around the theme of the "authoritarian personality." Having originated in Germany, this idea was introduced to the English-speaking public by Erich Fromm in his *Escape from Freedom* (1941). Fromm's thesis was that German National Socialism and other Fascist movements in Europe derived much of their mass appeal from the widespread incidence among the lower middle classes in these countries of a personality structure that he labeled "sado-masochistic" or the "authoritarian character." The authoritarian character combined a craving for power over others with a longing for submission to an overwhelmingly strong outside authority. Hitler himself, as revealed in *Mein Kampf,* was treated as an example, an "extreme form" of the authoritarian character. Continued research in this field led to the path-finding work by T. W. Adorno and his associates, *The Authoritarian Personality* (1950), which presented as a central theoretical construct the notion of an "F-syndrome" or potential fascism in the personality. A whole literature of criticism and discussion of this work has since arisen. The relevance of the theory and of research on the "authoritarian personality" (and related conceptions) to the study of totalitarian dictators as a personality type is obvious. On the other hand, it must be borne in mind that the conception of the authoritarian personality has grown out of efforts to improve our understanding of the psychology of authoritarian *followership,* and that the specific question of leader psychology has not been a conscious concern in much of this work. The researchers have primarily been interested in learning why large numbers of people in modern societies may be receptive to the appeals of authoritarian or totalitarian movements. The great importance of the problem is undeniable. But it cannot be taken for granted that the motives or personality traits that lead some persons to become followers of a totalitarian movement are the same as those which cause others to become its organizers and leaders. In this connection it appears to be a defect of Fromm's study mentioned above that it fails to reckon explicitly with the possibility that the personality needs which cause some people to want to lose their freedom are not the same as those which cause a Hitler, for example, to want to take it away from them. The relationship between the needs of the leader and the needs of the followers might well be one of complementarity rather than similarity.

II

Hardly less significant than the absence of a clear idea of the totalitarian dictator as a personality type is the absence of any resulting widespread sense that a need of political science is going unfulfilled. For evidence that this is so, and also for an explanation of why it is so, we may profitably turn to the literature of the recent past on the totalitarian dictatorship as a political system. Two overlapping stages may be distinguished in the growth of this literature. The first, extending from the late 1930's to the end of the 1940's, saw the emergence of the conception of the totalitarian state as a new, distinctively modern or non-traditional form of authoritarianism represented particularly in Nazi Germany and Soviet Russia. The second stage, coinciding with the growth of Soviet studies as an established branch of academic scholarship in postwar America, saw the detailed application of this conception to the Soviet system in its late Stalinist form, and also attempts at a kind of codification of the theory of totalitarianism.[6] It is only natural, of course, that in the late 1940's and early 1950's the attention of American scholars should have gravitated from the defunct Nazi case to the still very live totalitarianism of Stalin's Russia, and that in their studies of the latter they should have relied heavily upon the model of a totalitarian polity that had already been worked out in the first stage.

It is no monolithic doctrine that we find reflected in the literature on totalitarianism. We are confronted, rather, with a variegated body of thought developed over an extended period by thinkers of diverse intellectual background and research interest among whom differences of emphasis and opinion exist. Still, there are certain recurring themes, certain basic ideas that tend to be shared by various representatives of the school and may be taken as typical.

First, the totalitarian dictatorship is viewed as being, unlike most traditional forms of authoritarian rule, a dictatorship with a mass social base and having a popular or pseudo-popular character. "The totalitarian state is the state of the masses," wrote Emil Lederer, and other theorists have followed him in taking modern "mass society" or "mass-men" as a foundation or recruiting ground of totalitarian movements that speak in the name of the masses and assert their affinity with them.[7] On the road to power, totalitarian parties strive to create mass movements that indoctrinate their followers with the party's ideology by propaganda and agitation. Once in power in the single-party state, however, the totalitarian elite imposes upon its mass social constituency an unprecedented tyranny, under which political power emanating from a single source penetrates every pore of the social organism and all the resources of modern technology are used for control purposes. Autonomous social groups are destroyed, giving way to the controlled mass organizations that serve as the elite's transmission belts to the now "atomized" masses of the population.

"Modern totalitarianism, unlike the more traditional dictatorships, is a highly bureaucratized system of power."[8] This sums up a second characteristic theme in the literature on the totalitarian dictatorship. In *Behemoth,* for example, Franz Neumann depicts the Nazi dictatorship as a system ruled, albeit chaotically and competitively, by four great bureaucratic machines—the ministerial bureaucracy and the bureaucratized leaderships of the Nazi Party, the armed forces, and industry. The same basic theme receives a somewhat different emphasis from Arendt, who distinguishes "totalitarian bureaucracy" from bureaucracy of the traditional kind on the score of the former's "radical efficiency."[9] Both, however, share with other theorists of the school the view that totalitarianism carries the process of bureaucratization to its farthest extreme in modern society. There is, in fact, a tendency to regard the totalitarian state as a great bureaucratic monster functioning with machine-like impersonality in pursuit of its aims. Such an image is suggested, for example, by Arendt's later book, *Eichmann in Jerusalem,* which pictures the erstwhile director of operations in the Nazi "final solution" as a *kleiner Mann* of banal character who in supervising the murder of millions of Jews was dutifully carrying out his instructions as a higher functionary, a cogwheel in the totalitarian bureaucracy.

A third fundamental theme that has been both widely and heavily emphasized in the literature on totalitarianism has to do with systematic terror. Governmental use of terror is not itself held to be something distinctively new in the present age or peculiar to the totalitarian form of dictatorship. What distinguishes totalitarianism, according to the theorists, is rather the kind and degree of terror that is practiced, and also the characteristic predilection of totalitarian regimes for certain particular methods of spreading terror, such as the concentration camp and violent purges. Arendt, for example, differentiates "dictatorial terror," which is aimed against authentic opponents of the given regime, from an all-pervasive "totalitarian terror" that destroys not only actual political opponents but great numbers of wholly harmless people in purges, mass liquidations, and concentration camps; and she expresses the view that terror of the latter kind is "the very essence" of totalitarian government.[10] This view has found wide acceptance in the literature. Terror has variously been described, for example, as "the most universal characteristic of totalitarianism,"[11] "the linchpin of modern totalitarianism,"[12] and "the vital nerve of the totalitarian system."[13] So far as the question of the motivation of totalitarian terror is concerned, this is best considered under the next heading—the dynamics of totalitarianism.

The theorists of totalitarianism are in general and rather emphatic agreement that the totalitarian state is, in addition to its other characteristics, an extremely dynamic phenomenon. Sigmund Neumann, author of an outstanding work on the subject, saw the dynamics of the total state as revolutionary, and the political process in the totalitarian system as one of "permanent revolution." Others have used phrases like "permanent purge" and "permanent war" to describe essential aspects of the totalitarian dynamism in internal and external affairs. But why do totalitarian systems act in such ways? Whence their dynamics? The literature gives two kinds of answer to such questions. First, the characteristic behaviors of totalitarian regimes are explained by reference to postulated system-needs or functional requisites of totalitarianism itself as an operating socio-political system. A specimen of such reasoning is provided by Brzezinski when he writes, for example, that "The purge, arising as a combination of the rational motivations of the totalitarian leadership and the irrational stresses of the system, satisfies the need of the system for continued dynamism and energy," and further: "Totalitarianism is the system of the permanent purge. It promotes mobility and instability within totalitarianism. It necessitates constant reshuffling, and prevents the formation of too rigid lines of power demarcation within the system."[14]

A second and related line of explanation of the dynamics of totalitarianism stresses ideological motivation. The totalitarian ideology itself or the leaders' presumed obsession with it is treated as the source of the characteristic behavior of totalitarian regimes. Thus Friedrich describes Hitler's destruction of the Jews as "ideologically motivated."[15] On a higher plane of generality Arendt explains the action of totalitarian regimes by references to a "supersense" that drives the leaders to demonstrate at all cost the validity of their ideological world-image. "The aggressiveness of totalitarianism," she goes on, "springs not from lust for power, and if it feverishly seeks to expand, it does so neither for expansion's sake nor for profit, but only for ideological reasons: to make the world consistent, to prove that its respective supersense has been right."[16] The postulate of an ideological fanaticism as the driving force of totalitarian conduct reappears in Inkeles' conception of the "totalitarian mystique," which he sees as the defining characteristic of the totalitarian leader himself. The "mystique" is pictured as a compulsion in the leader and his lieutenants to force reality into conformity with an ideologically given "higher law" or ideal plan for man and society: "One may fruitfully view the dictatorial leader as the man who sees himself as the essential *instrument* of the particular mystique to which he is addicted."[17] In an application of this mode of reasoning, Friedrich and Brzezinski seek to explain totalitarian terror by ideological fanaticism. Having said that the terror is the "vital nerve" of the totalitarian system, they write: "This system, because of the alleged ideological infallibility of its dogma, is propelled toward an increase of terror by a violent passion for unanimity." Such passion, they go on to suggest, is what makes the terror totalitarian: "It aims to fill everyone with fear and vents in full its passion for unanimity. Terror embraces the entire society, searching everywhere for actual or potential deviants from the totalitarian unity. . . . Total fear reigns."[18]

Turning to the question of the dictator, it cannot be said that the theorists of totalitarianism have overlooked his presence in the system. It is true that the dictator's role has, on occasion, been explicitly disparaged. Thus Franz Neumann argued that despite its proclamation of the *Führerprinzip* and cult of the ruler, the totalitarian state should not be seen as a *Führerstaat*. For the doctrine of one-man rule was "merely a device to prevent insight into the operation of the social-economic mechanism," and this mechanism, in turn, was one in which "The decisions of the Leader are merely the result of the compromises among the four leaderships."[19] Nor do we find the role of the dictator singled out in the various efforts to define what has been called the "totalitarian syndrome," the cluster of elements that characterizes the totalitarian system as a distinctive political formation.[20] Most of the theorists, however, recognize at some point the reality of dictatorial rule by a single individual in a fully totalitarian system. Friedrich and Brzezinski, for example, refer to the Nuremberg trials and Khrushchev's secret speech of 1956 as sources of evidence for the view that Mussolini, Hitler, and probably Stalin too were "the actual rulers of their respective countries," and they conclude that the totalitarian dictator "possesses more nearly absolute power than any previous type of political leader."[21] Much earlier Sigmund Neumann described the dictator as the "moving spirit" of the total state, and Arendt writes of "the absolute and unsurpassed concentration of power in the hands of a single man" who sits in the center of the movement "as the motor that swings it into motion."[22]

But "chief cogwheel" would have expressed more accurately the way in which she and others among the theorists actually seem to conceive the dictator's role. She ascribes to the Leader's lieutenants the view that he is "the simple consequence of this type of organization; he is needed, not as a person but as a function, and as such he is indispensable to the movement."[23] This also seems to be Arendt's own view, arising out of the general conception of the totalitarian system as a mechanistic leviathan operating under pressure of its own system-needs and the "supersense." Thus she depicts the all-powerful dictator as essentially a chief executive whose role is to bind the totalitarian system together into a unity and, by assuming blanket responsibility for everything done in the name of the regime, to relieve all the lesser functionaries of any sense of individual responsibility for their actions. Hitlers, as it were, are needed by totalitarian states in order to enable Eichmanns and others to perform their genocidal and like deeds in good conscience. The system-needs remain basic, according to this way of thinking; *Führers* are functional requisites of totalitarianism as a peculiar kind of system.

"Not as a person but as a function"—this phrase takes us to the heart of an issue that particularly needs pursuing. We cannot say that the dictator is missing from the model of the totalitarian state that has been elaborated. But he is present in it raher as a function than as a person. This helps to explain why the theorists, while taking cognizance of the dictator, accord him no more than secondary importance in the theory of totalitarianism. He is seen as fulfilling certain needs of the system, which of course he does. But the system, or its politics, is not in turn seen as fulfilling certain personal needs of his. Insofar as the theorists take a psychological view of him at all, they see him simply as sharing with the rest of the leadership the postulated supersense or totalitarian mystique. The assumption of a generalized ideological fanaticism takes the place of psychological analysis of the dictator as an individual personality. His political motivations consequently are not really appraised in psychological terms; his manner of displacing "private affects" upon "public objects" remains outside the purview of the theory of totalitarianism. And this, in my view, is a very great deficiency of the theory.

III

A sense of the theoretical inadequacy of the conception of totalitarianism seems to have been growing in American political science in the 1960's. Increasingly the complaint is heard that this construct is too narrow and limited to serve as a useful basic category for comparative analysis of contemporary one-party systems. It leaves out of view the nationalist single-party systems that share very many significant characteristics with the Fascist and Communist systems. It does not fare well in the face of the recent growth of diversity among Communist systems themselves. Furthermore, the politics of post-Stalin Russia have become more and more difficult to analyze in terms of the theory of totalitarianism, the fall of Khrushchev being only one in a long series of events that do not easily find places in the model of a totalitarian polity; and efforts to modify the model so that it will fit contemporary Soviet communism—e.g., by introducing the idea of a "rationalist totalitarianism"—seem of little avail. And owing to the tendency to see totalitarian systems as examples of what might be called government without politics, with a unitary elite controlling an atomized population by organization and terror, the theory of totalitarianism has obstructed rather than facilitated awareness of the intra-elite politics of factional conflict and policy debates that rage constantly behind the scenes of the Soviet and other Communist systems, despite their official pretensions to monolithic unity and their claims that factions are forbidden. For these and other reasons, some students of the comparative politics of modern authoritarianism have become dissatisfied with the concept of totalitarianism and have begun to formulate alternative basic categories, such as "movement-regimes," "mobilization systems," and the like.[24]

But are we now to discard the concept of totalitarianism as an obsolete or obsolescent category in modern political science? Considering it an essential part of our theoretical equipment, I for one would not like to see this happen. In order to prevent it from happening, however, it appears necessary to carry out a more radical critique of the theory of totalitarianism than has yet been made, rather as medicine may have to resort to a more radical form of treatment in order to save a patient. So far criticism has concentrated upon the deficiencies of the theory in application to systems or situations that were not in view or in existence at the time the theory was devised. The more radical critique must address itself to a different question: How valid was the theory as a representation of political reality in the two historical cases that it was particularly devised to explain—Hitler's Germany and Stalin's Russia? The time is now especially propitious for pursuing this question, since we have far more documentary and other information on the two cases than was available in earlier years. Here the question will be considered only in the aspect relating to the role of the dictator in the system.

When we confront the theoretical model of a totalitarian polity with what we now know about the factual situation in Hitler's Germany and Stalin's Russia, it appears that the model was seriously deficient in its omission of the personal factor from the dynamics of totalitarianism, its obliviousness to the impact of the dictator's personality upon the political system and process. For not only do Hitler and Stalin turn out to have been, as already indicated, autocrats who at many crucial points individually dominated the decision-making process and behavior of their governments. The factual evidence likewise supports the further conclusions that (1) in both instances we have to do with individuals whose personalities would be classified somewhere on the continuum of psychiatric conditions designated as paranoid; and (2) in both instances the needs of the paranoidal personality were a powerful motivating factor in the dictatorial decision-making. The dictator did not, so to speak, confine the expression of his psychopathological needs to his private life while functioning "normally" in his public political capacity. Rather, he found a prime outlet for those needs in political ideology and political activity. In terms of Lasswell's formula, his psychopathological "private affects" were displaced onto "public objects." As a result, the dynamics of totalitarianism in Hitler's Germany and Stalin's Russia were profoundly influenced by the psychodynamics of the totalitarian dictator. The Soviet case is particularly instructive in this regard. For while our factual knowledge is less complete, we have here a system that survived the totalitarian dictator and thus some possibility of assessing the impact of his personality by studying the difference that his death made.

Before coming to power Hitler set forth in *Mein Kampf,* with its doctrine about a world-wide Jewish conspiracy to subvert the master race, a private vision of reality showing very strong parallels with psychiatric descriptions of a paranoid delusional system. Subsequently the vision began to be acted out inside Germany in the anti-Jewish terror, of which Hitler himself was the single most powerful driving force. Still later, when World War II was precipitated by the German invasion of Poland in 1939, it was Hitler's furiously insistent determination to (as he put it) "annihilate my enemies" that drove him, in the face of widespread apathy toward war in his own society and even in his own government, to push the world over the brink; and the story of his actions and reactions on the eve and in the uncertain early days of the conflict is like a page out of a case history of paranoia, save that this was likewise a page of world history. During the war the internal terror continued, now on the scale of occupied Europe as a whole. It was Hitler's own will to genocide that generated the relentless pressure under which Himmler's terror machine proceeded during the war to carry out the murder of European Jewry: "Himmler organized the extermination of the Jews, but the man in whose mind so grotesque a plan had been conceived was Hitler. Without Hitler's authority, Himmler, a man solely of subordinate virtues, would never have dared to act on his own."[25]

Stalin's career differed from Hitler's, among other ways, in that he did not come to power as the recognized leader of his own movement but gradually took over from above a movement that had come to power much earlier under other leadership, mainly Lenin's. Certain other differences flowed from this. Whereas Hitler's personal dictatorship was established rather easily through the blood purge of June, 1934, which took no more than a few hundred lives, Stalin's arose through the veritable conquest of the Communist Party and Soviet state in the Great Purge of 1936–1938, in which an estimated five to nine million persons were arrested on charges of participation in an imaginary great anti-Soviet counter-revolutionary conspiracy. In this case the dictator's private vision of reality was not set forth in advance in a bible of the movement, but was woven into the pre-existing Marxist-Leninist ideology during the show trials of 1936–1938, which for Stalin were a dramatization of his conspiracy view of Soviet and contemporary world history. The original party ideology was thus transformed according to Stalin's own dictates into the highly "personalized" new version of Soviet ideology that was expressed in the Moscow trials and in Stalin's *Short Course* of party history published in 1938. Contrary to the above-reviewed theory of totalitarianism, the Great Purge of 1936–1938 was not a product of the needs of Soviet totalitarianism as a system. Apart from the fact that it was only in the course of this purge that the Soviet state finally became a fully totalitarian one, especially in the sense of being the scene of permanent and pervasive terror, we have it now on highest Soviet authority that the purge was extremely dysfunctional for the Soviet state since it greatly weakened the ability of the country to withstand the coming test of total war. Not system-needs but the needs of Stalin, both political and psychopathological, underlay to a decisive degree the terror of 1936–1938.*

As in Hitler's case, we see in Stalin's the repetitive pattern, the subsequent reenactment in foreign relations of psychopathological themes and tendencies expressed earlier in the internal sphere. It was mainly in the postwar era of Soviet cold war against the West, against Tito, and so forth, that Stalin's psychological needs and drives found relatively uninhibited outlet in the field of external relations. Contributing factors included, on the one hand, the fact that an older and more deeply disordered Stalin was now less able to exercise restraint save in the face of very grave external danger, and, on the other hand, the capacity of a relatively more strong and less threatened Soviet Union to make its weight felt internationally with a large degree of impunity. We have the testimony of Khrushchev in the 1956 secret report that now "The willfulness of Stalin showed itself not only in decisions concerning the internal life of the country but also in the international relations of the Soviet Union," and that Stalin "demonstrated his suspicion and haughtiness not only in relation to individuals in the U.S.S.R., but in relation to whole parties and nations." The latter point is illustrated with a vivid recollection of Stalin in 1948 deciding on the break with Tito in a state of blind fury, exclaiming: "I will shake my little finger—and there will be no more Tito. He will fall."[26] Other postwar Soviet acts or policies that were influenced, if not directly caused, by Stalin's psychological needs include the imperious demands upon Turkey in 1945; the shutting down of cultural contacts and general isolationism of the 1947–1953 period; the extension of blood purges and show trials to Soviet-dominated Eastern Europe; the suspicion shown toward nationalist

* For a detailed elaboration of this argument, along with an analysis of the ideology of the purge trials in terms of the analogy with a paranoid system, see Chapter 3 of this book.

revolutions in Asia and elsewhere; and the unprecedentedly extreme Soviet psychological warfare of 1949–1953 against the West as manifested, in particular, in the savage propaganda campaign about alleged American germ warfare in Korea. There was, finally, the extraordinarily significant affair of the Kremlin doctors in January–February, 1953, which had a vital bearing upon Soviet foreign policy as well as upon internal affairs. The way in which Stalin's psychopathology found expression in this final episode of his career will be discussed below.

In both Germany and Russia, then, the dictatorial personality exerted its impact originally in ideology and the internal life of the country, and later found a major field of expression in foreign relations as well. The internal impact was felt, among other ways, in the form of terror; the external, in a special sort of aggressiveness that may best be described, perhaps, as an externalization of the terror. In other words, domestic terror, which may be viewed under the aspect of "internal aggression" against elements of the population, was followed by foreign aggression, which may be viewed as a turning of the terror outward upon the world. Parenthetically, since this temporal order of priority was and generally would be conditioned by objective factors in the situation (e.g., the necessity for the dictator to capture complete control of his own society before he can channel his personality needs into foreign policy), there may be a basis for relatively early identification of a rising totalitarian dictator of the type of Stalin or Hitler. This suggests, moreover, that the international community might possibly develop a politics of prevention based on stopping the dictatorial personality at the stage of "internal aggression." However, this would necessitate a modification of the traditional doctrine of non-intervention insofar as it sanctions the unlimited right of a nation-state to deal with its own population as the ruler or regime sees fit, provided only that it continues to observe the accepted norms of international law in relations with other states. Upon the willingness and ability of the international community to recognize this problem, and to institute means of preventing individuals of paranoid tendency from gaining or long retaining control of states, may hang the human future. Were Hitler and Stalin, for example, dictators of their respective countries in the 1970's instead of the 1930's, the probability-coefficient of civilization's survival would be very low.[27]

The evidence disclosed by the Stalin and Hitler cases on the connection between dictatorial psychopathology and the politics of totalitarianism strongly suggests that the personal factor should be included in the theoretical model of a totalitarian system. On the basis of the factual record in these cases, as just summarized, the contribution of the dictator's personality to the dynamics of totalitarianism should be recognized as one of the regular and important components in the "syndrome." Such a conclusion appears all the more compelling in view of the extremely heavy emphasis that the theory has placed, as noted earlier, upon pervasive and permanent terror as the very essence of totalitarianism. For in the Soviet and Nazi cases, the dictators themselves, driven by pathological hatred and fear of what they perceived as insidiously conspiratorial enemy forces operating at home and abroad, were responsible to a very significant extent for the totalitarian terror that did in fact exist in Hitler's Germany and Stalin's Russia. The Soviet case is especially instructive since it reflects the relation of Stalin to the Stalinist terror, not only positively in the form of direct evidence of his determining role, but also negatively in the form of the decline of terror that began to be felt almost immediately after his death and has since continued. As late as January–February, 1953, it may be said on the basis of the present writer's personal observations in Russia at that time, Soviet society was almost paralyzed with terror as preparations for another great purge developed to the accompaniment of ominous official charges that an anti-Soviet conspiracy, with threads leading to foreign intelligence services, was or had been abroad in the land. Stalin's death at that time not only cut short the purge operation but inaugurated the subsiding of the internal terror that had developed in a wavelike movement of advance and partial retreat ever since his rise to supreme power in 1929. Soviet citizens insistently refer to the subsiding of the terror as perhaps the most significant single expression of change they have experienced in post-Stalin Russia; and most foreign observers and scholars specializing in Soviet studies appear to agree with them on this point. Insofar as terror has continued to exist in post-Stalin Soviet society, it has become, to use Arendt's distinction, terror of the "dictatorial" rather than the "totalitarian" variety.

Given these facts and the premises of the theory of totalitarianism, certain conclusions concerning both Russia and totalitarianism would seem to follow. First, if total terror is the essence of totalitarianism, then a Soviet political system in which such terror has ceased to exist and in which terror generally has greatly subsided over a substantial period of years should be pronounced, at least provisionally, post-totalitarian. Second, if the terror in Hitler's Germany was connected in considerable degree with Hitler as a personality, and that in Stalin's Russia with Stalin as a personality, then the explanations of totalitarian terror in terms of functional requisites of totalitarianism as a system or a general ideological fanaticism in the ruling elite would appear to have been basically erroneous—a conclusion which derives further strength from the fact that the ruling elite in post-Stalin Russia remains committed to the Communist ideology. Third, the theory of totalitarianism should not only bring the dictator and his personality into the "syndrome," but also should give specific recognition to the role of the dictatorial personality in the dynamics of totalitarian terror.

The theory of totalitarianism has not, however, moved in this direction. The indicated critical post-mortem on earlier interpretations of the dynamics of totalitarian terror has not appeared. The evidence from Hitler's Germany and Stalin's Russia on the relation of the dictator as a terroristic personality to the practice of totalitarian terror, and for such peculiarly totalitarian characteristics of it as its tendency to grow over time, has been generally disregarded. And instead of provisionally pronouncing post-Stalin Russia to be post-totalitarian on the ground that the terror has subsided, some theorists specializing in Soviet studies have taken the very different path of eliminating terror from the definition of totalitarianism. This leads to the thesis that what we see in Russia after Stalin is a system of "totalitarianism without terror." Thus Brzezinski, who had earlier viewed terror as the "most universal characteristic" of totalitarianism, writes that we seem to be witnessing the emergence in post-Stalin Russia of a "voluntarist totalitarian system" and that terror must now be seen not as something essential to a totalitarian system but only "as a manifestation of a particular stage in the development of the system." In explanation of this point he states further: "Terror and violence may be necessary to change a primitive, uneducated, and traditional society rapidly. Persuasion, indoctrination, and social control can work more effectively in relatively developed societies."[28]

But such a view of the causation of the terror is open both to the objections already leveled against explanations running in terms of system-needs, and to others in addition. It is debatable, and nowadays increasingly being debated, whether the terrorism of forced collectivization and industrialization in 1929–1933 was a necessity for Soviet communism in achieving its goals of modernization. Such a prominent Communist theorist and politician as Nikolai Bukharin was profoundly convinced that there was no such necessity, and many others in Russia at that time shared his view. Moreover, some Western specialists on Russia and even, apparently, certain people in present-day Soviet Russia are increasingly of the opinion that his view was correct on the whole.[29] But even if we leave this question open, allowing for the possibility that terror and violence were in fact necessities of the modernization process in the Soviet case, the heightened terror by purge that was directed against the Communist Party and Soviet managerial elite between 1934 and 1939 and was mounting again in 1949–1953 cannot be explained by the need to "change a primitive, uneducated, and traditional society rapidly." By 1934 collectivization was a *fait accompli* and generally accepted as such even by the peasantry, the pace and rigors of industrialization had slackened, and there was no serious resistance among the population or within the ruling Party to the continuing process of modernization. Certainly there was no opposition to it on such a scale that it required to be quelled by terroristic means. And just at this time, when any need for terror and violence for modernization purposes had subsided, a vast new intensification of it occurred on Stalin's initiative and under his personal direction. Moreover, terror rose again in a post-war Soviet Union which, despite the devastation visited upon it by the Second World War, was basically the urbanized and industrialized country that we know in our time. These facts do not square with the thesis that the terror was a manifestation of a particular stage in the development of the Soviet system connected with forced modernization. Nor does this thesis explain why the postulated stage in the development of the system should have lasted as long as Stalin lived and ended with his death or very soon after. In actuality, what this fact and other positive evidence indicate is that the Stalinist terror was in large part an expression of the needs of the dictatorial personality of Stalin, and that these needs continued to generate the terror as long as he lived. In my view, the instinct that originally led the theorists of totalitarianism to treat total terror as belonging to the very essence of this phenomenon was a sound one. But if their insight is to be salvaged, it will be necessary to reckon in a new way with the personal factor in the totalitarian terror and the dynamics of totalitarianism in general.

IV

We seem to be confronted with a resistance to the idea that the personality of the dictator may play a decisive part in the politics of totalitarianism. In conclusion it may be useful to explore its intellectual sources, examining both sides of some issues involved. Such an analysis of underlying issues is all the more pertinent in view of indications that the position taken by various theorists of totalitarianism reflects not simply the views of this school of theory but a rather broad spectrum of thinking among practitioners of contemporary social science. The thinking in question has to do with the influence of personality, and especially psychopathology, in decision-making and action in large-scale organizations, governments in particular.

Social scientists generally reject the "great man" theory of history as obsolete on the ground that historical phenomena are to be explained by social, political, and economic conditions and processes rather than by actions of individual leaders, who themselves are constrained by these conditions and involved in these processes. And many may be inclined to deny a major determining role to the dictatorial personality in totalitarian systems in part because of a feeling that to do otherwise would mean going back to an outmoded theory of the way in which history is made. However, no such implication follows. We do not face here a choice between explaining history by reference to leader-personalities or assigning them no importance at all. Historical explanation in the social sciences requires multiple approaches and a flexible willingness to vary them in accordance with the nature of the individual problems under consideration. To recognize that the influence of an individual personality on political events may be very great in certain special circumstances—most notably, those obtaining in a totalitarian dictatorship—is not to argue that this is a common phenomenon or that no other factors than the individual personality need be considered even in explaining events in this particular kind of case.

Secondly, some scholars are opposed to highlighting the dictator and his psychological motivations on the specific ground that to do so is to divert attention from the features of the totalitarian system that make it possible for him to act as he does. Objecting, for example, to the attempt to explain Stalin's Great Purge as resulting from the "aberrations of one man," Professor Leonard Schapiro writes, *inter alia,* that such an explanation fails to illuminate "the reasons which enabled one man to impose his will on so many millions."[30] It will hardly be disputed that an explanation of the behavior of a totalitarian dictator should take account of such situational factors as the structure of the political system within which he operates. But it does not follow that psychological explanations should be avoided. The investigator who finds in "aberrations of one man" a major determinant of the actions of a regime need not—and should not—concentrate exclusive attention upon this one determinant to the exclusion of other relevant factors. Nor does the location in the dictator himself of supreme personal responsibility for certain events absolve his associates and subordinates of their share of responsibility for carrying out the instructions that they received from him.

We come, finally, to a number of complex issues arising out of what I propose to call the theory of organizational rejection of aberrant personalities from leadership positions. It may be that nobody has ever advanced this theory as a whole. In any event, no formulation of it as a single connected argument has come to my attention, although individual elements of it appear here and there in the contemporary literature of political science. It begins with the proposition that modern society, owing to what has been called the "organizational revolution," has increasingly come to be dominated by large bureaucratic organizations, among which national governments themselves are of foremost importance. It may be recalled in this connection that totalitarian systems have been described as those in which the organizing of social life and the process of bureaucratization have gone farthest of all. Now it is held that the behavior of individuals, including leaders, in the structured social situations obtaining in large bureaucratic organizations is regulated to such a degree by the nature of the patterned roles that they play, the role expectations of others, and what may be called the rules of the game, that the influence of individual personality factors is, if not nullified, at any rate greatly circumscribed. As one political scientist expresses it, referring specifically to foreign policy elites, they operate in bureaucratic social situations and are subject to conditions that "tend to inhibit the impact of personality-oriented pressures." He infers that in dealing with the behavior of nation-states as actors within the international system, "non-logical explanations, while not completely irrelevant, are of little use."[31] Taking a similar position, and again with special reference to officials representing nation-states in international relations, another political scientist writes: "The individuals who represent these entities are constrained by colleagues, decision-making processes, and role expectations."[32]

If the effect of personality-oriented pressures is in general limited by constraints inherent in the structured social situations obtaining in organizations, a logical next step in the argument is to hold that individuals with serious emotional disorders will be even less likely than well-integrated personalities to express personality-oriented pressures in organization action. For such disorders will normally incapacitate individuals from successful leadership careers in the big bureaucratic organizations, since these persons will lack the stamina, the ability to work cooperatively with others, the trust in others, and so forth, which such leadership demands. And if, in the exceptional case, such an individual comes close to the pinnacle of decision-making power, counter-pressures are generated within the organization that will greatly limit or even nullify his influence.[33] And such considerations may well seem applicable to totalitarian as well as other organizational settings. Moreover, it has been suggested that the peculiarly trying conditions of political life at the upper levels of a totalitarian state create an added obstacle to success of individuals with personality disorders. "So intense and continuous are the anxieties in a garrison-police state," writes Harold Lasswell, "that it is reasonable to suggest that only personalities who are basically integrated can endure. They must be in sufficient control of themselves to avoid over-suspiciousness, or they cannot identify confederates upon whom they can rely for common purposes."[34] Elsewhere Lasswell hypothesizes that while "anxiety-ridden persons" may be suitable for lower administrative niches in totalitarian systems, those in the top elite must have "relatively few internal conflicts" and be "comparatively free to make realistic appraisals of the environment," so that "It is probable that *a basically healthy personality is essential to survive the perpetual uncertainties of political life.*"[35]

The argumentation just outlined has merit; the question is, how much? Does it, in particular, warrant a conclusion that individuals with strong paranoid tendencies should not be expected to achieve and retain positions of supreme power in totalitarian movements and systems? I do not believe that it does. For the considerations that have been adduced here must be balanced against a series of countervailing considerations that appear to outweigh them. The countervailing considerations have to do with organizations, personality, and their interrelationships.

First, it seems inadvisable to discuss the problem on the plane of organization or bureaucracy in general. For distinctions between different sorts of organizations are quite important in assessing the likelihood that a given personality type or trait will be resisted, particularly if the type or trait falls in the category of psychopathology. We must distinguish, for example, between organizations that *are* bureaucracies, such as civil services, and organizations that merely *have* them, such as political parties. For psychological characteristics that might be a decided hindrance to success in the professional bureaucracy might be much less so, might in fact be a help, in a non-bureaucratic organizational milieu. Thus a Hitler would in all probability not have had a successful career in the *Reichsbank* under Hitler, who early in life rebelled against his father's wish that he become a civil servant and lacked many qualities requisite to success as one; but Hitler himself functioned in the very different organizational medium of the National Socialist movement and, later, of the higher Nazi leadership. Again, we must differentiate organizations in terms of their relative militance or non-militance, recognizing that at one extreme we find among political organizations some that are so militant in aim and outlook, so committed to political and psychological warfare as a mode of activity, that they may accurately be called "fighting organizations." Various revolutionary and extremist organizations would be cases in point—and cases that need to be considered because, as historical experience shows, under certain circumstances they achieve political power and furnish the leadership of modern states. Much of what has been said about organizational rejection of aberrant personalities is not applicable to organizations falling in this special category. Indeed, some of the very psychological characteristics that might tend to incapacitate an individual for a major role in other kinds of organizations may be potent qualifications for leadership of a fighting organization.

This organizational milieu is, in particular, favorable for the emergence in leadership positions of individuals of a type that may be called the "warfare personality." Hitler and Stalin were examples who also happened to be, in their respective ways, men of outstanding leadership ability. The warfare personality shows paranoid characteristics as psychiatrically defined,[36] but what is essential from the standpoint of this discussion is that it represents a *political* personality type. The characteristically paranoid perception of the world as an arena of deadly hostilities being conducted conspiratorially by an insidious and implacable enemy against the self finds highly systematized expression in terms of political and ideological symbols that are widely understood and accepted in the given social milieu. Through a special and radical form of displacement of private affects upon public objects, this world-image is politicalized. In the resulting vision of reality, both attacker and intended victim are projected on the scale of large human collectivities. Consequently, in proclaiming the imperative need to fight back against an enveloping conspiratorial menace, the warfare personality identifies the enemy not as simply his own but as the society's and, in particular, the organization's. His particular vision of reality may therefore furnish potent ideological inspiration for a fighting organization, especially at a time of acute social malaise and crisis when conspiracy-centered outlooks show a certain plausibility and have an appeal to very many in the membership of the organization and in its wider social constituency. There is thus a possible close "fit" between the needs of a fighting organization *qua* organization for militant orientation and leadership, and the needs of a warfare personality *qua* personality for a leadership role and a life of unremitting struggle against enemies. Paradoxically, the very enemy-fixation that would help incapacitate the individual for leadership of most other organizations is here the key to the confluence of organizational and personal needs.

There are other ways too in which psychopathological tendencies may prove highly "functional" for the warfare personality, both on the road to power in a fighting organization and also in his possible subsequent position as political ruler in a system of totalitarian character. Especially noteworthy is an extraordinary capacity for self-dramatization and self-deception. The presence of this quality in Hitler's personality has been mentioned above. We see it also in Stalin, and it appears to be a basic attribute to the warfare personality who is sufficiently gifted to qualify as a totalitarian dictator. He shows an outstanding ability, as it were, to project *mein Kampf* as *unser Kampf,* to pass himself off as merely the spearhead of the endangered group's resistance in a country-wide and ultimately world-wide struggle against the conspiratorial menace (however the latter is defined). What enables him to be so convincing in this capacity is his self-dramatization, which in turn is serious rather than playful. He carries conviction because he has conviction. He is like an actor who lives his role while in the process of playing it, with the difference that he rarely if ever stops playing it. He is—if the cases of both Hitler and Stalin as subsequently documented are indicative—extremely egocentric as a personality, yet able to project himself with signal success as utterly group-centered, as a person for whom self is nothing and the organization or the movement or the system is all; and he can do this because he himself is so persuaded of the fact, being the first to believe in himself in his own role. He thus appears, but deceptively, as a peculiarly selfless prisoner of an abstract "ideological supersense" or "totalitarian mystique." The psychological reality is much more complex. We may, then, hypothesize that a capacity for what may be called sincere simulation, for effective masking of his own psychological needs as those of the organization or system, is a characteristic of the totalitarian dictator as a personality type. And it may be in part for this reason that scholarly students of totalitarianism have, as argued earlier here, unduly emphasized "system-needs" as motivating forces of totalitarianism and left out of account the impact of the needs of the dictatorial personality. They too have been deceived by him.

In the career of a totalitarian dictator a time may come, of course, when his vision of reality loses its persuasive power within the leadership of the movement, when he can no longer successfully project his psychological needs as needs of the system, when simulation fails. This is what appears to have happened toward the close of Stalin's life, and it is one of the reasons why his case is so extraordinarily instructive for theoretical analysis. Owing to his psychological rigidity on the one hand and postwar changes in objective conditions of the Soviet state on the other, a rift opened up in his last years between his policy views and those held by others in the inner circle of top leaders. By about 1949 the Soviet state could no longer really be said to exist in a hostile external environment, and even the world beyond the limits of the great new surrounding belt of Communist-dominated states remained dangerously hostile only insofar as Soviet acts and attitudes served to sustain the prevalent fear, suspicion, and unfriendliness. To some forces high in the leadership it appeared that these new circumstances permitted, and Soviet interests dictated, a diplomacy of international *détente* in the cold war. In presenting this view to Stalin, they apparently argued that the old "capitalist encirclement" was a thing of the past now that the U.S.S.R. had a "socialist borderland" composed of friendly states.[37] However, Stalin, who for psychological reasons was obsessed with the omnipresence of "enemies" and convinced of the need to press the cold war in perpetuity, saw a diplomacy of *détente* as criminal folly, and relaxation of East-West tension, save on a momentary tactical basis, as out of the question.

In rejecting the *détente* policy, he put forward the psychologically very significant argument that the ideological postulate of a hostile capitalist encirclement must not be understood in "geographical" but rather in "political" terms, meaning that Soviet Russia must be seen as ringed with hatred and hostility even under the new circumstances when she had a "socialist borderland." And largely in order to demonstrate graphically that the hostile capitalist encirclement "still exists and operates," as the Soviet press put it at the time, he staged in the last year of his life the affair of the Kremlin doctors, which must be seen not simply as an "internal affair" but in its connection with Stalin's foreign policy. Analysis of this final (and probably fatal) episode in Stalin's political career shows that he was using the alleged Anglo-American–Jewish conspiracy for medical murder of Soviet leaders as a telling *riposte* against the high-level Soviet advocates of relaxation of international tension, and also as a basis for getting rid of these men and others with a new blood purge. The doctors' trial, which was apparently about to start at the very moment when Stalin providentially became "gravely ill," was to have dramatized—as the propaganda buildup for its January–February, 1953, showed—the continuing hostile machinations of what Stalin saw as a diabolical external enemy whose agents were operating internally in Russia, and even in the Kremlin, in the guise, for example, of Soviet doctors. All talk of a decrease of international tension, of improving relations with adversaries, would thus be exposed as a political absurdity. This interpretation of the affair is, incidentally, supported by Khrushchev's statement in the 1956 secret speech that Stalin, after distributing protocols of the doctors' confessions to members of the Politburo, told them: "You are blind like young kittens; what will happen without me? The country will perish because you do not know how to recognize enemies."* Stalin's politics of the "doctors' plot" were politics of paranoia. They represented the desperate effort of an aged warfare personality to continue acting out his private vision of reality and his bellicosity in the politics of his regime at a time when the vision had lost its credibility among the dictator's own entourage and the bellicosity endangered the system and all its beneficiaries.

If Stalin, as seems quite possible, was finally put out of the

* *Crimes of the Stalin Era,* S49. The evidence for the interpretation that has been offered here of the division over foreign policy at the close of Stalin's lifetime, and of the political meaning of the affair of the Kremlin doctors, has been presented in greater detail and with documentation in Chapter 4 of this book.

way so as to cut short the politics of paranoia on which he was engaged, this could be taken as evidence that even a totalitarian political organization has certain powers and a tendency to resist an aberrant personality in the role of dictator. But it would seem more reasonable to conclude that the developments toward the close of Stalin's life showed how fearfully weak these powers and this tendency can be. If action was taken against him, this happened only at the eleventh hour when the very lives of those who took the action were immediately and unmistakably endangered by his further survival. It speaks against, rather than for, the theory of organizational rejection of aberrant personalities, in application to the totalitarian leader, that an aged dictator who had lost much of his erstwhile vigor and flexibility, who no longer (as was the case in the 1930's) had the advantage of being able to deceive likely victims as to his intentions, and whose psychopathological symptoms were flagrantly apparent to those around him, nevertheless managed to carry through to the final stage his preparations for a violent purge of—among others—close associates. From this viewpoint, the cases of both Stalin and Hitler emphasize a failure of the theory of organizational rejection to consider to what extent a totalitarian dictator may be able to emancipate himself from those very constraints, decision-making processes, structured situations, and role expectations that the theory treats as operative in governments generally. The point easily overlooked is that structured situations can be restructured, role expectations confounded, and roles themselves decisively remolded to fit the needs of the dictatorial personality.

By subordinating the terror machine directly to himself, as both Stalin and Hitler managed to do, by using it to terrorize associates as well as citizens at large, and by various other devices, a dictator, particularly if he is still sufficiently young and vigorous, may be able personally to dominate decisions and policy to an extraordinary degree in the organizational setting of totalitarianism. Not least among the means of nullifying institutional constraints is deliberate disorganization of higher decision-making bodies. In speaking, for example, of the personal character of Hitler's decision in August, 1939, to attack Poland, Bullock points out that by then there was no longer in operation any supreme organ of government that might have organizationally constrained Hitler's power of making one-man decisions: "No Cabinet had now met for two years past, and anything that could be called a German Government had ceased to exist."[38] Stalin too, in his last years, disorganized the higher decision-making machinery of the Soviet Communist Party as a means of keeping himself in a position to decide important questions on his own. Plenary sessions of the Party's Central Committee were no longer convened after 1947 or 1948, and the normal functioning of the Politburo appears to have terminated in early 1949. Policy problems were assigned to powerless *ad hoc* Politburo commissions variously called "quintets," "sextets," "septets," and so forth, with the result, according to Khrushchev, that the work of the Politburo itself was disorganized and some members were kept away from participation in reaching decisions on the most important state matters. One of the members, Voroshilov, was usually excluded from the occasional meetings of the Politburo that occurred because of Stalin's suspicion that he was a British agent.[39]

The foregoing considerations do not speak in favor of the theory of organizational rejection of aberrant personalities from leadership positions in totalitarian movements and systems. An individual who might be psychologically disqualified for successful leadership in very many large-scale organizations need not be so in the very special context of a fighting organization, in which his very psychopathology may be "functional" for leadership purposes. And insofar as the personality disorder would in other ways be a serious handicap to the individual in the social role of supreme leader in a totalitarian system, this incapacitating effect would show up more strongly in his later years, when autocratic power may already be securely in his grasp, than in the critically important earlier years when he comes to power. We may recall in this connection that Stalin had emerged as Soviet supreme leader by 1929, when he entered his fiftieth year; that Hitler turned fifty as his power approached its zenith in 1938; and that Mussolini, much earlier, had become the head of the Italian government at the age of thirty-nine. Finally, we need to bear in mind that the bureaucratization of modern and especially of totalitarian society can foster as well as hinder the impact of personality. In particular, given a situation in which a warfare personality has managed, despite all obstacles, to climb to autocratic power in a totalitarian system, the very bureaucratic machinery that might resist personality-oriented pressures at lower levels may transmit them with terrifying results when they come from the very top. The bureaucratic organizations of the system then may become a conduit of the dictatorial psychopathology, so many machines for effectuating his will, serving his emotional needs, and acting out his private vision of reality.

For various reasons the repetition of this pattern, especially in modern states of major importance, may not be very likely at present. Organizational resistances are not, after all, negligible. Experience with totalitarian dictators is itself a force working against repetition, particularly in the countries that had the experience. Soviet leaders, for example, maintain that measures have been taken in the political system of the U.S.S.R. to prevent a recurrence of uninhibited personal rule on the order of Stalin's and the kinds of "errors" associated with it; and the fall of Khrushchev is only the most convincing of a long series of indications that the Soviet dictatorship after Stalin has not again become an autocracy. Moreover, it may be that the combination of outstanding leadership talent with the full range of psychological characteristics that mark the potential totalitarian dictator as a personality type is an extreme rarity in modern societies. But even if it should follow from these and other considerations that the phenomenon with which we have been concerned here would only occur in the rare exceptional case, the conclusion would not be a very happy one. For we live in a time when even a single case may be one too many. One thing that political scientists can usefully do under these circumstances is to improve our understanding of the totalitarian dictator as a personality type, and of the personal element in the dynamics of totalitarianism.

PART TWO

Stalin: Personality and Policy

3 STALIN, BUKHARIN, AND HISTORY AS CONSPIRACY

> BUKHARIN: *It must be said for the sake of historical exactitude. . . .*
>
> VYSHINSKY: *Don't trouble to speak for history, accused Bukharin. History will itself record what will be interesting for history.*
>
> FROM THE TRIAL

I

The court, like every human institution, is corruptible. Under certain conditions it comes to be employed for ends extraneous and alien to its proper primary purpose, which is to promote justice through the determination of guilt or innocence by the open examining and arguing of evidence. History has witnessed many examples of this misuse of the court in the form of political trials, in which governments exploit the courtroom for such aims as the defamation and defeat of their political opponents. A subcategory of the political trial is the show trial. Here the court proceedings become literally a dramatic performance in which not only the judge and the prosecutor but also the defendant or defendants play prearranged parts just as actors do on the stage. The crux of the show trial is the confession. The defendant plays the leading part by confessing in vivid detail to heinous crimes allegedly committed by himself and others as part of a great conspiracy. Such spectacles have antecedents going back to the medieval witchcraft trials in which the accused confessed to riding on

49

broomsticks at night and passing through keyholes for their evil purposes. In our time totalitarian regimes have adopted and perfected the show trial. Indeed, the propensity to stage these political dramas in the courtroom is one of the telltale symptoms of that still imperfectly understood phenomenon of the modern age called "totalitarianism."

Political trials have taken place throughout the history of Soviet Russia, from Lenin's time to the present. The show trial, however, is one of the special hallmarks of the Stalin era and of Stalinism. It began with the Shakhty case, in which a number of Soviet and foreign engineers who had worked in the Donets coal basin confessed to participating in a conspiracy to commit crimes of industrial sabotage, or "wrecking," on orders from abroad. This show trial was staged in 1928, the year of Stalin's emergence into ascendancy in the post-Lenin regime. Others soon followed: the trial of Professor Ramzin and the "Industrial Party" in 1930, the Menshevik trial in 1931, and the Metro-Vickers case in 1933. But all these were mere curtain-risers for the series of major show trials during Stalin's Great Purge of the Communist Party in 1936–1938. Then, after World War II, which brought a respite in this business, show trials were resumed on Stalin's orders and under the direction of Stalin's agents in a number of countries of Eastern Europe which had come under Soviet domination. And when Stalin died in March, 1953, he was in the midst of preparations for one more great and macabre show trial in Russia—the trial of a group of Kremlin doctors, most of them Jewish, on charges of conspiracy to commit medical murder of Soviet leaders on instructions from the Anglo-American intelligence services. This project may have been Stalin's own undoing, for it seems quite possible that he was put out of the way in order to prevent the doctors' trial—and the new party purge that would have accompanied it—from taking place. Since his death there have been no more show trials in the Soviet Union.

The three big purge trials staged in Moscow in 1936–1938 and widely known abroad simply as the "Moscow trials," hold a special place in this history. Whereas non-Party specialists, so-called "bourgeois remnants," had figured prominently in the earlier show trials, now the cast of the accused contained many of the great names of Bolshevism. In the prisoners' dock were most of the surviving leaders of the Bolshevik Old Guard, former People's Commissars in the Soviet government, former Soviet ambassadors who had served in major world capitals like Berlin and London, and, finally, a few obscure NKVD agents whose function in the trials was to assist the prosecution in special ways by blackening the principal accused. To see more clearly to what extent the Bolshevik Old Guard was on trial, it may be useful to recall that when Lenin, towards the end of his life, considered the problem of choosing a successor in a letter that became known in the Party as his "Testament," he mentioned the names of six prominent party figures: Trotsky, Stalin, Zinoviev, Kamenev, Bukharin, and Piatakov. One only—Stalin—was ruled out, for Lenin in a postscript to this letter directed the Party leadership to remove him from the post of General Secretary because of grave character defects that could, he said, prove of decisive significance. The other five, four in person and one in absentia, were leading defendants in the Moscow trials. Zinoviev and Kamenev headed the lists of sixteen accused in the trial of the "Trotskyite-Zinovievite Terrorist Centre" in August, 1936. Piatakov, along with Karl Radek, former Secretary of the Communist International, were the leading names in the group of seventeen accused in the case of the "Anti-Soviet Trotskyite Centre" in January, 1937. Bukharin, along with Alexei Rykov, Lenin's successor as Chairman of the Council of People's Commissars, led the list of twenty-one defendants in the trial of the "Anti-Soviet Bloc of Rights and Trotskyites" in March 1938. And Trotsky, although not physically present in the dock, was being tried in absentia. In fact he was the arch-criminal of Bolshevik political history according to the picture of events that unfolded in the course of the three Moscow trials. In passing sentence in the second trial, the court directed that he and his son be arrested and tried if apprehended on Soviet territory. This was an esoterically phrased death sentence and was carried out by the agent of Stalin who assassinated Trotsky in Mexico in 1940.

The 1938 trial of the twenty-one has good claim to be considered "the great purge trial." Here the series of show trials staged during the Great Purge reached its climax. The major accusatory themes introduced in the earlier purge trials were restated and brought together with new charges, one of them being that Marshal Tukhachevsky and fellow Soviet military leaders who were executed in June, 1937, after a secret trial, had headed a "military conspiratorial organization" linked with the larger conspiracy of which Bukharin and others had allegedly been ringleaders. The summing-up speech of the prosecutor, Vyshinsky, in the 1938 trial is the classic presentation of the ideology of the

Moscow purge trials in its full-blown development, and the trial itself may justly be regarded as the supreme production in the Stalin genre of political show trial. It was likewise, as I shall argue below, the scene of an encounter between Vyshinsky and the chief defendant, Nikolai Bukharin, who endeavored by a technique of indirection to transform his trial into an anti-trial. an indictment and conviction of his accuser, Stalin.

The problem of the Moscow trials, and of this one in particular, takes on still greater interest at present owing to the post-Stalin Soviet disclosures concerning the Great Purge and the purge trials. De-Stalinization has meant, in no small part, a process of exoneration and rehabilitation—posthumous in very many cases—of purge victims. In this process much significant information has been brought to light. Khrushchev's secret report on Stalin to the Twentieth Party Congress in 1956, although not published inside the Soviet Union to this day, was nevertheless the fountainhead of an official Soviet literature about the purges that went on accumulating during the years of Khrushchev's ascendancy and has continued to flow even after his fall from power in October, 1964. Although it still leaves many questions unsolved or incompletely answered, this body of Soviet material provides a basis not only for a fresh look at the trials and purges themselves but also for a critical re-examination of the ideas and assumptions underlying the voluminous Western literature on this subject, most of which was produced in the Stalin era.

A crucially important point that emerges from the post-Stalin Soviet revelations about the Great Purge is that Stalin personally conceived, initiated, and directed the entire process, including the planning, preparation, and actual conduct of the purge trials. It is true that testimony to the same effect had reached us from other sources much earlier. Stalin had been pictured as director-general of the purges and trials by high-ranking Soviet police officials with firsthand knowledge of the situation who escaped to the West at the time and published their stories.[1] However, this view of the matter, with all its profound implications, somehow failed to make the requisite deep impression upon the Western mind. Nor was it understood by the Soviet public and intelligentsia, who had no access to such sources of information. In memoirs published long after Stalin's death the writer Ilya Ehrenburg recalls what went on in the minds of Soviet intellectuals during the Great Purge: "We thought (perhaps we wanted to think) that Stalin knew nothing about the senseless violence

committed against the Communists, against the Soviet intelligentsia. Meyerhold said: 'They conceal it from Stalin.' One night . . .
I met Boris Pasternak in Lavrushensky lane; he waved his arms
about as he stood between the snowdrifts: 'If only someone would
tell Stalin about it.' "[2] Many purge victims reasoned similarly.
Some addressed anguished appeals to Stalin from NKVD cells,
protesting their innocence. General Yakir, one of those arrested in
1937 in the Tukhachevsky case, is said to have shouted at the
moment he was shot: "Long live the Party, long live Stalin!"
Khrushchev, who related this story at the Twenty-Second Party
Congress in 1961, explains: "He thought that enemies had infil-
trated the organs of the People's Commissariat of Internal Affairs."[3] Among some political prisoners in concentration camps
this belief took the form of a theory that fascists had wormed their
way into positions of power under Stalin. Another widely held
belief was that the events of the time were the work of the NKVD
chief, Yezhov; in fact, the climax of the Great Purge in 1937–
1938 became known in Russia as the *Yezhovshchina,* or "time
of Yezhov."

In reality it was the time of Stalin. The picture given earlier in
the accounts of NKVD defectors such as Krivitsky and Orlov has
been fully and convincingly confirmed by official Soviet sources of
the post-Stalin period. The man whom many believed to be incompletely informed about the Great Purge was in fact running it.
The man to whom some appealed for justice over the head of the
NKVD was in fact directing all its activity. In his secret report to
the Twentieth Party Congress, Khrushchev tells, for example,
how Yezhov would send to Stalin for his approval lists of persons
in NKVD custody with proposed sentences indicated upon them.
"In 1937–1938," he says, "383 such lists containing the names of
many thousands of Party, Soviet, Komsomol, Army and economic
workers were sent to Stalin. He approved these lists."[4] He tells
us further that Stalin rather than Yezhov made all the decisions
concerning arrests of high party leaders, many of whom were
arrested without the prosecutor's knowledge. "In such a situation," Khrushchev goes on, "there is no need for any sanction, for
what sort of a sanction could there be when Stalin decided everything? He was the chief prosecutor in these cases. Stalin not only
agreed to, but on his own initiative issued, arrest orders." Naturally, Stalin could not have engineered the Great Purge without
the zealous and capable assistance of many others, among whom
his police chiefs, Yagoda and Yezhov, deserve special mention.

But these men as well as their subordinates were essentially Stalin's accomplices and tools, not independent figures acting in their own right. Thus Yagoda, who had assisted Stalin in preparing the 1936 trial, was then removed (to become a defendant himself in the 1938 trial) and replaced by Yezhov, who in turn was eliminated after serving as Stalin's right-hand man at the height of the reign of terror.

Why did so many Russians, including some high-ranking victims of the purge, fail to understand that Stalin was the moving spirit and director of the whole business? Ehrenburg probably gives part of the answer when he speaks of their wish to believe otherwise. We must also take account of the traditional Russian habit of absolving the Tsar of personal responsibility for flagrant injustices, which were thought to be the work of evil ministers who kept the Tsar in ignorance of the people's sufferings. But a further and crucial part of the explanation is that Stalin contrived to hold himself aloof and in the background so that people would not understand his true role in the events of the time. His activity as stage manager of these events was carried on behind the scenes and was known only to a few, most of whom perished before the end. Even in the fateful Central Committee session of March 3–5, 1937, during which Stalin's two speeches were signals for intensification of the Great Purge as it entered the final period, he carefully posed as a force for moderation by cautioning in conclusion against "a heartless attitude toward people" and castigating unnamed Party leaders who were expelling Party members with reckless abandon and "think it a mere bagatelle to expel thousands and tens of thousands of people from the Party."[5] By such means Stalin successfully carried out one of the greatest acts of deliberate deception in modern political history. That is, he contrived to make the time of Stalin go down in Russian history as the "time of Yezhov."

As we re-examine the problem of the Moscow show trials, then, it is essential to bear in mind that these were basically one-man shows of which Stalin himself was organizer, chief producer, and stage manager as well as an appreciative spectator from a darkened room at the rear of the Hall of Columns, where the trials were held. Vyshinsky spoke for the prosecution, but we must understand that he spoke with the voice of Stalin. Although he did not claim personal authorship, Stalin was the chief playwright of the case of the "Anti-Soviet Bloc of Rights and Trotskyites" and the other cases enacted in the show trials.

II

"We have internal enemies. We have external enemies. This, comrades, must not be forgotten for a single moment." This was Stalin's "general conclusion" in a major speech of April, 1928, on the state of the Soviet Union. It flowed from his analysis of the Shakhty case, which he described as an economic counter-revolution plotted by bourgeois experts who "banded together in a secret group and were receiving money for sabotage purposes from former owners now living abroad and from counter-revolutionary anti-Soviet capitalist organizations in the West."[6] Here, in embryo, was the ideology of the later purge trials as elaborated by Vyshinsky with the assistance of the confessing defendants. Here was the *Weltanschauung* of those trials.

The world of the Moscow trials is one of long-drawn-out conspiratorial cold war waged for the purpose of destroying the Soviet state and the Revolution it embodies. It is a world dominated by the machinations of external and especially internal "enemies" who are diabolically cunning as well as totally vicious and evil. Abroad they may at times operate in the open, although their chief arm is the secretly functioning intelligence services of the major powers. But inside the Soviet Union they do all their nefarious work by stealthy and devious means, practicing deception as their primary technique of political warfare. They wear "masks" of loyal citizens and prominent party and government leaders until they are finally exposed as persons who, in the words of Vyshinsky's summing-up speech in the Bukharin trial, "spent the whole of their lives behind masks. . . ." And these internal enemies are no less a deadly danger to the Soviet state for the fact that they represent, in actual numbers, only a small minority of the total population. For, as Stalin explained in the March 1937 Central Committee meeting, "it does not at all need a big number of people to do harm and to cause damage. . . . Thousands of people are required to build a big railway bridge, but a few people are sufficient to blow it up. Tens of hundreds of such examples could be quoted. Consequently, we must not comfort ourselves with the fact that we are many, while they, the Trotskyite wreckers, are few."[7]

In this same speech Stalin represented the above-mentioned world-view as being "what Leninism teaches us," and Vyshinsky echoed the point in the 1938 summing-up speech. Though Stalin, in all probability, seriously believed this, he was mistaken. Lenin had provided a foundation for this world-view in his concept of an international class war between a "socialism" embodied in the Soviet Republic and a "capitalism" dominant in the rest of the world, which represented therefore a hostile "capitalist encirclement." But Stalin filled these old Leninist concepts with a new, distinctively Stalinist content, which found expression in the materials of the Moscow purge trials. The chief distinctive feature was the quite un-Leninist emphasis upon *conspiracy* as the hallmark of the present epoch. Although it did not exclude underhanded methods, the original Bolshevik or Leninist ideology did not view the international class war as a conflict being waged by essentially conspiratorial means. Nor did it see this conflict as centering in the hostile activities of masked enemies operating inside Soviet society. In Stalinism the Leninist notion of an international class war turns into the notion of a conspiratorial cold war against the Soviet Union. The final and finished expression of this conspiratorial interpretation of contemporary history is to be found in the pages of the trial transcript itself.

As we examine it we must bear in mind that the history of Lenin's party from its founding early in the century to the end of the 1920's was characterized by factional struggles and opposition movements supporting programs of Party policy that were at times openly debated. Shortly following the Bolshevik Revolution of 1917, for example, Bukharin, one of the outstanding leaders and theoreticians of the Party, headed a "Left Communist" opposition that favored revolutionary war as against Lenin's policy of accepting the annexationist peace dictated by the German government to Trotsky at Brest-Litovsk. Other opposition movements rose and fell in the Party during the turbulent first years of its rule, and factionalism flourished in spite of the formal prohibition of it in the resolution on Party unity adopted by the Tenth Party Congress in 1921. With Lenin's death the Party's inner conflicts intensified. In the mid-1920's the Trotskyite or "Left Opposition," joined in 1926 by Stalin's former allies Zinoviev and Kamenev, vainly opposed its program of rapid industrialization and "permanent revolution" to the platform of "socialism in one country." Though the latter became identified with Stalin, it originated with a group of "Right Communists" headed by Bukharin, who had now shifted to a moderate position, Alexei Rykov, and the trade-union leader Mikhail Tomsky. To these men "socialism in one country" meant a program of gradual industrialization without forcible measures to collectivize the Russian peasantry, continual alleviation of the harsher aspects of the dictatorship, and in foreign affairs a tendency to de-emphasize the policy of fomenting revolution in Europe in favor of efforts to cement diplomatic ties with and secure economic credits from the Western democracies.[8] Having taken over the slogan of "socialism in one country" from this source and used it with signal success against the Left Opposition, Stalin subsequently gave it an interpretation very different from that of the right-wing leaders, whose position was stigmatized at the end of the 1920's as the "Right Opposition." To Stalin "socialism in one country" meant a strengthening of the dictatorship and an orientation of the nation's economy towards preparation for total war. This was to be achieved through breakneck industrialization, emphasizing heavy industry and arms production, and exploitation of peasant labor by means of coercive collectivization. Stalin's program went into effect during the First Five-Year Plan (1928–1933) at ghastly cost to the country in strain, dislocation, privation, sacrifice, and suffering.

The right-wing leaders were opposed in principle to this Stalinist "general line" and fought it as hard and as long as they could. Bukharin, their foremost theorist and the soul of the Right Opposition, bore the brunt of the fight. In the course of it he made a move to secure support from Stalin's old left-wing opponents Zinoviev and Kamenev. On July 11, 1928, in an interview with Kamenev later published abroad by the Trotskyites, Bukharin said that his group considered Stalin's line fatal to the Revolution. Stalin, he said, was leading the country to famine, ruin, and a police regime with his program of exacting "tribute" from the peasantry for forced industrialization, and was ideologically justifying this line with an argument of "idiotic illiteracy" to the effect that resistance and therewith internal class conflict must grow as socialism grows. After comparing Stalin with Genghis Khan, Bukharin said that conditions were ripening in the Central Committee for dismissing Stalin but were not yet fully ripe. Meanwhile Stalin, who was at bottom interested only in power, was determined to strangle the opposition. "Stalin knows only vengeance," Bukharin declared. "We must remember his theory of sweet revenge." This was a reference to something that Stalin had said one summer night in 1923 to Kamenev and Dzerzhinsky: "To choose one's victim, to prepare one's plans minutely, to slake an implacable vengeance, and then to go to bed. . . . There is nothing sweeter in the world."[9] Publication of this interview proved extremely damaging to Bukharin and the Right

Opposition.

At the beginning of 1929 he was still editor of *Pravda,* and he made a final open attempt to oppose Stalin's course in an article on "Lenin's Political Testament" published in *Pravda* on January 21, the fifth anniversary of Lenin's death. He argued carefully and convincingly here that the essence of Lenin's final position was that the building of a socialist system in Russia should be achieved through a long process of *"peaceful organization and cultural work"* (Lenin's words, italics by Bukharin) and specifically without coercion of the peasantry. In short, it was Lenin's political testament, according to Bukharin's reading, that socialism could and should be built without an intensified class struggle in Soviet society and without such a violent "third revolution" as was plainly implicit in the Stalin program. In the following month matters came to a head in a stormy session of the Politburo during which the right-wing leaders attacked Stalin for one-man decisions and argued that his collectivization program was leading to what Bukharin called "military-feudal exploitation of the peasants."[10] From this point on the Right Opposition went down to defeat. Later in 1929 Bukharin was expelled from the Politburo and dismissed from his positions as editor of *Pravda* and member of the Executive Committee of the Comintern. Rykov was dismissed as Premier and Tomsky was removed from leadership of the trade unions. The three right-wing leaders publicly renounced their "deviation" in November, and open opposition came to an end. Earlier that year, it will be recalled, Trotsky had been deported from the country.

Though open opposition ceased, Bukharin, an exceedingly adroit thinker and talented writer, continued on occasion to convey criticism of Stalin by a technique of indirection, or double-talk, that was known, among the older revolutionists who had developed it under Tsarist censorship conditions, as "Aesopian language." Thus in a *Pravda* article of March 7, 1930, which was ostensibly a long polemic against the papacy in general and Pope Pius in particular for his newly published encyclical on communism, Bukharin skillfully conveyed that "popes" meant Stalin and his followers, "Jesuit order" the Stalinist NKVD, "heresy" the opposition viewpoint, and so on. Of special political significance was a passage that he quoted here from a book on Church history, saying: "If they (the popes, N. Bukharin) kill the soul, then why have they a right to call themselves the successors of Christ? Where is the similarity of their institutions?

Christ, speaking to Peter, once said: Feed my sheep! But what do the popes do? Do they not lead the Christians, *completely pillaged by papal plundering, to starvation? Do they not fleece their sheep continually, and cut into their flesh whilst shearing them?*" (Italics by Bukharin.) The "Aesopian" message here was that Stalin, who was pillaging the peasantry and leading the people to starvation with the catastrophic forced collectivization campaign then in progress, had thereby turned against the true heritage of Bolshevism as embodied in Lenin's political testament. That others in the party shared this view of the events of the time is shown by the clandestine circulation of the so-called "Riutin platform," in which a former follower of Bukharin bitterly assailed Stalin for his policies and called for his removal. By the time of the Seventeenth Party Congress in 1934, however, the situation in the country had eased. Such prominent former oppositionists as Bukharin, Rykov, Zinoviev, Kamenev, Piatakov, and Radek appeared on the platform to emphasize their approval of the general line and pay tribute to Stalin's leadership in carrying it out. Bukharin, though demoted from full to candidate membership in the Party Central Committee after the Congress, was appointed editor of *Izvestia,* a position he held until his arrest early in 1937.

Meanwhile there was one last episode of opposition to Stalin on the part of Bukharin. In the first of the great show trials, the Zinoviev-Kamenev trial of August, 1936, several defendants named Bukharin, Rykov, and Tomsky (the last-named committed suicide at this time) as co-participants in the criminal activities to which they confessed. A press campaign of vilification of the former right-wing leaders ensued, and in early September a meeting was reportedly called in the Central Committee to consider their expulsion from the party.[11] Presenting Stalin's case against them, Yezhov at this meeting moved for the expulsion of Bukharin and Rykov on the ground that they, along with Trotsky, Zinoviev, and Kamenev, had been involved since 1918 in a "monstrous conspiracy" in the course of which they had become agents of the Gestapo and were even now plotting, in concert with the Trotskyites, a *coup d'état.* Replying in his own defense, Bukharin agreed that a monstrous conspiracy was being carried out against the Party and state in the Soviet Union. But its leaders, he declared, were Stalin and Yezhov, who were plotting and acting to change the Bolshevik Party regime inherited from Lenin into an NKVD regime in which Stalin would enjoy unlimited personal power. He contended that the elimination of himself and Rykov was a necessary part of this conspiratorial plan and that what was now being decided, therefore, was not the "Bukharin question" but the fate of the country. Stalin's supporters in the Politburo supported the Yezhov motion in the ensuing discussion; others did not. When the vote was taken, the motion was supported by less than a third of the Central Committee members present. Stalin indicated his acceptance of the adverse decision, and a statement was published in *Pravda* on September 10 announcing that the case against Bukharin and Rykov was being closed because investigation had not established judicial bases for legal proceedings against them. Stalin meanwhile went on maneuvering. The Tukhachevsky military group, whose representatives in the Central Committee had supported the pro-Bukharin majority, were arrested and executed in June, 1937. In 1937–1938, according to data in Khrushchev's secret report, 98 members and candidates of the Central Committee, or 70 per cent of the total, were arrested and shot. It seems very likely that the physical liquidation of the overwhelming majority of this highest ruling body in the Soviet system was connected at least in part with the events just recounted. In any event, the way was now cleared for the trial of Bukharin and Rykov, which opened in March, 1938.

The case developed in this trial was an elaboration of the "monstrous conspiracy" charge made against Bukharin and Rykov in the reported secret Party meeting in 1936. It pictured the erstwhile Left and Right oppositions as two interconnected prongs of a conspiracy of many years standing to destroy the Revolution and the Lenin-Stalin regime. It was held that in 1918 Bukharin and his group of Left Communists and Trotsky and his group had plotted to frustrate the Brest-Litovsk peace, overthrow the Soviet government, arrest and murder Lenin and Stalin, and form a new government. Bukharin had helped inspire the terrorist attempt on Lenin's life by Dora Kaplan in August, 1918. Trotsky had entered the service of the German intelligence in 1921. Bukharin and Rykov had long been connected with foreign intelligence services through accomplices, and Krestinsky, Rosengoltz, and Rakovsky had been agents of foreign powers since the early 1920's. Both Trotskyite and Right oppositions had from the start been subversive movements motivated by criminal anti-Soviet aims rather than genuine oppositionist convictions. In 1932–1933, when the futility of further open opposition activity was clear, they had formed, on instructions of foreign intelligence services, a conspiratorial group called "Bloc of Rights and Trotsky-ites," on behalf of which Trotsky had negotiated an agreement with Nazi Germany looking to the overthrow of the Soviet government and the defeat and dismemberment of the U.S.S.R. in a coming war. The conspirators also had entered into a secret agreement with Japan under which she would render armed assistance in overthrowing the Soviet government and later be recompensed with the Maritime Region in the Soviet Far East. In preparation for functioning as a fifth column and opening the front in time of war, the conspiracy had engaged in espionage, wrecking activities, incitement of peasant risings, and the planning or execution of terrorist acts against Soviet leaders. The wrecking activities, aimed both at undermining the economy and at stirring up anti-Soviet feeling which would hamper the defense effort in time of war, included deliberate mismanagement of the ruble and state savings banks by Finance Commissar Grinko, deliberate infecting of pigs with plague through the efforts of Agriculture Commissar Chernov, and the mixing of glass and nails into butter by arrangement of the head of the consumer cooperatives, Zelensky. The terrorist acts had included the assassination of the Leningrad Party leader Sergei Kirov in 1934, and the medical murder of two other prominent Party leaders, Kuibyshev and Menzhinsky, and of Maxim Gorky and his son. The medical murders had been committed by well-known Soviet doctors on orders of the NKVD chief, Yagoda, who had made a deep study of the history of murder by poisoning and had planned, among other crimes, to murder Yezhov by poisoning the air in his office with mercury dissolved in an acid. Another and key unfulfilled aim of the conspirators had been the murder of Stalin.

How true or false was this conspiratorial view of Soviet history? It contained some sheer fabrications, such as the allegations about the espionage connections of the accused and their collaboration with Nazi Germany and Japan. But not everything falls in this category. Some actual facts have been mentiosed in the foregoing summary, and many more appear in the voluminous trial proceedings themselves. There was, as we have seen, a real history of opposition activity, a "Riutin platform," a 1928 anti-Stalin talk between Bukharin and Kamenev, and so on. Krestinsky, who was Soviet ambassador in Berlin in the 1920's, undoubtedly had conversations with German military men. Bukharin did, as mentioned in his testimony and final statement, have meetings in

Paris early in 1936 with the well-known scholar and Menshevik leader Boris Nicolaevsky. Some criminal acts mentioned in the trial actually occurred. Dora Kaplan did make an attempt on Lenin's life, Sergei Kirov was in fact assassinated, and it may be, although this is not definitely confirmed, that Gorky was murdered by poisoning. It is true that Yagoda, a one-time pharmacist, was knowledgeable in the history of murder by poisoning. Some peasant outbreaks did occur in the early 1930's and there was great loss of livestock then. Some savings banks were mismanaged, timber-floating operations were disorganized, the supply of school exercise books was in places interrupted, the sowing of vegetables was misplanned, and there were various goods shortages—facts which are mentioned in the trial—and these and like situations did create much popular discontent. It may even be that nails and glass had in places turned up in Soviet butter.

On the other hand, these real facts and incidents are all falsified in the manner in which they were presented at the trial. For they did not occur as elements in a vast anti-Soviet conspiracy. Thus Bukharin's opposition to Lenin over Brest-Litovsk harbored no anti-Lenin conspiratorial designs, and nothing in the world was more foreign to his makeup than a desire to harm Lenin. Although he came to loathe Stalin and wished it were possible to unseat him from power, he had not been involved in a terrorist plot to accomplish this. He met with Nicolaevsky in Paris in 1936 not for conspiratorial anti-Soviet purposes but in order to negotiate, on behalf of the Communist Party, for purchase of the Marx-Engels archives from the German Social Democratic Party. The peasant disturbances were a reaction to forced collectivization, not a product of right-wing plotting, and livestock was lost in great numbers because peasants slaughtered their animals in resistance to collectivization. The shortages, disruptions of supply, and general disorganization in the land were generated by Stalin's convulsive "third revolution" rather than by deliberate "wrecking" activity in connection with a conspiracy. Finally, the murder of Kirov was not organized by the accused but rather, it very strongly appears, by Stalin, who sought thereby both to remove a potential rival and to create a pretext for launching the Great Purge.

What unfolds before us in the trial, then, is a gigantic texture of fantasy into which bits and pieces of falsified real history have been woven along with outright fiction. It forms an elaborate unified system in the sense that everything hangs together in a coherent, logical, and internally self-consistent whole. The master theme running through it all and giving it a dramatic unity is the great anti-Soviet conspiracy. It furnishes the motivation and therewith the explanation for hundreds of events and incidents spoken of in the trial, many of which really happened. Now this scheme bears a definite and, as I shall suggest further on, understandable resemblance to textbook descriptions of a paranoid delusional system. Authorities describe a paranoid system as an intricate, schematized, and logically elaborated structure with a "central delusional theme" involving a hostile plot of which the person concerned is an intended victim. The plot is ascribed to a "paranoid pseudo-community," which is "an imaginary organization, composed of real and imagined persons, whom the patient represents as united for the purpose of carrying out some action upon him."[12]

That the conspiratorial master theme in the case of the "Anti-Soviet Bloc of Rights and Trotskyites" was fictional is no longer subject to dispute. The great anti-Soviet conspiracy around which the whole case is organized was quite imaginary. The "Bloc of Rights and Trotskyites" never existed as an organized conspiratorial group seeking to undermine the Soviet state and overthrow the Stalin government. As Bukharin correctly mentioned in his final statement, "the accused in this dock are not a group" and insofar as the "Bloc" actually existed it did so as a venture in back-stage opposition politics undertaken at the time of his conversation with Kamenev in 1928. Since that was prior to Hitler's rise to power, he went on, the group could not possibly have been formed on instruction of fascist intelligence services. That is, the basic conspiracy charge, relating to the alleged dealings of the accused with the Axis governments, was false. Bukharin's denial on this key point has been fully borne out. Had there been any foundation at all for the charge that the accused collaborated with the Nazis and Japanese, the captured archives of the defeated Axis powers and the memories of their surviving leaders should have furnished evidence of this collaboration. But they have not.[13]

The non-existence of the great counter-revolutionary conspiracy has been admitted by the Soviet regime since Stalin's death. A special commission of inquiry appointed by the Party Central Committee to look into the events of 1937–1938 found "nothing tangible" at the bottom of the treason charges brought against so many thousands of Party members at that time. This was reported by Khrushchev in his secret speech to the Twentieth Party

Congress. He says here that "when the cases of some of these so-called 'spies' and 'saboteurs' were examined, it was found that all their cases were fabricated." And further: "Many thousands of honest and innocent Communists have died as a result of this monstrous falsification of such 'cases.' " To illustrate the methods by which NKVD officials "manufactured various fictitious 'anti-Soviet centers' and 'blocs' " and "fabricated 'anti-Soviet plots,' " he cites the case of a survivor, one Rozenblum, who told the commission how, after being subjected to terrible torture, he was brought before the NKVD investigator Zakovsky. The latter informed him that the NKVD would work out the legend for his case: "You yourself,' said Zakovsky, 'will not need to invent anything. The NKVD will prepare for you a ready outline for every branch of the center; you will have to study it carefully and remember well all questions and answers which the Court might ask. This case will be ready in four–five months, or perhaps a half year. During all this time you will be preparing yourself. . . . Your future will depend on how the trial goes and on its results.' " This description, incidentally, accords with the accounts of surviving victims of the purge who found their way to the West and published stories of their experiences.

If the cases of so many thousands of "honest and innocent Communists" were fabricated, if mythical "anti-Soviet centers," "blocs," and "plots" were invented in full detail by expert NKVD political playwrights for acting out by prisoners in trials, then obviously the central super-conspiracy, with which all the lesser conspiratorial centers around the country were alleged to be linked, was similarly a fabrication. The Soviet regime has admitted this, although unfortunately it has not yet done so in a wholly unambiguous and comprehensive manner. Marshal Tukhachevsky and his fellow officers of the "military conspiratorial group" mentioned in the Bukharin trial are now declared to have been entirely innocent, patriotic Soviet citizens and devoted Party members done to death on trumped-up treason charges. As of this writing (December, 1964) several of the defendants in the Bukharin trial, including Krestinsky, Grinko, and Ikramov, have been similarly rehabilitated, which of course shatters the entire case, since their testimony interlocks at so many points with that of the other defendants. These others, particularly Bukharin and Rykov, have not yet been restored to places of honor in the history of the Party. It is notable, however, that the criminal conspiracy charges against Bukharin and Rykov have already been dismissed publicly. Speaking at a conference of Soviet historians late in 1962, P. N. Pospelov, director of the Institute of Marxism-Leninism, declared that "neither Bukharin nor Rykov of course were spies or terrorists."[14]

Since the Moscow trials a voluminous literature has grown up in the West on the question of why the defendants confessed. Certain points regarding the motives of Bukharin, who seems to have been something of a special case, will be made below. Here I should like simply to point out that Soviet post-Stalin disclosures corroborate earlier reports by NKVD defectors and purge victims who later escaped to the West that torture and extreme pressure, including threats of doing harm to loved ones, were employed. In the secret report to the Twentieth Congress Khrushchev cites a coded telegram sent out by Stalin to the heads of NKVD organizations and other officials on January 20, 1939, saying that methods of "physical pressure" in NKVD practice, which had been permissible from 1937 on, should continue to be applied "obligatorily" to "known and obstinate enemies of the people as a method both justifiable and appropriate." Khrushchev states further: "Confessions of guilt of many arrested and charged with enemy activity were gained with the help of cruel and inhuman tortures." This statement is borne out by testimony from a variety of sources. The defendants confessed because they were forced to.

III

The Moscow trials understandably aroused enormous interest in the West. In the discussion that started then and went on for a good many years, two questions were asked most insistently and discussed at greatest length: Were they guilty? Why did they confess? Inside Russia, on the other hand, attention focused upon a different question: Why the trials, and why the Great Purge as a whole? Ehrenburg recalls in his memoirs: "I realized that people were being accused of crimes which they had not and could not have committed, and I asked myself and others: why, what for? No one could give me an answer. We were completely at sea."[15] According to Beck and Godin, two purge victims who lived to write a book about it, the "enemies of the people" were asking the very same questions during their interrogation period and afterwards in the camps: "There was no question that excited the prisoners so much as that which the reader must already have asked himself time and again. 'Why? What for?' The question was endlessly argued. . . . The words 'Why? What for?' were to be found scratched with smuggled bits of broken glass on the inside walls of the 'black raven,' and the coaches of the prison trains. 'Why? What for?' "[16]

These Russians were asking the real main question, and it is one that scholars need to reopen in the light of the new information and better perspective that we now possess on the events of the time. One of the tendencies in Western writings has been to answer it by reference to postulated functional needs of the Soviet system as a form of "totalitarianism." Periodical blood purges, accompanied by such events as the Moscow show trials, have been viewed as a necessity or deep-lying tendency of totalitarianism *as a system*. This way of thinking is based upon an image of totalitarianism, in whatever form, as a fundamentally impersonal phenomenon, a system in which virtually all, including the highest functionaries of the state, are essentially cogs in a machine. Miss Hannah Arendt, whose important writings on totalitarianism have been one of the sources of this image, has suggested, for example, that blood purges such as those of the Stalin era, quite unlike the Party purges in the early years of the Russian Revolution, served as an "instrument of permanent instability."[17] Such instability, in turn, is treated as a functional requisite of totalitarianism as a system.

A different approach seems to be suggested by all that we now know. First, the phenomena in question were not at all functional necessities of the Soviet system. On the contrary, the system would have been better off and far more equipped to meet the coming test of total war had there been no Great Purge, which was, in effect, a great wrecking operation in Soviet society. We have testimony from the lips of no less an authority than Khrushchev that the Soviet order, far from requiring the Great Purge, was hard put to survive it. "Only because our party has at its disposal such great moral-political strength," he says in the secret report, "was it possible to survive the difficult events in 1937–1938 and to educate new cadres. There is, however, no doubt that our march forward toward socialism and toward the preparation of the country's defense would have been much more successful were it not for the tremendous loss of cadres suffered as a result of the baseless and false mass repressions in 1937–1938." We do not yet have any official Soviet statistics on the total losses resulting from the Great Purge, but it has been credibly estimated that around nine million persons were arrested during it.[18] And it must be borne in mind that the great majority of these victims were from the Party and non-Party governing strata of Soviet society, including professional people of all kinds and technicians.

Secondly, a great lesson to be learned from a study of the events of that time is that our theory of totalitarianism has unduly neglected the personal factor. It has not taken account, or sufficient account, of the role of the dictator and his personality in determining the conduct of the regime, the dynamics of totalitarianism itself, in such truly totalitarian situations as Germany under Hitler and Russia in the time of Stalin. Not the needs of the Soviet system but Stalin's own needs, both political and psychological, underlay the events of 1937–1938 in Russia. Not only was he, as noted earlier, the prime mover and director of those events; they occurred basically because he relentlessly willed them and was skillful enough to make others do his bidding, just as the "final solution" was perpetrated in Nazi Germany in the last analysis because Hitler fanatically desired to destroy European Jewry and succeeded in imposing his will upon the totalitarian machine of state. Of course, the Great Purge, once it started, acquired a self-propelling momentum of its own as a result, largely, of the NKVD system of forced denunciation under which each arrested person was coerced not only to admit participating in a non-existent conspiracy but also to name those who had recruited him into the imaginary conspiratorial center and those whom he himself had recruited. This helps to explain the probably unanticipated extent of the holocaust in Soviet society. But the key causal role was Stalin's. And his determination to force through the Great Purge and the trials was dictated by powerful motives that were peculiarly his own and not widely shared in the Soviet ruling elite. A full analysis of them is beyond the scope of this essay, but I will comment on three principal facets of the motivation.

We are here particularly concerned with the purge trials. But the reasons for staging them must be seen in the context of the motives for the total purge, in which thousands were executed or sent to camps by administrative order for every one who was placed on trial in public. For the purge trials had, in the first place, a political symbolic function, which was to provide a rationale for the purge, to make publicly meaningful the campaign of arrests that was going on night after night. The underlying assumption of the Great Purge was that treason was abroad in the land, especially among Party members, and that it had to be cleaned out and exterminated on the massive scale that this treason itself had assumed. The three great Moscow show trials and a number of lesser local trials held at this time were designed to dramatize this idea, to show the existence, enormity, and scope of the purported treasonable activity, which had—it was thus made to appear—been organized and directed by men at the pinnacle of the Party and state as well as their counterparts at the provincial level. Accordingly, the question of Stalin's motives is first of all the question of what he wanted to achieve by the purge as a whole.

A large part of the answer is that he wanted to achieve an unrestricted personal dictatorship with a totality of power that he did not yet possess in 1934. By the late 1920's he had become the acknowledged supreme leader of the Party and state. In the Bolshevik political tradition, however, this did not make him an absolute autocrat like the Russian Tsars, for no such position had been institutionalized in Lenin's one-party system. He could not dictate his will to the ruling elite at the level of the Politburo and Central Committee without fear of being contradicted. He could not count—as Lenin before him could not—on automatic acceptance of his policy designs without critical debate and opposition in the inner councils of the Party. And there are indications, as we have seen, that such debate and occasional opposition continued even in the early 1930's. The prime internal political purpose of the Great Purge from Stalin's point of view was to end all this, to eliminate the Bolshevik habits of criticism and opposition as well as the men who personified these habits, and to create for himself an autocracy as absolute as any that ever existed. To purge those Party members who had opposed him in the past was not enough for this purpose. Given the intricate system of patronage that prevailed at all levels in the Party and state bureaucracy, the purge of a major figure logically entailed the purge of his patronage group of associates and retainers, many of whom had lesser patronage groups of their own, and so on. Lack of objective incriminating facts about an individual was no obstacle to unmasking him, since he could be accused of *potential* oppositionism. Thus many of the purge victims were staunch Stalinists with no taint of real oppositionism in their records; their tragedies were caused by often quite accidental career associations. The outcome of the whole process was a veritable circulation of the Soviet elite. Total subservience to Stalin was now established as the first requirement for survival and political advancement.

Emerging from the events of 1936–1938 as a personal dictator in what was now a truly totalitarian system of power, Stalin had achieved the internal political purpose of the Great Purge.

But this political purpose was connected with psychological needs. Stalin has been called, and with good foundation, a technician of power. It would be a mistake, though, to see him as only that. He was not a cold-blooded cynic who viewed his villainy as villainy and accepted it as such. In making himself an absolute autocrat at so sickening a price in blood and misery, he thought he was serving the interests of the Party he was purging and the country he was terrorizing. We have evidence for the view that in engineering the events of 1936–1938 he really believed himself to be cleansing the Soviet land of treason. Some of it comes from Khrushchev, who says in the secret report: "Stalin was a very distrustful man, sickly suspicious; we know this from our work with him. He could look at a man and say: 'Why are your eyes so shifty today' or 'Why are you turning so much today and avoiding to look at me in the eyes?' The sickly suspicion created in him a general distrust even toward eminent party workers whom he had known for years. Everywhere and in everything he saw 'enemies,' 'two-facers' and 'spies.' " This description of a personality of pronounced paranoid tendency is supported by further testimony from a variety of sources, both Soviet and non-Soviet.

By what mechanism of thinking did Stalin apprehend "enemies," "two-facers," and "spies" all around him when, as we know, there was no real anti-Soviet conspiracy afoot? An essential part of the answer is that he regarded opposition to or criticism of himself—and there had been a great deal of both in the history of the Party—as evidence of profound malevolence and treasonable tendencies. Khrushchev points to this mechanism when he says in the secret report that the category "enemy of the people" was applied to "those who in any way disagreed with Stalin" as well as to "those who were only suspected of hostile intent" or "had bad reputations" (that is, politically). Stalin's tendency to identify oppositionism with treason was linked with his inability to tolerate the thought that oppositional or simply critical attitudes towards him could have any real basis in imperfections of his mind and character or in flaws in his leadership, and policies. Given this inhibition, which was rooted in his need to see himself as the perfect leader "of genius" (*genial'ny,* the term constantly used of him in Russia in his later lifetime), it followed logically that any opposition, whether open or merely a subtle suggestion of a critical attitude, must be a sign of hidden hostile designs and must stem from an enmity all the more deep and dangerous in that it was often concealed behind an appearance ("mask") of loyalty and friendliness. In short, it was evidence of probable participation in a criminal conspiracy or, at the very least, of an intention to participate in one. According to this logic, which is similar to if not actually paranoid logic,[19] the Party and country in the early 1930's, when Stalin began planning the Great Purge, were crawling with traitors.

The purge trials are constructed around this paranoid-like logic. It is to be observed that a great deal of the discourse between Vyshinsky and the defendants proceeds on the tacit understanding that an imputation of criminal conspiracy may be made on the basis of oppositional acts or attitudes. This idea defines the rules of the trial game, or "rules of translation" as they have been called.[20] A whole table of equivalences was accepted in which, for example, anti-Stalin = "counter-revolutionary," oppositional activity = "treason," anti-Stalin grouping = "conspiratorial terrorist center," anti-Stalin political orientation = "orientation on terrorism," etc., the general formula being that any opposing or criticizing of Stalin or his policies = "counter-revolutionary terrorism." In the 1937 trial Piatakov alluded to this system of equivalences when, in agreeing that he had given a certain man orders to make connections with German intelligence, he added that he had done this only in a "more algebraical formulation"— by having a talk with the man in an oppositional vein.[21] Similar allusions are made by Bukharin and others in the 1938 trial. The trials are thus in large part intricate exercises in the ferreting out of sinister terroristic *hidden meanings* in activities of the chief defendants which consisted mostly of critical or oppositional talk, especially about Stalin. The great counter-revolutionary conspiracy itself represents, as it were, the highly systematized sum total of all these hidden meanings, treated as true; it is the premise on which all of Stalin's most ominous suspicions about what was going on behind his back would have been well founded.

What I am arguing, then, is that the "algebra" of the Moscow trials was a reflection of the general way in which their organizer's mind actually worked. It is all the more understandable according to this view that Stalin, as has been reported, played a leading part in devising the legends for the trials. It need not be supposed that he believed them altogether literally. But they must have appeared to him as being true in principle and false, if at all, only in being embellishments on reality itself—embellishments, moreover, in which he could legitimately take a certain artistic pride. The implication is that the trials served not alone the above-mentioned political symbolic function of rationalizing the Great Purge but, at the same time, the psychological symbolic function of rationalizing Stalin's own paranoid tendency. The world of the Great Purge and the purge trials, peopled by multitudes of masked enemies conspiring to destroy Stalin's regime and Stalin himself, was Stalin's own mental world. Under his guidance the NKVD, assisted by Vyshinsky and others, was confirming the reality of it and making it appear still more concretely and convincingly real by arresting huge numbers of Soviet citizens, compelling them to *confess* that they had been masked enemies and putting on show trials in which leading former oppositionists and others publicly proclaimed themselves guilty of high treason. Accordingly, we may view the trials as vehicles for the acting out of something similar to a paranoid delusional system complete with central theme (the great conspiracy) and malevolent pseudo-community ("Bloc of Rights and Trotskyites," etc.). In this regard the verbatim report of the trial is a document out of the history of human psychopathology.

But there was much political method in this psychopathology. As indicated earlier, the thesis that the politics of the purge were psychological politics is in no way inconsistent with the view that practical political ends were pursued. Something has been said already about the internal political ends. But an interpretation of the trials must also take account of their external political purpose, their connection with Stalin's foreign policy.

IV

A widely shared opinion sees the Great Purge as an attempt to prepare the Party and the country for the coming test of total war by consolidating the home front in advance. The trials themselves, with their charges that the accused were plotting to act as a fifth column in a war with the fascist powers, invited such an interpretation. Probably not many informed people followed the former U.S. ambassador in Moscow, Joseph Davies, in taking the position (in his wartime book *Mission to Moscow*) that the treason charges had been factually true. But Western opinion has tended to accept the general idea that Stalin's major concern was to assure a solid internal situation in the face of the threat of German invasion.

According to a sophisticated version of it that has been expounded by Isaac Deutscher in his influential biography of Stalin, the point of the purge trials was to forestall any disruption of the future war effort, and Stalin's leadership of it, by eliminating those leaders with a record of political dissent who might be inclined to unseat him in a crisis. According to Deutscher, "His reasoning probably developed along the following lines: they may want to overthrow me in a crisis—I shall charge them with having already made the attempt. They certainly believe themselves to be better fitted for the conduct of war, which is absurd. A change of government may weaken Russia's fighting capacity; and if they succeed, they may be compelled to sign a truce with Hitler, and perhaps even agree to a cession of territory as we once did at Brest-Litovsk. I shall accuse them of having entered already into a treacherous alliance with Germany (and Japan) and ceded Soviet territory to those states."[22]

During and after World War II Stalin probably liked to view the events of 1936–1938 in retrospect as part of his preparation of Russia for the coming great conflict with Hitler. But the idea that this was his motive at the time he planned and directed those events appears unsound. First, the Great Purge, as has been re-marked above, was in effect a great wrecking operation in Soviet society. Stalin himself must have been aware that the onslaught upon the Soviet managerial elite was not calculated to make the Soviet system and economy better able to withstand the test of war. He must have realized too that the preparedness and morale of the army would scarcely be furthered by the purging of 35,000 officers (the estimated number of those affected) along with the high command headed by the immensely able Tukhachevsky. This military purge itself accounts in considerable measure for the Red Army's poor performance during most of the Finnish war and its staggering setbacks in 1941–1942; and those effects were easily predictable. Next, Stalin, for all his pathological suspicious-ness, was shrewd and discerning enough to realize that in a national crisis brought on by a Nazi invasion of Russia, even his worst old Party enemies would rally instantly and unreservedly around the war effort and his personal leadership of it. For these old Bolshevik leaders, and the Tukhachevsky group, were anti-fascist Communists. Finally, the view that the Great Purge and the trials were preparation for a coming conflict with Hitler collides with evidence that Stalin at this time was *not in fact preparing for conflict with Hitler but for collaboration with him*. He was preparing the diplomacy of the Soviet-Nazi pact that was finally concluded, on Stalin's initiative, in August, 1939. And insofar as the politics of the purge and the trials were externally oriented, they were, as I shall now try to show, a preparation for the active alliance of the two dictators which was thereby inaugurated.

It is a mistake to look upon the diplomacy of the pact with Hitler as the only possible course the Soviet government could have followed at the end of the 1930's. Nor was it a course that the Bolshevik leaders as a group could find politically compelling and psychologically acceptable, as Stalin did. For though there were strong resemblances between communism and fascism as institutional structures, the revolutionary intellectuals of the Bolshevik Old Guard, most of them Russian or Jewish by origin, felt that their aims and values if not their institutions were fundamentally different from those of the German Nazis. The one among them who voiced this feeling most effectively, the intellectual leader of Bolshevik anti-fascism, was Bukharin. His speech a the Seventeenth Party Congress early in 1934 was notable not only for his tribute to Stalin's policy and leadership but also for the impassioned warning and outcry against Hitlerism with which he concluded. Quoting the Nazi poet who had said, "Every time I hear the word 'culture' I reach for my Browning," he eloquently portrayed Hitlerism's cult of blood and violence, and foresaw for the Soviet Union an unavoidable collision with this irrational force: "This is what stands before us, and these are the ones whom we shall have to face, comrades, in all those stupendous historical battles that history has laid on our shoulders."[23] This part of the speech reportedly made a strong impression upon the assembly. After the Congress Bukharin became not only editor of *Izvestia* but also a member of the commission set up in February, 1935, to draft a new Soviet constitution, which was to show by its humanistic and democratic features the chasm that separated the Soviet order from fascism. There is reason to believe, moreover, that he was one of the leading drafters of this document.

Stalin's speech at the Seventeenth Congress reflected a very different line toward Hitler's Germany. He cautioned the Germans against thinking that the U.S.S.R. was now orienting itself toward France and Poland because fascism had come to power in Germany. "Of course, we are far from enthusiastic about the fascist regime in Germany," he said. "But fascism is beside the point, if only because fascism in Italy, for example, has not kept the U.S.S.R. from establishing the best of relations with that country."

Stalin went on to indicate clearly that a *rapprochement* with Berlin was not to be excluded, if Soviet interests would be served thereby and if, within Hitler's government, a pro-Soviet tendency should prevail over an anti-Soviet one.[24] If an anti-Hitler diplomacy was implicit in Bukharin's speech, the diplomacy of the 1939 pact was prefigured in Stalin's; and the divergence between them reflected a real division of tendencies in the Soviet leadership that was ended only by the Great Purge. According to Krivitsky, Stalin's inclination to make a deal with Hitler was strengthened by the latter's successful blood purge of Captain Roehm and his group on the night of June 30, 1934, an event that Stalin construed as evidence of the consolidation of Hitler's regime. But for some time Hitler showed no receptiveness to feelers from the East. In these circumstances Stalin was content to go along with the politics of the anti-fascist Popular Front and the diplomacy of collective security which Foreign Commissar Litvinov pursued vigorously in the middle 1930's.[25] If in the eyes of the anti-fascist Communists the Litvinov foreign-policy line was a correct political orientation, from Stalin's point of view it had at least the virtue of placing pressure on a reluctant Hitler to respond to his advances.

Hitler's unopposed occupation of the Rhineland in March, 1936, hardened Stalin's resolve to make a deal with Germany if possible, and this in turn spurred his efforts to proceed with the full-scale internal purge towards which he had long been moving for other reasons. It is notable in this connection that Party members (both Soviet and foreign) who could be suspected of being genuinely anti-fascist Communists were particularly hard hit *as a class* by the mass repressions of 1936–1938.[26] It was not simply that these people, including the great majority of Old Bolshevik leaders, would have found it very hard to stomach a treaty with the Nazis. To understand Stalin's special motive for getting rid of them, we must remember that he visualized the coming pact with Hitler as more than merely a way of securing temporary safety from invasion and buying time for further defense preparation. What he contemplated, as his alliance with Hitler in 1939–1941 showed in retrospect, was a kind of Moscow-Berlin axis, an active collaboration of the two dictatorships for territorial expansion, the division of spheres of influence in Eastern Europe, the Balkans, and even the Middle East. Now the Old Bolsheviks and other Party members who shared their outlook were revolutionaries, not old-fashioned Russian imperialists. They could have gone along, if reluctantly, with a simple non-aggression arrangement with Berlin. But a policy of outright imperialistic aggression in collaboration with Nazi Germany would have been extremely repugnant to very many of them, as Stalin knew. Nor could the Polish Communist Party (which was simply dissolved in the Great Purge) be expected to acquiesce supinely in a new partition of Poland between Russia and Germany. Consequently, to get a fully free hand for the diplomacy of the Soviet-Nazi alliance, Stalin needed to eliminate or expel thousands of foreign as well as Soviet Communists and to achieve in external as well as internal policy the absolute autocracy that, as we have seen. only the Great Purge brought him.

That this was his plan must have become clear to Bukharin upon his ill-fated return to Moscow from Paris in early April, 1936, and in his final months of circumscribed freedom he did what he could to resist. His last signed editorial article appeared in *Izvestia* on July 6, 1936, under the title "Routes of History" and with a sub-title ("Thoughts Aloud") that alerted the knowing reader, by its very unusualness in the Soviet press, to expect something significant. Starting with lavish praise of the "Stalin Constitution" that had by then been drafted and submitted for nation-wide public discussion, Bukharin expounded the theme that "real history" had not proceeded in our time along the routes previously predicted. Certain "false prophets" (by subtle allusion Stalin is indicated to have been foremost among them) had failed, for example, to foresee that fascism would emerge as the greatest international problem. Now it is a "paradox of history," the article goes on, that though the masses are regarded by the fascist ideologues as *Untermenschen,* the rulers in order to retain control must deceive the people by creating an illusion of being with and for the masses. In actuality, whereas socialism raises the mass, enriches the content of personality, and elevates the intellectual functions, fascism "creates a depersonalized mass, with blind discipline, with a cult of Jesuitical obedience, with suppression of the intellectual functions." Thus deception is the essence of fascism: "An intricate network of decorative deceit (in words and deeds) is the extraordinarily essential characteristic of fascist regimes of all kinds and complexions." And while the deceitful fascist elite allows that its people own the means of production only "spiritually," for its own part it means to own "cannon," "airplanes," and "lands in the east of Europe" not in a "spiritual" sense only, but materially. But this deception must sooner or later come to light: "Its perpetrators have it in mind to gain for themselves an historical respite by sending everything into the yawning abyss of war. However. this is a game of winner take all in which they will lose everything."

This most audacious and desperate of Bukharin's essays in anti-Stalin Aesopian polemics[27] may be translated as follows: Do not take the Stalin Constitution and its democratic phraseology seriously. It is only a decorative façade of political deceit behind which Stalin is moving to create, by means of a huge blood purge, a new Soviet regime of fascist complexion which will be a denial of the Marxist ideals of the Russian Revolution. It will be a totally despotic regime based on police terror and suppression of the Party leadership and the intelligentsia ("intellectual functions"). Stalin is seeking by these means to pave the way for an alliance with the German fascists which will precipitate a second world war in which he expects to remain at least temporarily uninvolved while we build cannon and airplanes and assimilate Eastern European territories that we will occupy under the deal. But the whole plan will lead only to disaster. Why Bukharin thought Stalin's plan would lead to disaster was explained shortly after in another editorial, which was unsigned but bore indications (for example, the characteristic touch of quoting from Shelley's "Masque of Anarchy") of Bukharin's personal authorship. "It would be unforgivable blindness," it said, "not to see that it is the land of Soviets that attracts the most savage hatred of the unbridled adventurists." It was folly, in other words, to suppose that Hitler could be deflected for long from attacking the U.S.S.R. The editorial also made an emotional appeal to the British ruling circles to take a firm stand against the Nazis. Picturing Lords Lothian, Londonderry, and others as "fawning on Hitler," it recalled the war dead of 1914–1918 and asked: "How are the sons of England sleeping in Flanders fields?" This editorial, entitled "War and Peace," appeared in *Izvestia* on August 1. Later that month the trial of the sixteen began, and with it the public denunciations of Bukharin.[28]

For Stalin the purge trials had a foreign-policy motive beyond those just discussed. He wanted to use them as a means of communicating to Hitler the seriousness of his interest in a collaborative arrangement, and simultaneously as a way of softening the shock that a Stalin-Hitler pact would inevitably cause in Russia and especially in the world Communist movement. These motives may seem implausible in view of the fact that negotiating a deal with the Nazis was presented, particularly in the 1937 and 1938 trials, as one of the most heinous acts of treason on the part of the accused. Did this not impart a strongly anti-fascist coloring to these trials? Superficially it did, but let us take a closer look. The men in Berlin well knew that the charges of treasonable dealings with Nazi Germany were baseless. But if negotiating with the Nazis was not their real crime, was it, in Stalin's eyes, a crime at all? If the German Embassy in Moscow followed the 1938 trial closely, it must have noted that the defendant Bessonov, who had been counselor of the Soviet Embassy in Berlin at the start of the Nazi era, pleaded guilty in the very first session to receiving and acting on orders from Deputy Foreign Commissar Krestinsky and also from Trotsky to obstruct a "Normalization of relations between the Soviet Union and Germany." This charge, repeated later in the trial, carried the significant implication that the anti-Stalin Communist opposition had been standing in the way of developing fruitful diplomatic relations between the Soviet and Nazi governments. Moreover, the Germans could not but know that many of the principal trial defendants, above all Bukharin, had been foremost among the anti-fascist Communists, and that a sizable proportion were Jews. Putting all this together, the fascist leaders could very reasonably infer from the trials that Stalin was seriously getting ready to do business with them. Evidence that the trials were so interpreted is to be found in a foreign-affairs commentary printed in the Italian fascist paper *Popolo d'Italia* on March 5, 1938. Reacting to the Bukharin trial then taking place in Moscow, the commentary asked whether "in view of the catastrophe of Lenin's system, Stalin could secretly have become a fascist." In any event, it went on: "Stalin is doing a notable service to fascism by mowing down in large armfuls his enemies who have been reduced to impotence." The commentator was Benito Mussolini.

The trials had, finally, the function of softening in advance the shock that the treaty of alliance with Hitler would administer to Soviet and world Communist opinion. This function was served, in particular, by the charges against the Trotskyite and Right Oppositions of negotiating a deal with the Nazis. In developing these charges in the trials, much was made of the theme that such prominent anti-Stalinist Communists as Trotsky and Bukharin were not only prepared to have dealings with the Nazis but were themselves pro-fascist. Thus the defendant Ivanov pictures himself and Bukharin as having, politically speaking, "arrived directly at fascism," and Vyshinsky, in the summing-up speech, says of Bukharin: "Like a true watchdog of fascism, he barked joyfully expressing his admiration for German fascism." This smearing of the accused as both fascist in mentality and bent on collaborating with the Nazis was preparation for *Stalin's* collaboration with them—in the sense that it undermined the whole idea that communism stood for anti-fascism, and spiked in advance the thought (which certainly would have occurred to many in Russia and the Communist movement) that the Old Bolsheviks, unlike Stalin, would have avoided the Soviet-Nazi pact *on antifascist principle.* In short, it paradoxically tended, if not to establish in advance the political respectability of Stalin's plan for the pact with Hitler, at least to diminish its disreputability. In these terms the trials were saying: If the anti-Stalin Communists were ready and willing to bargain with the Nazis for *anti*-Soviet purposes of defeating and dismembering the U.S.S.R., what is so bad about striking a bargain with Berlin that will *serve* Soviet interests by expanding our territorial possessions and keeping us out of war while the Germans and the West fight it out? To a considerable extent the trials fulfilled this devious design. For while the pact of August, 1939, came as a shock to the international Communist movement, which suffered significant defections as a result of the disgust many felt at this turn of events, the shock would have been all the greater and more damaging to the movement and to Stalin had he not, by means of the purge trials, compromised the notion that no Communists, and no Old Bolsheviks in particular, would have friendly dealings with the Nazis.

v

The conduct of Bukharin at his trial has long fascinated the Western mind. Rubashov, the Old Bolshevik hero of Arthur Koestler's well-known novel about the purge trials, *Darkness at Noon,* appears to have been drawn, at least in part, upon the model of Bukharin. In 1947 the French philosopher M. Merleau-Ponty published a small book, *Humanisme et Terreur,* which was devoted largely to a critique of what the author called Koestler's "Rubashov-Bukharin" and to an interpretation along different lines of Bukharin's decision to confess. Others too have contributed to this literature, and no examination of the great purge trial would be complete without an effort to solve the problem of Bukharin's motivation. What I should like to do here is to outline some of the evidence for an interpretation of it that relies in part on what is called "Kremlinology," that is, the analysis of Soviet political processes as reflected in esoteric communication or veiled controversy in published Soviet materials. For it seems to me that in one of its many aspects the verbatim report is a kind of laboratory for the study of Soviet politics by the Kremlinological method.

We must recognize, to begin with, that Bukharin agreed to participate in the trial only under some kind of duress. There were others, such as Yenukidze and Karakhan, who refused to do this and went to their death without public trial. Bukharin himself hints at his resistance. He was under arrest for well over a year before the trial, and says in his final statement: "For three months I refused to say anything." To have resisted pressure for so long was in itself a remarkable feat. For as Bukharin put it in an Aesopian passage of his final statement, speaking of his confession: "But here we also have the internal demolition of the forces of counterrevolution. And one must be a Trotsky not to lay down one's arms." This was a way of saying: Stalin and his men have ways of demolishing a person's resistance by playing upon his innermost feelings, ways that hardly anyone can resist unless he is a Trotsky, that is, unless he is living in Mexico or somewhere else outside the reach of the NKVD. What were the feelings in question? We have no evidence that physical torture was used in Bukharin's case, or that a deal was struck to spare his life if he cooperated, for he made it rather clear in the trial that he expected no mercy for himself. The lives of others, however, do appear to have been at stake. What was reportedly used as the chief means of coercing Bukharin into agreement to go on trial was the threat to retaliate against his young wife and little boy if he should refuse.[29] This was an all but irresistible form of pressure to which Stalin had also resorted in other cases, notably Kamenev's.

It is very likely, however, that in the case of Bukharin, as in some others involving former leaders of the Party, Stalin and his men also made use of certain blandishments, including the invitation to play the trial role as a "last service" to the Party and the Revolutionary cause. As a person whose whole life had been bound up with the Party and the Revolution, Bukharin could hardly have been insensitive to such an approach. Perhaps on this account the theory of the "last service" figures prominently in the Western literature about Bukharin on trial. In *Darkness at Noon,* for example, the Stalinist investigator Gletkin appeals to Rubashov-Bukharin to render a final service to the Party by going on trial and thereby helping to consolidate the country behind the

Stalin regime in the face of an imminent danger of war, and Rubashov performs this service, although with deepening doubt of the moral validity of the revolutionary cause to which he had devoted his life and was now sacrificing it. Merleau-Ponty, on the other hand, in effect makes out Bukharin to be a man who dialectically arrived on his own at Gletkin's kind of reasoning. On this view Bukharin, though not guilty of the counter-revolutionary crimes with which he was charged, nevertheless sees in his dialectician's mind that he *was* guilty, since oppositionism in any form was tantamount to treason under the precarious conditions of existence of the Soviet state in the 1930's. Thus Merleau-Ponty ascribes to Bukharin an acceptance in principle of that peculiar Stalinist algebraic formula according to which any opposing of Stalin = "counter-revolutionary terrorism."

If we suppose (as seems reasonable) that Bukharin's consent to take part in the trial represented in some sense a deliberate political choice as well as a bowing to coercion, then the idea that he wanted to render a last service to his cause is highly plausible. But the versions of the theory just mentioned, and others similar to them, encounter certain objections. First, we have reason to doubt that the Moscow trials were in fact a means of preparing the country to withstand the test of war. Bukharin, moreover, certainly saw them as a means of preparing for the Soviet-Nazi alliance, and it is unimaginable that he could have brought himself to a decision to take part in the show trial in order to help Stalin pave the way for his pact with Hitler. Furthermore, the theory of the last service in its conventional forms would lead us to expect Bukharin to play his part in the show trial in active co-operation with the prosecutor or at any rate in a spirit of resignation. But this he did not do. He did make a point of admitting and even underlining the enormity of his guilt; and this is a salient fact that our interpretation must account for. But at the same time we have a mass of textual evidence and eyewitness testimony to the effect that there was a play within the play of the show trial, and that the inner play was a real contest between Bukharin and Vyshinsky.

During the trial Bukharin, even though he had to speak in broad conformity with a script prepared in advance to suit his accusers, fought constantly. Thus he intervened on occasion to impugn by a single question the credibility of a defendant who had testified against him (a case in point is his question to Ivanov in the morning session of March 3), and at one point he directly described two of the defendants, Ivanov and Sharangovich, as police agents ("agents provocateurs"). He pleaded guilty to "the sum total of crimes committed by this counter-revolutionary organization," but thereupon suggested that not only did he not take part in but he even lacked knowledge of "any particular act" involved. He denied, as we have seen, that the defendants constituted a con- spiratorial group in the sense of the trial indictment. He dis- claimed all knowledge of his alleged connections with the German fascists, denied ever having spoken of opening the front in time of war, rejected the charge of plotting the assassination of Lenin, Stalin, and Sverdlov in 1918, failed to recall ever having directed anyone to engage in wrecking activities, categorically denied all connection with foreign intelligence services as well as any com- plicity in the assassination of Kirov, Gorky, and his son, and so on. During Vyshinsky's summing-up speech, which preceded his own, he was observed furiously taking notes. His own final state- ment was so little pleasing to Stalin that it was not, like the preceding parts of the verbatim record, printed in full in the next day's *Pravda* but only briefly summarized. And foreign observers present at the trial were profoundly impressed by his fighting demeanor. According to the *New York Times* correspondent, "Mr. Bukharin alone, who all too obviously in his last words fully expected to die, was manly, proud and almost defiant. He is the first of the fifty-four men who have faced the court in the last three public treason trials who has not abased himself in the last hours of the trial."[30] Fitzroy MacLean, who attended the trial as an offi- cial representative of the British Embassy in Moscow and later wrote a vivid account of it, pictures Bukharin, in giving his final statement, as standing there "frail and defiant," admitting in principle the justice of the case against him and then proceeding "to tear it to bits, while Vyshinsky, powerless to intervene, sat uneasily in his place, looking embarrassed and yawning ostenta- tiously."[31]

That Bukharin was putting up a fight is clear enough, but what was he fighting for? It is evident that he was not fighting in any real sense to defend himself or to save his life, since any small chance of saving his life would only have been erased by the very fact that he put up this fight. I suggest, therefore, that his aim in the contest was offensive rather than defensive. Not to defend himself but to convict his accuser was the purpose. That he would have *wanted* to do this, if he could, is quite clear from evidence already cited in these pages. He had long before begun to view

Stalin as a coarse bungling political leader who was ideologically illiterate on crucial points and was leading Lenin's party and the Bolshevik Revolution to ruination out of a monstrous appetite for personal power. Before his arrest he had even pictured Stalin as engaged in transforming Soviet communism into a Soviet form of fascism, and he had attempted to warn the Party and the world that Stalin was scheming to make common cause with Hitler in a great and ill-starred political gamble that would bring on World War II and destroy the Soviet Union. By no stretch of political imagination could he now identify Stalin's regime with historic Bolshevism or see Stalin himself as other than anti-Bolshevik. Is it not clear, then, that for Bukharin a last service to the Party and the Revolution could consist only of a last denunciation of Stalin for betraying and ruining both? That such an idea would occur to him was all the more likely, moreover, in view of a certain tradition in the Russian revolutionary movement before 1917—the tradition of turning trials into anti-trials. The crux of this maneuver was that a revolutionist on trial for attempting to overthrow the existing order would seek to turn the tables upon his accusers and place them on trial before the court of public opinion and history. He would do this by foregoing a speech of defense and delivering instead a revolutionary oration, a denunciation of his accusers, their motives, their policies, and their social order.

Now there was no possibility for Bukharin to deliver such an oration in one of Stalin's show trials. Nor would the course followed by Krestinsky meet the needs of the anti-trial strategy. In the initial session Krestinsky publicly retracted his pre-trial confession, intimating that he had confessed under duress. But this gesture availed him nothing, for a little later on in the trial, after unknown events transpired behind the scenes, he retracted his retraction and from then on played his part unresisting. Bukharin must have been fully aware of the futility of such a course. Nevertheless, he appears to have found and put into practice a method of achieving his purpose. It required, first of all, simply a decision to go on trial—something that he in any event was being coerced to do. Secondly, it required the pursuit of certain tactics during the trial which I shall comment upon presently. Stalin was insisting that he appear as chief defendant in the trial. Well and good. He would do so, and try to save his family by complying with that basic and irreducible demand. But he would do so in his own way, speaking his lines according to the Stalin-Vyshinsky script but at the same time saying between these lines whatever he could say to make *his* point. Stalin, knowing Bukharin well, undoubtedly realized that he would do this. But he evidently thought it a tolerable price to pay for the great success of persuading Bukharin to go on trial and confess himself guilty of counter-revolutionary conspiracy. And he probably assumed that Vyshinsky and Ulrich, with the help of many of the trial defendants who would in effect be prosecution witnesses in the guise of defendants, would together manage to hold Bukharin in check.

Bukharin thus has a twofold objective in the trial—to comply with Stalin by confessing and at the same time to turn the tables on him. He wants to make it two trials in one. He himself tells us this in a brilliant display of Aesopian language in his final statement. Taking up the theme of the puzzlement that Western European and American intellectuals were showing over the Moscow trials and particularly over the confessions, Bukharin stresses that he has retained his "clarity of mind" and he dismisses fanciful hypotheses that would explain the confessions as based on hypnotism or a mysterious "Slavic soul" or a Dostoyevskyan psychology of self-abasement, etc. He says further that "the first thing to be understood" is that he and any others like him ("the enemy") have "a divided, a dual mind." What he meant by this is indicated by further statements a little later on.[32] The trial, he says, has an aspect of confession, but this is not the crux of it: "The confession of the accused is not essential. The confession of the accused is a medieval principle of jurisprudence." Here Bukharin is saying between the lines that in one of its aspects this trial is a sort of medieval witchcraft trial, and that we should not take the confession *per se* seriously, since in such a trial the witch, as a matter of course, has to confess. And the other aspect? Bukharin communicates this point by way of observing that Lion Feuchtwanger's *Moscow 1937,* a little piece of pro-Stalinism apologetics for the trials that had been shown him in prison, did not get to the core of the matter, "when, as a matter of fact, everything is clear. *World history is a world court of judgement"* (my italics). The crucial message is contained in Hegel's dictum on world history as the world's court of justice. In its second aspect, Bukharin was saying, this trial is taking place before the bar of history.

If in the one aspect it was a trial of Bukharin, in the other it was obviously, in Bukharin's eyes, a trial of Stalin. On the basis of his pre-trial political past we can see that the crime for which he would have wanted, if possible, to condemn Stalin before the court of history was that of desecrating the memory of Lenin, betraying what the Revolution stood for, and crushing the Party. Since it would be out of the question to say such things openly in the courtroom, they would have to be conveyed by indirection. Now the essence of convicting someone of a crime is to demonstrate that he has committed it. In the present instance the task would be to demonstrate by indirection that Stalin was committing what in Bukharin's eyes was the supreme political crime—destroying Bolshevism. How could he accomplish this? One way, and under the circumstances the only way, was simply to go on public trial and thereby permit Stalin, his accuser, to convict himself symbolically of destroying Bolshevism by committing the judicial murder of *him*. What enabled Bukharin to accomplish this purpose by this means was his own stature in the Russian Communist movement. He himself was a symbol. If any surviving Old Bolshevik had special claim to represent the original Bolshevik heritage and the link with Lenin, who was the founder and moving spirit of Bolshevism, it was Bukharin. In the "Testament" Lenin himself had said of him: "Bukharin is not only the most valuable and biggest theoretician of the Party, but also may legitimately be considered the favorite of the whole Party." More than Trotsky, who had always been something of an independent quantity, more than Zinoviev and Kamenev, and unquestionably more than Stalin, who claimed the title, Bukharin had a basis to be considered "Lenin today." And though he had been bested by Stalin in the post-Lenin struggles in the Party, his prestige in the eyes of a generation of Party members was very great. Indeed, it was over the "Bukharin question," as we noted earlier, that Stalin appears to have encountered finally a real if belated attempt in the Party leadership to oppose his plans for the Great Purge.

Bukharin was thus in a position to dramatize by his own self-immolation in the show trial what Stalin was doing to Bolshevism. By undergoing the ordeal of defamation to which Stalin and Vyshinsky systematically subjected him all through the trial, by permitting and indeed inviting Vyshinsky to cover him with a torrent of vituperative abuse as "the acme of monstrous hypocrisy, perfidy, jesuitry and inhuman villainy," Bukharin was able not only to convict Stalin of putting Bolshevism on trial but to catch him, as it were, red-handed in the act and show him up before the world in the process. Unquestionably it cost him great agony to go through this experience of having his whole revolutionary past besmirched and being accused of what to him would be quite inconceivable acts such as conspiring to kill Lenin or to destroy the Soviet order. But he evidently decided upon it, in part, because it would be a meaningful political act in terms of all that he had set store by in his previous political life. And this is what I believe he was trying to communicate when he said in his final statement that in the face of "the absolutely black vacuity" confronting him, he wanted to die for something. In the next breath he said it would be something that would cost him the sacrifice of his revolutionary reputation and pride: "And at such moments, Citizens Judges, everything personal, all the personal incrustation, all the rancour, pride, and a number of other things, fall away, disappear."

But the anti-trial was much more than a passive act of self-sacrifice designed to dramatize by Bukharin's own fate that Stalin was condemning Bolshevism. There was an active effort on Bukharin's part to transform the trial into an anti-trial. The fight that he put up against Vyshinsky was entirely dedicated to this purpose, and his tactics all through the trial were precisely calculated to fit the needs of the anti-trial strategy. First of all, as mentioned earlier, he made a special effort to underline his own great guilt. Thus he accepted full responsibility for the mass of counter-revolutionary acts with which the "Bloc" was charged, although in doing so he insisted that this was *political* responsibility, that as a leader of the alleged conspiracy he was guilty for whatever acts were committed, either by himself or by others in carrying it out. Still more to the point, he repeated several times in the trial that he wished not to defend but to accuse himself. "I did not want to minimize my guilt, I wanted to aggravate it," he said in one place. "This is not my defence, it is my self-accusation," he said elsewhere. "I have not said a single word in my defence." All this was to say: My tactics in the anti-trial are tactics of self-accusation. By emphasizing in this manner how terribly guilty I, an Old Bolshevik leader, am in Stalin's eyes, I am showing implicitly how guilty *he* is of murderous attitudes and acts against the people who embody historic Bolshevism. Hence my tactics of self-accusation are my way of placing my accuser on trial for his crimes against our party.

This view that Bukharin was not trying to defend himself may seem to be contradicted by what was said earlier here about his denial of guilt under the specific criminal charges. But only in a surface sense was this a defensive move. Bukharin rejected the criminal charges not with a view to pleading innocent in the trial but rather with a view to making more clear where his real guilt lay—in the political field. For this purpose, of course, it was necessary to indicate that he was *not* guilty of certain things. Thus the denial of the criminal charges was an organic part of the whole strategy of exposing and convicting Stalin through his own self-accusation. Only if the public saw the accused Bukharin as a political man would it see that the accuser Stalin was destroying a political tendency, condemning Old Bolshevik's for their Bolshevism. Only in this event would it be clear that when, as Bukharin put it, "out of certain deviations monstrous conclusions are formed by the logic of the struggle," these monstrous conclusions and the paranoid-like logic that produced them were Stalin's.

So it was vital to Bukharin's whole case in the anti-trial to show that he had been a Bolshevik oppositionist in relation to Stalin and not, as Vyshinsky was trying very hard to show, a criminal element masquerading for long years as a Bolshevik revolutionary. The duel that rages between the two all through the great purge trial is thus one in which Vyshinsky argues that all Bukharin's purported political acts were really crimes and Bukharin maintains that all his alleged crimes were really political acts. If Bukharin came off remarkably well in this encounter, despite all the disadvantages of his situation compared with Vyshinsky's, one reason lay in the fact that his contention was true.

4 THE STALIN HERITAGE
IN SOVIET POLICY

The materials available to us do not make it possible to form a detailed picture of the policy debate that went on in Moscow from 1945 to 1952, the time of the Nineteenth Party Congress. They do reflect, however, the broad outlines of it. By an analysis of the principal published documents, and particularly of Stalin's papers published in 1952 under the title *Economic Problems of Socialism in the U.S.S.R.,* which were a kind of authoritative summation of the whole discussion, it is possible to arrive at a reasoned view of the chief issues and the positions taken on them.

In its ideological expression the discussion had to do with the further development of Soviet society on the path of "transition from socialism to communism." In the official view, the U.S.S.R. was now in the "lower phase of communism" ("socialism"), and the problem of its future development was that of determining how, when, and under what conditions it would move into the "higher phase" that had been predicted but not concretely outlined by Marx and Engels. It is apparent that one of the causes for the strange delay in the convening of the Nineteenth Congress was the prolonged and involved behind-the-scenes wrangle over this issue.

According to Tito's biographer Dedijer, Georgi Malenkov told delegates to the Cominform meeting in Warsaw in 1947 that preparations for the Nineteenth Congress were in progress in Moscow. He also informed them privately that this Congress was to adopt a "fifteen-year plan of transition from socialism to communism," and that those concerned with charting this program were "drawing in detail upon the utopian socialists."[1] These remarks of Malenkov, and especially his reference to the "utopian" directions of

Moscow's thinking on Soviet internal evolution, had the flavor of the immediate postwar atmosphere in Russia, that interlude of comparative calm and popular hopefulness between the great war that had just ended and the great cold war that was about to begin. The experience of victory in 1945 had a very special quality for most Russians. In some countries, the ending of a great war brings with it a yearning, which always proves illusory, for a "return to normalcy." This was not so in Russia, because "normalcy" there did not mean tranquility but rather the furious pace and the privations of the prewar years. Consequently, the immediate postwar attitude in Russia was forward- rather than backward-looking; it was a hope for a "new period," different from what they had known before the war, not for a "back-to-normal" move.

Now, it seemed, the oppressive era of total preparation for war need not return. Now Russia would no longer pursue a *compulsive* course of internal policy dictated by adverse international circumstances, by the implacable hostility of a powerful external environment. The year 1945 seemed to bring with it a national opportunity to choose the future in accordance with inner developmental needs. The "utopian" trend in the official thinking of the immediate postwar period was in some sense an *obeisance* to this mood of the nation, an ideological echo of it in the counsels of the Soviet regime. The theme of a meaningful transition to a "higher phase" would have the effect of confining to "safe" channels the urge that was abroad in Soviet society toward new directions of national life. It conveniently coupled the popular yearning for something new, which was nonideological in inspiration, with the realization of the ideological grand design of Soviet Communism.

If the ending of World War II had placed the problem of Russia's internal development on the agenda, the advent of the East-West conflict profoundly modified the terms of reference. The visionary overtone of Malenkov's remarks in Warsaw was anachronistic by the time those remarks were made. It was at the Warsaw meeting of Communist delegates that Andrei Zhdanov, on behalf of the Stalin regime, issued a declaration of cold war against the Western democracies. His "Report on the International Situation" was far more than a denunciation of the Marshall Plan. Its primary purpose was to apprise everyone, friend and foe alike, of Stalin's doctrine that the world was split irrevocably into two great opposing "camps" and that the next stage of history would be dominated by the antagonism and conflict between them. Here Zhdanov was spelling out the full implications of the programmatic speech that Stalin gave on February 9, 1946, in Moscow. In the speech, Stalin had conjured up the specter of another great war, latent in the "capitalist system of world economy." He said that further "military catastrophies" were inevitable because there was no way for countries to divide up markets and raw materials by "coordinated and peaceful decisions." Therefore, Russia would have to devote its resources and energies in the coming years to developing the basic industries to the point at which she would be "guaranteed against all contingencies." "This will take perhaps three new Five-Year Plans, if not more."[2]

Stalin's speech was, in effect, a denial of the idea of a "new period." By clear implication, if not in so many words, it said: back to prewar "normalcy," back to a time in which a postulated external danger is the primary fact of national life and the internal policies of the government are a compulsive response to it. Stalin's speech was at bottom a denial of national choice, a rejection of the view that the internal wants and needs of the country could now be the principal determining factor in the policy-making of the regime. It said in effect that policy-making would have to be rigidly subordinated to the one great overriding imperative of arming, so that Russia, standing alone in a potentially hostile world, might be and feel safe. Finally, it implied that there was no other way of coming to terms with this potentially hostile external environment. The degree of external danger was an independent variable, unmanageable by the devices of diplomacy or any other action (or abstention from action) on Russia's part. These twin concepts of the primacy of the external danger and the impotence of diplomacy to allay or alleviate it were crucial in Stalin's thinking, and to a very profound extent the internal political struggle in Stalin's last years and after revolved around them.

By means of what policy, inquired Stalin in his speech, had the Party ensured Russia's ability to withstand the recent war and emerge victorious? The answer: industrialization and collectivization. And here he reviewed, with studied emphasis, the distinctive feature of what he called the "Soviet method of industrialization." In capitalist countries, industrialization ordinarily begins in the sphere of light industry, where the return on investment is higher and quicker. The Soviet Union had followed a different path. The Party knew that "war was approaching, that it was impossible to arm the country without heavy industry, that the development of heavy industry had to be tackled as soon as possible, that to be late in this undertaking meant to lose." Hence industrialization in Russia began with heavy industry, which had proved "very difficult, but feasible." The Soviet Union had likewise rejected the capitalist path of developing large-scale modern agriculture because it "presupposes too long a path of development." What especially recommended the "method of collectivization" was that it enabled the regime to cover the land with big collective units "in the space of a few years," and thus to obtain "more marketable produce." All the oppositional trends in the country had basically pursued one purpose: to retard the cause of industrialization and collectivization. But the regime had not been deflected by this resistance. It had not accommodated itself to the backward forces, it had not "feared to go against the stream."[3]

The virtue of this exposition of Stalinism by Stalin was its curious candor. During the stormy post-NEP years, when the Stalinist pattern was being imposed on Soviet society, the controversies had been waged very largely in ideological terms. Stalin had recommended his policy plan as the proper way to go about "building socialism," and he no doubt thought that it was. But the content of the conception was not derived from a "Marxist blueprint" of the organization of life in a future socialist society. The historic impulse behind the Stalinist pattern of internal policy, as the speech of February 9, 1946, revealed so clearly, was to organize a relatively backward agrarian society, in a short time and by ruthless methods, for total war. Forced industrialization and the revival of something comparable to serfdom in the framework of the kolkhoz were the primary elements in this pattern, as Stalin indicated, but they in turn were the basis for the complete totalitarianization of Soviet society that occurred in the 1930's. From the program of salvation by heavy industry and collectivization flowed the hypertrophy of the Soviet state machinery, the bureaucratization of all phases of the life of the people, the steady growth of the role of organized terror, the binding of all strata to service of the state in a manner reminiscent of the "binding of all classes" in the Muscovite state of the seventeenth century. Thus the repressive social pattern of Stalinism was a reflection of the policy pattern. The policy pattern was the forced concentration of all resources and energies on preparing the country for a coming conflict. The social pattern was the total subjugation of society to the direct control of the state in the course of this process. Both had their source in the postulated primacy of the external danger.

In the speech of 1946, Stalin reasserted the validity of this historic structure of Stalinism, its "general line," not only with respect to the past but with respect to the future, too. His orientation was reactionary in the literal sense of the word. It meant that the postwar period would have to be transformed, in idea if not in actual fact, into a *new prewar period,* for this was the necessary matrix of the Stalinist pattern. Did Stalin discern that the anticipation of a "new period," and its echo in the idea of voluntarism in national policy-making, were an implicit challenge to the perpetual validity of the Stalinist pattern? Was his subsequent cold war against the West, in part at any rate, a way of arresting the historical process in Russia itself? Whatever the answer to these questions, the speech was an envisagement of the post-1945 period as a repetition, under new conditions, of the post-1928 cycle of events.

II

In reimposing the general line in 1946, Stalin did not discard the idea of the coming transition from socialism to communism. This perspective belonged to the ideological self-image of the system and could not be abandoned. What happened was that Stalin while preserving the principle of transition, progressively drained out of it all implications in conflict with the perpetuation of the general line. The "higher phase" was thus made consonant with the continuation of the policy pattern in the present "lower phase." This involved the suppression of numerous trends of thought that had to seem deviationist from a Stalinist standpoint. In his final years, Stalin was much occupied with the extirpation of these heresies.

First, he tried to enforce an understanding of the "inevitability of gradualness" in Soviet economic development. Here he pitted himself against the persistent habit of reasoning about Soviet social development in dialectical terms. It had seemed to Soviet theoretical minds that at some point in the "transition," there must come a dialectical break in development, a turning point that would mark the advent of the higher phase. In his essay on linguistics of 1950, Stalin dealt harshly with such notions. He emphasized that the development of a language from an old to a new quality ("phase") does not take place, as Soviet linguists had believed, by means of an "explosion" or revolutionary destruction of the old quality, but rather by the "gradual accumulation of the elements of the new quality." He then applied his evolutionism to phenomena other than language:

> In general it must be said for the information of *comrades who are engrossed in explosions* that the law of transition from an old to a new quality by means of an explosion is inapplicable not only to the historical development of language—it likewise is not always applicable to other social phenomena of a foundational or superstructural nature. [Italics added.][4]

Stalin's reference here, as materials published subsequently made clear, was to the idea that the transition to the "higher phase" of communism would entail a revolutionary change in the pattern of policy applicable at the lower phase.

Almost at the very time that his essay on linguistics was printed in *Pravda,* a discussion of the transition to communism was taking place in the Soviet Academy of Sciences. The remarkable feature of this discussion was that it dealt primarily with the question of the free distribution of goods in the projected higher phase. This reflected the persistent idea that at some point in the transitional period, the Soviet regime would have to devote its attention and effort directly to the problem of the depressed Soviet standard of living. The main issue discussed was whether all goods would become free at the same time or whether free distribution would begin with certain selected categories of goods and services, such as bread, telephone services, subway tickets, etc. This distributive orientation was the next heresy with which Stalin had to deal. The whole idea of the discussion in the Academy was condemned in *Pravda* as harmful and erroneous. "Such a narrowly distributive and consumptionist approach is anti-Marxist, harmful to the practical task of building communism." Questions of distribution and consumption were merely "derivative." Soviet economists should focus their entire attention on the problem of production, on "creation of the material-technical base of communism."[5] Again the message was the same—the general line must prevail, the concept of the "higher phase" must be emptied of all content that would constitute it a *different* phase. The idea that Soviet society might at some point move consciously in the direction of material plenty was "anti-Marxist." Material welfare could only be envisaged as a remote possible by-product of the development of heavy industry, never as a direct goal of Soviet governmental policy.

The final outcome of the heresy-hunting was Stalin's *Economic Problems of Socialism in the U.S.S.R.* Here, for the last time, he vented his wrath on those whom he called "voluntarists." In his terms, these were people who believed that the Soviet regime "can do anything." Sternly he informed them that the policy of the Soviet regime must conform to "objective economic laws" dictating, among other things, the "preponderant growth of the production of means of production," i.e., the priority of heavy industry. Rigid controls must be instituted over market factors in the economy (the "law of value") that might impel the government to "abandon the primacy of the production of means of production in favor of the production of consumer goods."[6] And in full consistency with this basic conservatism in economic policy, Stalin proposed the transformation of kolkhoz property, theoretically cooperative in character, into state property and also a system of direct "product-exchange" between the central government and state farms. Thus Stalin treated the problem of the transition to communism not as one of creating an abundance of goods for the people, but as one of establishing state controls over market factors and perpetuating the preferential position of heavy industry in economic development.

We may say in fact that in these papers, prepared not long before his death, Stalin was attempting to cram the future development of Soviet society into the framework of the general line. And this final word of his on the Soviet future was not intended simply as a theoretical statement but as a practical guide to Soviet policy. In one of its resolutions, the Nineteenth Party Congress decreed that it was time to revise the 1919 Party Program. It set up a commission headed by Stalin to prepare the new program and instructed the commission to make its proposals on the basis of the fundamental theses of *Economic Problems of Socialism in the U.S.S.R.* Clearly, the pattern of Soviet internal policy in the coming years was to conform to the Stalinist general line.

III

Throughout these postwar discussions on economic problems of socialism, Stalin was protecting the general line on what might be called its internal flank. Now we must review indications that the occasion also arose to protect it on the external flank, on the issue of Soviet foreign policy.

The Stalinist policy pattern, resting on the postulate of overwhelming external danger, became vulnerable in the later postwar years to undermining from this angle. During the period from 1944 to 1949, while the great postwar expansion of the Communist sphere was in progress, no element in the Soviet regime was likely to suggest that the process of expansion be checked. But by late 1949, after China's entry into the sphere, the opportunities for further expansion were narrowed and the dangers had increased. By this time, the Western powers had undertaken in earnest to redress the balance and form interlocking defensive coalitions against further Communist advances. It is at this point that dim signs begin to appear of an opposition within the Soviet regime to continuation at full intensity of the cold war. The idea with which this opposition seems to have associated itself is that of calling at least a temporary halt to Soviet foreign expansion in order to diminish the degree of external danger. The threat to the general line implicit in this reasoning was that if the degree of external danger could be manipulated by measures within Soviet control, such as lessening aggressive pressure or making minor concessions, then it might become possible to deal with the internal problems of economic development in a more "voluntaristic" manner. Thus it became imperative for Stalin to prove that it was impossible for the Soviet Government to diminish international tension.

The foreign policy heresy manifested itself first in a contention that the "capitalist encirclement," the fundamental presupposition of the entire Stalinist pattern of policy, no longer existed in the sense that it had from the Revolution up until that time. The U.S.S.R., so this contention ran, now existed in the midst of a "socialist encirclement." It was bordered for the most part by friendly countries. "Certain comrades," wrote the Party journal *Bolshevik* in 1951, had "construed the establishment of the people's-democratic system in a number of countries bordering on the U.S.S.R. as liquidating the capitalist encirclement."[7] The "certain comrades" were never identified by name. But one prominent Soviet leader who publicly voiced an opinion of this kind was Malenkov. In the opening portion of his report of November 6, 1949, he gave an unusual review of the situation on the Soviet borders. "Never in all its history has our country had such just and well-ordered state frontiers as it has now," he asserted. "Never before in all its history has our country been surrounded with neighboring countries so friendly to our state."[8]

It is true that Malenkov did not here say in so many words that the "capitalist encirclement" had been replaced by a "socialist encirclement." But this was the conclusion suggested by his words, by the spirit of geopolitical complacency that they breathed. Such an inference is also suggested by the fact that no Soviet leader had ever dealt with this theme in this way since the war's end. Whether or not Malenkov was among the "certain comrades," the conception of the decline of the capitalist encirclement was itself condemned very strongly in 1951 and after. The supporters this interpretation were said to have made the mistake of thinking of the capitalist encirclement as a "geographical" notion, whereas they should have seen it as a "political conception."[9] The inference was that no favorable readjustment in areas contiguous to the Soviet territory could bring the encirclement to an end. In January, 1953, the journal *Kommunist* confirmed this inference in the remarkable statement that "So long as capitalism remains in the principal capitalist countries, it would be wrong to speak of the liquidation of the capitalist encirclement."[10] This metamorphosis of the idea of the capitalist encirclement is one of the most revealing incidents in the postwar evolution of Stalinist ideology. The determination to preserve the general line at all cost led, in internal policy, to a doctrine of indefinite industrialization. In foreign policy, the counterpart of this orientation was the new theory of an ever-present capitalist encirclement that could not be canceled by the mere fact that it receded from the Soviet borders. This was a rationalization for indefinite continuance of the cold war.

The issue of the capitalist versus socialist encirclement disclosed the contradiction inherent in the Stalinist position. On the one hand, the incorporation of Eastern Europe and China into the Soviet orbit was advertised as an enormous strengthening of the Soviet Union, a historic increment of Communist power. But this very emphasis upon increased power could give rise to inferences subversive of the Stalinist pattern of policy. Since the Soviet Union was so vastly strengthened now, was it not possible to relax a little abroad and concentrate upon internal tasks? This was the real issue implicit in the argument about the capitalist encirclement. And its importance in the early 1950's was amply borne out by such acts of political stagecraft as the "doctors' plot." This episode, the final act of Stalin's career, must be seen in part as his desperate attempt to dramatize the postulated persistence of the capitalist encirclement, to demonstrate the hopeless unreality of any notion of relaxing international tension. The trial of the culprits, the Jewish doctors, was to furnish the Soviet people with tangible proof that capitalist encirclement not only continued to exist, but that it continued to represent the greatest threat and danger to the Soviet Union.

This intention was made transparently plain in the course of the propaganda campaign following the announcement of January 13, 1953, that a doctors' plot had been uncovered. For example, *Pravda wrote*:

> Certain would-be theoreticians have argued to the point of contending that, now that a mighty camp of socialism has taken form, *imperialism ceases to represent a danger to us.* . . .
>
> It is beyond doubt that the detachment of a number of countries of Europe and Asia from the capitalist camp, the establishment of a people's-democratic system in these countries, the incorporation of these countries in the camp of socialism—all this has radically altered the international situation, struck a shattering blow at the imperialist camp, strengthened the front of peace, socialism, and democracy. *But this does not signify by any means that from now on the capitalist encirclement no longer exists.* It exists and operates actively. . . .
>
> *All talk to the effect that the capitalist encirclement is supposedly a thing of the past* can only give rise to attitudes of complacency and lightheartedness and blunt the feeling of revolutionary vigilance. [Italics added.][11]

We see here that a real and decisive political issue underlay the tissue of morbid fabrications about the "doctor-plotters" and their alleged relations with the governments of the United States and Britain. The case of the Kremlin doctors was a calculated political move on Stalin's part in the context of the internal conflict over foreign policy. It was a sensational way of supporting his insistence that capitalist encirclement was really a "political conception," that the external danger and hostility to the Soviet Union were greater now than ever before, and that there could be no realistic thought of taking steps (e.g., the conclusion of a formal armistice in Korea) to reduce the extremes of tension between the Soviet bloc and the West.

This interpretation of the political rationale of the affair of the doctor's plot is indirectly supported by Khrushchev's statement in the 1956 secret speech that Stalin, after distributing protocols of the doctors' confessions to members of the Politburo, told them: "You are blind like young kittens; what will happen without me? The country will perish because you do not know how to recognize enemies."[12] This shows that the people to whom Stalin wanted to "prove" by means of the doctors' case that no reduction of international tension was possible were members of the Politburo itself, that the opposition against which he was battling in the foreign-policy debate was an opposition at the very highest levels. What Stalin wanted to show by means of the alleged machinations of the doctors was the need to "recognize enemies" in the sense of abandoning all idea of improving relations with the Western powers.

Other evidence that such an opposition existed came out in an article published in January, 1953, concerning Stalin's concluding speech at the Nineteenth Congress. The author was D. Chesnokov, a former professor of philosophy who had recently risen meteorically to a position in Stalin's entourage. His article was an exegesis of the short final speech in which Stalin had pictured Soviet Russia as a "shock brigade" of world Communist revolution. Its main thesis was that "so long as the capitalist encirclement exists, the imperialists will not leave us alone." Chesnokov followed this statement with an almost frenzied denunciation of unnamed proponents of a policy of "concessions and concessionlets* to the imperialists." There were some, it appeared, who fancied that the external enemies could be "appeased" by concessionlets. But:

> Leninism teaches that the imperialists cannot be "appeased" by concessionlets, as suggested by various liberals who have broken with the theory of the class struggle and descended into right-wing opportunism. Concessions and concessionlets to the imperialists in basic issues of principle weaken the positions of the socialist country and encourage the imperialists to increase the pressure on the socialist and democratic countries, to put forward fresh and ever more insolent demands. *Plainly, only people who break with Marxism can go along this path.* As Comrade Stalin teaches, the laws of the class

* The word here translated "concessionlets" was *ustupochki,* the diminutive form of "concessions." This usage is significant. Had the reasoning been about general principles only and not about a concrete issue that had arisen in the inner circle of the Soviet leadership, it is quite doubtful that such a special and unusual turn of speech would have been employed.

struggle demand an intensification of the offensive against the positions of reaction and not concessions to reaction and the reactionary
classes. Successes on the front of the class struggle are won in the
course of a fierce struggle against the enemy. This likewise applies
in full to the struggle for peace and democracy, against imperialist
reaction and war. [Italics added.][13]

This authoritative pronouncement reveals clearly that Stalin was
not contemplating an international détente toward the end of his
life, as some foreign observers have supposed. On the contrary, he
was defending with all the force of his autocratic authority the
opposite view that no *détente* was possible, that no "concessions
and concessionlets" could achieve the relaxation of the international situation which to some seemed desirable. The statement by
Chesnokov also attests that this was not an academic question but
a burning political issue in Stalin's regime. Of particular interest in
this regard is the sentence underlined in the passage quoted above,
which refers to the oppositional point of view in the present tense.
The "liberals who have broken with the theory of the class struggle
and descended into right-wing opportunism" were not figures of
the past, but living Soviet politicians.

One further aspect of the discussion merits brief consideration
here. The Chesnokov article and other materials of that time presented the paradoxical thesis that greater Soviet strength meant
greater external danger. The argument was that Soviet internal successes intensify the hostility toward Russia in the shrunken imperialist world: "The Soviet people knows that the greater our
successes, the more intense the hatred on the part of the bourgeoisie. . . . The hatred on the part of the bourgeoisie will increase
in direct proportion to the growth of the forces of peace, democracy, and socialism; this hatred will drive it on to fresh adven-
tures."[14] This line of reasoning might be dubbed the "theory of
ever-growing hostility." Its manifest purpose was to check all talk
and thought of an international *détente* by deriving the East-West
tension from the imaginary glowing achievements of "Soviet reality." Obviously, if "our successes" are the source of the imperialists'
fanatical hostility, if in other words it is what the Soviet Union *is*
at home rather than what it *does* abroad that creates growing
international tension, then to suppose that Soviet diplomacy can
reduce tension is preposterous. International tension must always
be growing.

IV

Stalin's commitment to indefinite continuation of cold-war hostilities found expression, finally, in his discussion of the world
situation in *Economic Problems of Socialism in the U.S.S.R.* Contrary to some Western interpretations, which have seen in it a
signal of impending Soviet switch to a "softer" line in foreign
policy, this part of Stalin's final work carried as its implicit theme
and message the need for the Communist world to wage political
war against the West without letup.

He addressed himself here to the task of refuting arguments by
"some comrades" (no names given) to the effect that Lenin's
thesis on the inevitability of wars under imperialism was now "obsolete" and that wars were no longer inevitable. Their position, as he
stated it, was that wars between capitalist countries were no longer
inevitable since the capitalist leaderships had learned the lesson of
two world wars, since the United States was now able to control
events in the capitalist camp, and, finally, since "contradictions"
between capitalist countries were now less acute than those between the capitalist and socialist camps. He further attributed to
them the argument that another world war had ceased to be inevitable since there now existed powerful forces for peace that
could check such a development. Stalin rejected all these arguments. Intercapitalist wars were still inevitable, he maintained, because various capitalist countries would eventually turn against the
United States. Far from being less acute than the contradictions
between the hostile camps, the intercapitalist contradictions were
more acute. And as for the peace movement, the most that it would
possibly achieve would be to effect a "temporary postponement" of
a *particular* war. It could not eliminate the inevitability of war.
For that "it is necessary to abolish imperialism."[15]

Reconstructing the position against which Stalin was polemiciz-
ing here, we can see that the high-level proponents of a relaxation
of tension had devised a rather ingenious line of argument in favor
of their policy views. It was an argument to the effect that the
Soviet Union both could and should seek an improvement in East-
West relations, partly in order to reduce the danger of a major
war and partly because it would work to the political advantage of
Communism. The thesis that wars were no longer inevitable things
was a necessary presupposition of advocacy of a deliberate policy
of reducing the war danger, for it makes no sense to endeavor to

avoid something not subject to conscious control.* The thesis that
intercapitalist contradictions had now been eclipsed by those between the two camps was, on the other hand, a way of arguing that
it would serve Soviet and other Communist political interests to
ease the tense international situation in the 1950's.

What this argument was saying, in effect, was that the United
States had succeeded during the cold war in mobilizing most of the
countries of the non-Communist world into something verging on
a world-wide anti-Communist defensive coalition, and because
East-West tension remained so high—in the Korean War, for example—the underlying inner conflicts in the Western coalition were
held in check by the transcendent need for unity under Communist
pressure; if this pressure were relaxed by decision of Moscow, the
divisive forces within the non-Communist world would re-emerge
onto the surface and do their work to the advantage of the
U.S.S.R. and her allies. Such an "argument from *détente*," as we
may call it, was in fact put forward publicly soon after Stalin's
death. In his important address to the Supreme Soviet of August
8, 1953, Malenkov asserted that "if now, under conditions of a
tense international situation, the North Atlantic bloc is rent with
inner struggle and contradictions, a relaxation of this tension may
lead to its disintegration."[16]

What I am suggesting is that Malenkov and others had voiced
this same argument in private before Stalin died, and that this
was the real target of Stalin's above-mentioned disquisition on the
fatal strength of intercapitalist contradictions, which were, he
affirmed, even more acute than those between the two camps and
which would inevitably generate future wars between capitalist
countries. Some foreign observers have, I believe, misinterpreted
the intent of this argument because they have not seen it in the
total context of the issues in Soviet politics at that time. They have
inferred an intention to soften Soviet policy from Stalin's reference
to the greater acuteness of intercapitalist contradictions. But on
closer analysis in the context of the policy debate as sketched in
above, it becomes apparent that this point was integral to Stalin's
attack on the "argument from *détente*."

Stalin was tilting against Soviet proponents of a relaxation of
international tension. In order to invalidate the rather sophisticated

* See Chapter 11 for a discussion of the political logic of the thesis on
noninevitability in the context of the revised post-Stalin doctrine of coexistence.

argument that they had hit upon, he was compelled to maintain that the intercapitalist contradictions were so deep and powerful that eventually they would split the capitalist world wide open *quite independently of any Soviet initiative to relax international tension.* He had to contend that the unity of the Western coalition would break down even if the Soviet Union kept up the cold war indefinitely. "These comrades," wrote Stalin in reference to those whom he was opposing, "see the externals glittering on the surface, but they do not see the forces down below which, even though their effect is as yet unnoticeable, will nevertheless determine the course of events."[17] In other words, the argument from *détente* is based upon a superficial view of world realities, one which pre-supposes that Soviet pressure might cause the Western powers to compose their differences permanently in the common cause of defense. But the differences run too deep for that; in the long run, economics will prevail over politics and divide the countries of the capitalist world in warlike opposition to one another. The Soviet Union need not take measures to relax East-West tension (if that were possible) in order to divide her adversaries; the "forces down below" will do that! Thus Stalin's argument in his final work is all of one piece. He is still defending the general line.

In this essay I have attempted to explore the divided mind of the Soviet leadership in Stalin's last years. Those years show the Stalin regime moving insistently "against the stream," striving to reimpose, in the new postwar setting, a basic pattern of policy that emerged earlier and corresponded to a significantly different con-figuration of internal and external realities. The pattern of policy was represented as an involuntary course, dictated not by desires but by the compulsions of safety. It posited an indefinite suppres-sion of actual Soviet wants and needs, of national economic de-velopment in any natural form, as a compulsory response to mortal danger emanating from a hostile environment. Partly, this proved a self-fulfilling prophecy: Large sections of the world reacted with real hostility to Stalinist foreign policy, and with rather successful efforts to combine forces against it. After the new Soviet empire was established, approximately from 1949 on, it became harder for Stalin to maintain the thesis of a necessarily constant or rising ex-ternal threat over which Moscow could exercise no alleviating in-fluence by its action or abstention from action. Hence the idea of the leadership's freedom to choose the course, which had been expelled earlier from the discussion of internal policy, returned at last to plague Stalin in the realm of foreign policy. He was occupied all the while with extirpating what must have seemed a hydra-headed heresy, one that reared up first in one quarter and then somewhere else. Behind each of its manifestations lurked the specter of voluntarism.

One of the lessons to be drawn from this analysis is the realization that Stalin's heirs did not receive their policy inheritance as a set of axiomatic truths or copybook maxims about the proper way to conduct the affairs of the Soviet Union. Not only did Stalin leave behind him a crisis of governing methods. On the great substantive issues of policy there were no formulas to which usage and common acceptance had imparted a character of self-evidence. It is true that Stalin had swung the full weight of his autocratic authority behind the blueprint for future policy implicit in his final work. Toward the end, this projection of policy had apparently prevailed. Stalin had lived to see it enshrined in a resolution of the Nineteenth Party Congress that was supposed to guide the drafters of the Party's revised program. But this "testament," if one can call it such, was heavy with associations of a controversy still fresh in the minds of the surviving Soviet leaders. It had "unified" the Soviet leadership only at the cost of repressing certain deviant ideas whose proponents were still in positions of power and unlikely to have been inwardly dissuaded from their points of view. Stalin had played a crucial part in all this. His death, coming at the time it did, inevitably affected the situation profoundly. It opened the sluice-gates of change, and they have remained open ever since.

5 SEVERAL STALINS

I

The best-known Stalin biographies were produced while their subject was still alive and able to control the sources of information about, *inter alia,* himself. Souvarine's *Stalin* was completed in the late 1930's. Trotsky's was still unfinished when the assassin sent by Stalin struck him down in 1940. Deutscher's came out in 1949 and was only enlarged by a chapter, not revised, in the new addition published in 1966. The classic Stalin biographies, along with many others, were written without the benefit of the mass of new evidence now at our disposal.

Some of the new material, such as Milovan Djilas' revealing *Conversations with Stalin,* has come from sources outside of Russia. But the great bulk is Soviet in origin and a product of the Khrushchev period's experiments in de-Stalinization. As a Soviet politician desirous of reforming the Stalinist system and yet opposed by conservatives to whom such reform politics spelled danger, Khrushchev found it necessary to legitimate his position and clear a way for action by impugning certain events of the Stalinist past, most notably the Great Purge of the 1930's. To accomplish this object, he had to set some historical facts on the record, as he did in the report to a closed session of the Twentieth Party Congress in 1956—a report that did not remain secret for long. This opening of the floodgates for hitherto unknown or suppressed information on Stalin and the Stalin years may or may not have been Nikita Khrushchev's main service to Soviet Russia, but it unquestionably was a great service to Russian studies.

The flow continued in many forms. Other, public, speeches by Khrushchev and some of his associates contributed further infor-

103

mation useful to the Stalin biographer, as did scolarly writings by historians like Burdzhalov and Nekrich; protocols of party meetings in 1917; previously unpublished writings of Lenin; diaries of his secretaries; press articles on posthumously rehabilitated purge victims; and memoirs by Soviet writers, officials, military officers and others. This new material, taken in its entirety, still leaves a great many important questions about Stalin unanswered or only partially answered. Like any historical testimony, it must be used with critical caution. But all this being said, the fact is that the student of Stalin and his time is far less in the dark now than twenty years ago. He is much better informed about Stalin as a personality and about various key points in Stalin's political life, such as 1917, the Civil War, the last months of Lenin, the collectivization drive, the Great Purge, and the Second World War. Even on the most carefully guarded subject of all—Stalin's role in Soviet foreign policy—we have at least somewhat more information than before.

The regime of Khrushchev's successors has been less kind to Russian studies. Its gradual reinstatement of Stalin in a place of honor in Soviet history has necessitated and been accompanied by a new censorship of historical facts and testimony at variance with this effort. Meanwhile, however, a vital new source of historical information has opened up through *samizdat*—the circulation of uncensored writings in typescript—and this source has yielded much material of interest to the Stalin biographer. Some notable examples are: a verbatim report of a critical discussion by rehabilitated Old Bolsheviks on a draft volume of the official party history dealing with the revolutionary period; the memoirs of Evgenia Ginzburg and Galina Serebriakova, two purge victims who survived and wrote about it; Zhores A. Medvedev's story of what happened to Soviet genetics in the Stalin period and after.[1] and Nadezhda Mandelstam's magnificent account of the road to Calvary on which she and her husband embarked in 1934 after word of his unpublished (and unflattering) sixteen-line poem about Stalin reached Stalin.[2] Svetlana Alliluyeva's *Twenty Letters to a Friend,* originally written in 1963 "for the drawer," may be viewed as a sort of contribution to the *samizdat* literature, and the glimpses it affords of Stalin as perceived by his daughter while growing up and in adulthood are of no less value to the scholar for the fact that he may not always accept her interpretations. Further, we know that the *samizdat* literature includes a major work by Roy Medvedev, the historian brother of Zhores, about

Stalinism and Stalin. Since this book has not yet appeared abroad, we can only hope that it will, and soon. Finally, in *Khrushchev Remembers*—which I take to be Khrushchev's own material, however raw, arbitrarily edited and incomplete the text may be —we have a major addition to the unofficial memoir literature on the Stalin period and a source of many a significant new historical detail concerning Stalin, particularly in his later years.

Still another genre of *samizdat* literature useful to the scholar is the work of fiction in which Stalin appears as a character. In Solzhenitsyn's novel *The First Circle,* to take the best-known example, there is a sequence of scenes, dated late 1949, in which the aging Stalin has a nocturnal soliloquy, starts writing his papers on linguistics, and talks with his secret police chief, Abakumov. Those who consider this fictionalizing of Stalin a weakness of the novel seem to me to miss a point. Solzhenitsyn, like many other intellectuals in Russia, finds the Stalin question endlessly interesting because of the deep connection with the greater question of the Russian Revolution itself and its paths of development. In addition to being contemporary Russia's best novelist, Solzhenitsyn is something of a sovietologist. Witness, in *The First Circle,* the author-like character of Nerzhin, who became interested in the Stalin question as a boy when he read his works and found them, by comparison with Lenin's, "a sort of mush," and who, as a prisoner later on, writes secret notes on Soviet history because of a compulsion—as he puts it to himself—to "grapple with the riddle of the inflated gloomy giant who had only to flutter his eyelashes for Nerzhin's head to fly off." Whether or not the nocturnal Stalin scenes in *The First Circle* contain any new items of historical fact,* they are valuable as a partial record of Solzhenitsyn's "grappling," his interpretation of Stalin as a personality.

One further source of new evidence concerning Stalin is material that earlier biographers have tended to overlook. In all branches of scholarship, the appearance of new evidence often turns on changes in what is regarded as significant. Such changes are occurring in biography now through the Freudian revolution and the resulting new appreciation of the importance of childhood and youth in people's lives. Erik Erikson's exploration of the

---

* The possibility that they do is not excluded. On internal evidence, for example, Solzhenitsyn appears, in writing them, to have had access to the Alliluyeva manuscript, *Twenty Letters to a Friend,* or knowledge of material contained in it.

"identity crisis" in *Young Man Luther* opened, in this respect, a new epoch in the field of biography—an epoch, however, which has yet to be felt in Stalin biography. Here the standard form has been the ordinary political biography, with relatively little attention to the formative years that Stalin spent before, at the age of nineteen, he became a seminary dropout and professional revolutionary. What *brought* him to this crucial decision, psychologically speaking, is not a question satisfactorily answered in the literature of Stalin biography, although some of the material relevant to the answer has been available to us for thirty years or so. Since the question has not been treated as central, the significance of pertinent recorded facts about Stalin's seminary years has not been fully perceived.

II

If Stalin is fated to become the subject of a new biographical literature in the coming period, how is our picture of him likely to be affected? One way of approaching this question is to reconsider some past views in the light of present knowledge. I am referring not to particular works of biography so much as to general images of Stalin that have been influential both in the biographical literature and the public mind.

In Trotsky's view, which has undoubtedly been one of the most influential, Stalin was in essence a man of the bureaucratic apparatus, and his qualities—the very qualities, in fact, that explained his success—were those typical of the apparatus-man: practicality, strong will, persistence, primitive theoretical equipment, stubbornly empirical mind, lack of creative imagination, and mediocrity—above all, mediocrity. Trotsky's theory of Stalin was thus part and parcel of a larger theory of the takeover of the Bolshevik Revolution by a new ruling stratum, the "Thermidorian bureaucracy." It all came to him in a flash one day in 1925 when he was talking with his deputy Sklyansky, who asked for his view of Stalin. "Stalin," Trotsky replied, "is the outstanding mediocrity in the party," and in that short conversation, as he later recorded in his autobiography, he grasped for the first time, in all its psychological and social complexity, the problem of the Thermidor. "For the thing that matters is not Stalin, but the forces that he expresses without even realizing it."[3] Or, as he summed it up later in *The Revolution Betrayed*: "Stalin is the personification of the bureaucracy. That is the substance of his political personality."

It is hard to resist the thought that this theory of Stalin had elements of unconscious rationalization. At the moment of its formulation, Trotsky was losing out to Stalin in the post-Lenin political struggle. To succumb to a man he saw as a third-rater must have been intensely galling to this proud revolutionary, but less so if what he was succumbing to was a whole new social stratum of which Stalin was merely the representative figure and symptom. But whatever view one takes of the origin of Trotsky's theory, it seriously misread the situation. Lenin had the truer perception when he wrote in the document of late 1922 that later became known as his "Testament" that Trotsky and Stalin were the two most able men in the party leadership. As many were later to point out, Stalin was no mediocrity as a man of politics. He was in fact *besting* Trotsky in the fight for the succession. And not simply because he had certain "qualities" that endeared him to the bureaucracy, or because of his power over appointments, but because he was making effective use of themes to which wide circles of the party were responsive, such as the theme of the possibility of constructing socialism in one country. To the extent that it existed, the peculiar affinity that Trotsky perceived between Stalin and the rising Soviet bureaucracy was largely a result of Stalin's staking out a position that the new men of power found convincing. The appearance of such an affinity was therefore a tribute to Stalin's formidable political talents.

Not having risen as the bureaucracy's creature, Stalin never was that. But neither, for a long while, was he its absolute master. He achieved this position with the great terror of the 1930's, through which he destroyed not only the Bolshevik Old Guard but the bulk of that very bureaucracy which had given him its support in the 1920's and executed his policies of forced collectivization and industrialization in the sequel. The new bureaucratic generation that succeeded to the command posts during the Purge was, in the fullest possible sense, Stalin's own creature and servant. One of Solzhenitsyn's services to sovietology is his gifted portrayal of this fact in the imaginary scene between Stalin and Abakumov. He shows us this man—the first apparatus-man of Russia in 1949 —cringing before Stalin, knowing that "one mistake in his presence could be that one mistake in life which set off an explosion, irreversible in effect. Stalin was terrifying because he did not listen to excuses, made no accusations; his yellow tiger eyes simply brightened balefully, his lower lids closed up a bit—and there, inside him, sentence had been passed, and the condemned man didn't know: he left in peace, was arrested at night, and shot by morning."[4]

III

Professor E. H. Carr, whose many-volumed history of Soviet Russia through the 1920's is almost the only truly monumental work of scholarship produced in Soviet studies in our generation, does not regard Stalin as either a mediocrity or a mere embodiment of the bureaucracy. He sees him as an historical figure in his own right, and a great one. Countering Trotsky's remark that it was not Stalin who created the machine but the machine that created him, Carr observes: "But it required something more than a machine to 'create' Stalin and put him in power."

Yet, the influence of Trotsky is still to be seen in Carr's own interpretation of Stalin's as "the most impersonal of great historical figures," not a molder of events and circumstances but one molded by them. To illustrate this thesis, and what he calls "the essentially impersonal character of Stalinist policy," Carr asserts that no element of personal conviction, and certainly no originality of conception, was involved when Stalin assumed leadership of the industrialization drive. The aims he pursued in his vigorous and ruthless way were those "dictated by the dynamic force inherent in the revolution itself." His qualities, like his convictions, were those of his milieu; they "mirrored the current stage of the historical process." His role in Soviet history was that of an outstanding organizer and administrator, an *executor* of revolutionary policy with no vision of where it would lead. His distinctively Russian orientation in socialist construction betrayed the absence from his makeup of the western European influences imbibed by the other Bolshevik leaders as part of their Russian intelligentsia tradition. Their Marxism had unconsciously assimilated the Western cultural foundations. His, reflecting the anti-Western educational tradition in which he was reared, had the character of a "formalistic creed rather than that of an intellectual conviction," faith being a more important virtue to him than reason.[5]

Carr's view of Stalin corresponds in a number of ways to the characterization given by Isaac Deutscher, who had earlier spoken of Stalin's "almost impersonal personality." Deutscher does not see Stalin as a man of ideas or Marxist theorist. Rather, Stalin appears in his biography as essentially a pragmatist, concerned more with making things work than with theory. Here, too, Stalin is the one who accomplished by ruthless means a revolution that others had conceived and designed; he is the executor of other Bolsheviks' ideas. Thus, Deutscher maintains that the ideas behind Stalin's revolution from above in the early 1930's were "not his," that Stalin embarked upon this second revolution in an "unpremeditated, pragmatic manner," and that he was "precipitated into collectivization" by the chronic danger of famine in 1928 and 1929.[6]

One need not rate Stalin among the foremost Marxist thinkers in order to disagree with the Trotsky-Deutscher-Carr view of him as basically a non-intellectual with no great concern for theory. The fact is that Stalin from early youth gravitated not simply to revolution but to Marxism as an overall philosophy and as a theory of society, history, and revolution. It is true that he was self-taught as a Marxist, but so were those Bolsheviks with whom Carr contrasts him; Marxism was not among the subjects officially offered in Russian universities in those days. During and after his years in the Tiflis seminary, Stalin mastered the writings of classical Marxism then available, along with the Russian Marxist literature and the histories of European socialism. The exposition of Marxism that he published in 1906–07 (in his work *Anarchism or Socialism?*) set forth some of the ideas he would express in his essay of 1938 on dialectical and historical materialism. His treatise of 1913 on *Marxism and the National Question* was generally recognized as a significant contribution, at any rate to Bolshevik Marxism; and although he wrote it with the help and under the direction of Lenin, the work itself was no more Lenin's than any successful dissertation is the work of the man who supervises it. In 1924 he produced, in *The Foundations of Leninism,* an erudite compendium of Leninist thought that was to prove serviceable as a handbook of theory for several generations of Party members.

In a 1928 conversation with Kamenev that became widely known in Soviet circles at the time, Bukharin, then in close contact with Stalin, remarked that Stalin was "eaten up" by the craving to be recognized as a theoretician. In the last years of his life Stalin was still striving to fulfill this ambition. In 1950, when extremely grave economic and social problems urgently pressed for his attention, he lavished time and energy on the effort to produce a *magnum opus* in his papers on *Marxism and Linguistics;* and he delayed the postwar Party congress for years so that he could give it an epoch-making Marxist theoretical revelation with his booklet *Economic Problems of Socialism in the U.S.S.R.* (1952). Stalin was an intellectual of some little learning, limited but not negligible talent, and grandiose pretensions. He never became the eminent Marxist thinker that he yearned to be, but he also never ceased trying. One could call it a classic intellectual's story were it not for the tragic consequences—for others —that failure had in this instance. Needless to say, none of what has been said obviates the fact that Stalin also wanted to go down in history as the doer, the man of practical deeds who translated the Marxist-Leninist revolutionary program into reality. His pretensions to historical greatness were not only far-reaching, but many-sided.

The impersonal Stalin of Carr and Deutscher is a case of the mistaking of historical appearance for reality. It would have been (had it been so offered) a perfect characterization of Molotov, who was indeed the "almost impersonal personality," a man of commonplace qualities, a doer who was not a thinker, and one who became an instrument of the historical process. But Stalin is a different matter. Not only did he have political ideas and a Marxist-Leninist mind of his own, whatever its crudities and limitations; some of his personal qualities—qualities that affected his political style or policies—were out of the ordinary. Such diverse observers as Milovan Djilas and George Kennan, both of whom saw Stalin at close quarters, concur, for example, in the view that he was (in Kennan's words) "a consummate actor."[7] Paradoxically, Stalin's extraordinary histrionic ability may help explain the appearance of impersonality that he frequently conveyed, and also why it was only an appearance. It may account, too, for the fact that a man we now know to have been morbidly sensitive to the least possible slight, irascible, moody, hyper-suspicious, given to occasional fits of rage, and capable of the kind of panic and depression that came over him when Hitler attacked Russia in 1941 could delude some of his biographers into believing that the pseudonym *Stalin* ("man of steel") was not simply his wish for himself or pose but a true summation of his personality.[8]

Another personal quality of Stalin's pertinent to our argument was his intense Great Russian nationalism, which was accompanied by an anti-Semitism that grew quite obsessive in his final years. Great Russian nationalism was not peculiar to Stalin, although he felt it with a special intensity that was bound up with other aspects of his personality as well as with his non-Russian ethnic origin. It was an attitude that he shared with a certain section of the Party in the early post-revolutionary years, but not with the Party as a whole. There were forces working in both directions, as shown, among other things, by the conflict that developed between Stalin and Lenin over this very issue in 1922.[9] The forces of resistance to what one Bolshevik called "Russian Red patriotism" were then still strong in the Party. Their defeat in the later years undoubtedly owed something to the fact that an extreme exponent of Russian nationalism became leader of the Party. In this instance, then, Stalin possessed an attribute that could not be ascribed simply to his time and place; and his possession of it proved influential for the subsequent course of events.

Stalin is not rightly seen as a pragmatic leader who simply led in the direction that events were tending. Even accepting Professor Carr's contention that in the Party struggles of the 1920's he molded himself to events rather than vice versa (which seems at best partially true), we have to recognize the great change that occurred between that period and after, between Stalin rising and Stalin risen. As early as the end of 1929, the year of victory in his long fight for the supreme leadership, Stalin took advantage of his new-won ascendancy to place his strong personal imprint upon the first great policy act of the Stalinist era—the plan for total collectivization of agriculture. Archival information released in Soviet publications during Khrushchev's time shows that he intervened in the bureaucratic policy-making process to impose far swifter tempos than the drafters of the plan had thought feasible. and that he quashed certain provisions that had been written into the plan to safeguard against panic reactions on the part of peasants whose holdings were to be collectivized. This in turn contributed materially to the catastrophic course that events took, culminating in the great famine of 1931–1933, which claimed millions of lives. Very probably, collectivization in some form and according to some timetable was a foregone conclusion after the grain crisis of 1927–1928. But this does not mean that it had to take the form it did, that brute events "precipitated" the breakneck course Stalin followed. History—as it usually does—offered alternatives, and there was no lack of Bolshevik minds to grasp them. Much light has been shed on this question by the revisionist Soviet history of collectivization that emerged during the Khrushchev period and by the recent work of Western scholars like Lewin and Nove.[10]

The evidence is strong, although it has not yet been adequately presented in our scholarship, that Stalin did not embark upon the second revolution in "an unpremeditated pragmatic manner." He acted on certain rather distinctive ideas that had been maturing in his mind for several years before 1929. Even if they showed some influence of the thinking of Preobrazhensky and the Left opposition, these ideas cannot simply be ascribed, as Deutscher has done, to that source. The use of coercion to effect a swift total collectivization had never, for example, been a part of the Left opposition's program, nor did it envisage the pace of industrialization that Stalin sought to enforce. The developments of that time do not support the thesis of the essentially impersonal character of Stalinist policy.

Stalin's career before and after 1929 provides an illustration of Sidney Hook's paradigm of the "event-making man," who is dependent upon a social class in coming to power but subsequently emancipates himself from this dependence and makes himself into a force for the shaping of the historical process.[11] In Stalin's case, as was indicated earlier, the Great Purge of the 1930's was the ultimate radical means by which he emancipated himself from dependence upon his bureaucratic social constituency. This gigantic act of terrorism was itself one of the supreme modern manifestations of the impingement of personality upon history, and paved the way for others. One of them was the conclusion of the pact of August, 1939, which freed Hitler to unleash the Second World War. Many more followed in the postwar years of Stalin's rule.

IV

One further Stalin remains to be considered here, among the larger number that might have been discussed: Khrushchev's Stalin.

In this instance we are dealing not with a biography but with material for one, material of a rare documentary kind, full of significance for Stalin biography. The special report that Khrushchev gave before the closed session of the Twentieth Party Congress on the night of February 24–25, 1956—or rather the condensed version of it that reached the West and was published in *The New York Times* on June 5 of that year—is a close-up portrait of Stalin as observed behind the scenes by political associates over a period of years, together with the results of a posthumous inquiry into aspects of his rule that remained more or less obscure even to these associates, or many of them, while he was still alive. All future Stalin biographers will have to take this document into account and contend with its implications.

Scholars have taken issue with a number of specific points in the secret report. It has been noted, for example, that Khrushchev was not correct in saying that Stalin originated the concept "enemy of the people." Some (including Soviet military memoirists) have questioned Khrushchev's remark that Stalin planned military operations during the Soviet-German war on a globe. But on the whole, the informational content of the report is accepted, and rightly so, as historically true. Some have even contended that it revealed little that had not already been known or surmised in the West, and that it was chiefly significant as an official Soviet confirmation of these facts. It is true that such subjects of the report as Lenin's "Testament" and certain particulars of the Great Purge were already known to us. But the view in question does not really do justice to the fundamental novelty of Khrushchev's Stalin-portrait, as regards both many specific details and general significance.

Apart from the question of basic factuality, there is the matter of fairness. After all, selectivity can combine elements of truth into a false or deeply distorted overall picture. Is this true of Khrushchev's picture? An essential part of the answer, it seems to me, is that no one should take the secret report as a full, rounded account of Stalin's life and work. Nor, for that matter, did Khrushchev offer it as such. He began it by observing that Stalin's merits in the Revolution, the Civil War, and the following years had been sufficiently written about to be well known to all his audience. Far from denying these merits, he praised Stalin, in a later passage, for having been "one of the strongest Marxists" in the 1920's and for having played a constructive part in the party struggles of the post-Lenin years and the drives for collectivization and industrialization. Furthermore, Khrushchev did not portray Stalin as a man villainous in his motivation, but rather insisted that he was not that. While presenting an appalling record of cruelties and brutalities toward party members and others—a record that makes Stalin at certain later periods of his life look like a homicidal maniac—Khrushchev declared:

> . . . Stalin was convinced that this was necessary for the defense of the interests of the working classes against the plotting of enemies and against the attack of the imperialist camp. He saw this from the position of the interest of the working class, of the interest of the laboring people, of the interest of the victory of socialism and communism. We cannot say that these were the deeds of a giddy

despot. He considered that this should be done in the interest of the party, of the working masses, in the name of the defense of the revolution's gains. In this lies the whole tragedy!

The future Stalin biographer would do well to ponder these words seriously. Stalin may have been one of the great villain-figures of history, but he was not aware of it; he considered himself a *good* Bolshevik.

How, then, should we characterize the secret report as an historical document? In essence, it is a study in the abuse of power —indeed, an indictment on this charge, supported by a massive array of pertinent facts. Abuse of power is the leitmotif; these very words occur over and over in the document. Having reached the pinnacle of power, Stalin turned against the party that had placed him there, destroyed many thousands of its loyal members and terrorized the rest, including those who worked most closely with him in high Party and state positions. In doing this, he acted on the vivid belief that he was surrounded by stealthily conspiring enemies who must be destroyed lest they destroy both him and the state of which he was leader. By eliminating those whom he perceived as enemies, many of whom were in the Soviet armed forces, he gravely weakened the country's preparedness for war; and his leadership on the eve of and during the Soviet-German war showed many failings. Imbued by a grandiosity that knew no bounds, he made use of his tyrannical power for—among other purposes—his own self-glorification. And in the final, postwar years his sense of being surrounded by malevolent plotting forces grew still more obsessive: "Stalin became even more capricious, irritable, and brutal; in particular his suspicion grew. His persecution mania reached unbelievable proportions. Many workers were becoming enemies before his eyes."

The indictment for abuse of power in Khrushchev's theme; the particulars with which he supports it are what are of chief interest to the Stalin biographer. Especially useful are those particulars that say or imply something about Stalin as a personality. I have given only a very rough sketch of them here. But this summary may be sufficient to suggest what is essentially novel about the secret reports as a contribution to Stalin biography: it is the description at first hand of a person whose behavior falls somewhere on the continuum of psychiatric conditions usually designated as "paranoid." Khrushchev himself did not use this term or indicate that Stalin might have been considered a psychiatric case; he was *indicting* Stalin as a man and leader. However, the factual testimony presents the picture of a personality of paranoid tendency. Moreover, this testimony is supported and supplemented by reports from other knowledgeable Soviet sources, including such an indubitably non-hostile witness as Stalin's daughter, Svetlana Alliluyeva. Her observations corroborate Khrushchev's at a number of critical points, particularly with respect to the "persecution mania" (her words) and its progression to a peak in the postwar years.[12] Here it may be remarked in passing that the "progressive" nature of paranoia, that is, its tendency to develop in early adulthood and grow increasingly pronounced in later life, is regularly emphasized in textbooks of clinical psychiatry.

Khrushchev's Stalin was a bombshell, and scholarship is still feeling the shock. For various reasons, the field of Russian studies was less primed to assimilate the message than to resist it. None of the better-known Stalin biographies, so far as I am aware, had propounded the hypothesis of a paranoid Stalin and examined the evidence that may be adduced in its support. Nor had those few Westerners who saw Stalin on rare occasions noted the sorts of behavior in him that associates were observing behind the scenes, although there were occasions when, as George Kennan reports, someone would see "the yellow eyes light up in a flash of menace and fury as he turned, momentarily, on some unfortunate subordinate. . . . " ;[13] and Charles Bohlen, Roosevelt's wartime interpreter, recalls "a rather acrimonious accusation by Stalin, at one of the dinners, that Churchill had secret sympathies for the Germans."[14] Furthermore, students of the Soviet and other modern dictatorships had evolved a kind of "systems approach" to the explanation of some of the facts to which Khrushchev made reference in the secret report. The terroristic purges of the 1930's and after in Stalin's Russia appeared, on the basis of this approach, to express the dynamics of totalitarianism as a system, not the personal politics and psychodynamics of its leaders. Indeed, the behavior in question was generally viewed not as the leader's behavior or a product of it, but as behavior of the system —which to *some* extent, of course, it was.

Accordingly, the impact of Khrushchev's Stalin upon scholarship has been somewhat muted. The specific historical details and episodes to which the secret report makes reference have been assimilated without difficulty, but the broader implications are still, in a sense, being weighed in the scholarly mind. Some believe that what should remain uppermost is the responsibility of

Leninism or the Soviet system *for* Stalin and his actions, whatever psychological motives drove him to act so. There is also some skepticism that a person of psychotic tendency could have acted as methodically as Stalin did in destroying those whom he perceived as enemies. As Professor Leonard Schapiro has written, apropos of Stalin's motives for the *Ezhovshchina* of 1936–1938, "the assault on the party showed too much careful preparation, planning and system for madness to be the explanation."[15] In this instance, the objection appears to be based on a misunderstanding. The major authorities, starting with the father of modern psychiatry, Emile Kraepelin, have found paranoia to be a condition characterized (in Kraepelin's words) "by the gradual development of a stable progressive system of delusions, without marked mental deterioration, clouding of consciousness, or involvement of the coherence of thought."[16] Not only are "careful preparation, planning and system" not foreign to individuals of this category; they are among the characteristics attributes of them. With mental powers fully intact, the paranoid organizes his life around methodical planning and scheming to strike at those who, he unshakably believes, are doing just this to him. Stalin's preparation of the events of 1936–1938 in Russia gives every sign of having been an historic case in point.

The testimony of the secret report on this point, and in general on Stalin as a personality, receives both corroboration and further elaboration in the memoir material published in the West in 1970 under the title *Khrushchev Remembers.** Especially significant is the wealth of fresh fact and observation concerning Stalin in the postwar years, when his paranoidal reactions became so pronounced—and at times even grotesque—that close associates needed no psychiatric sophistication to recognize them for what they were. His suspiciousness reached such boundless extremes

* The circumstances under which this book appeared were unusual and remain (at the time of writing—February, 1971) unclarified. A publisher's note states that the material emanated "from various sources at various times and in verious circumstances," and leaves it an open question whether Khrushchev "intended or expected his words ever to find their way into print, either in his own country or in the West. . . ." Questions as to authenticity have been raised, partly on the basis of errors of fact that seem to some reviewers implausible as coming from Khrushchev. But on internal evidence the authorship of the material, or at least the great bulk of it, appears indubitably Khrushchevian. Pending further clarification of the circumstances of origin, editing, etc., however, the scholar would do well to be guarded in his use of the book as an historical document.

that he was overheard on one occasion saying, "I trust no one, not even myself," and Khrushchev, after quoting the remark, comments: "All of us around Stalin were temporary people. As long as he trusted us to a certain degree, we were allowed to go on living and working. But the moment he stopped trusting you, Stalin would start to scrutinize you until the cup of his distrust overflowed. Then it would be your turn to follow those who were no longer among the living."[17]

Stalin's vivid sense of being surrounded by conspiring enemies found lethal expression in the "Crimean" and "Leningrad" affairs. When a group of prominent Soviet Communists who had headed a Soviet Jewish Anti-Fascist Committee during the Second World War proposed to him afterwards that the Crimea be made into a Soviet Jewish Republic, Stalin perceived in their proposal a Jewish conspiracy to establish an outpost of American imperialism on Soviet shores, and he consigned its authors—in whom he now saw agents of American Zionism—to fates ranging from death to long-term exile. Molotov's wife, one of the Committee's leaders, was sent into exile; and Molotov himself, although still a member of the Politburo, came under a cloud of suspicion in Stalin's mind. Stalin decided that Molotov must have sold out to the Americans during a wartime visit to confer with President Roosevelt, and he cabled the Soviet Union's U.N. Ambassador, Andrei Vyshinsky, for confirmation of his theory that Molotov must have owned a personal railway car in America, as he had traveled by train from Washington to New York at that time.[18] The "Leningrad affair" of 1949 took the lives of several high officials whom Stalin suspected of involvement in an anti-Soviet conspiracy, and threatened the lives of many more. In this connection, and in a significant departure from the secret report, Khrushchev speaks of "the sickness which began to envelop Stalin's mind in the last years of his life."[19]

But after recognizing classical symptoms of paranoia in Khrushchev's Stalin and searching in the appropriate sources for any light they can cast on this type of personality and the patterns of experience that normally go with it, the future Stalin biographer will still find himself face to face with the classical biographical task. He must try to reconstruct the life history of Stalin and as much of the associated *inner* life history and motivation as possible; he must relate them both to the changing culture and milieu; and he must explore the interplay of personality and society in this particular instance. Psychology or psychiatry may aid him—in part to discover how much more complex and difficult the task is than he realized when he started—but it can no more resolve the problem for him than it can relieve the clinician of the biographical effort involved in developing the case history of an individual patient. By virtue of their very generality, psychiatric categories (like other categories) are limited in what they can reveal about any individual person and how he became the person that he is, or was. No matter how inwardly and outwardly disturbed the life is or may have been, it still requires to be seen as a life. So, if the clinician must be a kind of biographer, how can the biographer find a short cut to his objective in the lore of the clinician?

PART THREE

Stalinism and After: Internal Affairs

6 THE IMAGE OF DUAL RUSSIA*

I

When Ilya Ehrenburg hopefully put the word "thaw" into currency soon after Stalin's death, by making it the title of a novel, he may or may not have known that it had a previous history in Russia. According to some pre-Revolutionary sources, Russians began to talk of a "thaw" at the end of the reign of Iron Czar Nicholas I, who died in 1855. The thaw was manifested in a change of atmosphere, a relaxation of censorship, and other signs of softening of the bureaucratic regimentation of society that had marked Nicholas' long reign, especially in the so-called years of official terror after 1848. The image of the thaw pictured the period lived through as a gray, interminable Russian winter of despotism above and paralysis of society below. The incipient relaxation of state controls was seen as the harbinger of a coming "spring" of liberalization.[1] The comparison with the official terror of the last years of Stalin's reign, and with the atmosphere in Russia as felt in the early months after his death in 1953, is very striking. No knowledge of obscure history books was needed for the word "thaw" to come back into circulation. For Russia had just lived through another long, gray winter of despotism above and paralysis of society below, and was now, once again, awakening to hope for change.

The symbolism of the thaw is particularly revealing in its implicit comparison of the Russian state with a bleak elemental force that holds the land in its grasp and is a blight on the life of society. This points to an element of Russian thought and feeling about the state that has been relatively constant in its core through a large part of the history of the country, relatively independent of

* This chapter appeared in slightly different form in C. E. Black, ed., *The Transformation of Russian Society* (Cambridge: Harvard University Press, 1960). © 1960, by the President and Fellows of Harvard College. Reprinted with permission.

the shift of political seasons. I propose to call this the image of dual Russia. It embraces, first, a consciousness, which remained more or less inarticulate for a long time, of Russia as a double entity: Russian state and Russian society. On the one hand, there is *vlast'* or *gosudarstvo,* the centralized autocratic state power, embodied in the person of the Czar and operating through a hierarchy of bureaucratic institutions and their local agents. In the nineteenth century, everything pertaining to *vlast',* including the autocrat, the court, the bureaucratic officialdom, the official customs, official uniforms, official truth or ideology and so on, came to be subsumed under the concept of "official Russia." On the other hand, there is the population at large, the society, nation, or people (*obshchestvo, narod*). It came to be conceived as a separate and distinct Russia with a life and truth of its own. This we may call unofficial or "popular Russia."

The image of dual Russia is not simply a conception of the state and people as two different Russias. It also comprises an evaluative attitude, or rather a range of such attitudes. Their common denominator is the apprehension of the autocratic state power as an *alien* power in the Russian land. The relation between the state and the society is seen as one between conqueror and conquered. The state is in control, but in the manner of an occupying power dealing with a conquered populace. It is the active party, the organizing and energizing force, in the drama of dual Russia, whereas the population at large is the passive and subordinate party, the tool and victim of the state's designs. An alien power is, of course, one toward which a great many different positions may be taken, ranging from active collaboration through resignation and passive resistance to outright rebelliousness. However, there is a unifying thread in this whole range of responses. The liberal scholar and statesman Miliukov, writing in exile after the 1917 Revolution, summed it up by saying that the state power had always remained in Russia "an outsider to whom allegiance was won only in the measure of his utility. The people were not willing to assimilate themselves to the state, to feel a part of it, responsible for the whole. The country continued to feel and to live independently of the state authorities."[2] In what follows I wish to examine the background of this attitude and to outline the view that the story of the Soviet period in Russian history is partly a tale of how the state became an outsider again in the consciousness of the Russian people.

The image of dual Russia is grounded in the actualities of Russian historical experience with the state. The consciousness of the state as an alien power grew out of a real separation of the state from the nation. According to Miliukov, the two foundations of the Russian system as it evolved in Muscovy from the sixteenth century onward were the "autocratic power" on the one hand and the "population" on the other, the two "more or less imperfectly linked by a system of mediating governmental organs."[3] Far from developing as a dependent political "superstructure" over the social-economic "base," the Russian state organism took shape as an autonomous force acting to create or recreate its own social base, to shape and reshape the institutional pattern of society, in a series of revolutions from above. The state showed itself in what might, broadly speaking, be called a totalitarianizing role in relation to society. It brought the society under its centralized control and direction. The fastening down of serfdom upon the peasants in the seventeenth century was only one great phase in the historical process of the "binding of all classes" in compulsory service to the autocracy. A system arose whose guiding principle was the idea of the servitude of all sections of society to the state. Claiming ownership of the land, the state power destroyed the boyars as a class and created a controlled nobility of "serving men" whose landed estates were allotted on condition of military service to the state. This was the foundation of the subsequent growth of the Russian system of an "aristocracy of rank" (*chin*), under which bureaucratic distinction rather than birth became, in principle, the highroad of entry into the nobility.

The mainspring of the whole "binding" process was the drive of the autocratic power to aggrandize the national territory, its "gathering of lands," through which Muscovy expanded from an area of about 15,000 square miles in 1462 to one-fifth of the earth's surface in 1917. The expansionist drive placed a great premium upon military strength. Because of the country's economic backwardness and technological inferiority to its Western neighbors, the government sought to mobilize the resources for war by enlisting the population directly in its service. The exploitative relation of the state to the society brought an extension of coercive controls and the hypertrophy of the centralized governmental system. In his summation of modern Russian history from the sixteenth to the mid-nineteenth centuries, the historian Kliuchevsky writes that "the expansion of the state territory, straining beyond measure and exhausting the resources of the people, only bolstered the power of the state without elevating the self-confidence of the people. . . . The state swelled up; the people grew lean."[4]

The image of dual Russia was an outgrowth of this entire process. But one particular episode in the process, Peter the Great's revolution from above, did most to make the people conscious of the state as a separate and alien power in their midst. Peter particularly aspired to borrow technology from the West, and not civilization in the wider sense. But in the process, he reorganized the state administration along new centralized lines, set up the governmental bureaucracy in a new capital separate from the rest of the country, and proceeded by forcible means to carry through a cultural revolution designed to change the old Russian way of life. The group most immediately affected by the cultural revolution was the bureaucratic serving class itself, so that the rift between the state and the people became a visible fact of manners, language, and dress. Consequently, later writers tend to date the division of Russia into two entities from Peter's time. Alexander Herzen, for example, wrote in 1853, "Two Russias came into hostile opposition from the beginning of the eighteenth century." He explained:

> On the one hand, there was governmental, imperial, aristocratic Russia, rich in money, armed not only with bayonets but with all the bureaucratic and police techniques taken from Germany. On the other hand, there was the Russia of the dark people, poor, agricultural, communal, democratic, helpless, taken by surprise, conquered, as it were, without battle.[5]

So foreign did the Russian Government become in the eyes of its own peasant people, wrote Herzen elsewhere, that Russian officials in uniform seemed to the peasant to be representative of the German Government. In the military officer, he saw a policeman; in the judge, an enemy; in the landowner, who was invested with the authority of the state, a mighty force with which he was unable to cope.[6]

Thus, *gosudarstvo* came to seem, in the eyes of a majority of the people, a kind of occupying power in the Russian land. Summing up this development, Sir Donald MacKenzie Wallace wrote at the close of the nineteenth century:

> It was in the nature of things that the Government, aiming at the realization of designs which its subjects neither sympathized with nor

clearly understood, should have become separated from the nation. . . . A considerable section of the people looked on the reforming Tsars as incarnations of the spirit of evil, and the Tsars in
their turn looked upon the people as raw material for the realization
of their political designs. . . . The officials have naturally acted in
the same spirit. Looking for direction and approbation merely to
their superiors, they have systematically treated those over whom
they were placed as a conquered or inferior race. *The state has thus
come to be regarded as an abstract entity,* with interests entirely different from those of the human beings composing it; and in all
matters in which state interests are supposed to be involved, the
rights of individuals are ruthlessly sacrificed. [Italics added.][7]

The fact that the state, by virtue of its role in Russian historical
experience, had come to be widely regarded as an alien and "abstract entity" is of great importance for an understanding of the
turbulent course of events in Russia between 1855 and 1917. It
helps to explain the paradox that liberalizing reform from above
in the 1860's coincided with the rise of an organized revolutionary
movement from below, and also the circumstance that in February,
1917, "A few days of street disorders in St. Petersburg, and the
refusal of the soldiers of the city garrison to put them down, were
enough to topple the Tsarist regime. It made no real attempt to
defend itself, for *it proved to have no supporters.*" (Italics added.)[8]

II

The thaw at the close of Nicholas I's reign marked the beginning
of a new period in the life of Russia, in which the direction of the
earlier Russian historical process was decisively reversed. It was
the time of "unbinding." The government itself remained autocratic; the system of administration, centralized and bureaucratic.
However, the reforms of the 1860's, beginning with the abolition of
serfdom, inaugurated the emancipation of Russian society from the
all-encompassing tutelage of the bureaucratic state. Official Russia
contracted, so to speak, permitting unofficial Russia to emerge into
the open from behind the "shroud" with which, as Herzen expressed it, the government had covered up the life of the country.
Forces in Russian society acquired a certain scope for independent
self-expression. The monologue of the state with its agents gave way
to a dialogue between the state and society, above all, between the
state and that element of society that called itself the "intelligentsia."

Peter Struve, writing in the early twentieth century in *Vekhi,* suggested that the spiritual hallmark of the Russian intelligentsia was "its estrangement from the state and hostility toward it."* This statement may have been made in a spirit of polemical exaggeration, yet it is certainly true that a sense of apartness from the official world, and of closeness to the world of the Russian people— or to what this world was imagined to be—was characteristic of the intelligentsia. A consciousness of the fundamental duality of Russia permeated its mind; its heart was with the people and against the state, with the muzhik and against the *chinovnik.* This educated minority, drawn from different strata of society, formed an image of itself as the "self-aware people," the thinking organ of the *narod.* That image underlay its major movement in the second half of the nineteenth century, the *narodnichestvo,* or Populism, and in particular the crusade of "going to the people" in the 1870's. The intense Russian national feeling characteristic of the intelligentsia was a feeling that tended to delete *gosudarstvo,* the whole official world, from the concept of the nation. It was a peculiar form of antistate nationalism that inspired Herzen, for example, to say that "The Russian Government is not Russian. Its usual direction is despotism and reaction. It is more German than Russian, as the Slavophiles say. This explains the sympathy and love of other governments for it."[9]

One of the most original and influential creations of the mind of the Russian intelligentsia was Slavophilism, a philosophy of life that revolved in great measure around the image of a dual Russia. Konstantin Aksakov provided a classic statement of this philosophy in a memorandum of 1855 to Czar Alexander II, "On the Internal Condition of Russia." This memorandum was one of the expressions of the nineteenth-century thaw. In it, Aksakov argued that the Russian people, being probably the only truly Christian people on earth, was "unpolitical" (*negosudarstvennyi*), i.e., fundamentally uninterested in government, constitutions, revolutions, political representation, and so forth. The un-Christian power-principle embodied in the state as an institution was foreign to this people's

---

* *Vekhi. Sbornik statei o Russkoi intelligentsii* (5th ed., 1910), p. 160. The theme was not new with Struve. Much earlier, for example, Herzen recalled the following about the young Russians of the 1840's who formed the nucleus of the future intelligentsia: "The main trait of all of them was a deep sense of alienation from official Russia. . . ." (*Byloe i dumy,* 1946, p. 226.)

nature. It was essentially a "social people," concerned with spiritual, moral, cultural, and economic freedom in a Christian communal society, of which the Russian village commune (*mir*) was the nucleus. Accordingly, it had originally invited the northern Vikings to come and exercise the governmental function in Russia, and there had taken shape in ancient Russia a peculiarly Russian system, a marriage of convenience between "state" and "land" founded on the principle of "mutual noninterference." The state authority was freely accorded the right to govern autocratically, while for its part the "land"—that is, the people—was left free and undisturbed in the practice of its Christian communal way of life and culture, and also enjoyed the opportunity to voice its opinions on national affairs to the state authority at periodically convened "gatherings of the land." Later this system of alliance broke down. In the person of Peter the Great, the state invaded the land, assaulted the customs, infringed upon the religion, suppressed all freedom. As a result of this revolution from above, "the previous alliance was replaced by the *yoke* of the state over the land, and the Russian land became, as it were, the conquered party, and the state the conqueror."*

The present condition of Russia, Aksakov continued, could be traced to the Petrine aggression of the state against the land, and to the refusal of Peter's successors to admit and rectify this wrong. What was the present condition? Russia was sick, and the cause was the unnatural relation of the state to society, the repression of spiritual and social freedom. The imposing external position of the Russian Empire contrasted with the profound and pervasive moral crisis within. The bloated bureaucratic organism of official Russia was shot through with venality and corruption. There was no spontaneity of social self-expression. In the stifling atmosphere of unfreedom, no one dared to speak the truth aloud, and nothing was

* N. L. Brodsky (ed), *Rannie slavianofily* (1910), pp. 72, 80, 86. The Slavophile aversion to the idea of the state was a powerful contribution to the development of anarchist thought in Russia. The Slavophile doctrine was a quietistic anarchism. Although it accepted the state as necessary, it was in no doubt that the state was evil. Aksakov said: "The state is evil in principle; the lie is not in this or that form of the state, but in the state itself as an idea or principle; it is not a question of which form is better and which worse, which true and which false, but of the fact that the state *qua* state is a lie." Mikhail Bakunin, who was to become the leading philosopher of revolutionary anarchism, highly commended Aksakov for this view.

heard but official lies and fulsome adulation of the Czar. Above all, the government and the people were mutually estranged:

> The present condition of Russia is a condition of internal division covered up with shameless lies. The government, and with it the upper classes, have separated themselves from the people and become alien to it. . . . The government and the people do not understand each other, and their relations are not friendly.[10]

What was the remedy for the internal crisis? In the long run, it was for the state to undo the historic wrong done to the land, to withdraw to its proper governmental sphere and stop encroaching upon the nonpolitical life of the people. Meanwhile, the urgent immediate need was to let the fresh air and light of free speech exert a medicinal effect. The liberation of public opinion was the means by which the government could cleanse out the bureaucratic corruption and repair the moral estrangement between itself and the people: "To the government, unlimited state power; to the people, complete moral freedom, freedom of life and spirit. To the government, the right of action and thus of law; to the people, the right of opinion and thus of speech."[11] Putting it in contemporary terms, the Slavophile program for Russia was in essence anti-totalitarian, aspired to roll back the encroachments of the state on the territory of society, and looked to establishment of a system of peaceful coexistence between an absolutistic Russian government and an apolitical Russian people.

According to an old saying in Russia, the Populists (*narodniki*) were Slavophiles in rebellion. The foundations of the philosophy of Russian Populism were laid by Herzen. He had been a leader of the Slavophiles' opponents, the Westerners so-called. As they saw it, the Slavophiles' idealized image of ancient Russia as a voluntary alliance of the state and the land was but a "retrospective utopia," and Russian Orthodoxy had never been anything but "apathetic Catholicism."[12] But Herzen, after taking up voluntary exile in Western Europe, discovered deep Slavophile affinities in his thinking. The Slavophile conception of the Russian people as essentially a "social people" became the cornerstone of Herzen's "Russian socialism." It pictured the muzhik as the man of the future in Russia and the *mir* as the foundation of a socialist society. Herzen also, as already noted, accepted the Slavophile image of dual Russia.

But Populism wrought a far-reaching change in the picture of the relation between the two Russias. The Slavophile program of

peaceful coexistence between the state and the land by courtesy
of a repentent Czarist authority was discarded, as was the conception of the Russian people as "nonpolitical." Popular Russia
became "revolutionary Russia" (Herzen's phrase), and the image
of dual Russia became an image of *two Russias at war*. Revolutionary Populism called the land to arms against the state. Herzen,
writing in his London paper *Kolokol* in 1861, issued a declaration
of war against official Russia on behalf of the Russian people. The
occasion was the suppression by troops under the command of
General Bistrom of student disturbances at the University of St.
Petersburg over the peasant question. Addressing the imprisoned
students, Herzen wrote: "Where shall you go, youths from whom
knowledge has been shut off? . . . To the people! . . . Prove to
these Bistroms that out of you will emerge not clerks but soldiers,
not mercenaries but soldiers of the Russian people!"[13] The declaration of war evoked a powerful response among the Russian student
youth, and the following year saw the rise of the secret society
"Land and Freedom." Revolutionary Populism had come into being as an organized movement. At this time there appeared in Russia a manifesto, "Young Russia," which expressed a philosophy of
revolutionary terrorism against the state. Dividing all Russia into
two parts—the party of the people and the party of the Emperor—
it called for the physical extermination of all those who stood or
even sympathized with the party of the Emperor. Inscribed on the
banners of the nascent Russion revolutionary movement was the
image of a dual Russia.

But popular Russia was not then the "revolutionary Russia"
imagined by Herzen and the revolutionary Populists. The conception of two Russias at war was not realistic, and the would-be
soldiers of the people found themselves rather in the position of
generals without an army. The failure of the movement of "going
to the people" in the 1870's revealed the chasm between the
peasantry and the revolutionary intellectuals. Although there were
many isolated instances of local peasant disorders in the latter half
of the nineteenth century, the peasantry in general proved politically inert. Here it should be noted that the peasant mind did not
equate official Russia and the Czar. On the contrary, it tended to
look to the Czar—as distinguished from his bureaucracy—for help
in satisfying its claim to the land that still remained in the possession of the nobles after 1861. On the whole, as Miliukov later
observed, the rural population, while always remaining in a sense

"natural anarchists," tended to render passive obedience to a state authority that did not get too much "under their skin." This peculiar combination of peasant characteristic helps explain the events of the Russian Revolution.[14] That is, the anarchist tendency got the upper hand in the special conditions prevailing in 1917, and the tendency to render passive obedience made for acceptance of the new dictatorial state authority that emerged out of the storm.

Decline of faith in the peasantry as a revolutionary force, and in terrorism as the prime revolutionary weapon, led some Populists to turn to Marxism as the ideology of revolution. The 1890's witnessed a contest between Populists and Marxists for hegemony over the revolutionary movement, followed by the rise of Leninism or Bolshevism as claimant to the role of sole authentic voice and organ of Russian Marxism. The relative success with which Marxism "took" among the radical intelligentsia of Russia may seem surprising in view of Marx's vision of history as turning on the axis of class struggle. The basic realities of mankind, according to Marx, are social-economic classes at war, culminating in a final battle between bourgeoisie and proletariat. But not only were these two forces still only developing in Russia; Russian history, as noted earlier, turned not on class struggle but on the issue of relations between the state and society.* Despite this, the Russian revolutionary mentality found no difficulty in adjusting itself to Marxism, or Marxism to itself. Part of the explanation is that this mentality was, even in pre-Marxist days, hostile to capitalism. But the chief facilitating circumstance was the fact that Marx conceived of the class struggle in political terms. He argued, that is, that the war between class and class had to to be decided in the final analysis by overthrowing the existing *state*. Further, his doctrine appealed to the anarchist streak in the Russian revolutionary mentality, for it visualized the withering away of government after the proletarian revolution. Hence it was entirely possible for a Russian revolu-

* Donald MacKenzie Wallace has this to say on classes and class conflict in Russia's past: "Certain social groups were, indeed, formed in the course of time but they were never allowed to fight out their own battles. The irresistible Autocratic Power kept them always in check and fashioned them into whatever form it thought proper, defining minutely and carefully their obligations, their rights, their mutual relations, and their respective positions in the political organization. Hence we find in the history of Russia almost no trace of those class hatreds which appear so conspicuously in the history of Western Europe" (*Russia*, 1912, pp. 368–69.)

tionary whose mind was obsessed with the image of a dual Russia
to become a Marxist and continue in that capacity the indigenous
revolutionary tradition of warfare against official Russia. He could
march to battle against the state with the war cry of "class struggle"
on his lips. He could talk as a Marxist while thinking and feeling
as a Russian revolutionary Populist. As Ivanov-Razumnik points
out, "the Russian Marxists of the 1890's identified the social with
the political by contending that 'every class struggle is a political
struggle'; this was an expression in new form of the old People's
Will [i.e., Populist] thesis, 'To the social through the political.' "[15]

All this applies particularly to Lenin and his political creation—
Russian Bolshevism. He emerged during the 1890's as one of the
leaders in the Marxist polemic against the Populists. Against them
he contended that not the muzhik—who still comprised nearly
nine-tenths of the Russian population—but the industrial worker
was the man of the future in Russia, and that the rise of Russian
capitalism was to be seen as a hopeful and not a deplorable phenomenon from the revolutionary standpoint. However, the political
personality of Lenin was shaped in very significant degree by the
tradition of the Russian revolutionary Populists of the 1860's, especially Chernyshevsky. The principal motivating force was a con-
suming hate for *gosudarstvo,* for official Russia and everything it
connoted. Lenin married the old image of two warring Russias
with Marxism. His theory of the Marxist party as a small disciplined body of revolutionaries drawn from the intelligentsia and
acting as the politically conscious "vanguard" of the working class
revived in a new form the old image of the intelligentsia as the
"self-aware people." Finally, in his *State and Revolution* and other
writings, he accentuated the anarchist theme in Marxism. "The
proletariat needs the state only temporarily," he wrote. "We do
not at all disagree with the anarchists on the question of the
abolition of the state as an *aim.*" The immediate purpose of the
revolution would be to smash *gosudarstvo* to pieces, to raze the old
state apparatus to the ground, and then to replace it with a system
of direct rule by the armed people *without* bureaucrats ("privileged
persons divorced from the masses and standing *above* the masses"),
preparatory to the withering away of all statehood.[16] Lenin thought
of the revolution as the rising of popular Russia against official
Russia. In his mind, the Marxist concept of the "dictatorship of
the proletariat" took concrete shape as a vision of *popular Russia*

in power.* Thus Leninism was a subtly Russified Marxism, a fusion of Marxist symbols and concepts with much of the content of thought and feeling characteristic of the old Russian revolutionary Populism. Lenin conceived his mission in the international Marxist movement as that of resurrecting its "revolutionary soul." But it was a very Russian spirit of revolution that he breathed into Marxism.

III

If the February Revolution of 1917 completed the process of "unbinding" Russian society, the Bolshevik seizure of power in October and establishment of a new centralized and dictatorial state authority laid the foundation for a reversion of Russia to the past. The results of sixty years of Russian history in emancipating society from the aegis of the state were nullified. In practice, the dictatorship of popular Russia meant the dictatorship of popular Russia's self-appointed organ of consciousness, the Bolshevik Party. This, along with the nationalization of the economy, made *gosudarstvo* again the dominating force. "The most pressing and topical question for politics today," wrote Lenin in September, 1917, "is the transformation of all citizens into workers and employees of one big 'syndicate,' namely, the state as a whole."[17] In his wildly utopian imagination, he thought that this could be done without recreating a governmental bureaucracy standing above society. Before he died, however, he is reported to have remarked ruefully: "We have become a bureaucratic utopia."

Lenin's legacy was the one-party dictatorship and the New Economic Policy, under which the state retained only the "commanding heights" of the economy and permitted 25 million private peasant farms to exist and contribute to an economic revival. During this transitional period, the situation in Russia fell once again into the historic pattern of duality. In Miliukov's formula for the system in Muscovy, there was the "autocratic power" on the one

---

*Speaking of Chernyshevsky and like-minded Russian revolutionists of the 1860's, Wallace writes: "Their heated imagination showed them in the near future a New Russia, composed of independent federated Communes, without any bureaucracy or any central power—a happy land in which everybody virtuously and automatically fulfilled his public and private duties, and in which the policemen and all other embodiments of material constraint were wholly superfluous." (*Russia,* p. 616.) In some ways, this accurately sums up Lenin's image of a future Communist society.

hand and the "population" on the other, the two "more or less imperfectly linked by a system of mediating governmental organs." This was reflected in the concept of the soviets, cooperatives, and other mass organizations as "levers" of the Party's influence and authority among the population. Thus the outcome of the Revolution, politically speaking, was that Russia had reverted to a situation strongly paralleling the remote past. However, since the new dictatorial state authority permitted the population, or very large sections of it, to carry on some nonpolitical pursuits more or less autonomously, the state, at the height of the NEP, was not experienced by the Russian people as a highly oppressive power. The NEP was, in a way, a period of semipeaceful coexistence between the state and the land. That, at any rate, is the way it tends to be remembered. It has become a kind of "retrospective utopia" for very many among the older generation. Just as the Slavophiles once pictured the pre-Petrine past as a satisfactory time in the relations between the government and the people, so now the NEP is recalled by very many Russians as the golden age of Soviet Russia, when the state, dictatorial though it was, did not trespass too much upon the popular domain, on the way of life of the people. In both instances, the past is evaluated in relation to what was experienced in the historical aftermath.

In Soviet Russia, the aftermath was Stalinism, the essential meaning of which was the dynamic resurgence of *gosudarstvo*. Lenin and the Bolshevik Party had, by the seizure of power and establishment of a centralized dictatorial state structure, created a medium in which this movement could arise and flourish. But it was Stalin, a man in whom the spiritual affinities with the revolutionary antistate Russian intelligentsia were quite tenuous, who became its conscious instrument and architect. In the peculiarly Russian terms whose meaning has been considered above, Stalinism meant, to begin with, the invasion of the land by the state. Reviving the historic pattern of revolutionism from above, Stalin moved to bring every element of society under coercive state regimentation and control. He re-enacted the "binding" of all strata in servitude to the state authority. The outstanding single manifestation of this totalitarianizing process was the terroristic collectivization of the peasantry and the reimposition of serfdom within the framework of the kolkhoz. Here the state acted quite literally in the role of conqueror of rural Russia. As Stalin observed to Churchill during World War II, his conquest of the Russian peasantry was the hardest of all his campaigns, the casualty list totaling 10 millions. As before in Russian history, the process of totalitarianization was actuated in large part by the central authority's overriding concern for external defense and aggrandizement, which dictated a policy of direct exploitation of the human resources of the economically backward country for amassing military power through industrialization. Total exploitation necessitated total control. There took place, therefore, an enormous hypertrophy of state functions of command and control of society, an immense expansion of bureaucracy. One of Stalin's Bolshevik opponents, Bukharin, caught the historic implications of this whole pattern of policy when he labeled it "military-feudal exploitation."[18] Russian history in the Stalin period retraced the course that Kliuchevsky epitomized in his phrase cited earlier: "The state swelled up; the people grew lean."

Stalinism meant the resurgence of *gosudarstvo* not only in fact but also in idea. The new Stalinist order became an order of statism in the fullest sense of the word: *Gosudarstvo* was its supreme symbol and object of glorification. Its philosophy was succinctly summed up by Georgi Malenkov in a speech in 1941: "We are all servants of the state."[19] Otherwise expressed, the motto read: "Place the interests of the state above all else!" In the new conception, the whole of society was regarded as a single great "interest group" identified with the goal of the unlimited expansion of the power and glory of the Russian Soviet state. The old Leninist Bolshevik idea of the Party as popular Russia's authoritative organ of consciousness and rule gave way, in practice if not entirely in theory, to the concept of the Party as the apostle and agent of the interests of the Soviet state. One of the probable sources of Stalin's murderous fury against the surviving Bolshevik old guard, whom he exterminated wholesale in his purges of the 1930's, was the ingrained inability of many of these men, schooled as they were in the *Weltanschauung* of the revolutionary antistate Russian intelligentsia, to see things in the "state way" and assimilate fully the ideal, very new and yet very old in Russia, of the "state-oriented man" (*gosudarstennyi chelovek*). As Russian Marxists of the Lenin Bolshevik school, they could not easily adopt the historic Russian standpoint of *gosudarstvo*. In exterminating them, Stalin saw himself as acting after the manner of his chosen model, Ivan Grozny, who had undertaken, as it were, to liquidate the boyars as a class; the Bolsheviks were Stalin's boyars. Using his

NKVD as Ivan had used his *oprichnina,* he broke the back of the Party, eliminated it as a living political organism and ruling class, and refashioned it as a lever of a new absolute autocracy.

The change of regime from Bolshevism to Stalinism was registered in various changes in the ideological system. The Marxist reading of Russian history had to be criticized and radically revised in order to permit the official glorification of *gosudarstvo* to be projected upon the Russian past. Stalin corrected Marx and Engels—not to mention Lenin—on the embarrassing point about the desirability of the earliest possible withering away of the state. Despite all this, however, he performed the phenomenal mental feat of continuing to regard himself as a Marxist. How he did this is suggested by his papers of 1950 on Marxism and linguistics, in which he frowned upon the notion of revolutionary "explosions" from below and recommended, as the proper revolutionary process, the "revolution from above" carried out "at the initiative of the existing regime."[20] Having identified himself with the historic pattern of revolutionism from above, he mentally assimilated Marxist revolutionism to this pattern. He thus became, in his own self-image, a kind of Marxist Czar. It was a standpoint from which he could see himself as the legitimate successor of *both* Ivan Grozny and Lenin. If Lenin fused Marxism with antistate revolutionary Populism, Stalin fused it with pro-state revolutionary Czarism. If the one merged Marx with Chernyshevsky, the other merged Marx with Ivan the Terrible.

IV

The full implications of the recapitulation of the earlier Russian historical process under Stalin emerged into clear view only in the final period of his reign, the years following World War II. This was the heyday of Stalinist statism, and also the time when it became plain in innumerable ways that Stalinist statism meant the resurrection of official Russia. This new official Russia found its visible incarnation in the huge hierarchy of officialdom, the privileged stratum of bureaucratic serving men, dressed many of them in uniforms similar to those of the old *chinovniki,* and organized according to a new "table of ranks" that was analogous in substance if not nomenclature to that which Peter had created. This bureaucracy itself was the only ruling class, but it was not really that; its mission was to serve the goals, needs, and whims of the absolute autocrat. It did, however, consist of (to use Lenin's phrase) "privileged persons divorced from the masses and standing *above* the masses." The separation of this stratum from the people was reflected in an image of the government that Stalin used in 1945. In a toast proposed at a victory banquet in the Kremlin, he spoke of the great mass of "ordinary" people in Russia, the workers, peasants and lower employees who held no ranks or titles, as "cogs in the wheels of the great state apparatus" and, again, as "cogs who keep our great state machine going in all branches of science, national economy, and military affairs." "They are the people who support us," he told the assembled dignitaries, "as the base supports the summit."* The Iron Czar might have spoken in a similar vein.

This was the view from the summit looking down. What was the view from the base looking upward? What picture did the millions of "cogs" form of the "great state machine?" Broadly speaking, the processes that had led to the resurrection of official Russia had led also to the resurrection of popular Russia as something separate from the official world. They had produced a revival of the popular consciousness of the duality of Russia, of estrangement from *gosudarstvo*. This is particularly true if we consider the situation as it stood at the climax of Stalin's reign, the years between 1945 and 1953, when the people discovered that the hopes for liberalization that the regime had covertly encouraged during the war years were not to be fulfilled, and that life in Russia, far from becoming more tolerable, was in fact much less so than in the period before 1941. By now, the "great state machine" had become, in the minds of millions of ordinary Russians, a great alien "It," which commanded their fear or even their awe but did not inspire any affection or sense of identification. When one spoke to them in private, one found that they referred to the government as *"Oni"* —"They." Very many of them seceded spiritually from the life of the Russian state, "emigrated" inwardly. They felt themselves in it, but not of it. It was an attitude of resignation rather than rebelliousness. The state was seen as an alien oppressive force, but as a force in firm control, a force to which the individual had to adapt himself somehow while hoping secretly for change.

---

* *Pravda*, June 27, 1945. The first published critical comment on that utterance was made seventeen years later by V. Karpinsky, a surviving Old Bolshevik: "It seems to me that when Stalin compared the ordinary working people to 'cogs,' he was distorting Leninism in highly important matters." (*Pravda*, September 19, 1962.)

The popular mind dimly sensed that this hope was bound up with the death of the autocrat. This thought was reflected in an anecdote that circulated in Russia in 1947. It concerned a citizen who, in a letter to a relative in America, remarked: "He is getting old now. I wonder when he will die." The censor marked this passage and forwarded the letter to the secret police, to whose offices the citizen was summoned. A police officer asked him: "Whom were you thinking of when you wrote that passage?" "Churchill," replied the citizen after a moment's deliberation. He was then excused, but as he departed he turned and asked the officer: "And whom were *you* thinking of?" The implication, of course, was that the death of Stalin was secretly on everybody's mind in Russia, from bottom to top.*

The revival of the consciousness of the state as an alien power was governed by the basic facts of the historical situation: the invasion of the land by the state; the mercilessly exploitative relation of the state to the people; the politicalization and regimentation of all public pursuits; the punitive attitude of the central authority toward those guilty of any infraction of its impossible rules; the presence of a bureaucratic officialdom whose behavior was increasingly characterized by soulless formalism, worship of red tape, servility toward superiors, and arrogance toward inferiors. The fact that the new bureaucracy had largely been recruited from the common people made no essential difference. To the ordinary person, the "great state machine" was a force that was constantly mobilizing him; calling upon him for fresh sacrifices; taking all and giving nothing; breaking its promises to him; lecturing, scolding and indoctrinating him; constricting his choice of occupation, his ability to employ his talents profitably and productively, his opportunity to travel and move around, his freedom to speak his mind above a whisper. It was a force whose bureaucratic organs were callous to his concerns, whose institutions had become "bureaucratic fortresses," to use the Soviet novelist Dudintsev's phrase, whose system of

---

* In this connection, it may be of interest to recall the relative lack of popular reaction in Moscow at the time of Stalin's death. In four days of observation in the streets, I saw only one person, a girl of high-school age, crying. The mood of the crowds, and of the many who stood patiently waiting in line for the chance to see Stalin lying in state in the Hall of Columns, seemed to be one of stolid reflectiveness, with a suggestion of suppressed cheerfulness in the attitude of some. In 1945, by contrast, a shock wave of sorrow swept over Moscow with the news of the death of President Roosevelt.

administration forced one to bribe one's way through life, whose press and radio disseminated a mass of boring harangues, whose economic policies compelled a rich country to live miserably, whose secret agents were everywhere in society, listening to hear what one might say in an unguarded moment. This, roughly, was the Stalinist Russian state as experienced by millions of its subjects from 1946 to 1953. It suggests why the idea of a "thaw" carried so much meaning in the period just following Stalin's death, when the tension broke and the atmosphere changed.

The press of official Russia propagated the image of the country as a monolithic unity of state and people. It maintained the pretense that the people lived the life of the state, that its goals and interests and values were theirs too, that the millions at the base were willing and eager cogs in the great machine. In effect, it continued to propagate the myth of the Revolution, according to which the new state system was the political incarnation of popular Russia. At the same time, it revealed in many indirect ways how far the monolithic picture was from the truth. When Malenkov, for example, spoke at the Nineteenth Party Congress in 1952 of the need for "Soviet Gogols and Shchedrins," he implied, whether wittingly or not, that there had arisen a new official Russia basically similar to the one satirized by Gogol and Shchedrin. Again, internal propaganda constantly complained that "some" citizens were attempting to get what they could *from* the state and give as little as possible *to* it. This showed that the exploitative attitude of the government toward the people was being reciprocated insofar as conditions permitted, that the ordinary person had developed an opportunistic code of behavior in his relations with the governmental apparatus. Finally and most revealingly, the leaders and their press began, approximately from 1946 onward, to castigate regularly what was called *apolitichnost'*—the "apolitical attitude." This went along with *bezideinost'*—the "nonideological attitude." Taken together, they signified a failure of response, an alienation from the official world, and a tendency among the people to live, as best they could, a life apart.

Russia had again become a dual entity. Despite the spread of literacy and education in the Soviet period, the country experienced a revival of the cleavage of cultures. The culture of official Russia, with its apotheosized autocrat in the Kremlin, its aristocracy of rank, its all-powerful bureaucracy, its pervasive atmosphere of police terror, its regimentation of all activities, its rituals of prevarication, its grandiose "construction projects of Communism," its great new foreign empire, its official friendships and enmities, its cold and hot wars—this was one thing. There was also a suppressed and little-known unofficial Russia with a life of its own. In the late Stalin period, this was largely an underground life. For very many, it meant a life of underground private enterprise in various forms. For the peasant, it typically meant the effort to evade work on the state fields and concentrate his effort on the family's private garden plot. For the artist, thinker, and writer, it often meant an underground creative life over which the state had no control, an escape from the dreary official culture to real self-expression in secret.* Among some youthful elements, there was a revival of evangelical religion, carried on underground, and the old Populist tradition came alive again when university students at Moscow, Leningrad, and elsewhere formed secret circles to discuss among themselves oppositional political ideas with an anarchist tinge. Unofficial Russia also developed other forms of expression, in which the life apart from the state was a life of crime or sought the consolations of vodka.

This picture finds considerable confirmation in the works of post-Stalin imaginative literature that have stirred up interest in Russia and abroad. Some of these writings are, in fact, representative of the underground literature of the late Stalin period, and many of them are concerned with the life of the country during that time. From Ehrenburg's *Thaw* and Pomerantsev's powerful tract *On Sincerity in Literature* down to Dudintsev's *Not By Bread Alone,* the theme which emerges is that of a duality in Russian life and consciousness, of division between the official and unofficial Russias. Ehrenburg's hero is an underground artist who cuts himself off completely from the official art world in order to be able to work creatively. Dudintsev gives a portrait of the underground

---

* A young painter with whom I spoke in Russia in 1946 said: "All the good work in the arts here is being done underground." Once in a great while, some hint of this situation penetrated the press. For example, during the "philosophical discussion" of 1947, one speaker referred to the "dualization" of philosophy resulting from the authorities' fear of passing for publication any work containing a trace of originality. Owing to this "protectionism" and "mystical fear of mistakes," there had come into being a "second" and "hidden" social science and philosophy: "There exists a manuscript and typescript literature on philosophy and the history of philosophy that is richer, fuller, and deeper than the one we know." (*Voprosy filosofii,* No. 1, 1947, pp. 375, 376, 377.)

life of invention. His hero does battle with the state bureaucracy, for which Dudintsev has created a significant literary symbol in the figure of Drozdov, and goes to a concentration camp for his pains. The wide, interested response that these writings have aroused among Russians is closely related to the fact that they raise, between as well as in the lines, the deeply meaningful question of the two Russias and their relations.

One of the significant themes of this recent literature is that the line of division between the two Russias may run through the individual person. The image of a dual Russia becomes here an image of the Russian functionary as a dual personality. He has a role and self-identity in official Russia, but also a hidden unofficial existence and identity. He is "two persons in one man," as a character of Dudintsev's expresses it. There are "two sides—the hidden one and the visible one."[21] Alexander Yashin's story "The Levers," published in the almanac *Literary Moscow* for 1956, is constructed around this theme. It introduces us to a group of persons conversing informally in a room of the administration building of a collective farm. Out of their quiet, uninhibited talk unfolds a picture of the farm as an utterly run-down institution where the peasants earn only a mere pittance, where there are no more cows, where the planning of crops remains a jealously guarded prerogative of district officials, etc. They comment acidly about the district Party boss who, while knowing all this, pretends that it is not so and repeats catch phrases about "animal husbandry growing from year to year," the steady upsurge of the peasants' "welfare," and so on. Then, suddenly, a meeting is called to order, and it transpires that this group of persons composes the collective farm's Party organization. A metamorphosis of personality occurs: "Their faces all became concentrated, tense and dull, as though they were preparing for something long familiar to them but nevertheless ceremonial and important. Everything earthly and natural vanished, and the action shifted to another world. . . ." The action has shifted to the world of official Russia. The individuals have changed selves. Now they are acting and speaking in the capacity of representatives of official Russia, its "levers" in the countryside. They proceed to repeat the official catch phrases of the district Party boss, the very phrases they have just been ridiculing. They pass the requisite official "resolution," and the meeting ends.

The question arises: Who really *are* these people? Yashin leaves no doubt that the real selves are the unofficial ones: "They quickly departed, and it seemed that each had in his soul a sense of duty done, but at the same time of uneasiness, of dissatisfaction with himself."[22] In the tradition of the Russian intelligentsia a century earlier, Yashin senses the existence of a rift between the state and society, between official and popular Russia, and morally aligns himself with the latter. As might be expected, the official press has denounced this point of view. It strikes at the heart of the myth of the Soviet regime as the political incarnation of popular Russia.

The death of Stalin, like the death of Nicholas I, was the end of an era and posed the problem of internal change and reform. In both instances, the autocratic system revolved around the autocratic personality, and the situation toward the end of the reign assumed the aspect of a profound national crisis, a crisis of paralysis and compulsion. Pent-up forces for change and reform were released in the aftermath. Before many years passed after Stalin's death, however, the limits of the official conception of reform had become abundantly clear. The reform idea with which the regime has operated under the leadership of Khrushchev, and to some extent after, does not envisage the new period as one of a new "unbinding" of society. It sees the solution in terms of reorganizational schemes, the decentralization of the bureaucracy, the restoration of Party rule, the relaxation of police terror. It attacks the agrarian crisis by the cultivation of virgin lands and corn rather than by the abolition of the kolkhoz. More recently, it has been emphasizing material things, adumbrating, as the new formula for "communism," the Soviets-plus-supermarkets. The regime, it would appear, looks to a rise in the material standard of consumption as a means of reconciling the Russian people to unfreedom in perpetuity.

But it is doubtful that a policy of reform operating within these narrow limits can repair the rupture between the state and society that is reflected in the revival of the image of a dual Russia. A moral renovation of the national life, a fundamental reordering of relations, a process of genuine "unbinding," or, in other words, an alteration in the nature of the system, would be needed. The state cannot resolve the situation satisfactorily so long as it clings to the positions won in its reconquest of the Russian land, just as it cannot work out firm relations with the peoples of Eastern Europe so long as it holds on to the structure and idea of empire. But of reforms on this major scale the present leadership appears to be, for various reasons, incapable. So it goes on attempting to square the circle, to make the system function well by merely tinkering with it rather than by fundamentally altering it. This is the dilemma of Russia today.

7 STALIN AND THE USES OF PSYCHOLOGY

The influence of ideological conceptions upon the men who make Soviet policy has been frequently and rightly emphasized. Some observers are so deeply impressed by this influence that they tend to regard the Soviet system as a kind of ideocracy. It is undeniable that ideology has been one powerful factor in the shaping of Soviet policies and actions from the time of the October Revolution to the present. But one must not lose sight of the fact that, in Soviet Russia, the relationship between ideology and policy is one of interaction. It is a two-way process in which theoretical conceptions affect the making of policy and practical considerations affect the content of the ideology. The ideological system is not a completely static thing. It has evolved over the years, and the realities of Soviet politics have been the driving force behind this evolution.

The immediate purpose here is to investigate certain Soviet ideological trends of Stalin years in their relation to the regime's policy in internal affairs. These trends cluster around the militant revival in Soviet psychology of Pavlov's teachings on the conditioned reflex. The Pavlovian revival, which began in 1949, will be examined in connection with various developments in biology, political economy, and other fields, and the entire ideological complex will be related to a central policy motivation to which I have given the name "transformism." The final part of the study will consider various indications of a post-Stalin retreat from transformism and from the ideology associated with it. The study can then serve as a basis for a tentative interpretation of some of the changes in Soviet internal policy since Stalin's death that have aroused interest abroad.

I

A prominent tendency of Soviet thought during the last years of Stalin's reign was the quest for formulas by which reality could be transformed and remolded to the dictates of the Soviet regime. The idea of transforming things in accordance with a formula was not in itself new; the notion of a revolutionary transformation of capitalist society is as old as Marxism and is rooted particularly deeply in the ways of thought characteristic of Russian Bolshevism. But in Stalin's later years this transformist concept seemed to acquire an obsessive hold upon the regime. Along with it went a mania for bigness and a tendency to apply the various formulas with a dogmatic and indiscriminate rigidity.

During the postwar period, transformism became the reaction of the Stalin regime whenever it was confronted with a genuinely difficult domestic situation that clearly called for remedial measures of some kind. Instead of using the materials at hand and adapting its conduct to the realities present in the situation, it habitually responded with a grandiose project of transformation. In 1949, it came out with the so-called "Stalin Plan for the Transformation of Nature," an immense and costly undertaking of irrigation and afforestation that was to convert rural Russia into a fertile, blooming garden. Closely linked with this was the scheme for transforming the industrial landscape of the country by a series of giant "construction projects of Communism"—canals, dams, and hydroelectric power stations that, it was boasted, would eclipse the best and biggest accomplishments along this line in the United States or any other country. To cite a further example, the Soviet regime, faced with an acute shortage of housing and office space in Moscow, responded with a plan for "transforming the face of the capital." This was to be accomplished by the erection of an ensemble of skyscrapers that would rival those of New York, although, unlike New York, Moscow had abundant space for less ambitious structures, which would have resolved the problem more quickly and economically.

This transformist outlook was reflected in the "biological discussion" of 1948, at which the Michurin-Lysenko doctrines on heredity were accepted officially, with the full authority of the Central Committee of the Communist Party and of Stalin himself. "Michurinism," as these doctrines were called, was a perfect model of transformist thinking. Their founder, the Russian naturalist

I. V. Michurin (the "Great Transformer of Nature"), had, it was said, taken a "gigantic step forward" in the further development of Darwinism. Darwin had merely explained the evolutionary process, while "I. V. Michurin made evolution."[1] Michurin, it was said, had discovered laws and methods by which it would be possible to "mold organic forms."

The Michurin-Lysenko teachings are associated with the Lamarckian principle of the inheritance of acquired characteristics. This was the practical crux of the matter. However, the biological issue was only one aspect of an ideological problem. Underlying the controversy over the inheritance of acquired characteristics was a clash between two radically different conceptions of the relationship between the organism and its environment. The Soviet geneticists whose work was based upon the Mendelian school postulated "autogenesis"—evolution under the influence of certain hereditary forces inherent in the organism itself. In this view, the so-called "internal factors of development" assume primary importance, and the role of external environmental conditions in the evolutionary process is reduced to either a "starting mechanism" or a limiting factor. It was essentially this "autogenetic" conception of the organism that Lysenko and his followers, backed by the full authority of the Soviet state, denied and attempted to expunge from Soviet biological thought.

Lysenko was led to this standpoint not by the weight of carefully sifted scientific evidence, but by the imperatives of transformist ideology. Transformist thinking is fundamentally opposed to any conception that endows the object that is to be transformed (in this case, the organism) with developmental autonomy; it must not have spontaneous internal forces for growth or change that the transformer has to reckon with and respect, because that would impose unwanted limits upon the extent to which the object could be transformed from without.

The Michurinist doctrine arose out of this need to conceive the active factor of evolutionary change as residing not in the organism but in controllable conditions of the environment. For transformism, the role of these conditions must be decisive. Accordingly, Michurinism proclaims the "unity of the organism with the environment," a conception that holds that the organism has no separate existence apart from the particular configuration of environmental conditions that sustain it. In other words, the organism and its environment constitute an adaptational system in which the forces for change reside *exclusively* with the environment. Changing environmental conditions make the unity of the organism with the environment a "contradictory unity," and the organism then resolves the contradiction by successive adaptations that become hereditary. Or else it falls by the wayside: "Organisms that cannot change in accordance with the changed conditions of life do not survive, leave no progeny."[2] The Darwinian concept of a natural selection of chance variations of organisms engaged in a struggle for existence is thrown overboard. Michurinism rules out both chance variations and an intraspecies struggle for existence. The struggle for existence takes place between the individual organism and its environment. Variations are the organism's strictly determined responses to environmental change. They are its weapons in the struggle to survive when the external conditions change. The law of evolution is: Change or die.

If, as this doctrine holds, environmental change is the sole active agent of the evolutionary process, then man's power of control over the environmental conditions of plants and animals enables him to direct their evolution according to his needs and purposes. He can then, as the participants of the 1948 session declared in their message to Stalin, "govern the nature of organisms by creating man-controlled conditions of life for plants, animals, micro-organisms." The relationship of this trend of thought to the transformist motivation of the Stalin regime becomes transparently clear. The Michurinist agrobiology, said the final resolution of the session, is "a powerful instrument for the active and planned transformation of living nature." The validity of this claim is debatable. But between 1948 and 1953, Lysenko's theory was an integral component of Stalinism. It provided a rationalization in the biological sphere for Stalinism's effort to impose its dictates upon the world, to transform reality according to its wishes.

II

But while reality can be transformed, the "scientific" laws that govern the transformation are themselves fixed, necessary, and immutable. The will to transform reality was coupled with a vehement denial that there was anything arbitrary, subjective, risky, or unpredictable about the various schemes for transformation that the regime put forward. In this respect, Stalinism made a break with a deep-seated tradition of Bolshevism. The characteristic Bolshevist belief in determinism, its general "denial of accidents," had always previously coexisted with belief in an "indeterminist tendency" with respect to the details of the future, with an allowance for the future's "partial unpredictability."[3] In 1948, this tempered view gave way to an absolutely rigid and all-embracing determinism. All the processes of nature and society began to be viewed as working themselves out with an iron necessity; they were seen as perfectly predictable provided one could grasp their "regularities." Nothing whatever was left to chance. Lysenko's oft-quoted slogan "Chance is the enemy of science" formulated the new attitude. Mendelian genetics, resting as it does upon the concept of chance mutations, was derided by Lysenko for having to "resort to the theory of probability" and for reducing biological science in this way to "mere statistics."[4] Michurinism, on the other hand, not only posed the far-reaching goal of transforming organic nature, but guaranteed the attainment of the goal by absolutely predictable scientific means. It had worked out the "laws and methods" of obtaining directed variations and of perpetuating them in the species concerned. It was all based upon the discovery of "necessary relationships" in organic nature. And so, promised Lysenko, "We will expel fortuities from biological science."[5]

The mounting obsession with necessity, determinism, and the expulsion of chance from every area of Soviet policy came to a climax in Stalin's last work, *Economic Problems of Socialism in the U.S.S.R.,* published in October, 1952. Until its appearance, it had been an accepted practice for Soviet theorists to maintain that the all-powerful Soviet state, because of its control over every aspect of economic life, could repeal or transform the laws governing its economic operations and create new ones in their stead. But in 1952, Stalin protested vehemently against this idea of the transforming of laws. Those who had spoken in such terms were denounced as economic adventurists whose disdain of "objective regularities" was fraught with great danger.

For what would happen if the Soviet state would regard itself as competent to create or transform economic laws? It would lead, said Stalin, to "our falling into a realm of chaos and fortuities; we would find ourselves in slavish dependence upon these fortuities; we would deprive ourselves of the possibility not only of understanding, but even of finding our way around in this chaos of fortuities." Therefore, the Soviet state must base its economic policy upon "scientific laws." Scientific laws, in turn, were reflections of "objective processes in nature or society, taking place independently of the will of human beings."

But Stalin simultaneously protested against what he called the "fetishizing" of laws: "It is said that economic laws bear an elemental character, that the effects of these laws are inexorable, that society is powerless before them. This is untrue. This is a fetishizing of laws, the surrender of oneself into slavery to laws. It has been shown that society is not powerless in the face of laws, that society, by perceiving economic laws and relying upon them, can restrict their sphere of action, use them in the interests of society, and 'saddle' them, as happens with the forces of nature and their laws."[6]

There is thus a contradiction in Stalin's doctrine about scientific laws. On the one hand, he insists that Soviet policy must conform with "objective processes taking place independently of the will of human beings." This would eliminate choice and spontaneity from Soviet economic development, which would now be subordinated completely to the dictates of economic necessity. On the other hand, he cannot endure the thought of slavery to laws. He must regard his regime (or himself) as somehow superior to them, able to "saddle" them, subdue them, or "attain mastery over them," as one saddles and subdues the elemental forces of nature. He endeavors to resolve this conflict through the medium of the knowing mind. The function of the mind, he says, is to discover, grasp, study, and apply scientific laws. This intervention of the knowing mind enables him to feel that subordination to objective regularities is different from slavery to them. To settle this point, he cites the statement of Engels (derived from Hegel) equating freedom with "apprehended necessity."

Why was it that Stalin, while set on saddling, subduing, or attaining mastery over the supposedly objective laws of social-economic development, found utterly intolerable the thought of creating, repealing, or transforming them? What explains the enormous importance this quasi-verbal distinction evidently had for him? The answer may lie in "externalization," a process by which a person experiences his own thoughts, drives, or standards as operative in the external environment. In Stalin's case this tendency eventually found expression in a legislative attitude toward reality. In other words, what he referred to as "objective scientific laws" were an externalization of his inner policy dictates; they were a projection upon future Soviet history of the formulas for social-economic development generated in his own mind. *His own ideas appeared to him as natural necessities governing the development of society.*

This process of externalization performed for Stalin a double psychological function. First, it stilled any gnawing uncertainty in his own mind about the validity of the formulas and directives that he evolved; there could be nothing arbitrary or capricious about formulas that represented "objective processes taking place independently of the will of human beings." Subjective considerations entered only in the sense that his mind was the first to discover them, as Newton had been the first to discover the law of gravity. Secondly, this mental operation shut off all possible argument. It is reasonable to question a proposition about Soviet policy, even if its author be Stalin, but to question a law of nature is pure impertinence. With this in mind, we can understand how irritated Stalin became at the idea of creating, repealing, or transforming the objective laws of nature and society; such an attitude toward laws was a potential threat to his infallibility, a challenge to his externalized policy dictates. His heavy-handed insistence on the objectivity of all scientific laws, on their independence of the will of human beings, was a means of backing up his own claim to legislate the future course of nature and society. On the other hand, he could easily admit the possibility of "saddling" or "subduing" the laws, because this did not in any way affect their validity but only the manner in which society reacted to the discovery of them. It was his role as Supreme Architect of Communism to discover the laws, and it was the business of Soviet society to study them and put them into effect, and thus to "attain mastery" over them.

These considerations make it plain that the frantic preoccupation with causality, objectivity, and scientific laws that emerged in Soviet theoretical writings and the press during 1952 did not signify a retreat into a more empirical and pragmatic temper. Far from implying adoption of a scientific outlook, in the proper sense of the term, this tendency was part and parcel of the drift of the regime (under the commanding influence of the dictator himself) into the realm of political fantasy and wish-fulfillment. The extreme and at times almost hysterical emphasis upon necessity, iron regularities, objective scientific laws, etc., apparently expressed an imperative need to cover up the arbitrary and willful character of the decisions to transform things to suit the dreams and dictates of the autocracy. The further Stalin went in his schemes for the transformation of nature and society, the more he needed the reassurance that everything was proceeding in accordance with objective laws. The appeal to mechanical causality was a rationalization of rampant adventurism in Stalinist policy.

We have noted Lysenko's expression of scorn for Mendelian genetics because it "resorts" to the theory of probability and relies on "mere statistics." In later years this attitude led to a conscious rejection of any concept of scientific method that ruled out the absolute character of scientific laws. The physicist Bohr, for example, was attacked in 1952 for attempting to transform the law of the preservation of energy from an absolute law of nature into a statistical law that only holds good on the average. The "indeterminacy principle" enunciated by Heisenberg in connection with the quantum theory proved highly bothersome to Soviet philosophers of science, who felt called upon to contend that beneath the superficial appearance of indeterminacy the microparticles of quantum theory must fully conform to a law of "deeper causal determination" of the microprocesses.[7] Especially strongly did they react against the speculation of Western quantum theorists to the effect that the electrons "choose their path," as it were, and thus (metaphorically speaking) possess a certain amount of "free will"; in other words, that there are certain moments when "nature makes a choice." The emotional intensity with which such thoughts were flayed reflects the psycho-ideological motivation of the Stalinist position. To the Stalinist mind it was imperative that nature at all its levels, from the microprocesses to man, be governed by mechanical laws of causality. For only on that condition could it be regarded as infinitely manipulable. The behavior of every single object must be reducible to a rigid, hard-and-fast formula, discovery of which would make it possible to saddle or subdue the object, to gain complete mastery over it, to transform it at will. Therefore, autogenesis was unacceptable. Nothing can behave in spontaneous ways not completely reducible to its objective formula. Everything "subjective" becomes suspect. The endowing of electrons with spontaneity was similar to the endowing of living organisms with developmental and mutational tendencies inherent in their genes. In either case the ideal of total control and transformability would be jeopardized. Here was an outlook that might fairly be described as the projection of totalitarianism upon nature.

III

Inevitably, the postulates of transformism and mechanical causality penetrated the areas of Soviet thought concerned with the behavior of man. There were also special reasons for this. The most difficult problem faced by the Stalin regime in the postwar years was the profound passivity of the Soviet populace, its failure to respond positively to the goals set before it. Throughout all classes of Soviet society, the hopeful moods which had prevailed widely during the war years evaporated as the regime's endeavors to mobilize them for fresh exertions in the postwar period got under way. The root of the matter was not the incapacity of people to endure another season of privation, but rather the meaninglessness of the sacrifices they were called upon to make, the pointlessness of Russia's being in eternal conflict with the rest of the world, the total lack of prospect for tranquility in their time. The result was widespread apathy, resignation, spiritual disengagement from the goals of the Stalin Government.

Stalin evidently decided that the problem could be solved, or at least greatly alleviated, by a massive propaganda effort coupled with improved controls over an intermediate element—the artists and writers—whose work in the service of the goals of the state would in turn influence the public in the required ways. This was one impulse behind "Zhdanovism," the drive that started in the summer of 1946 to enlist and organize the creative intelligentsia of the Soviet Union as a corps of conscious instruments of state policy, as missionaries of patriotic enthusiasm among the dispirited multitude of the Russian people. The attempt to elicit popular enthusiasm by means of a propaganda campaign continued through the postwar years, but with little apparent success. The whole undertaking was an example of Stalinism's characteristic overevaluation of the potentialities of propaganda.

As indicated earlier, the typical reaction of the Stalin regime to a situation in which certain forces in the environment were proving recalcitrant to its goals was not to re-examine the goals, but to search for a formula by which it could transform or remold the forces and thereby overcome their recalcitrance. If the material at hand was showing itself perverse to the dictates of the regime, then some way had to be found to conquer its perversity. The dictates themselves were righteous and unalterable; their frustration only evoked redoubled insistence upon their realization. In the case in question, the regime was faced with persistent popular apathy and passive resistance to its control in various sections of Soviet society, especially the peasantry. People were not responding in the expected way to the techniques of political education and indoctrination. This led the Stalinist mind to seek a formula for making people respond properly. If Russians were failing to respond to the goals set before them, then something was the matter with the Russians and with the means employed to elicit their response. Their minds had to be remolded to the point where inner acceptance of the Soviet ideology and all the behavior patterns it imposed would come as a matter of course. But for mind control to become a reality, it had to be based upon scientific bedrock. What was required was a *formula for man.*

By 1949, when the need for a new formula in terms of which human nature could be scientifically explained and "saddled" had become more or less obvious, Stalin found in the Michurin-Lysenko doctrines a theory of the transformation of organisms on the biological level. Could he not draw in some fashion upon these doctrines for the purpose of constructing a more perfect science of man? We know that he tended to employ the biological analogy in his sociological thinking. In his essay on "Dialectical and Historical Materialism" published in 1938 as a chapter of the *Short Course,* he had written that the science of society "can become as precise a science as, let us say, biology, and capable of making use of the laws of development of society for practical purposes."[8] Lysenko, with Stalin's blessing, had become the reigning authority of a new biology which boasted of its ability to "expel fortuities" from this area of knowledge. If Michurinism could produce new species of plants and animals, might it not serve in the hands of the all-powerful Soviet state as a means of eventually creating a new species of "Soviet man"?

Actually, a "Michurinism for man" was germinating during the aftermath of the genetics controversy of 1948, but it did not come forth as a Soviet version of eugenics. It was a transference to man not of the specific biological concepts and techniques of Michurinism, but of its basic underlying ways of thought, of its general theory of the relationship between the organism and the environment. In his search for a counterpart of Michurin in the field of psychology, for a Russian who could qualify as the "great transformer of human nature," Stalin rediscovered Pavlov. *The formula for man was the conditioned reflex.*

This rediscovery heralded a Pavlovian revolution in the Soviet behavioral sciences. The principle of the conditioned reflex was made the basis of a new Soviet concept of man. According to this concept, man is a reactive mechanism whose behavior, including all the higher mental processes, can be exhaustively understood through a knowledge of the laws of conditioning, and can be controlled through application of this knowledge. The new movement began in 1949, and continued with ever-increasing momentum during 1950, 1951, and 1952. From the fields of physiology and medicine, where it took its rise, it radiated out into numerous adjacent areas of science, including psychiatry, pedagogy, and psychology.

It must be emphasized once again that the motivating springs of this movement were not scientific but political, not intellectual in the proper sense but psycho-ideological. That is, the neo-Pavlovian movement did not grow spontaneously out of the scientific investigations of Soviet physiologists, pathologists, and psychologists working independently at their respective problems. It was, on the contrary, imposed upon them from above by political authorities whose interest in the matter was nonscientific. According to Academician K. Bykov, who played a part in the Pavlovian revolution similar to that of Lysenko in genetics, the whole development took place "under the directing influence of the Party" and was inspired by Stalin personally: "The initiator of the events that have elevated the teachings of Pavlov in our country, the initiator of the creation of the most favorable conditions for the development of Soviet physiology for the benefit of the people is the brilliant architect of Soviet culture—Joseph Vissarionovich Stalin. We are indebted to Comrade Stalin for the victory of the Pavlovian cause in our country and for the creative upsurge we now observe in the development of this most important field of contemporary natural science."[9] There appears to be no reason to doubt the testimony of Bykov on this crucial point.

IV

The year 1949 was the turning point in the official Soviet attitude toward Pavlov. Prior to that time, Pavlov's memory had been venerated in Soviet writings. But in the new phase, which began in 1949, veneration gave way to a positive glorification of both the man and his teachings. As the potential practical use of these teachings dawned upon the Stalin regime, they began to receive official endorsement in a new spirit of dogmatic authority. Symptomatic of Pavlov's apotheosis was the nationwide observance in September, 1949, of the hundredth anniversary of his birth. Although the Pavlovian revolution was at that time still in its formative stages, some of the themes of the centenary materials were highly indicative of the direction in which the thought of the regime was moving. The mounting antipathy toward "subjectivism" was evident in the boast by Academician Bykov that Pavlov "drove the soul out forever from its last refuge—our minds."[10] The logic of facts, wrote Bykov, led Pavlov to the necessity of "putting an end forever to the conception of the soul." And *Pravda,* in its anniversary editorial, said that Pavlov had invaded the sphere of spiritual phenomena, established the material basis of higher nervous activity, and in this way had smashed for all time the "idealistic fables about the supernatural character of our minds." Moreover, this editorial revealed vividly the relationship of the new official interest in Pavlov to the transformist trend of thought: "To master nature, to subjugate her to the interests of man, to achieve unlimited power over the most intricate type of motion of matter—the work of the brain—such was Pavlov's ardent dream. Like another great Russian scientist, I. V. Michurin, Pavlov did not wish to await 'favors' from nature, but took the view that it is possible and feasible for man himself to take these 'favors,' actively to intervene in nature, to remake her."[11] The coupling of the names of Pavlov and Michurin was far more than a casual rhetorical flourish.

The tendencies toward an official enthronement of Pavlov came to fruition in June, 1950, shortly after the publication of Stalin's papers on linguistics; this was an event with which the Pavlovian revolution was closely connected. One June 22, 1950, *Pravda* announced the convocation of a joint session of the Academy of Science of the U.S.S.R. and the Academy of Medical Sciences to discuss problems of the physiological theories of Pavlov. The session opened in Moscow on June 28. There were two keynote reports, given by Academician K. M. Bykov and Professor A. G. Ivanov-Smolensky, respectively. Seventy-five others followed. The theme of the occasion was struck by Vavilov, President of the Academy of Sciences, in the opening speech. The development of Soviet physiology since Pavlov's death, he said, had diverged from the "direct paths laid down by the great Russian scientist" into secondary bypaths. The center of gravity had shifted considerably from the "Pavlov line." The present session would be a turning point beyond which Soviet physiology would develop squarely in the Pavlovian heritage. This basic theme was developed by Bykov. It was a mistake, he stated, to think of Pavlov's teachings as a mere addition to physiology or a new chapter in its development. It would be more correct to divide all physiology, and all psychology as well, into two phases: the pre-Pavlov phase and the Pavlov phase.

Bykov and Ivanov-Smolensky attacked the leaders of all the "deviationist" tendencies in Soviet physiology and medicine. Academician Orbeli, who until 1948 had directed the main Pavlovian institutes in the U.S.S.R. and had been recognized as the principal custodian of the Pavlovian heritage, was the foremost target. He was criticized primarily for his view that the principles of the conditioned reflex can explain only the more elementary forms of behavior, and that the existence of a "subjective world" must be reckoned with at the human level. Orbeli had written in 1947 that "in those temporary connections that Ivan Petrovich [Pavlov] studied, we have only the most elementary process of higher nervous activity." And he had called attention to the phenomenon in man of *resistance* to the formation of conditioned reflexes. Both of these propositions were now totally unacceptable. The conditioned reflex was to be regarded as a universal formula for all higher nervous activity, and no exceptions could be allowed, even at the human level, to the principle of total determination by conditioning. "Also incomprehensible," added Ivanov-Smolensky, "is Academician L. A. Orbeli's assertion that a qualitative singularity of man is the rise in him of a 'subjective world.' "[12]

The relationship of the Pavlovian doctrine to the transformist goals of the Soviet regime and to the Michurinist ideology was made explicit by Bykov and· Ivanov-Smolensky. Pavlov, declared the latter, had aspired not only to study but also to *master* the phenomena being studied, to direct them, command them, change them in the required directions. Through a knowledge of the laws of conditioning combined with control over the environment, behavior could be conditioned in whatever ways were considered desirable. In addition, the conditioned connections, repeated for a number of generations, could "by heredity turn into unconditioned ones." The organic relationship between Michurinism and Pavlovianism in the minds of the Soviet proponents of these doctrines was reflected in the later appearance in Soviet writings of a new hyphenated expression: the "Michurin-Pavlov biology." According to this conception, the common basic principle of the two doctrines was the "law of the unity of organism and environment." The difference between them related only to the spheres of application of the basic principle. Michurinism applied it to agriculture, while Pavlovianism applied it to physiology, psychology, and medicine.

A notable detail of the Pavlov session was the frequent reference to hypertension as foremost among the diseases that would prove amenable to therapeutic methods derived from the Pavlovian arsenal. This is interesting in view of the fact that Stalin himself apparently suffered from chronic hypertension; according to the official announcement of March 4, 1953, his fatal brain stroke was caused by hypertension. Whether or not the clinical interests of Soviet medicine were guided in part by Stalin's personal medical needs, the fact remains that the participants in the Pavlov session of 1950 devoted a remarkable amount of attention to the problem of hypertension. Both of the leading speakers, in particular, laid special stress upon a Pavlovian approach to the cure of this disease. The Pavlovian view, as they developed it, was that this, like other internal diseases, e.g., ulcers, is ultimately caused by a disordered state of the cerebral cortex. In technical Pavlovian terms, employed by A. L. Myasnikov in his speech at the session, hypertension is based upon "disorders of the first and second signal systems," i.e., the nonlinguistic and linguistic systems of conditioned reflexes. This being so, therapy should concentrate upon bringing influence to bear upon the patient via the central nervous system. Ivanov-Smolensky mentioned sleep treatment, hypnosis, and suggestion as three specific techniques for possible use in this connection. Bykov alluded to some sort of linguistic therapy, saying that "speech can cause deep changes in the whole organism." Can it be that Stalin was in effect mobilizing the Soviet medical profession to discover a Pavlovian miracle treatment for his high blood pressure? The answer to this question must remain for the time being one of the intriguing mysteries of Stalin's reign. However, in view of what is known about the sustained efforts of Soviet specialists to satisfy Stalin's interest in pushing back the frontiers of human longevity, an affirmative answer to the question must be regarded as entirely possible.

Although problems of physiology and medicine largely dominated the deliberations of the Pavlov session, its momentous implications for Soviet psychology did not escape the minds of those present. A "reconstruction of psychology on scientific principles" was one of the tasks the session's decree laid down for the specialists in this field of knowledge. Among those who addressed the session were two of the most prominent Soviet psychologists, B. M. Teplov and S. L. Rubinstein. Teplov's speech was a piece of abject self-criticism on behalf of Soviet psychology as a whole. The task of constructing a system of psychology based upon the teachings of Pavlov had not, he said, been fulfilled.* All of the existing textbooks and treatises on psychology were "utterly unsatisfactory." Soviet psychologists had suffered from "a fear of the simplicity and clarity of the Pavlovian teaching," a fear that reflected in part the regrettable influence on Soviet psychologists of certain fashionable foreign schools in psychology. Now, however, Soviet psychology was entering upon a new stage of its development, the Pavlovian stage.[13]

There is abundant evidence to show that during the early postwar years, the professional psychologists of the U.S.S.R. were quite oblivious of the impending revolutionary reorientation of their science on the basis of the reflex principle. Reflexology in all its forms was generally viewed as an aberration of the 1920's, a stage that had been traversed and transcended once and for all. Furthermore, there is nothing to suggest that the majority of psychologists regretted this. Reflexological concepts, especially of an extreme and rigid variety, do not appear to be particularly congenial to their ways of thought. In any event, the irrelevance of the reflex concept to an understanding of the higher forms of human experience was by many taken more or less for granted. Teplov, for example, had written in 1947: "The explanation of all the phenomena of psychic life by the principle of the formation of associative or conditioned-reflex connections is, of course, utterly wrong. . . . By itself, the theory of conditioned reflexes is not even adequate for understanding the physiological foundation of human behavior."[14] At the time it was made, this statement merely expressed a view that had come to be accepted with the force of dogma by many of the leading figures of Soviet psychology.

That was how matters stood in 1950, when the command was issued for Soviet psychology to be radically reconstructed on the basis of the reflex principle. Implying as it did that this discipline had been on the wrong track for the past twenty years, the com-

* For understandable reasons, Teplov failed to add that this task had also not previously been set.

mand came as a shock to those on the receiving end. It forced the psychologists to raise again the most fundamental problems concerning the concepts and methods of psychology. The pessimism and perplexity that this prospect aroused among the psychologists were reflected in an incident that occurred some time after the Pavlov session. A number of psychologists wrote a collective note to Ivanov-Smolensky, inquiring, "What is the subject of psychology and what are its tasks?" The note was signed: "Group of Psychologists Seeking the Subject of Their Science."[15] There is no record that they received a reply. According to a Soviet source, in the aftermath of the Pavlov session many of the psychologists were "at a loss" in the face of the necessity it had proclaimed for a reconstruction of their science. This found expression "either in liquidator attitudes toward the subject matter of psychological science or else in efforts somehow to cut themselves off from the Pavlovian teaching, to stand aside and wait it out until the reconstruction had taken place."[16]

The next major development was a conference on psychology held in Moscow in July, 1952, and attended by more than 400 psychologists from all parts of the country. Its task was to take stock of the results already achieved in the Pavlovian revolution and to chart its future directions. The conference admitted in its final resolution that the reconstruction of psychology was proceeding at an "inadmissibly slow" pace, and urged that the task be approached more boldly and resolutely. Professor A. A. Smirnov, the main speaker, declared that the reconstruction had to be fundamental and decisive. It had to extend to "the entire content of psychology." The psychological concepts had to be radically recast, purged of "all elements of idealism, subjectivism, introspectionism."[17] However, this did not mean, according to Smirnov, the reduction of psychology to physiology, the dissolving of psychological concepts into physiological ones. The concept of consciousness, for example, was not to be discarded, as some psychologists had proposed in the aftermath of the Pavlov session. Instead, it was to be so reinterpreted that all the phenomena of conscious experience could be strictly correlated, on the basis of the reflex principle, with their environmental determinants. Far from facing liquidation, psychology was destined to occupy a position of crucial importance among the sciences. By employing the theory of Pavlov, it would open up the subjective world of man to objective study and thereby to regulation.

V

The leading Soviet psychologies of the 1920's showed an exclusive interest in overt behavior and an emphasis on environmental influence. But in the new model of personality that emerged in the 1930's, the center of gravity shifted to the subjective side. The individual recovered his psyche. His overt behavior was now seen as a product of processes taking place inside him as shaped by his previous experience and the educational efforts of the Soviet state. While the principle of causality was not abandoned, there was a significant shift away from exclusive stress on environment. Soviet man was accorded in psychological theory a capacity for self-determination, for consciously regulating his conduct by norms and ideals which, though assimilated from the "socialist environment," were a genuine part of him and hence, supposedly, commanded his sincere and spontaneous allegiance.[18] This was in essence an optimistic conception. It presupposed that people growing up in the Soviet social order and subject to the formative influences that the state could bring to bear upon them through the family, the school, the press, and all the other channels of control would, in the vast majority of instances, develop true "Soviet selves." Once formed in this manner, the personality system would become an autonomous force in the individual's life, ensuring his loyalty to the regime, his conformity to its doctrines, and his allegiance to its goals.

Seen in this perspective, the Pavlovian revolution of the early 1950's marks an event of historic significance: the breakdown of the optimistic conception of man with which the Stalin regime had officially been operating for nearly two decades. It was a reflection of the quiet resistance of the majority of Russians to the Sovietization of their real selves, a resistance that had proved relatively immune to the massive propaganda pressures of the postwar years. The fact was that Soviet society, with all its controls and its immense resources for indoctrination of the citizenry, was not producing a generation of New Men. The optimistic model of personality endowed the individual person with a capacity of spiritual self-determination, but the results did not bear out the confident prediction of the 1930's. And there was nothing in the working model that would point the way toward the attainment of better results. These implications were not openly acknowledged in the writings of the early 1950's that centered around the teaching of

Pavlov. But they were omnipresent below the surface of these writings, and occasionally showed through unmistakably.

The attempted reconstruction of Soviet psychology was far more, though, than a confession of the bankruptcy of the optimistic model of personality. It was also an expression of Stalin's determination to elaborate a new model that would answer the needs of his regime, a truly workable model based upon a perfected technique of soul-forming that would leave nothing to chance and, if properly mastered, could not fail to achieve the goal. In his address to the psychological conference of 1952, Professor Smirnov formulated the goal rather candidly: "Soviet psychologists are confronted in all definiteness with the problem of the *formation of the personality of man,* the formation of it in the concrete social-historical conditions of people, in the conditions of our socialist reality, under the influence of the educational work of the school [italics added]."[19] Since the master formula for the attainment of the goal was to be the conditioned reflex, the model of personality had to be revolutionized: *Man had to be understood as a being whose character and conduct are controlled at every step by the conditioning process, whose every psychic act is a reflex.* As Smirnov put it, "I. P. Pavlov's teaching on temporary connections is a firm basis for understanding *all* the conscious activity of man."[20] Thus the reflex mechanism was to be seen as an all-inclusive key to the workings of the mind. The basic premise of the new Pavlovian model of personality was that there is nothing in man that transcends in principle the conditioned salivary responses of Pavlov's dog.*

From this starting point, Soviet psychology inevitably moved back into a rigid environmental determinism. The leading spokes-

* For the sake of historical accuracy, it should be recorded that one N. P. Antonov, a psychologist from the city of Ivanovo, raised a lone and ineffectual voice of protest against this basic premise. In the article referred to in note 15, he wrote: "By attempting to reduce the whole psyche to reflexes, to temporary connections, we are thereby equating the salivation of a dog at the sound of a metronome with the most intricate phenomena of the spiritual life of man, with the conscious activity of people, with the brilliant creations of human intelligence in poetry, art, science, social and political life." (*Voprosy filosofii,* No. 1, 1953, p. 197.) Antonov's article immediately became the object of severe and concerted attack on the part of the other psychologists. But the quoted statement is valuable as an acknowledgment from a Soviet source of the full implications of the neo-Pavlovian trend.

men of the neo-Pavlovian movement never tired of pointing out that the Pavlovian model of personality was deterministic. The psyche's existence was not denied, but all causal determination was shifted to the external environment, natural and social. "The causes of psychological facts," said Smirnov in a typical formulation, "are influences emanating from without, primarily influences of a social character."[21] According to another authority, "Determinate agents of the external world are the cause, the impetus, of determinate activity of the organism."[22] In taking this position, the Soviet psychologists saw themselves as applying to psychology the principle of the unity of organism and environment that the Michurinist doctrine had applied to biology. Just as Michurinism denied the existence of autogenetic forces in animals and plants, so neo-Pavlovianism denied the existence of psychogenetic forces in man. The result was to deprive the human being of all spontaneity, all inner sources of activity. He is jerked into motion, tugged this way and that, by "determinate agents of the external world" in which all causal efficacy resides. This is a view that might have been summed up in the slogan: Overboard with self-determination! It marked a clean break with the conception of the New Man. Employing the terminology of the American sociologist Riesman, the transition from the New Man to the Pavlovian model of personality can be described as a shift from an "inner-directed" type, whose character operates as an autonomous determining force in his life, to an "other-directed" type, whose behavior is guided by signals received from outside. In the Soviet version, however, the sole source of the signals to which the "other-directed" person responds is the state.

To the outsider who studies the materials of the neo-Pavlovian movement, nothing is more striking than its insistent endeavor to empty man of all inner springs of action, to visualize human nature as motivationally inert. Man is "hollow." He has no wishes, instincts, emotions, drives, or impulses, no reservoir of energies of his own. No motive is allowed to intervene between the stimulus emanating from the environment and the person's reflex response. Rubinstein, for example, protested vigorously against the notion that the individual has "inner impulses" (drives, instincts, tendencies, etc.) which underlie his reflexes and "guide the action of the reflex mechanisms in a direction desirable to the organism." His new view was as follows: "The Pavlovian conception of reflex action does not require and does not allow for any 'motive,' drive or impulse lodged behind the reflex, in the depths of the organism, which by some means unknown to us sets the reflex mechanism in motion."[23] True, a person's responses are seen as influenced to some extent by his habits, but these in turn are a crystallization of past conditioning and consequently an integral part of the system of reflex mechanisms.

The linguistic orientation that Stalin imparted to the neo-Pavlovian movement has already been touched upon above. In the reconstruction of Soviet psychology, the conception of the regulative function of language took on decisive importance. And it was at this point that Stalin's theoretical interests impinged most directly upon the new movement in psychology. In emphasizing the all-important role of language in conditioned-reflex behavior at the human level, the Soviet psychologists referred constantly to Stalin's *Marxism and Questions of Linguistics,* a series of papers published in the summer of 1950. The first and longest of these papers appeared in *Pravda* only two days prior to the announcement of the forthcoming Pavlov session, and this close coincidence in time is probably an indication of the intimate relationship in Stalin's mind between the linguistic doctrines that he enunciated and the revival of Pavlovianism in physiology and psychology. Such a relationship was, at any rate, taken for granted by the psychologists themselves.

The passages of Stalin's work on linguistics most frequently quoted by the psychologists are those in which he stresses the enormous significance of language in all departments of social activity, and the inseparability of language and thought. On the first point, he writes that language is directly linked with every activity of man "in all areas of his work." It "embraces all the spheres of activity of man" and is "virtually unlimited."[24] Moreover, Stalin equates language with *word language,* rejecting the notions about gesture language and wordless thought that had been emphasized by the founder of Soviet linguistics, N. Ya. Marr. Thus, language to Stalin means word language exclusively; it is inseparable from thought, and it penetrates and pervades every aspect of the social behavior of man. Those propositions formed a starting point for constructing the new Pavlovian model of personality, which pictured man as a creature whose behavior is controlled and regulated by verbal signals.

The concept of the "second signal system" provided a connecting link between Stalin's generalities about language on the one hand and the theory of conditioning on the other. This concept is one that Pavlov casually developed in some of his later writings and in conversations with his students. The minor part that it played in his system can be judged from the fact that there are scarcely more than a dozen brief references to it in all his writings and recorded conversations. His idea seems to have been that word language functions in the context of the individual human being's behavior as a system of verbal signals, higher-order conditioned stimuli that evoke indirectly the same responses as those conditioned to non-verbal stimuli. One of the most striking features of the neo-Pavlovian moment was the disproportionately heavy emphasis that it placed upon this minor appendage of the original Pavlovian system. Until 1950, the concept of the second signal system had been generally ignored by Soviet psychologists. Among the physiologists, the only two who gave it much attention were—significantly enough—Ivanov-Smolensky and Bykov. Then, however, it was lifted out of obscurity and erected as the central pillar of the new Stalin-Pavlov system of psychology. According to Rubinstein, "all the specifically human characteristics of the psyche" are revealed in the functioning of the second signal system.

The Pavlovian revolution placed great emphasis upon the semantic side of Pavlov's theory of conditioned reflexes. In fact, the Soviet neo-Pavlovianism of the early 1950's was essentially a theory of semantics constructed on a physiological basis. The foundation upon which the whole structure rests is, in the words of Bykov, the "principle of signalization." The concomitant of a stimulus, such as the sound of the metronome in Pavlov's well-known experiment with the dog, becomes a "signal" of the presence of the stimulus (in this instance, food) and evokes the reflex action appropriate to it. The totality of concomitants that in the natural life conditions of the organism take over the stimulus function and serve as signals constitute, in Pavlov's terminology, a "first signal system of reality." The first signal system is common to man and animals. But at the human level an "extraordinary addition" emerges in the form of speech. Speech is a system of signals of the second order—"signals of signals," in Pavlov's phrase. It forms in its totality a "second signal system of reality" which is peculiar to man and which, according to Pavlov, operates on the same fundamental laws as those that govern the conditioning process at the lower level. Finally, the generalized verbal signals comprised in the second system are assigned a position of hegemony in the life of man; the second system takes precedence over the first in orienting the human being in his environment. This is the substance of Pavlov's "wonderful idea" of the second signal system, which, according to Bykov and others, had heretofore been mistakenly ignored by Soviet science.

In using the phrase "signals of signals," Pavlov apparently had in mind the view that the word is a generalized "substitute signal" of the object it denotes and, as such, evokes the behavioral reaction appropriate to the object in the same way that the sound of the metronome evokes in the experimental dog the behavioral reaction appropriate to the signalized food. Since this line of speculation was outside the direct purview of his scientific work, he did not pursue it further. However, his present-day Soviet followers accepted it as the literal truth and made it the cornerstone of the new psychological theory that they had been ordered to build on a Pavlovian basis. The theory rests squarely on Pavlov's surmise that verbal substitute signals evoke behavioral tendencies or reactions in the same way that ordinary conditioned stimuli do. One writer, for example, illustrated the thesis as follows: "By mastering the word, that is, by learning to pronounce the appropriate auditory complex and to relate this complex correctly to specific objects, the child masters the significance of the given word. After that the word can play the part of a signal of signals: the word 'apple' can signalize the very same stimuli as those evoked by a real apple."[25] If, in other words, the sight of an actual apple lying on the table will cause a hungry child's mouth to water, hearing the word "apple" will eventually, after the proper language training, evoke a similar reaction. The function of words is, then, to trigger behavioral responses appropriate to the objects that people have been trained to associate with the words.

We may note here that this Pavlovian concept of the function of language is appropriate to a hypothetical primitive condition of man in which speech was exclusively an instrument of social control and had not yet acquired an autonomous representative function. By treating words as second-order signals to action, it overlooks the acquired *symbolic* function of language. The distinction between words used as signals to action on the one hand and purely as symbols of their objects on the other is illustrated by an American semanticist in the following way: "A term which is used symbolically and not signally does *not* evoke action appropriate to the presence of its object. If I say: 'Napoleon,' you do not bow to the conqueror of Europe as though I had introduced him, but merely think of him. If I mention a Mr. Smith of our common acquaintance, you may be led to tell me something about him 'behind his back' which you would *not* do in his presence. . . . Symbols are not proxy for their objects, but are *vehicles for the conception of objects.*"[26]

The failure of the Soviet psychologists to recognize and take account of this crucial distinction was not accidental. The practical importance discerned in the neo-Pavlovian movement, its electrifying educational implications to the Stalinist mind, depended entirely upon reducing language to its signal-function exclusively, upon regarding words as "proxy for their objects." The whole movement would have collapsed instantly had its initiator forced himself to consider the possibility that words can be employed purely symbolically as neutral vehicles for the conception of objects. The goal was to treat language as an instrument of social control. For this purpose it was imperative that words should always be signals that touch off responses appropriate to their meaning. Here was the needed link between semantics and politics. As Smirnov expressed it, the Pavlovian teaching reveals the conditions under which stimuli, including verbal stimuli, become signals *"and by virtue of this fact regulate the behavior of man* [italics added]."[27] On this view of the function of language, a person hearing the word "Napoleon" should indeed make at least a mental bow to the conqueror of Europe, or whatever other gesture his earlier conditioning had linked with this verbal signal. Or, to take a familiar example from the Soviet context, on hearing the signal "warmonger," a properly Pavlovianized Russian should respond with a shudder of fury. Granted the initial premise that the word is in every case primarily a call to action, linguistics logically takes its place at the head of the list of policy sciences. Of all the monopolies enjoyed by the Soviet state, none would be so crucial as its monopoly on the definition of words. The ultimate weapon of political control would be the dictionary.*

At this point it may be useful to summarize briefly the argument of the foregoing pages. I have suggested that the movement initiated by Stalin to reconstruct Soviet psychology marked a decline of the optimistic conception of man that had officially prevailed in the U.S.S.R. since the early 1930's. This in turn was an indirect reflection of the fact that millions of Russians, especially under the

---

* It is interesting in this connection to note the extraordinarily intense activity, after 1950, in the writing and rewriting of dictionaries in the Soviet Union.

impact of their experiences during and after World War II, showed tendencies to deviate radically from the norm of Soviet selfhood, which, according to the optimistic conception, they should have naturally assimilated as a result of their education and spontaneous personality development. In the face of this disturbing fact, Stalin resorted to the peculiar mode of coming to terms with perverse situations that we have termed "transformism." In the Pavlovian model of personality he found a formula that seemed to place human nature in the arbitrary power of a state-controlled educational environment. Emptied of all inner springs of character and conduct, man appeared in this model as a passive plaything of determining influences from without, particularly influences of a social character brought to bear through the medium of language. By mastering the "objective scientific laws" of the language-conditioning process, the state could—theoretically—bring about the "directed alteration of psychic processes," i.e., it could transform the minds of its citizens, mold them in the Soviet personality image. The crowning concept of this theoretical edifice was the second signal system. In the Stalin-Pavlov model of man, the second signal system is the mechanism of mentality. Consciousness is the distinctive capacity of human beings to respond to and regulate their behavior by verbal signals. Man is basically a signal-receiving animal. And since it is the state that calls the signals, an appropriate name for this theoretical new species of Soviet humanity would be "state-directed man."

VI

The interpretation offered here of the neo-Pavlovian chapter of Soviet thought assigns a crucially important place to Stalin. The evidence for such a view converges from a number of directions. First, there is the direct public testimony of Bykov, Rubinstein, and others that Stalin initiated the back-to-Pavlov movement. Secondly, the neo-Pavlovian movement was in its way an outgrowth, an extension to man, of the Michurin-Lysenko line in biology, which enjoyed Stalin's personal patronage. Further, it was closely linked up with the ultradeterministic conception of scientific law that he developed in his final work on political economy. Finally, in its medical aspect, the movement impinged upon an area in which Stalin had shown all along, and especially toward the end, a most intense personal interest. These various indications of Stalin's role as the instigator and guiding spirit of the Pavlov revival lend special interest to the course the movement took after Stalin died.*

The Stalin-Pavlov line was not altered immediately. As late as August, 1953, Bykov was quoted in a Soviet journal as saying: "We must preserve the purity of the Pavlov teaching, which has affected all major issues of contemporary natural science."[28] But then subtle signs of a countertrend began to appear. One of these was the move to topple Lysenkoism from its monopolistic position in biology. This emerged into the open in early 1954. Later in that year, the countertrend went further. A prominent physicist, S. L. Sobolev, was permitted to publish an article in *Pravda* stating that scientific progress "is always connected with the abandonment of preconceived points of view, with the bold breaking-down of old norms and conceptions." Sobolev attacked the previous disparagement of Einstein's physical theories by physicists of the Moscow University. He coupled this with a caustic reference to the unmerited claims of certain Soviet scientists to monopoly of the truth, mentioning three names in this connection: Lysenko, Bykov, and Ivanov-Smolensky.[29] To the psychologists, the inference could only be that the twin dictators of Stalin's neo-Pavlovian movement had fallen from the pedestal of official infallibility. The way was now opened for a reaction against this movement.

The reaction came shortly afterward in an editorial summation in *Problems of Philosophy* of the whole discussion of recent years on psychology.[30] The editorial did not attack Pavlov or question the importance of his teachings for psychology. But in various significant ways it undermined the Stalin-Pavlov line. It redefined psychology in pre-1950 terms as "the science of the psychic activity of man." Next, it announced—with something of an air of discovery—that psychic activity is both real and subjective in nature: "The subjective—man's psyche—really exists." It reproached the 1952 conference on psychology for banning the introspective method. It told the psychologists not to be afraid of describing the rediscovered subjective world of man in terms of the traditional psychological categories: mind, feeling, will, imagination, etc. "This observation," it added, "we address to certain nihilistic tendencies

* Some materials published as part of the new wave of exposures of Stalin in the aftermath of the Twenty-second Party Congress carry indirect confirmation of the hypothesis that Stalin's personal role was a very important one. See especially *Voprosy filosofii*, No. 7, 1962, pp. 72, 81.

in the matter of the so-called recasting or redefinition of the psychological terms and concepts on the basis of the Pavlovian physiology." The reader will recall that these "nihilistic tendencies"
were part and parcel of the Stalin-Pavlov line. They expressed the
very crux of what Stalin was directing the Soviet psychologists to
do. Finally, the editorial referred in sharply negative terms to those
who would "dogmatically apply to man" all the methods that Pavlov evolved in the study of animal behavior. The effect of all this
was, of course, to revise the whole orientation imposed on Soviet
psychology from high political spheres in 1950.

The new admission that "the psyche really exists" reflected something quite crucial—the abandonment of *total* environmental determinism in the sense that was implied in the Stalin-Pavlov line.
This was made explicit in early 1955 in the first issue of a new
Soviet journal, *Problems of Psychology*. The programmatic leading
article was contributed by Rubinstein. In it he rejected the idea of
determinism "as the theory of a cause that operates as an external
impetus and directly determines the terminal effect of the external
stimulus." This, as noted earlier, is precisely the kind of determinism implicit in the model of the state-directed man. The verbal signals called by the state were supposed to determine directly his attitudes and acts. No intervention of the psyche as an autonomous
inner force in man was allowed; no self-determination, no spontaneity, no motives were to be presupposed by psychology. Having
formulated the deterministic principle as implicit in this model,
Rubinstein continued: "It is easy to understand the invalidity of
such determinism. All the facts of science and everyday observation testify against it. We may convince ourselves at every step that
one and the same stimulus can evoke various different reactions
in various different people. One and the same stimulus evokes different reactions in one and the same individual under various
different conditions of that person. . . . External causes operate
through the medium of the internal conditions which represent
the foundation of the development of phenomena."[31] Here the
principle of "autogenesis," the idea that the personality is to some
extent an autonomous determining force in the person's life and
behavior, is restored. The core of the Stalin-Pavlov line is cut
away. The model of the state-directed man presupposes a one-to-
one correspondence between the verbal propaganda stimulus and
the individual's reflex response. It implies "direct" determinism
in the sense here denied. Such determinism, concluded Rubinstein,

"would signify the *complete disintegration of personality* and would lead to a defective mechanistic conception holding that each influence on a person has its own 'separate' effect irrespective of the dynamic situation. . . . The central link here is the 'psychology of personality.' This is the point of departure and the point of arrival for an adequate theory of motivation [italics added]."[32] Not only did this statement alter the model of the state-directed man in Soviet psychology. It admitted by indirection that the Stalin-Pavlov line envisaged nothing less than the complete disintegration of human personality.

Turning from these early post-Stalin writings in Soviet psychology to some representative writings of the present (1962), we find that the countertrend already visible then has continued. The existence of "the subjective," of inner forces and faculties and tendencies in man that exert one of the determining influences upon his behavior and are a legitimate object of psychology inquiry, is recognized. And it has become common practice among Soviet psychologists, especially since the Twenty-second Party Congress and the new wave of de-Stalinization initiated there, to criticize what is called the "dogmatization of Pavlov's teachings." The critical voices have been surprisingly frank and forthright in some instances. As an example one might cite an article on "The Authority of Facts" by Professor V. V. Parin of the Academy of Medical Sciences, who was apparently one of the many Soviet scientists exiled to distant places in Stalin's last years. Science, he says, breathes only one air—the oxygen of facts. Its growth and progress are incompatible with dogmatism and the administrative pressure used in 1950 and after to impose a rigid set of Pavlovian formulas upon various disciplines. In Soviet medicine this had the crippling effect of driving a wedge between theory and practice. It turned medicine into a kind of "double-bottomed suitcase with phrases about cortical-visceral medicine in the upper part and, underneath, therapy founded on common sense and personal experience." Furthermore, writes Professor Parin, the great Pavlov, who was above all an experimental scientist and innovator, could "never have imagined that his works would one day be turned into a combination of prayerbook and club for the terrorizing of the heterodox."[33]

Similar statements were made in a more formal and official setting at an important new conference held in Moscow in May, 1962, to discuss philosophical problems of psychology and the physiology of higher nervous activity in the light of post-Stalin developments. According to Academician P. N. Fedoseev, who gave the opening address, "the cult of Stalin's personality left its imprint also on the development of physiology and psychology. It fettered the creative initiative of scientists, generated dogmatism, an atmosphere of uncritical acceptance of certain particular dubious and inaccurate formulations presented at the session [the reference is to the 1950 Pavlov session]. . . . Conducted in the spirit of the cult of Stalin's personality, the session in many ways distorted the idea of scientific criticism, supplanting comradely, free exchange of opinions with the pinning of derogatory labels on and wholesale condemnation of the heterodox. In the ensuing years there appeared a tendency, associated with vulgar-materialist views, to biologize man. Wide currency was given to a wrong attitude to the science of psychology, whose subject matter scientists tried to dissolve into the physiology of higher nervous activity."[34]

Thus Soviet psychology has continued emancipating itself from the extremes of a dogmatic Stalinist Pavlovianism. It has been doing so, moreover, in the face of resistance from those whom Professor Parin, in the article cited above, calls the "dogmatists" or "orthodox Pavlovians." However, this continuing countertrend is not a counterrevolution. The conference of May, 1962, criticized the Pavlov session of 1950 not for giving a wrong general direction to Soviet psychology, but only for its excesses and wrong methods of giving it a right direction. Soviet psychology in the early 1960's still shows a fundamentally Pavlovian orientation and no tendency to depart from it. What has apparently been discarded is, specifically, Stalin's idea of finding in Pavlov the scientific key to mind control.

What are the policy implications of the countertrend? The Stalin-Pavlov line, as shown earlier, was an expression of the Will to Transform that was operative in Stalin's postwar policies. It was a search for a sure formula of mind control that would yield techniques for the psychic transformation of human beings, rendering them plastically receptive to the official propaganda image of the world and of themselves and their tasks in Soviet society. Underlying it was the idea that "propaganda can do anything" if only the psychic conditions of receptivity to it could be scientifically set and controlled. This was a theory of environmentalism in which the state-operated organs of education and indoctrination were seen as the sole active sector of the environment, the determining environmental force. The remainder of the environment, including the material living conditions of Soviet people, would *not* have to be ameliorated in order to accomplish the transformist objective. The illusion of a happy life could be built up and maintained in Soviet minds no matter how miserable the actual living conditions might be.

If this aspect of transformism were subsiding in Soviet official thought, how might we recognize the shift? There would be some sign of recognition that propaganda, as it were, "cannot do everything," that actual living conditions would have to be improved in order to assure a better popular response to the regime and its goals. Policy, in other words, would be governed by a more pragmatic approach, one that combined continued heavy stress on indoctrination with some effort to ameliorate the real environment of the masses of Soviet citizens. Manifestations of such a shift in the policy orientation of the Soviet regime have, in fact, appeared. One of the most interesting is the recognition of the limitations of coercion and propaganda persuasion as means of controlling mass behavior. For example, the Central Committee's journal, *Party Life,* has written that private commercial "speculation" (classed as a "survival of capitalism") cannot be combated by legal regulation and propaganda alone. It is also necessary "to show concern for the all-round development of Soviet trade, the improvement of supplies for the population, and the creation of an abundance of consumer goods. Only on this condition will all ground for speculation disappear."[35] It is questionable whether "this condition" will soon or ever be realized under the Soviet economic system, but the statement itself is significant as an indication of the decline of transformism in the regime's official thinking. An even clearer indication comes in a direct criticism by the Soviet philosophical journal of the tendency to overvalue the potentialities of propaganda. Some, it states, have reasoned "as though the survivals of capitalism in the minds of people could be overcome *solely by means of propaganda,* by means of education, while neglecting the solution of economic tasks, the necessity of steadily developing social production, which creates objective conditions for improving the material position and cultural standard of the people [italics added]."[36] But such reasoning, it contends, is mistaken. A policy operating "solely by means of propaganda" will not do. The inference is that the new Soviet leadership recognizes direct mind control of the kind Stalin sought as, at the least, an impractical proposition. In other words, it recognizes the imperative need to combine indoctrination with improvement of "objective conditions" if Soviet popular attitudes and behavioral patterns are to be altered in its own favor. No revolutionary shift of internal Soviet economic policy has resulted from such recognition. But there has been evident in the post-Stalin period, at times more clearly than at others, a cautious, pragmatic orientation toward economic meliorism. This does not seem to have been basically affected by the various shifts in the leadership during these years.

To paraphrase an epigram, politics as practiced by Stalin in the final years of his reign was the art of the impossible. Under the regime of his successors, Soviet policy appears to have executed a strategic retreat into the realm of possibility.

8 THE POLITICS OF SOVIET DE-STALINIZATION

I

An inquiry into the political situation in post-Stalin Russia may well begin with a reflection on its historical uniqueness. Stalin, who sponsored the "Russia first" theme in Soviet propaganda, established a real momentous "first" for Russia by his own death. Never before had a totalitarian dictator of one of the world powers died, or been put to death, before his totalitarian system collapsed, or came near collapse, in war. Hitler and Mussolini, who lived long enough to bring down their systems in ruins, furnish no parallel.

The post-Stalin years in Russia, therefore, provide a spectacle of what may happen in a totalitarian political system when the dictator who shaped it leaves it intact and technically at peace.

The history of those years is a story of conflict over power and policy among the heirs of Stalin, of starts and stops and fresh starts in the attempt to carry out reforms from above, of ambitious new departures and shattering setbacks in Soviet policy, and, finally, of the gradual political awakening of popular forces in Russia and Eastern Europe. Through it all runs a fundamental theme and problem: *change*. The great question that Stalin posed by his death was not, Who shall take the place of Stalin? It was, rather, What shall take the place of Stalin*ism* as a mode of rule and pattern of policy and ideas? The issue around which Soviet politics and Soviet history have largely revolved ever since Stalin died is the issue of de-Stalinization. The death of the dictator exposed the integral relationship between Stalin as the ruling personality and Stalinism as the system of rule.

In order to set out the elements of the problem of de-Stalinization analytically, we will first sketch a picture of the foregoing process of Stalinization, viewing Stalinism as a political form that evolved over a period of years, beginning approximately in 1928, and that went through a sequence of phases. Such a sketch will make possible a systematic approach to a whole cluster of questions involved in de-Stalinization, such as: Why did Stalin's death necessitate de-Stalinization? What might de-Stalinization mean in terms of changes in the Soviet political system? How much of this meaning is embraced in the official concept of de-Stalinization with which the ruling group has been operating? To what extent does the popular concept of it diverge from the official concept? How has the process of de-Stalinization been influenced by the struggle for factional ascendancy within the post-Stalin regime? In what follows, my purpose is to cast some fresh light upon this complex of intimately interrelated questions.

The Bolshevik Revolution in October, 1917, followed by the establishment of a one-party dictatorship and the nationalization of the Russian economy, nullified the previous sixty-five years of Russian history, during which, despite many setbacks, a trend of basic liberalization had been making itself felt. The Revolution thus created conditions for a reversion to that long period in Russian history that had been characterized by the ascendancy of the state over society, and by government through bureaucracy, with the Czar as head bureaucrat. Bolshevism set the stage for a rebirth of elements of the classical political system of Russian Czarism as it had existed before the great reforms of the mid-nineteenth century.

It was Stalin, however, not Lenin, who made himself the key instrument of this process and restored the institution of the autocracy in all but name. In the later years of Stalin's rule, Czar Ivan the Terrible, the supreme historical apostle of Russian absolutism, became the dictator's favorite figure among those whom he regarded as his forerunners. In 1947, Stalin called in a Soviet film producer and ordered him to make a film showing Ivan as a "great and wise ruler." He commented that, of all the leaders in Russian history, Ivan and Lenin were the only two who had introduced a state monopoly of foreign trade.[1] This remark indicates the nature of Stalin's understanding of socialism. It did not seem to him an ideological error to look upon Ivan the Terrible as his great historical forerunner. He saw in Ivan a true socialist, a Stalinist of the sixteenth century. This is significant for an understanding of Soviet

Russia's history in the Stalin period, and of the events that followed.

The governmental system as Stalin left it might be described as an elaborate, completely centralized bureaucratic mechanism for the command and control of society. The centralization of effective governing authority in Moscow was so extreme that semiofficial Soviet idiom divided the whole Soviet realm into the "Center" (Moscow) and the "periphery" (all the rest of the U.S.S.R.). For example, a high official of the theoretically sovereign government of the Ukraine at Kiev might informally describe himself as "a worker of the periphery." This was the actual situation behind the façade of Soviet federalism, according to which the U.S.S.R. consists of a number of independent "union republics." The actual status of the republics is illustrated by the fact that in July, 1956, one of them, the Karelo-Finnish Republic, was abolished by a stroke of the governmental pen in Moscow, and was incorporated as a subunit into the huge central territory, the Russian Republic, or R.S.F.S.R. This reduced the number of republics to fifteen, including, in addition to the R.S.F.S.R., the Ukraine, Belorussia, Moldavia, and the three Baltic, three Transcaucasian, and five Central Asian republics.

There are three main systems of governing organs: (1) the soviets, forming the nominal machinery of local government, plus the Supreme Soviet; (2) the system of ministries, subordinated to the Council of Ministers of the U.S.S.R., which is the government in the technical sense; and (3) the Communist Party, headed by its Central Committee. The last-named now has a total membership of about 300, and might perhaps he described as a periodic gathering of the Soviet power elite. Its permanent machinery functions under the control of the Secretariat.

In soviets, ministries, and Party, actual authority is concentrated to a very great extent in small and closely interlocking presidiums: the Presidium of the Supreme Soviet; the Presidium of the Council of Ministers, consisting of its chairman and vice-chairmen; and the Presidium of the Central Committee, or the Party Presidium, which is not known to have a regular chairman. Among the three organs, the Party Presidium is pre-eminent in real power.

Below these peak levels, each of the three systems is a hierarchical structure of administrative-managerial organizations with networks of primary organs of various kinds extending throughout the country. Thus, the system of soviets consists of many thousands of province, town, district, and rural councils, with a membership of about two million all told, and with each unit directed by an executive committee or bureau. The Party has its parallel structure of committees at all levels, from union-republic central committee down to the town and district committees; each of these is directed by its secretariat. The Party committees are the most important nuclei of local authority. Then there is a network of about 300,000 primary Party cells in factories, farms, and institutions of every kind. These perform a variety of functions of control, surveillance, agitation for plan fulfillment, and systematic indoctrination of the Party membership, now numbering about 10 million. There are a number of other governing systems of lesser importance, including the trade-union structure, with its Central Council in Moscow, and the Komsomol, or youth organization, with a membership today of 19 million.

The system of ministries, as Stalin left it, was an enormous bureaucratic complex charged with the planning and administration of the national economy, operation of banks, factories, stores, and state farms, administration of the police system and courts, the armed forces, education, cultural activities, and foreign relations. It came to a head in the U.S.S.R. Council of Ministers, consisting of the chairman, the vice-chairmen, about fifty ministers, and the heads of state committees, such as the State Planning Committee, or Gosplan. In addition, each of the fifteen union republics had (and has) its own local council of ministers, as well as its own local supreme soviet. The ministries themselves fall into three groups: all-union, union-republic, and republic.

The direct jurisdiction of the all-union ministries extends to all organizations throughout the country in the particular field concerned. For example, an industrial ministry directly controls all enterprises in its system, regardless of their location in the country. The union-republic group, which includes the Foreign Ministry, the Defense Ministry, the Ministry of Culture, and others, directs its subordinate units in territories of the union republics through affiliate-ministries of the same name in the capitals of these republics. Hence these affiliate-ministries operate according to the so-called principle of "dual jurisdiction," being subordinate both to their local Council of Ministers in the given union republic and simultaneously to the head ministry in Moscow. The third group, the republic ministries, are those operating under the direct jurisdiction of the councils of ministers in the capitals of the union republics. Most of these administer industrial enterprises of local importance to the given union republics.

Every ministry in the Stalinist system was a governmental empire, a vast realm of bureaucracy. A ministry of one of the branches of heavy industry—say, the steel industry—could be described as a gigantic monopolistic concern, with its own permanent board of directors, planning bureau, subdivisions, trusts, distributor agencies, down to and including the actual steel mills and hundreds of subsidiary enterprises. It had its own means of transport, internal communications system, technical-training colleges, housing fund, recreational facilities, company trade union, and police department. This bred a big-business mentality in the top managers. In the autumn of 1955, the author and a party of Americans visited Russia and Eastern Europe. At a diplomatic reception in Moscow, Mikhail Pervukhin, then a member of the Party Presidium, remarked to us: "You call it General Electric, we call it the Ministry of the Communications Equipment Industry." Pervukhin wanted to suggest that these two industrial giants were pretty much the same thing. It was the voice of Soviet big business speaking.

II

This great bureaucratic structure of command and control did not come into being all at once; it evolved. The October Revolution and Lenin's Party dictatorship laid the foundation and paved the way. But the evolution itself took place under the direction and pre-eminent influence of Stalin. Without in any way relaxing the iron rule of the Party, Lenin, in 1921, announced the so-called New Economic Policy, or NEP, under which the state retained only the "commanding heights" of the economy, giving some scope for private enterprise and allowing 25 million private peasant farms to exist and contribute to economic revival. This is one reason why, in the Russia of the 1930's and 1940's, many looked back on Lenin and his era with a certain nostalgia.

Stalin, using the Party, of which he had gained control by about 1929, and the secret police, which he increasingly succeeded in wielding as a personal instrument, ended the NEP and then shaped, perfected, and vastly expanded the command and control structure. His aim was to effect in this manner the total state regimentation of society, creating in the totalitarian political structure a mechanism for unlimited exploitation of the human and natural resources of

Russia with a view to amassing power in the hands of the Center. The industrialization, beginning with the First Five-Year Plan in 1928, and the terroristic collectivization of peasant farming in the succeeding four years were the twin policy programs on the basis of which he carried through the process of total state regimentation of society. This was the period of the emergence of a full-blown, as distinguished from a merely embryonic, totalitarian state system. The policy programs called for more and more coercion and controls, including domestic passports, massive regimentation of the labor force, more and more concentration camps, and police terror as an integral part of daily life. Expansion of controls and governmental functions called for more and more bureaucratic regulation; and this in turn further augmented the need for controls, including controls over the bureaucratic controllers, and so on in a vicious circle. Stalin, possibly with the image of Ivan the Terrible already in mind, christened the whole process the "building of socialism." Actually, it was the first great stage of Stalinization.

No sooner was the basic work accomplished (approximately in 1933) than Stalin turned his attention to the next and culminating step, which was to reconstitute the autocracy. This occupied five years, from 1934 to 1939. That period witnessed the virtual suppression of the Bolshevik Party, carried out by Stalin in the name of Lenin and Bolshevism.

Every true totalitarianism is a one-man system and comes to power through the subversion of a pre-existing political regime. In the case of Hitler, the pre-existing regime was the Weimar Republic. In the case of Mussolini, it was the Italian constitutional monarchy. In those instances none could doubt that a regime had been subverted. Stalin's case was exceptional, and therefore deceptive, because here the pre-existing regime was a ruthless party dictatorship, and the destruction of it was effected without any official admission or overtly obvious sign that a continuity of political life was being broken. So authoritarian was the rule of the Bolshevik Party in Russia that it could be eliminated as a living political organism and replaced by the autocracy of Stalin without the world's quite realizing that something of real consequence had happened. But Stalin himself was at least subconsciously aware of what he had done, and showed it when, in 1952, he expunged the very word "Bolshevik" from the title of the Party and the official vocabulary of the regime. He banned the use of the word "Bolshevik" in the Soviet Union, evidently feeling uncomfortable at the sight and sound of it. The word was revived immediately after he died.

This is a point of critical importance for the analysis both of Soviet politics of the 1930's and 1940's and also of the post-Stalin period. We are accustomed to thinking in terms of a continuity of Party rule in Soviet Russia from October, 1917, to the present. Actually, however, after Stalin's blood purges of the middle 1930's, there was no longer in any real sense a ruling *party*, just as there was no real ruling *class*; there was at most a privileged stratum of bureaucratic serving-men who lived well and wore medals but who were instrumentalities rather than real holders or sharers of power. To call this stratum an "elite," as is sometimes done, is to invite misconception of the actual situation that had come to prevail under Stalin; it was only an ersatz elite.

The one-party system had given way to a one-person system, the ruling party to a ruling personage. Through the massacre of the bulk of the Bolshevik leadership and the exile of many thousands more, Stalin completed the transformation of the former ruling party into a transmission belt of autocracy, an administrative-bureaucratic mechanism totally submissive to his will. Only the *local* Party bosses retained a measure of actual authority. They became little dictators, ruling their localities at the pleasure of the big dictator in the Kremlin. And they had to watch out for the local head of the secret police, who was also working for Stalin.

Accordingly, although the Soviet Union continued to be a party-ruled state in Stalinist ideology, the former ruling party became in fact merely the first in importance of the mass organizations in the totalitarian system. This suppression of the Party was especially accentuated after World War II. The post-Stalin regime has not openly admitted this. Its euphemistic formula is that the "cult of personality," as Stalin's despotism is called, merely "diminished the role of the Party."

However, Khrushchev's secret report at the Twentieth Congress and other more recent revelations cast more light on the matter.[2] It revealed that of the 139 Central Committee members elected at the Seventeenth Congress in 1934, 98, or 70 per cent of the supreme governing body, were arrested and shot in the purges; of 1,966 delegates to the Congress, 1,108 were purged. Even this was only one major part of the slaughter. Khrushchev uses the phrase "many thousands of names" when he mentions the lists of selected victims that were sent to Stalin for his personal approval before sentence was carried out. Of course, some Bolsheviks survived, including Khrushchev, at the price of serving Stalin vigorously in the process just described.

But what happened to the Party as a party in the process is best reflected in those sections of the secret report that deal with the postwar period. The Central Committee, according to the Party statutes then in force, was supposed to meet in plenary session once every four months. Khrushchev says: "In the last years, Central Committee plenary sessions were not convened." Actually, the last officially reported plenary session was that of February, 1947. Thus, the supreme governing body not only did not govern; it did not even meet. As for the Politburo, often regarded in the outside world as the real organ of dictatorship in Stalin's Russia, Khrushchev says that its sessions "occurred only occasionally, from time to time." Its regular functioning ceased, it appears, early in 1949, when one of its members, Nikolai Voznesensky, chief of Gosplan, was shot on Stalin's orders, along with a number of other very high officials.

Stalin formed various committees of Politburo members, which he called quintets, sextets, and septets, to deal with particular matters that he assigned to them. The Politburo, supposedly the top policy-making body, ceased in any effective sense to exist. In 1952, at the Nineteenth Party Congress, Stalin changed its name to the Presidium and enlarged the total membership to about thirty-five, including a large number of younger men. According to Khrushchev, Stalin was planning to kill off the old guard. The case of the Kremlin doctors, announced in mid-January, 1953, was an apparent preparation by Stalin for a new blood purge. Six weeks later he was dead. It seems possible that he was killed just prior to the scheduled opening of the trial of the doctors, to prevent the purge process from starting down its deadly path to members of the erstwhile Politburo.

Thus, in the second major phase of Stalinization, which took place in the mid-1930's, Stalin created an absolute autocracy through the suppression of the Bolshevik Party. This meant, in effect, the suppression of the Soviet ruling class.* Here again we must refer to Ivan the Terrible in order to elucidate the subjective

* The concept of the Party as the ruling class was introduced by Lenin, who said in August, 1917: "Russia used to be ruled by 150,000 landlords. Why could not 240,000 Bolsheviks do the same job?"

rationale of Stalin's actions, the method in what might seem to be merely madness.

In directing the treason trials and executions of Party cadres, Stalin imagined himself to be acting as Ivan had acted in asserting his absolutism against the ancient landed aristocracy, the boyars, who were bloodily suppressed on charges of treason and sedition. He even used the pseudonym "Ivan Vasilyevich" (the first name and patronymic of Ivan the Terrible, the initials of which corresponded to those of his own first name and patronymic, Iosif Vissarionovich) in some secret inner correspondence of the purge period.[3] Later, in the conversation with the film director in 1947, he allowed himself to criticize Ivan on just one point. Ivan, he said, had made the mistake of failing to liquidate five remaining feudal families, had not carried through the suppression of the aristocracy to a finish; but for this omission, he suggested, there would have been no Time of Troubles in Russia after Ivan's death. "And then Iosif Vissarionovich added humorously that 'Here God interfered with Ivan': *Grozny* liquidates one feudal family, one boyar line, and then for a whole year repents and prays forgiveness for the 'sin,' whereas what he should have done was to act still more decisively!"[4] Stalin not only took Ivan the Terrible as his political model; he conceived himself as the pupil who surpassed the master in the politics of the blood purge.

One further important point requires mention here. Ivan created an institution known as the *oprichnina,* which was an instrument for the repression of the boyars and a mainstay in his administration of the state. The prerevolutionary Russian historian Kliuchevsky describes the *oprichnina* as an all-powerful security police. It was organized as a kind of state within the state. The *oprichniki* wore black and rode black horses; their special insignia consisted of a dog's head and a broom attached to the saddle. In the folk memory of the Russian people, the *oprichnina* lingers as a symbol of black crimes and terror, as does its chief, Ivan the Terrible. Stalin modeled his NKVD quite consciously upon it. The Soviet security police, originally the terrorist weapon of the Bolshevik Party's dictatorship, became the weapon with which he broke the back of the ruling party. Its functions expanded as its importance rose during the 1930's, until finally, under Stalin's direct guidance, it became a kind of state within the state, an *oprichnina* of Stalinist Russia, inspiring terror, practicing torture, watching over everything and everybody, carrying on the kidnaping of selected Soviet citizens as a matter of official policy. In the later Stalin years, the idealizing of Ivan the Terrible was extended to include the idealizing of the *oprichnina*. Stalin inspired this, too. In the 1947 conversation in the Kremlin, "Iosif Vissarionovich noted also the progressive role of the *oprichnina*."[5]

If Stalin destroyed the Bolshevik Party as a political organism and ruling class, how, we may ask, did he take its place all by himself? What was the Stalin autocracy, considered as an institution? The basic political system has been described here as a complex, three-way, state-party-soviet structure of command and control of society. The autocracy, as Stalin reconstituted it, was a superstructure of command and control, superimposed upon this basic structure, making the Soviet system one single organization in the most literal sense of the word. Concerning the title and detailed operation of the organ of the autocracy, there is still some uncertainty. Some sources speak of a personal Stalin "secretariat." But according to one account that seems authentic, the organ was something enmeshed more closely with the actual machinery of rule.

It was the so-called "Special Sector" of the Central Committee apparatus, operated by and for Stalin along the lines of a personal secretariat. Through its own special representatives stationed at control positions, this organ operated the police system in accordance with Stalin's bidding. All his directives for trials and purges were funneled through it. All information was channeled into it. It had a foreign section through which Stalin conducted Soviet foreign policy, and so on. The superstructure controlled and commanded the control and command apparatus at all key points. It was, as it were, a little gear box through which the massive machinery of Soviet rule over nearly 900 million human beings on about one-third of the earth's surface was operated. By manipulating the levers in the control panel, Stalin could cause all kinds of things to happen. He could play politics as though playing a piano, touching a key here and striking a chord there, with results as diverse as a blast in *Pravda* against Churchill, a purge in the Ukraine, a plan for a new power station on the Volga, a propaganda campaign about germ werfare, a re-evaluation of Einstein, or a government change in Bulgaria.

Naturally, this supercontrol system was not an efficient instrument for governing a third of the earth. For various reasons, it failed to transmit upward much necessary information. Many needed decisions were not taken; many that were taken were not needed. The policy line—and there had to be a policy line on almost everything—remained completely rigid until, at length, a particular key was touched, whereupon the shift was radical and instantaneous, and often quite demoralizing to the officialdom that had to implement it. The rigidity forced policy into maladjustment with ever-changing reality, and the radical shifts often widened rather than narrowed the gap. So the system, plainly, was not efficient. But it satisfied Stalin's craving for total control and command, and that, essentially, is why he built it up and perfected it, and also why he clung to it with compulsive tenacity despite all evidence that it was inefficient, sluggish, contrary to Soviet state interests, harmful to international Communism, or anachronistic in an age of modern technology and swift events. It is not surprising that in his final years Stalin became a hidebound conservative in almost everything that had to do with the Soviet system: He wanted everything to stay just as it was—namely, under control.

One earlier incident testifies to the neurotic character of this need for total control. Khrushchev in the secret report notes Stalin's refusal, in 1941, to believe that Hitler intended to attack Russia—despite all warnings received—and also his great panic when the attack came. This behavior is explicable when we consider that the threat of attack, and later the attack itself, seemed to Stalin to jeopardize the entire control and command structure he had built up, which represented his life's work and his way of life: He needed it in the same way that an addict needs dope, and reacted to the threat of its downfall as the addict would react to a threat to the dope supply—with panic. He said at the time, according to Khrushchev, "All that which Lenin created we have lost forever." This, perhaps, was his way of saying: "All that *I* created is tottering, and I feel lost." Danger to Russia could not, as such, have caused these panic reactions in Stalin; but danger to his super-control system would. This helps to explain why nothing much could change in the Soviet Union until Stalin died, and also why various things immediately began to change when he did die. De-Stalinization did not start with Khrushchev's denunciation of Stalin in early 1956. The first and the essential act of de-Stalinization was the death of Stalin.

This analysis may have some bearing upon the much-discussed question of the relation between the Stalin autocracy and the Soviet order. It is often maintained that Stalin was a necessary product of the "system." One objection to this argument is that it tends to regard the Soviet system as a static being, born whole and intact out of the October Revolution. In reality, as the foregoing discussion indicates, there was a parallel and interactive evolution of the system and the autocracy. Thus, the Stalin phenomenon must be viewed as historical cause as well as historical effect. It is true that the pre-existing Party dictatorship provided a highly favorable political milieu for Stalin's drive to absolute power. The Russian national tradition of centralized bureaucratic rule and passive popular acceptance of it also helped to smooth the path for Stalin. However, these objective circumstances did not make the rise of the Stalin autocracy inevitable; at most they made it a possible or probable tendency.

What converted the tendency into a historical reality was not the nature of Russia or the nature of Bolshevism: It was the nature of Stalin. His personality was a factor of crucial importance in shaping the history of the Stalin period. Furthermore, once in existence, the autocracy became an autonomous historical force, reshaping its own political milieu, transforming the whole Soviet system into a mechanism for the projection of Stalin's power and personality. In this sense it may be said that the Stalinist political system was a product of Stalin. It is precisely the latter point that is overlooked, no doubt deliberately, by the Soviet view as voiced by Khrushchev in the secret report. That view treats the autocracy as a kind of regrettable excrescence on the otherwise healthy organism of the Soviet system, something that just grew and eventually caused all sorts of painful complications, now happily in the past. The elimination of the excrescence, it is held, restores the organism to its normal state of health. The official Soviet concept of de-Stalinization is founded on this tendency to minimize the meaning of Stalinization.

What general conclusion may be drawn concerning the historical inevitability of Russian Stalinism? Inevitability is a retrospective idea. That is to say, whatever happens in the world *becomes* inevitable in retrospect by virtue of the fact that it happened: Everything having been precisely as it was beforehand, the event in question resulted. Therefore, the meaningful question is not whether Stalinism was inevitable, for the fact that it "happened" makes it so in retrospect, but rather, What were the critical conditions of its inevitability? In particular, would the Leninist party dictatorship have been transformed into a Stalinist-type totalitarian autocracy, into something resembling Soviet fascism, if there had been no

Stalin; if, say, J. Djugashvili had died in infancy? The answer to which the foregoing discussion points, and which the pages to follow will bring out more clearly, is: perhaps, but not necessarily. For the pathological personality of Stalin was a critically important factor in the outcome. It could be argued, with this in mind, that if Stalin had never existed, some other equally and similarly pathological personality would have certainly been there to capitalize on conditions and shape events in like fashion. But this position is impossible to substantiate. How a Soviet Russia minus Stalin would have developed from the 1920's to the 1950's must remain, to some extent, an open question.

III

The period from the end of World War II, in 1945, to Stalin's death, in early 1953, forms the climax and concluding chapter in the development of Stalinism. It was the period of Stalin's greatest autocratic eminence in the affairs of Russia and of his personality's greatest impact upon the affairs of the external world. It might well be called the *Stalinshchina*—The Time of Stalin. The story of the currents and countercurrents of events inside Russia during those years is one of enormous inner complexity, which has not yet been fully and satisfactorily understood in the Western world.

One of the most important new developments of the postwar period was the externalizing of the Stalinization process. This had started with the Soviet occupation of the Baltic republics and eastern Poland in the period just prior to the war, but was interrupted by the Soviet-German hostilities. When the war ended, Stalin pushed ahead with an empire-building effort that carried Stalinization to most of Middle Europe and parts of Asia. Like the process inside Russia, Stalinization abroad proceeded through a series of consecutive stages. Now, however, the pattern having been laid down and the techniques learned and perfected, the agencies of Soviet power were able to compress the re-enactment into a very short span of years. The formation of the satellite empire meant the incorporation of the countries concerned into the Moscow command-and-control structure, their reduction to the status of Soviet "union republics" in all but name. Communist China, for various reasons, appears to have occupied a somewhat exceptional position in this picture, and Yugoslavia successfully rebelled against full-scale Stalinization. Otherwise, the process was carried through consistently and to the fullest possible extent.

In the countries that were to become satellites in the complete sense, Stalinization meant, first, the process of *Gleichschaltung*. This Nazi term connotes a forcible bringing into conformity. In the process of *Gleichschaltung,* the institutional structures of the satellites-to-be were brought into line, in all essentials, with the basic structure built up earlier in the U.S.S.R. This corresponded to the first phase of internal Soviet Stalinization. Secondly, Stalinization in the satellites meant the establishment of firm Soviet control over the native ruling groups and apparatus of power. In these external territories, the two phases of the process proceeded more or less simultaneously. One of the reasons for this is that some elements of the native Communist leaderships, instanced by Gomulka in Poland, were reluctant to cooperate in all aspects of the *Gleichschaltung*. For example, they were not eager to push through the full-scale and forcible collectivization of the peasantry. Hence the snuffing-out of any tendencies toward independence in the local Communist leaderships was a prerequisite for unrestricted imposition of the Soviet structure on all the satellite countries.

The Stalin-Tito conflict was, from Stalin's point of view, an unhappy incident in the general process of clamping down total control upon the Communist leaderships in all the satellite countries. Perhaps he even felt that it had its "constructive" political uses, since it afforded him a pretext for the savage repression of elements in those leaderships (Kostov, Rajk, etc.) that were suspect of independent tendencies, for the appointment of Marshal Rokossovsky as Russian viceroy in Warsaw, and so on. The trials and repressions of Communist leadership elements that Stalin engineered in the satellite countries from 1949 onward, culminating in the Slansky trial in Czechoslovakia in 1952, were the counterpart in external Stalinization of the extermination of Russian Bolshevism in the 1930's. The aim was to make political "dead souls" of the satellite ruling parties as had been done with the Bolshevik Party in Russia. Henceforth, they would exist as well-oiled transmission belts of the superstructure of command and control in the Kremlin.

From the internal Soviet point of view, the *Stalinshchina* meant, to begin with, "back to Stalinist normalcy." It is precisely for this reason that the year 1945 may be taken as the historical starting point of the internal political unrest that began to make itself evident on the surface of Russian life in the post-Stalin period, and especially in the latter part of 1956. For the reimposition of Stalinism-as-usual was precisely what the Russian people as a whole did not want and did not expect in 1945. Popular sentiment was epitomized in the remark of a Russian army officer in Moscow on VE-Day: "Now it is time to live."

The term "reimposition" does not refer to the institutional structure, for that did not alter during the war years. However, the atmosphere of life in Russia did alter. In the face of the ordeal of invasion and the dread possibility that the Russian people would not support the defense effort, the Stalin regime relaxed its police controls somewhat, and particularly police terror. Equally important, it took steps to encourage the belief among the people that the postwar period would be the beginning of a "new period" of growing internal abundance and freedom. For example, peasants were encouraged to hope that the kolkhoz system would be abolished, or at least drastically liberalized, after the war. Soviet intellectuals were allowed to look forward to what they called a "postwar breathing spell," meaning a relaxation of official controls on the country's intellectual and artistic life. There were rumors in wartime Moscow that, after the war, the United States and Great Britain, Russia's highly popular allies, would be permitted to open department stores in the Soviet capital, and so on.

These were some of the expectations of the Russians. *In effect, the people expected a beginning of de-Stalinization.* They expected to hear from Stalin at the war's end a speech similar to the one given by Malenkov in August, 1953, when he announced a new course in which Russian energies would be invested, at least in part, in raising the Russian standard of life. Instead, when Stalin addressed them over the Soviet radio on February 9, 1946, he gave a lecture on the timeless virtues of the 'Soviet method of industrialization," eulogized the collectivization of agriculture as its counterpart, sketched a vista of many further five-year plans oriented toward heavy industry, signalized a new period of international tension, and extolled the Stalinist order as "superior to any non-Soviet social order" and "a form of organization of society that is perfectly stable and capable of enduring."[6]

This was Stalin's credo of conservatism in all that concerned the Stalinist structure of command and control. The system was to remain intact; nothing was to change. Thus were the popular hopes for a measure of postwar de-Stalinization dashed to pieces. "We were deceived!" echoes down the postwar years in the statements of Russians who escaped. They had fought for a decent Russia. When it was all over, they received the *Stalinshchina.* Then and there, the prerequisites began to develop for an oppositional tendency in Soviet society.

However, this was not evident on the surface of events in the early postwar years. The popular attitude was not then notably rebellious; rebellion will appear only when desperation is ignited by a spark of hope. There was very little hope left in the people of Russia during the postwar years of Stalin's reign. What happened was that most people came to look upon the command-and-control structure as an alien environment, something that had to be lived in perforce, but which was not a real home. There were a great many manifestations of this attitude, which might be summed up as passive resistance to the conditions of Soviet existence, a failure of response. Examples were the shirking of work on the kolkhoz; low or declining labor productivity; juvenile delinquency in many forms; utter indifference to politics (*apolitichnost'*); total lack of interest in official ideas (*bezideinost'*); alcoholism as a way of life for very large numbers of Russian men; hack work in every profession; erosion of artistic creativity. Among elements in whom the need for inner integrity was still strong, especially among the youth, there was a rebirth of evangelical religion, carried on in underground forms, and there were tendencies toward oppositional political thought with an anarchistic tinge. For example, secret circles of university students in Moscow, Leningrad, and elsewhere disseminated among themselves the idea that Stalinism was a betrayal of socialism. In all save a few special fields of national life, such as military production and heavy industry, signs of regress appeared. The system flourished; the society entered into decline.

No amount of propaganda and indoctrination could counteract this decline. Propaganda cannot either create or abolish feelings; at most, it can influence or channel feelings that already exist. This is one explanation for the steady growth of official anti-Semitism in the U.S.S.R. after 1946. It was, in part, the regime's way of endeavoring to divert the popular resentment of a life lived in a maze of controls. But the very fact that this was done shows how ineffective the regular lines of indoctrination were proving. The secret police, which reinstituted an atmosphere of continual pervasive terror in the postwar years, could not correct this situation. The terror could do no more than hold popular attitudes in check, combat outward manifestations here and there, enforce a sense of hopelessness. As we now know, hard-bitten Soviet officials in high places saw this phenomenon of estrangement and failure of response, and the resulting damage; and they realized that it was in the regime's own interests to try by other means than terror and propaganda to counteract it. But who would explain all this to Stalin? Who would tell him that the Russian people, or large elements of it, were inwardly emigrating? No one, of course. For Stalin doted on the image of himself as the darling of the people and the international working class, as the beloved "Leader and Teacher" of a prosperous nation and progressive empire. To call in question the condition of the realm would be to call in question this glorious, idealized self-image of Stalin, and woe betide the Soviet official—be he high or low—who dared do this.

What happened, then, was that, by mobilization of submissive artists and intellectuals, a servile officialdom made reality *seem* to do Stalin's bidding. That is, it created for Stalin a fantasy-picture of Soviet reality, transforming it in *Pravda* and films and novels into a beautiful world of happy workers and peasants and ever-advancing progress and productivity, marred only by a few "alien elements" that occasionally penetrated and caused something to go wrong. This was no isolated Potemkin village; it was a Potemkin Russia, fabricated not out of wooden façades but out of words and pictures and symbols of all kinds—an image of a Russia that did not really exist but was *supposed* to exist. And because, in these circumstances, no real remedial measures could be taken— for the crisis and the need for reforms could not even be mentioned aloud—the discrepancy between the dream-reality fabricated for Stalin and the actual reality experienced by Russia grew greater and greater as the postwar years wore on.

In one area, agriculture, the practical consequences became so serious that the fearful subordinates took heart and brought up the question—very gingerly, no doubt—with Stalin. Here is what Khrushchev tells about the incident in his secret report: "All those who interested themselves even a little in the national situation saw the difficult situation in agriculture, but Stalin never even noticed it. Did we tell Stalin about this? Yes, we told him, but he did not support us. Why? Because Stalin never traveled anywhere. . . . He knew the country and agriculture only from films. And these films had dressed up and beautified the existing situation in agriculture. Many films so pictured kolkhoz life that the tables were bending from the weight of turkeys and geese. Evidently, Stalin thought that it was actually so." Thus was a picture created in which reality *appeared* to conform to the specifications set by Stalin's self-image. Needless to say, Khrushchev and his collagues cooperated in a multitude of ways in the maintenance of this official illusion.

IV

It is not hard to see why Stalin's death *had* to mean de-Stalinization. The Stalinist political order was a one-person system. The personality of Stalin was, by virtue of the intricate control mechanism described here, the focal force of Soviet politics, the sun around which the whole Soviet political universe revolved. Consequently, his death revolutionized the internal political situation in Moscow overnight.

There was no new Stalin-personality in the inner circle to take his place and operate the system as he had done. Stalin would not have tolerated such a personality close by for long; he would have seen in it an unendurable rival. He needed in his subordinates a combination of compliance and technical competence—that is, personality-types quite different from his own. He gathered around him skillful and sycophantic executors of his slightest wish, such as Molotov and Kaganovich; a fellow-Georgian expert in applying the screws of terror, such as Beria; an efficient managerial mind, such as Malenkov's; a respectful courtier, intelligent and totally dependable, such as Bulganin; a bulldozing ex-provincial boss who would drive the bureaucrats to action, such as Khrushchev; young technocrats, and a brace of old cronies. This was the entourage. "Not Stalin's heirs, but his heritage," Tito reportedly remarked of it on one occasion.

No one of its members had been built up even for the *appearance* of a true succession. The fact that Malenkov gave the main report at the Nineteenth Congress in 1952 did not constitute a real grooming for the succession; and the quick collapse of the effort to portray him as successor just after Stalin died is one indication of this. Stalin could not groom anybody even for an apparent succession because, no doubt, he could not brook the thought of being succeeded. Meanwhile, Soviet medical science was mobilized to solve the problem of rejuvenation. Stalin was encouraged to believe that a real solution was in the offing, and that he would be in the Kremlin for many more years. When death came, it left a vacuum of individual supreme rule that no one was in a position to fill.

It also left the majority of the subordinates in no mood to permit a continuation of the autocracy. The infinite oppressiveness and universal insecurity associated with Stalin's personal reign were in some ways most painfully felt at the very top, in the terrorized ex-Politburo. The stifling repression of new ideas and programs, of fresh thoughts on politics that might be practicable and serve Soviet state interests, was also painfully experienced. As Khrushchev put it in the secret report, Stalin "choked a person morally and physically. A situation was created where one could not express one's own will."

From this standpoint, Stalin's death was a great moment of liberation from the cramping confines of the autocracy as he had shaped and practiced it; and the thought would inevitably arise that the autocratic superstructure of control and command should be dismantled, and precautions taken to see that it could not easily be restored in future. The urge for personal security demanded it, and the urge of all concerned to participate actively in policy formation reinforced the demand. Finally, the crisis in Soviet affairs was evidently perceived with greater or lesser distinctness and depth by all concerned. They felt that the autocracy was largely responsible for the extreme acuteness and aggravation of the situation in the postwar years.

All this, then, contributed to the next step of de-Stalinization, which was revealed as early as March, 1953, when the Soviet press began to talk emphatically about the principle of "collective leadership" and the harmfulness of what it called "one-man decisions." The real political fact reflected in these verbalisms was, apparently, the determination at the top to bar a Stalin succession and to eliminate the autocracy as an institution. The phrase "collective leadership" involved the assertion, in the first place, of a *negative* principle: "There shall be no new Stalin." No one individual would be permitted to assume autocratic command and control of the Soviet system.

Elimination of the supercontrol system of the autocracy involved a rather intricate set of readjustments at the apex of the Soviet regime, especially as regards the status and functions of the security police. Stalin, as mentioned earlier, had transformed the police into his *oprichnina,* the special executive mechanism of the autocracy. It became an enormous organization practicing permanent and pervasive terror against the population and government hierarchy at the pleasure of the boss in the Kremlin. From the very outset, the regime of collective dictatorship set about clamping control upon this organization and placing certain restraints upon its arbitrary activities of terrorization.

This all began as early as April, 1953, when Beria was in charge of the unified interior ministry. Thus, de-Stalinization was associated from the start with the denunciation of police terror and with moves to bring the police under collective control. Khrushchev's denunciation of terror in the secret speech was only the culminating step in this campaign. It has been a question not of doing away with the Soviet secret police, but of reforming its official manners and administration. In other words, the police, according to the official concept of de-Stalinization, were no longer to be permitted to function as an *oprichnina,* as a state within the police state that Russia continues to be. It is interesting to note the reflection of this idea in post-Stalin historiography. An article in the Soviet historical journal in 1956 raises the question of Ivan the Terrible's *oprichnina.* It concludes that, together with the tyranny of Ivan which it served, it not only failed to play a "progressive role" (as Stalin affirmed in 1947) but "led Russia to the well-known events of the beginning of the seventeenth century."[7] That is, it led to the Time of Troubles. It is interesting to compare this view with Stalin's own, mentioned earlier.

We have seen that the early phase of Stalinization brought society under the total command and control of the state, and that a later phase brought the state under the total command and control of Stalin, curtailing Party rule in the process. De-Stalinization has been conceived mainly in terms of the repudiation and partial rectification of the second phase. This, as suggested earlier, exposes the dilemma at the heart of post-Stalin Soviet politics; for, in actuality, the two phases were consecutive steps in a single organic process of historical development. Consequently, the repudiation of the latter inescapably poses in the mind of the public the question of repudiating also the earlier phase and its consequences, such as the kolkhoz. But the Soviet regime has striven, and will no doubt continue to strive, to divide the indivisible, to separate phase two from phase one and hold on to the latter. In short, it will seek to preserve intact the underlying structure of command and control of Russian society, although not without significant readjustment.

The intention to separate the two phases of Stalinization shows through very clearly in the documents of the official de-Stalinization campaign, notably in Khrushchev's secret report and in the Party decree of June 30, 1956 (which was the version of the anti-Stalin line published for the Russian people). "It would be a gross error," states the decree, "to draw conclusions, from the existence of the cult of personality in the past, concerning some kind of changes in the social system of the U.S.S.R."[8] This was published after word of the secret report had circulated through the country and it had become evident that elements of the intelligentsia were showing just such a tendency to "draw conclusions" about the need for changes in the social system, i.e., for the undoing of the first as well as the second phase of Stalinization.

It should not be thought, however, that any change had taken place meanwhile in the official concept of de-Stalinization. Even in the secret report, with its savage attack on Stalin, a line is clearly drawn between the two phases. Khrushchev in effect condemns Stalin for the second phase, for the whole sequence of events beginning in 1934 that has been described here as the suppression of the Bolshevik Party and the restoration of Russian autocracy. His condemnation focuses almost entirely upon this, and upon Stalin's later arbitrary uses of the despotic power so gained. So far as the first phase is concerned, Khrushchev flatly states in the secret report: "Here Stalin played a positive role." The direct reference of this laudatory note in the great philippic is to Stalin's political battle against the oppositional trends in the Party in the late 1920's and early 1930's, especially the Bukharinist opposition, with its notions of "cotton-dress industrialization" and cooperation with the peasantry. But, indirectly, this is an endorsement of the policies Stalin advocated in those battles, and hence of the whole first phase of Stalinization.

So intent is Khrushchev on establishing the point that he refrains from even a mild criticism of Stalinist coercive methods in collectivization and industrialization, although at the same time he amply documents the sadistic brutality of the methods Stalin used in dealing with the Party. There is no word, for example, of the dreadful human toll exacted by the terroristic collectivization of the Russian peasantry. In effect, Khrushchev suggests that Stalinist methods, intolerable when employed to break the Bolshevik Party, were acceptable when employed to break the Russian peasantry. His double standard of moral evaluation of Stalin is governed by the determination to preserve and perpetuate the basic institutional order that evolved out of the first phase of Stalinization.

This same intent also governs a fresh falsification of Soviet history that began well before the official de-Stalinization campaign and is continued in it. Briefly, the Stalinist trademark is removed from a basic policy pattern of Stalinism. The first phase of Stalinization is not attributed primarily to Stalin—who merely "played a positive role"—but to Lenin and "the Party." As the decree of June 30, 1956, puts it, "Fulfilling the Leninist behests, the Communist Party set course toward the socialist industrialization of the country, the collectivization of agriculture, and the carrying out of the cultural revolution."[9]

The political logic of this version of Soviet history is transparent: If the institutional order that evolved out of the first phase of Stalinization is to be extolled and perpetuated while the absolute autocracy established in the second phase is condemned and dismantled, Stalin's role in the first phase must be retrospectively downgraded to that of a mere accessory of "the Party." The inspiration of the Stalinist full-scale totalitarianizing of Russian society must be attributed wholly to Lenin. The first phase must be "de-Stalinized" only in the special sense of detaching Stalin's name from it. Re-falsification of Soviet history intertwines with restoration of historical fact in the official de-Stalinization campaign.*

The post-Stalin regime has managed so far to enforce this rigid separation of phases in the process of de-Stalinization. But there are various signs—including the admonition to the public not to "draw conclusions" concerning changes in the system—that an unofficial concept of de-Stalinization more far-reaching in scope than the official one has been developing in Russia, especially since the Twentieth Party Congress. It does not operate under the same constraint of separating the two phases. It envisages changes in the control structure that the present regime would deny, such as the partial emancipation of artistic and literary work from official censorship and tutelage, freedom from the straitjacket of ideological conformity, the right of limited political dissent. It shades off at one extreme into a tendency not only to chafe at the limits of de-Stalinization, but also to question the Leninist legacy of dictatorship and one-party rule.

Although official de-Stalinization has in mind mainly the un-

---

* This process of refalsification was prepared in Soviet official documents published in late 1953 and early 1954, and was analyzed in some detail in the writer's study "The Metamorphosis of the Stalin Myth," *World Politics*, vii, No. 1 (October, 1954), pp. 38–62, and in a review article, "Party History—What It Is and Is Not," *American Slavic and East European Review*, xx, No. 2 (April, 1961), pp. 296–97.

raveling of the second phase of Stalinization, even this limited process has many complexities when it passes beyond the enunciation of the negative principle of "no new Stalin." To rehabilitate the reputation of a majority of a party's murdered leadership is not tantamount to the resurrection of those murdered. To bring back Old Bolsheviks and others from Siberian exile does not restore the Party as they once knew it. Nor is it easy to reinfuse a real *esprit de corps* in a demoralized political organism inured for decades to a regime of complete servility to the supreme dictator and his local agents. Hence the revival of Party rule in post-Stalin Russia has been a slow and partial process. The Presidium, reduced to its pre-1952 size immediately upon Stalin's death, became a "collective"—that is, a talking, freely debating, voting, fighting, and feuding—organ of government, with some apparent effort to introduce political order into its workings (although one problem, the Beria issue, was reportedly settled with a pistol at one of its meetings).

The Central Committee was brought back from post-1947 oblivion to become, at least in theory, the supreme arbiter of the Presidium's squabbles; it acted as such in the June, 1957, political leadership crisis and perhaps has done so on other occasions as well. In any event, it has been functioning as a periodically convened conference of the Soviet power elite for discussion of major policy issues. Although the published proceedings have been tame and stereotyped for the most part, there is reason to believe that the closed sessions held concurrently with the publicly reported ones have often been scenes of turbulent controversy. One example that has been reported in some detail by a Communist official who escaped to the West was the Central Committee's plenary session of July, 1955, when Khrushchev and Molotov clashed violently behind closed doors over fundamental issues of Soviet foreign policy and relations between the Soviet and other Communist-ruled states.[10]

Although de-Stalinization left the basic command and control structure intact, merely cutting off the superstructure of autocracy and making appropriate adjustments stemming from that, in practice the matter has not been so simple. For the basic structure itself is not simply a structure, but broadly includes its habitual mode of operation, its spirit, techniques, and conceptions of rule; and all this was formed over many years under the peculiar conditions of the superstructure's mode of operation and conceptions, down to and including Stalin's own nocturnal work schedule. Everything was geared to the requirements of total autocratic control of the situation throughout the Soviet world realm. Consequently, the elimination of the superstructure has posed many questions relating to reform of the workings of the basic structure and, especially on the economic side, to its partial reorganization. An important aspect of de-Stalinization on this plane has been decentralization, the diffusion of administrative authority, combined with the encouragement of discussion so long as it is thoroughly loyal, and the unbinding of bureaucratic initiative so long as it works in the interests of the regime. In the field of economic administration the reform movement has shown, at times, a tendency to take more account of objective conditions for rational operation of a modern industrialized and urbanized economy. In this connection, the underlying reorientation of concepts and methods of administration may be described as a transition from the direct and absolute centralized control that was so characteristic of Stalinism to indirect and manipulative forms of control. A good illustration of the latter would be the modified profit-incentive system of plant management suggested by the Kharkov economist Liberman in proposals published in September, 1962, for purposes of public discussion.

v

De-Stalinization has been viewed here as a process that was not only made possible but actually initiated by the death of Stalin and therewith the removal of the dictator-personality whose psychodynamics were integral to Stalinism as a political formation and system of rule. Beyond this, it has been described as a process of reform in the structure and workings of the Soviet system that was and is dictated by the interests of the post-Stalin regime as a whole. However, it must now be added that the dynamics of de-Stalinization have been, in significant measure, dynamics of internal political conflict in the Soviet Union and Communist world at large. The general interest of the ruling group cannot explain all aspects of Soviet de-Stalinization. Some aspects, including its peculiar tempo, cannot be explained without reference to the struggle over power and policy that has gone on continually in the post-Stalin period, even in periods of outward political calm, and still continues today. With regard to de-Stalinization as well as to most other aspects of policy, the Soviet political mind has been a divided one.

Here a general reflection or two on the place of conflict in Soviet political life may be appropriate. Probably the most important single failing of Soviet studies in the West has been a general tendency to take pretty much at face value the Communist pretension to a "monolithic" system of politics. In Communist theory or ideology, unity and harmony are the rule in the Party and conflict is the exception, something that regrettably occurs from time to time but remains an abnormality; and this has been an underlying assumption of much Western thinking about Soviet politics. The truth seems to be, however, that the unity and harmony in Soviet politics are largely a matter of external show and pretense, and that in Soviet politics as it is carried on *behind* the scenes they are the exception and conflict is the rule. Not monolithic unity but the fiction of it prevails in Soviet politics. The ruling party has rarely if ever been the disciplined phalanx pictured by its image-makers, and Lenin's well-known Resolution on Party Unity of 1921 has largely been honored in the breach. Lenin himself, who after all founded the Bolshevik Party as a venture in factional politics within the Russian revolutionary movement, helped set this precedent. Even under the terroristic regime of the later Stalin period, when the Party's machinery became a transmission belt of the autocracy and a kind of paralysis of political life ensued, a clandestine factional contest apparently still went on, with Stalin's own encouragement and instigation, and political debate took place.

In the new situation created by Stalin's death—with no clear line of succession marked out, with old animosities dividing the top leaders—the conflict for factional ascendancy not only continued but grew in force and intensity, and on several occasions has erupted onto the surface of Soviet public life in full view of a startled world. The first four post-Stalin months saw a Beria-Malenkov factional ascendancy, followed by Beria's fall and a kind of interregnum, during which Malenkov headed the Council of Ministers and Khrushchev, his chief rival, headed the Party apparatus as First Secretary. Early in 1955, Khrushchev managed to oust Malenkov and install his own confederate, Bulganin, as Premier, inaugurating the Khrushchev-Bulganin factional ascendancy. In the shifting pattern of back-stage factional politics in the ensuing period, there took shape in the Party Presidium an anti-Khrushchev majority faction that included Molotov, Malenkov, Kaganovich, Voroshilov, and Premier Bulganin himself, among others. Branded an "anti-Party group" following the defeat of its bid in June, 1957, to depose Khrushchev, this anti-Khrushchev faction might well have won victory had not Marshal Zhukov intervened on Khrushchev's side, apparently for reasons connected with personal hatred of the leading oppositionists owing to the prominent role most had played in the purge of the Red Army High Command in the late 1930's. He thereby sealed his own political doom, for neither Khrushchev nor the other Party politicians could be happy about a situation in which this war hero and professional military man had become unofficial high arbiter of their differences and disputes. They soon found a way of removing him from active political life.

By the end of 1957, Khrushchev had emerged as the supreme leader, the dominant figure of the post-Stalin Soviet regime. Many foreign students of Soviet affairs then concluded that the Stalin succession crisis had been resolved and that Khrushchev, like Stalin before him, was now the "unchallenged" leader of Soviet Russia. But this conclusion was erroneous. Khrushchev did not, in the full sense, become Stalin's successor. He did not, that is, become an autocrat standing above the need to persuade the politically influential elements in the Soviet Union of the rightness of his own policy ideas. One of the great political operators of our age, Khrushchev had to fight for his success in the face of formidable political pressures from within the regime and oppositional currents that made themselves felt not only in the international Communist movement but also within the Soviet Communist Party itself. He did not elevate himself above the political battle that waxes and wanes behind the scenes of the Soviet "monolith." Khrushchev has been a challengeable leader. His overthrow in 1964 was not the first indication of this fact; it was only the final confirmation.

Of course, his dual primacy as First Secretary of the Party Central Committee and Chairman of the Council of Ministers (a post in which he replaced Bulganin in early 1958) carried great political weight, partly because of the resultant scope for maneuver and the ability, within limits, to manipulate the massive Soviet publicity apparatus to his own advantage. But in dealing with Soviet government and politics, we must carefully distinguish between "power" and "powers." The Soviet Premiership or First Secretaryship is not the American Presidency. The actual power of a man who holds those two high posts cannot, that is, be inferred completely from the constitutional nature of the posts themselves. It rests on arrangements and factors that are in many ways informal and largely invisible—at least to us. It is a variable that may rise and fall in dependence upon obscure, shifting alignments and combinations in the high-level factional competition regularly going on in the inner world of Soviet politics.

One of the principal issues around which the factional politics has swirled ever since Stalin's death is de-Stalinization—its desirability, forms, limits, and tempo. And the curious wavelike course of de-Stalinization, a course marked by convulsive starts and stops and restarts, reflects also the fact that the regime has been inwardly divided over these questions. Such differences have aggravated the contest for factional ascendancy, and in turn have been aggravated by it. For the question of de-Stalinization arose not simply in the form of "Shall we de-Stalinize, and how far?" It arose also in the form of *"Who* shall de-Stalinize?" and "Under the auspices of which group shall the process be carried out?" The enormous importance of the latter issue derives from the fact that de-Stalinizing moves, including such significant symbolic moves as the public criticism of Stalin, were bound to be popular among various elements of the Soviet people, and political credit would redound especially to the leader or the group that the public mind associated with the idea and program of de-Stalinization. This has at times had an accelerating and at others a retarding effect upon the process, and may thus help to explain its wavelike course.

For a faction already in the ascendancy but not securely so, as the Beria-Malenkov faction was just after Stalin's death, one promising way to consolidate its ascendancy was to take the lead in de-Stalinization, particularly in such aspects of it as the curbing of the secret police, the amnesties, the banishment of terror, and the denunciation of the widely hated Stalin. And here the factional interest might conflict with the underlying conservative bent of the regime as a whole, by dictating an unsettlingly swift policy tempo. However, if it was in the factional interest of the temporarily dominant element to associate itself with the policy of de-Stalinization, it was *ipso facto* in the interest of the rival faction to *oppose* this policy for the time being, until its opponents were dislodged from places of authority, perhaps forming a bloc with extremely conservative elements of the regime in the process. This peculiar situation helps to explain the pattern of post-Stalin Soviet politics, in particular the starts and stops in de-Stalinization.

The first wave of de-Stalinization began almost on the day of Stalin's funeral, sooner than the regime's general power position necessitated or its over-all interests dictated. It did in fact start on that day, for it was in his funeral oration that Beria cryptically announced the forthcoming series of moves having to do with the curbing of police terror. This first wave was presided over by Beria, the head policeman, who exonerated the accused Kremlin doctors, denounced their subjection to torture, sponsored the first amnesty, espoused the idea of cultural autonomy for non-Russian nationalities of the country, reportedly started to get in touch with Tito, made overtures to the West, and so on. Abroad, this haste toward reform was widely misconstrued as a sign of the regime's weakness. Actually, it reflected the weakness of the momentarily dominant Beria-Malenkov *faction* and its desperate desire to consolidate itself in popularity and power by spearheading de-Stalinization. Later, the June, 1953, uprising in East Germany gave a coalition of opponents its chance to move against Beria, and his fall brought to an end the first wave of accelerated de-Stalinization. During the ensuing interregnum, Khrushchev and his supporters, guided by their factional interests, pursued a fairly conservative course with regard to de-Stalinization. They were concerned, first, to prevent too much political credit from accruing to Malenkov, who had proclaimed a new, consumer-oriented economic course in August, 1953; and, second, to ensure that a highly conservative or pro-Stalinist group in the Party Presidium, centering around Molotov, Kaganovich, and Voroshilov, would support them in the eventual ouster of Malenkov from his post of head of the Soviet Government.

But hardly was this accomplished in early 1955 than Khrushchev, no longer inhibited by such political considerations, turned against the conservative line and took the lead in a new wave of accelerated de-Stalinization. This second wave gathered momentum during 1955 with such actions as the attempted reconciliation with Tito and came to a peak in the following year with the Twentieth Party Congress and its aftermath. In addition to formalizing some new departures of the post-Stalin period in both internal and external policy, this Congress marked, in its public criticism of the "cult of personality" and its historic secret session on Stalin, an effort to burn the political bridges to the Stalinist past. It might in fact be described as a congress of de-Stalinization. The ruling group was not, however, unanimously agreed that it should be such. It was deeply divided over the issue, rent with an inner conflict that raged during the congress itself and continued afterwards. This, at any rate, is the testimony of Khrushchev, who asserted in his closing address to the Twenty-second Party Congress in October, 1961, that the record of Stalin's actions had been laid before the earlier gathering in the face of the most strenuous opposition of the Molotov group in the Party Presidium and even then only after he, Khrushchev, had threatened to take the issue to the floor of the congress over the opposition's objections. He then went on: "But the factionalists did not cease their struggle even after the congress; they did everything they could to hamper an investigation of abuses of power, afraid that their role as accomplices in mass repressions would be revealed."[11]

The latter statement, along with much other material of the Twenty-second Congress, both confirms that the Soviet leadership has at times been deeply divided over de-Stalinization and reinforces the belief expressed above that a policy of accelerated de-Stalinization has been used as a weapon in the factional struggle for power. In addition to the motive of direct self-identification with a potentially popular cause, there has been operative, it seems, in Khrushchev's politics of de-Stalinization the motive of tarring his opponents with their complicity in Stalin's misdeeds, thereby discrediting them politically. The Twenty-second Congress itself provides the most dramatic evidence on this count. There Khrushchev and his closest confederates opened a new campaign of vilification against the leaders of the erstwhile anti-Khrushchev oppositional group, Molotov in particular. Whether their main concern was to attack unnamed new oppositional elements through Molotov or to eliminate him once and for all as a potential rallying point for an anti-Khrushchev movement in the Party, the Khrushchev faction evidently felt an imperative need to blacken Molotov's name forever in the annals of Communism and, if possible, to read him out of the Party altogether. To this end they depicted him as a mean and heartless man, a low, scheming, political intriguer, a virtual warmonger opposed to the policy of coexistence, a bumbling bureaucrat who indeed "worked with Lenin," as he liked to boast, but so badly that Lenin was appalled, and, finally, as a principal accomplice of Stalin's in many of the latter's most heinous actions during the great purge. The latter line of argument involved them, of necessity, in a resumption of the anti-Stalin campaign of the Twentieth Party Congress, with the difference that this time the recounting of Stalin's crimes was performed not in secret session but in public, culminating in the amazing final episode in which the resolution on the removal of Stalin's remains from the mausoleum was adopted.

Khrushchev and the men of his faction were thus led by the logic of the internal political struggle to inform the populace publicly and in some detail that it had been ruled for many years by a murderous psychopath and that some of the highest officers of his government, including former Premier Molotov, had been his knowing helpers in terrible misdeeds. The Twenty-second Congress became in this way a second congress of de-Stalinization and the starting point for yet another wave in the process. The outcome is uncertain, but one thing can be said with confidence: The dynamics of Soviet de-Stalinization cannot be fully explained without reference to the processes of political conflict that have gone on and are still going on, however obscurely, behind the scenes of Soviet politics.

PART FOUR

Stalinism and After: Foreign Affairs

9 RULING PERSONALITIES IN RUSSIAN FOREIGN POLICY

The ruling personality has been one of the important factors in Russian foreign policy, both before and after the Bolshevik Revolution of 1917. It has also been a somewhat neglected factor. For various reasons, including the modern fashion of explaining history by reference to impersonal social or economic forces and tendencies, the part that governing individuals have personally played in the determination of Russia's foreign policy and the conduct of its foreign relations has been insufficiently appreciated.

On occasion, the omission of the autocratic personality from the picture of Russian foreign policy has been predicated on a positive theory according to which some particular group or class has determined Russia's policy. A notable representative of this school is Friedrich Engels. In his article of 1890 on "The Foreign Policy of Russian Tsarism," Engels argued that Russia's policy had been guided for centuries toward world domination by a "gang of adventurers," mostly of foreign extraction: "The Russian diplomatic corps forms, so to speak, a modern Jesuit order, powerful enough in case of necessity to overcome even the whims of the Tsar and to become master of the corruption within Russia, in order to disseminate it abroad the more plentifully; a Jesuit order recruited originally and preferably from foreigners . . ."[1] This might be described as the cabalistic theory of Russian foreign policy.

The testimony of historical fact does not speak in favor of this theory. In actuality, the foreign policy of Russian Czarism was very much a foreign policy of the reigning Russian Czar. This was so from the rise of the Russian autocracy in sixteenth-century Mus-

covy to its fall in 1917, which was due in part to the blundering
diplomacy of an autocrat who was reluctant to permit his own
Council of Ministers to *discuss* Russian foreign policy, much less
decide it.* Even after the constitutional reforms of the early years
of the twentieth century, the fundamental laws of 1906 proclaimed
(Article 12) that "The emperor is the supreme director of the external relations of the Russian state with foreign powers; he also
sets the course of the international policy of the Russian state." In
this instance, the official rule accurately reflected the realities of
political practice.

To appreciate the influence of the personal factor in Russian foreign policy, it is essential to realize that the Czarist system of government was an absolute autocracy in the fullest sense of the word.
The historical background of this autocratic system was the Mon-
golian occupation of Russian lands in the thirteenth century. Later,
the grand princes of Muscovy took the lead in overthrowing the
alien yoke, but at the same time modeled their kingdom in many
ways upon the realm of the Golden Horde. Czarism arose as a Russian adaptation of Oriental despotism with an ideology drawn
largely from Byzantine sources. The subsequent Europeanization
of Russia altered the form and façade of the governmental system,
but the institution of absolute autocracy was preserved intact. Thus
Peter the Great shaped the Russian nobility, which his predecessors
had already reduced to dependency upon the autocratic power, into
a bureaucratic governing class of servants of the state.

The high tide of Russian autocracy was the thirty-year reign of
Nicholas I in the nineteenth century, during which the Czar's own
secretariat ("Personal Chancellery of His Imperial Majesty") was
the hub of the governmental system. The role of the autocrat in the

---

* G. H. Bolsover, "Aspects of Russian Foreign Policy, 1815–1914," in
R. Pares and A. J. P. Taylor, eds., *Essays Presented tô Sir Lewis Namier*
(New York: St. Martin's Press, 1956), p. 328. Speaking of Nicholas II's
reluctance to let the Council of Ministers discuss foreign affairs, Bolsover
adds: "Constitutionally the council was entitled to discuss them whenever
the Czar commanded it or the foreign minister considered it necessary or
they affected other ministries. But Nicholas II still thought of them as
essentially his own concern, to be treated between himself and the foreign
minister with the minimum of interference from the council of ministers
and its chairman." I am much indebted to Bolsover's excellent summary
of the main facts on the role of the autocrat in Russian foreign policy of
the nineteenth century.

system was described by a well-informed Russian at mid-century as follows:

> It is known that the sovereign in Russia is autocratic, but it seems to me to be insufficiently realized that he is *autocratic* in the full sense of this word. . . . Not a single one of the more or less orderly forms of rule commonly called unlimited is or ever has been so autocratic as the Russian form of government, wholly concentrated in the person of the emperor. In all countries ruled by an unlimited power there has always been and is some class, estate, some traditional institutions, which in certain instances compel the sovereign to act in a certain way and set limits to his caprice; nothing of the sort exists in Russia.[2]

In such a system of complete one-person rule, the policy of the state in internal and external affairs was literally the policy of the one person, subject only to those influences to which he might prove susceptible. Moreover, the personality of the Czar could and did set limits to the range of information his advisers dared give him. We learn, for example, from the source just quoted that one of the functions of the Russian Ministry of Foreign Affairs was to extract material from foreign journals for the information of the emperor: "And yet the editors of these extracts put them together sometimes in such a way that the abridged version no longer resembles at all the original articles, and this is done because the latter might not please the autocrat."[3]

Naturally, the personal factor in Russian foreign policy and diplomacy was most consequential in the reigns of such strong, energetic, and willful autocrats as Ivan the Terrible, Peter the Great, Catherine the Great (of whom a foreign diplomat in Petersburg remarked that the whole of the Russian government could be located between her brow and the back of her head), and Nicholas I. Some not only determined Russia's foreign policy but acted as their own foreign minister and first diplomat. The role of Ivan the Terrible, for example, has been described as follows:

> He felt entirely in his element in international affairs, and in it felt superior to all his rivals. No wonder he was so fond of personally entering into diplomatic negotiations, of giving foreign ambassadors extremely lengthy audiences, of overwhelming them with scholarly references, entering into dispute with them and putting to them difficult or unexpected questions. . . . As regards the direct conduct of foreign policy, even to the extent of coming out as an orator and controversialist, Ivan IV was unique among the rulers of his time.[4]

But the diplomacy of such a Czar-diplomat as Ivan reflected the compulsions of his "turbulent, imperious nature," which often inspired him to "by no means diplomatic and sometimes tactless sallies against second-class rulers, or those enjoying only limited power." And further: "Ivan Grozny's arrogance began to be reflected in official notes addressed to foreign powers as soon as he began to direct foreign policy himself."[5]

Peter the Great was another dynamic Russian autocrat whose foreign policy was in every sense his own and who supervised even the details of its execution. Although this policy was oriented primarily toward Europe, he found time amidst his incessant foreign wars to draw up detailed plans for geographical expeditions designed to extend and consolidate Russia's position in the Far East. And the historian Florinsky finds in the autocratic personality of Peter himself the chief explanation of the wars that filled his long reign:

> The incredibly costly wars of Peter are often represented as the more or less inevitable and in the end beneficial stages of the inexorable historical process which eventually led to the creation of a unified empire with outlets on the Baltic and on the Black Seas. . . . A closer examination of the facts . . . leads to the highly unsatisfactory conclusion that the wars which filled the reign of Peter were largely of his own making, that they were embarked upon without any realization of what they actually meant, and without any definite and clear object in view.[6]

Peter's death inaugurated a lengthy period of political instability after which the tradition of a strong autocratic regime was revived by Catherine the Great, who conducted her own foreign policy. And it was the personal factor that brought changes afterward. Under her son and successor, Paul, "Foreign policy was conducted with a cavalier disregard for what, in the reign of Catherine II, had been considered Russia's vital interests, and diplomacy was subordinated to the romantic infatuations and caprices of the Emperor (as, for instance, his championship of the Order of Malta)."[7]

The autocratic tradition in foreign policy was upheld by all five Czars who ruled Russia in the nineteenth century and the early part of the twentieth. Not only Nicholas I, of whom special mention has been made here, but his predecessor Alexander I and his three successors on the throne—Alexander II, Alexander III, and Nicholas II—directed Russia's foreign relations as autocrats. They varied considerably, however, in character and ability, and likewise in the degree of their interest in foreign policy and the manner of participating in it. Both Alexander I, who had notable diplomatic ability, and Nicholas I, who as already indicated fully deserved his reputation as the "Iron Czar," personally dominated Russian foreign policy to an extent not matched by their successors. Alexander II is said to have shown strong interest in this field of activity and also the capacity to take a coherent over-all view of it, something that Alexander III, on the other hand, was intellectually too limited to do. The latter, moreover, was a retiring man not much given to direct dealings with foreign statesmen and ambassadors. Nicholas II was more active in this way, but "in matters of state he was sadly lacking in comprehension and will-power, and in foreign affairs he merely fumbled and blundered through problems of growing complexity and importance which he mistakenly imagined that he understood and could cope with."[8]

Although the decision-making authority in foreign policy was thus wholly concentrated in the hands of the Czar, it was not always possible under conditions of Imperial Russia to maintain centralized control in this sphere. Agents of the Czar in far-off places occasionally found themselves in a position to take important decisions independently of St. Petersburg, and there was considerably more delegation of authority to negotiators than was to be the case in Soviet Russia. One of the best known instances of independent action by an agent of the Czar was the incident in 1850 when a young Russian naval officer, Nevelskoi, went beyond his official orders and led an expedition up the Amur to begin on his own the occupation of territory that was nominally Chinese. Nicholas I was persuaded to pardon him, however, and on that occasion made the famous remark: "Where the Russian flag has once been hoisted it must not be lowered." Again, in 1854, Nicholas delegated to Muraviev, the Governor-General of Eastern Siberia, the right of conducting all diplomatic negotiations in the Far East on his own and independently of the Russian Foreign Ministry.[9] Here it should be recalled that this happened during the Crimean War, when communications by sea were difficult between St. Petersburg and the Russian Far East.

But the relative independence occasionally enjoyed by such distant agents of the Czar as Nevelskoi and Muraviev was not possessed by the Czar's foreign minister. He was typically an executor of the wishes of the sovereign rather than a genuine maker of foreign policy. His activities were more concerned with the execution of policy than with its formulation. Thus Lamsdorff, who served as foreign minister for a time under Nicholas II, was described by the French Ambassador at Petersburg as "a minister of foreign affairs *à la russe*, which is to say that he does not have charge of the foreign policy but only of the diplomacy of Russia, with the mission of adapting the latter to the former."[10]

This foreign diplomat's observation is amply reinforced by the testimony of Russian foreign ministers themselves. The relation between Nicholas I and Foreign Minister Nesselrode has been described by a Russian historian as follows: "He studiously examined the reports of Nesselrode and learned from him, but in essence conducted his own policy; Nesselrode was not particularly exaggerating when he called himself 'a humble instrument of his designs and organ of his political calculations.' "[11] In later years, Gorchakov gave a similar account of his own position as foreign minister under Alexander II: "In Russia there are only two people who know the policy of the Russian cabinet: the emperor who makes it and myself who prepares and executes it." And according to Bismarck, this Russian foreign minister used to compare himself "to a sponge that is caused by pressure from the emperor's hand to emit the liquid with which it is filled."[12]

It would not be accurate, however, to infer that Russian foreign ministers had no influence upon foreign policy. In so far as the Czar was prepared to turn to his foreign minister for information and advice, the latter could and often did play an influential role without being a powerful figure. Moreover, efforts by foreign ministers to exert a moderating influence upon the imperial makers of Russian foreign policy were rather common in the nineteenth century. The outstanding instance of success in such efforts occurred in the reign of Alexander III, whose foreign minister, Giers, is credited by historians with dissuading the "Czar peacemaker" from taking actions that might have precipitated a general European war. On the other hand, Nesselrode's moderating influence was not sufficiently effective to prevent the imperious and passionate Nicholas I from pursuing on his own a line of diplomacy that helped to precipitate the Crimean War. Speaking of Nicholas' individual role in the diplomatic prelude to this war, Florinsky remarks: "The personal element, so contemptuously dismissed as trivial by the believers in economic determinism, played probably a decisive part in shaping the course of events."[13] The same might perhaps be said, *mutatis mutandis,* of Nicholas II and the outbreak of the Russo-Japanese War. In the confused prelude to this conflict, Nicholas circumvented his own Ministry of Foreign Affairs and War Ministry and acted at the prompting of a group of political adventurers whom the Russian War Minister described as a "black cabinet."

This episode illustrates the pattern of unofficial government that existed in Czarist Russia. The formal institutions of state authority had no real power in the autocratic system; the Czar was under no obligation to act through them or even to consult with them. Thus, the Committee of Ministers (later Council of Ministers) was not a cabinet in the ordinary sense, but merely a coordinating conference of ministers who were wholly responsible to and dependent on the Czar himself and dealt with him directly and separately on matters within their domains—when he chose to permit them to do so. The Czar in these circumstances could and sometimes did turn elsewhere for information and advice. A well-informed Russian pictured the situation early in the present century as follows: "In Russia there are really two Governments: one official, consisting of the cabinet; the other non-official, consisting of the Court *camarilla.* This *camarilla* holds all the threads of foreign as well as home politics."[14] This practice of unofficial or "backstairs" government under the autocracy is perhaps what underlies, and in any event confers a certain plausibility upon, the cabalistic theory of Russian foreign policy. But the historical evidence indicates that the crucial figure in Russian foreign policy under the old regime was the Czar himself.

II

The Bolshevik regime was in many ways a novel phenomenon in Russia. It was not originally a dictatorship of one person like the Czarist autocracy, but a dictatorship of one party—something quite new in a country that had never known party rule of any kind and had little experience with political parties. With it came not only new patterns of Russian foreign policy, but also new ways of deciding foreign-policy problems and conducting the country's foreign relations. In particular, the autocratic tradition in Russian foreign policy was interrupted for a period after 1917.

Lenin was of course the supreme leader and dominating figure, and his personal role in decisions concerning foreign policy and the conduct of external relations was correspondingly great. His decision-making power was not a function of the state office that he held as chairman of the Council of People's Commissars (Sovnarkom), but of the enormous authority he enjoyed within the ruling party, which he himself had organized and led on its revolutionary career to power. This authority rested not only upon his demonstrated capacity for outstanding revolutionary leadership and resulting prestige, but also upon his remarkable persuasiveness within the circle of men controlling Russia. His ultimate sanction for enforcing political decisions upon the Party was the threat to resign.

This indicates the nature of the break with the autocratic tradition. Autocracy in the historic Russian sense meant the authority of the supreme leader both to determine state policy and decree the course of political action and the composition of the regime individually, independently, and arbitrarily, with or without consulting and heeding the views of others no matter how high their office. Putting it otherwise, Russian autocracy—and autocracy in general—might be characterized as a mode of government under which the supreme leader has no need and does not make it a regular practice to *persuade*. It differs from oligarchy in that the latter is a mode of government in which persuasion is a vital function within the governing authority. An oligarchical system is one in which the supreme leader (if there is one) must, or at any rate regularly and reliably does, decide questions of high policy in company with a group of the politically powerful whose consent to his views is won by means of persuasion. If wide circles of the population outside the regime also have to be persuaded, then the mode of government may be called democratic.

On these criteria, the Leninist system was basically oligarchical rather than autocratic. Soviet politics in the Lenin period were, in their way, a continuing drama of persuasion of the ruling minority by its own acknowledged supreme leader. In the field of foreign policy, the Central Committee's debates on the negotiations with the Germans at Brest-Litovsk and on the signing of the Brest-Litovsk peace treaty provide the best illustration. In February, 1918, Lenin's motion in the Central Committee on acceptance of the Germans' terms was passed by a plurality of seven votes to four, with four abstentions, after a scene that Louis Fischer has described as follows:

The Central Committee of the Communist Party met that day. . . . Lenin arose first. He demanded the acceptance of the terms. . . .

Otherwise he would resign from the Government, and from the Central Committee. This was his ultimatum. He would not withdraw it.[15]

One who abstained, Felix Dzerzhinsky, expressed his regret that the Party was not sufficiently strong to risk the resignation of Lenin.

The decision-making process was concentrated during the first period (1917–19) within the Central Committee, which then had a membership of only about twenty-five. Sovnarkom dealt with the practical implementation of policies decided upon by the high party organ. Trotsky spoke of this relationship in a speech to the Second Congress of the Comintern:

> Today we have received from the Polish Government proposals for the conclusion of peace. Who decides this question? We have Sovnarkom, but it must be subject to a certain control. What control? The control of the working class as a formless chaotic mass? No. The Central Committee of the party has been called together to discuss the proposal and decide whether to answer it.[16]

By the time this statement was made, however, the still smaller Politburo of the Central Committee (consisting of Bukharin, Dzerzhinsky, Kamenev, Rykov, Stalin, Tomsky, Trotsky, and Zinoviev, in addition to Lenin) had become the focal point of the decision-making process, and the Central Committee itself was well on its way to becoming a sort of "superior Party conference" as Lenin later characterized it—a body meeting every two months or so to discuss and ratify decisions taken by the Politburo.[17] Thus Lenin reported to the Ninth Party Congress in 1920 that the Politburo had decided all questions of foreign and domestic policy during the past year.

It became the established practice, then, for the Politburo to formulate the policy line of the Soviet Union in foreign affairs; and its role as a collective decision-maker and policy-planning staff was accentuated in the last year or two of Lenin's life, when illness greatly restricted his scope of activity. The Politburo's directives were transmitted for implementation to Foreign Commissar Chicherin, who at that time was not even a member of the Central Committee. In 1923, Lenin recommended this "flexible amalgamation" of the policy-making Party Politburo with the policy-executing Commissariat of Foreign Affairs (Narkomindel) as a model of Party-Government relations that might be profitably emulated elsewhere in the Soviet system of government:

Do we not all see that such an amalgamation has been very bene-
ficial in the case of the People's Commissariat for Foreign Affairs,
where it was brought about at the very beginning? Have not we on
the Political Bureau discussed from the Party point of view many
questions, both minor and important, concerning the "moves" we
should make in reply to the "moves" of foreign powers in order to
forestall their, say, cunning, if we are not to use a less respectable
term?[18]

Within the Politburo, however, Lenin was undoubtedly the
principal deviser of "moves" until his health failed. If Russian
autocratic tradition was broken in the sense that persuasion by the
supreme leader became a vital part of the policy-making process,
Lenin nevertheless left an indelible personal imprint upon the
formative period of Soviet foreign policy and diplomacy. He exercised dynamic personal leadership both in the formulation and
execution of policy. It was not without reason that Chicherin, in
a memorial article on "Lenin and Foreign Policy," written just
after the leader's death, spoke of "his foreign policy."[19]

It was Lenin's own policy, first of all, in that he was primarily
responsible for the theoretical conceptions underlying it. Although
he was much influenced by the thinking of such close revolutionary
associates as Bukharin and Trotsky, Lenin was the one who worked
out for the first time a more or less comprehensive "Marxist" theory
of contemporary international relations, especially with his wartime treatise on *Imperialism: The Highest Stage of Capitalism*.
Basic Soviet strategy in world affairs, under which Comintern and
Narkomindel operated as two arms of a "dual policy," the one
working to overthrow capitalist governments while the other tried
to do business with them, was essentially Lenin's creation. So,
finally, was the concept of a Soviet diplomacy that would lessen the
insecurity of the revolutionary state by aggravating the "contradictions" between its enemies so as to prevent the formation of a
fatal anti-Soviet coalition.

Lenin's personal leadership was also manifested in various practical aspects of foreign policy. Here his fertility of political imagination, his tactical skill and ingenuity, and his concern for detail
found ample scope of expression, and one is tempted to draw a
parallel with Peter the Great, the only Russian autocrat for whom
Lenin ever had a favorable word. Lenin devoted a great deal of
time and energy to the work of organizing the Soviet diplomatic
service, a task in which Trotsky, during his brief tenure as foreign

commissar, had shown little interest.[20] He was largely responsible for the peculiar propagandistic style and tone that Soviet foreign policy showed from the beginning in such acts as the peace decree and the denunciation and publication of the secret treaties of the Czarist regime. Moreover, he exercised close personal supervision of the practical conduct of foreign relations by Narkomindel so long as his health permitted, and likewise furnished guidance regularly to those in charge of Comintern affairs. As Zinoviev later recalled in his speech to the Thirteenth Party Congress, "The procedure followed was that we Comintern workers mapped out the line ourselves and conferred personally with Comrade Lenin. That was sufficient, and the whole Central Committee knew that things must be in good shape."[21]

That Lenin was in a very real sense his own foreign minister is well attested to by Chicherin's memorial article of 1924, which gives the following account of the relations between the two men in the conduct of Soviet foreign relations:

> In the first years of the existence of our republic, I spoke with him by telephone several times a day, often at length, and had frequent personal interviews with him. Often I discussed with him all the details of current diplomatic affairs of any importance. Instantly grasping the substance of each issue and giving it the broadest political interpretation, Vladimir Ilich always provided in his conversations the most brilliant analysis of the diplomatic situation, and his counsels (often he straightway suggested the text of a reply to a foreign government) were models of diplomatic art and flexibility.[22]

According to Chicherin, Lenin supervised the details of the negotiations with Estonia in 1919, and with Finland in 1920. He likewise directed (by telephone) the peace talks with Poland at Riga, in which the Soviet negotiators followed his "remarkable idea" of offering Poland more territory than Clemenceau and Curzon had done. He originated the appeal to economic interest as a basic instrument of Soviet diplomacy vis-à-vis the major European powers. He directed the development of this diplomacy, including the preparations for the Genoa Conference (his critical comment on a draft of Chicherin's opening speech was: "Never mind the hard language"). Finally, Chicherin stresses Lenin's personal role in guiding the Eastern policy of Soviet Russia toward *rapprochement* with such countries as Afghanistan, Persia, and Turkey. Their last conversation, held in 1922, dealt with the problem of the Turkish

Straits in connection with Soviet preparations for the Lausanne Conference. This, it appears, was Lenin's final intervention in the conduct of Soviet foreign relations.[23]

III

Lenin and Stalin are comparable figures in that each dominated a period of Russia's history. Yet they differed greatly in motive and manner of rule, and in the way in which their personalities impressed themselves upon the shape of historical events. The difference in mode of rule was qualitative: Lenin's power rested upon his authority *in* the Party, whereas Stalin's authority rested upon his power *over* the Party. This power was acquired in the political revolution from above described in earlier chapters.

In the transition from Lenin's era to Stalin's, the method of formulating policy, both internal and external, underwent a change comparable to that which had taken place in the earlier revolutionary transition from the Czarist period. This was in the strictest sense a reactionary change, a reversion to the ways of Russian Czarism. Moreover, as has been shown earlier, Stalin consciously conceived it as such; his model was Ivan the Terrible, and his destruction of the leadership of the Bolshevik Party was patterned upon Ivan's death struggle against the boyar aristocracy in the sixteenth century. As a consequence of his victory over the Party, the previous oligarchical pattern of Soviet politics gave way to a system of one-man command, an autocracy in the sense in which this term has been defined above. Stalin, that is, emancipated himself from the practice of persuasion and from the need to persuade in order to secure adoption of his ideas about policy. After the Great Purge, according to testimony by Khrushchev, "Stalin thought that now he could decide all things alone and all he needed were statisticians; he treated all others in such a way that they could only listen to and praise him."[24]

The revival of Russian autocracy under Stalin brought with it the decline of the Politburo as a decision-making body. By the early 1930's, it had become a mere high-level advisory panel for the Boss. The following description by a former Soviet diplomat is based upon a firsthand acquaintance with its workings at that time:

> A thin appearance of collective work is still kept up at Politburo meetings. Stalin does not "command," he merely "suggests" or "proposes." The fiction of voting is retained. But the vote never fails

to uphold his "suggestions." The decision is signed by all ten members of the Politburo, with Stalin's signature among the rest. Yet everyone knows that there is only one boss. The phrases used, the forms of address, follow traditional Party terminology; but behind them all Comrade Stalin's word is law. . . . Stalin not only is generally called "the Boss" by the whole bureaucracy, but *is* the one and only boss.[25]

It was Stalin's practice to assign individuals or groups within the Politburo to oversee this or that important sector of government operations and report on policy problems pertaining to it. There was, in particular, a Politburo Commission for Foreign Affairs whose task was to supervise the work of the Commissariat for Foreign Affairs, which continued to function on the basis of directives from the Politburo itself. In the later 1930's, this commission reportedly consisted of Molotov as chairman, Mikoyan as the member chiefly concerned with foreign trade matters, and Zhdanov as the member principally responsible for Comintern affairs.[26] During World War II, it was apparently enlarged, becoming a six-man body or "sextet" in Stalin's language. In 1946, he gave it responsibilities pertaining also to internal affairs and transformed it into a "septet" by the addition of the planning director, Voznesenskii, who was later executed on Stalin's orders for reasons that remain obscure.[27]

Having been reduced even before the war to a semblance of a collective policy-making body, the Politburo gradually sank into total eclipse during the postwar years, when Stalin's autocracy reached its height. According to Khrushchev, it was then convened "only occasionally, from time to time," and its functioning was disorganized by Stalin's increased penchant for dealing directly with the sextets, septets, etc.[28] Actually, it appears to have ceased normal functioning in early 1949, and to have been virtually dissolved by Stalin in early 1951,[29] although it was reconstituted as a Presidium, with an inner bureau of unspecified membership, shortly before he died. Meanwhile, however, Stalin's dictatorial command and control of every aspect of Soviet foreign and internal policy had long since been institutionalized in an organ of government quite separate from the Politburo. This, it appears, was the so-called "Special Sector" (*osobyi sektor*) of the Central Committee, sometimes referred to abroad as his private secretariat.

If Stalin was ultimately able to dispense entirely with the Politburo, this was largely because he had built up, in the Special Sector, a highly organized personal machine of autocracy that may be compared with (and may even have been consciously modeled after) Nicholas I's "Personal Chancellery of His Imperial Majesty." Through this organization, the sovereign will of the autocrat radiated over Russia, its empire, and the world. According to the most detailed report on it that has yet come to us:

> Through the Special Sector Stalin directed the foreign Communist parties, received all reports on the work of the military and political intelligence services abroad, gave his directives to ambassadors, guided the fifth columns and issued instructions to them such as those on the assassination of Trotsky, the kidnaping of General Kutepov, atomic espionage, and so on. . . . Foreign policy was made in the Kremlin by Stalin and transmitted downward through the Special Sector. The activities of the Ministry of Foreign Affairs, the foreign department of the MGB, the military intelligence and the Cominform were coordinated in the Special Sector.[30]

This source also reports that the Central Committee did not have a foreign department in those years; the control of foreign policy was placed directly in the Special Sector in order to ensure the absolute subordination of this entire field of activity to Stalin alone.

All this is essential background for understanding many aspects of foreign policy in the Stalinist period. As in the time of some earlier Russian autocrats, so again under Stalin the personality of the leader became not simply a powerful influence upon policy, but the driving wheel of the entire mechanism of Russia's relations with the external world; and the technology of autocratic control was of course perfected by the use of certain modern totalitarian devices not available to the earlier Czars. Molotov, who replaced Litvinov as Foreign Minister in 1939 and served in this post for a decade, might well have paraphrased his Czarist predecessor Gorchakov and said, "In Russia there are only two people who know the policy of the Party: Stalin who makes it and myself who prepares and executes it." The now available documentary record of Nazi-Soviet relations in 1939–41 provides factual evidence that such a situation had been created. In general, Stalin's unrestricted autocratic command of Soviet foreign policy dates from the Great Purge, and it is notable that his first major move afterward was to initiate the diplomacy of the Soviet-Nazi alignment with his speech to the Eighteenth Party Congress in March, 1939. There is reason to believe that the Great Purge itself may have been motivated in part by his desire and determination to clear the way for the con-templated alliance with Hitler by destroying the old Leninist revo-lutionaries and other Bolshevik elements (including Marshal Tuk-hachevsky) who could not easily have resigned themselves to such a policy.[31]

The ways in which the personality of Stalin affected the foreign policy of Russia in his time were manifold. First, it should be em-phasized that the re-establishment of an absolute autocracy was not the only expression of the revival of Russian Czarism under Stalin; the movement of return to the past embraced likewise the revival of certain ways of thought and action characteristic of Czarism. Without ever abandoning the Marxist-Leninist ideology of world revolution, Stalin consciously identified himself and his regime with the cause of historic Russia—particularly the Muscovite Rus-sia that had seen itself besieged in a hostile world (the precapitalist encirclement, so to speak) and did not belong to the European system.

This attitude was clearly visible in his famous speech of 1931 to the business executives, in which he recounted the "beatings" that old Russia had suffered through the ages as a result of weak-ness and backwardness. It showed itself after World War II in claims such as those for the "return" of certain Turkish territories and for control of the Straits; in Soviet press descriptions of Stalin as the great "gatherer of Russian lands," a title originally applied to the grand princes of Muscovy; and in his remarkable V-J Day statement that the return of southern Sakhalin and the Kuriles to Russian possession would remove the "dark stain" of defeat in the Russo-Japanese War. ("For forty years have we, men of the older generation, waited for this day."[32]) We see it, too, in the pattern-ing of the Stalinist diplomatic service upon that of the Czars, down to the details of diplomatic uniform, and in the stilted, arrogant style and tone that Stalinist diplomatic correspondence increas-ingly assumed in Stalin's later years, just as Ivan the Terrible's did in *his* later years. And, needless to say, the official glorification of Ivan included the praising of his diplomacy and his manner of conducting the foreign relations of Russia. In all this, the person-ality of Stalin was the decisive driving force, as is witnessed by the fact that the orientation began to change as soon as he died.

Stalin's basically statist orientation was manifested, among other ways, in a view of the uses of diplomacy that deviated from the Bolshevik tradition. As noted earlier, diplomacy had been accorded a limited, if highly important, place in the total complex of Bolshevik foreign policy; it was regarded as essentially a defensive weapon in the struggle of the Soviet state to survive in a hostile "system of states." Stalin, however, looked upon diplomacy as a powerful offensive weapon, an instrument of Soviet Russia's territorial aggrandizement. This was shown in his diplomacy of the Soviet-Nazi alliance, which opened the empire-building phase of his career. It was manifested again in his wartime diplomacy of the anti-Hitler coalition. And he stated it bluntly in a toast to his foreign minister at a victory reception in the Kremlin in 1945: "Don't forget that a good foreign policy sometimes counts for more than two or three armies at the front. To our Viacheslav!"[33]

However, in the final period of Stalin's reign, the era of the cold war from 1947 to 1953, diplomacy ceased to play a large part in Soviet relations with the external world. The psychology of the autocrat unquestionably stands in first place among the reasons for this change. The postwar years marked not only the high tide of Stalin's autocracy, but also the climax of his personality disorder. "After the war," as Khrushchev has put it, "Stalin separated himself from the collective even more. Everything was decided by him alone, without any consideration for anyone or anything."[34] Moreover, the autocracy was now, so to speak, turned outward upon the world. Having earlier emancipated himself from the need to persuade in internal governmental affairs, Stalin now emancipated himself—or acted as though he had—from the need to persuade in external affairs, including many of the affairs of the newly formed Communist bloc. Since the practice of persuasion is a vital ingredient of the diplomatic process, this necessarily brought about the decline of diplomacy in Soviet external relations. Serious negotiation was possible only in such a situation of Soviet adversity as that created by the failure of Stalin's blockade of Berlin.

The turning of the autocracy outward upon the world is dramatically reflected in a small incident related by Khrushchev in his secret speech to the Twentieth Party Congress: "Once, when I came from Kiev to Moscow, I was invited to visit Stalin, who, pointing to the copy of a letter lately sent to Tito, asked me, 'Have you read this?' Not waiting for my reply, he answered, 'I will shake my little finger—and there will be no more Tito. He will fall.' "[35] The episode was cited as an example of Stalin's "willfulness" in international affairs and to show that "he demonstrated his suspicion and haughtiness not only in relation to individuals in the U.S.S.R., but in relation to whole parties and nations." In the text of this speech published abroad, Khrushchev did not expand upon this point, but confined himself to the further general comment that "during Stalin's leadership our peaceful relations with other nations were often threatened, because one-man decisions could cause, and often did cause, great complications."[36]

It must ruefully be recorded that the Western mind failed at the time to comprehend that an absolute autocracy had been re-established in Russian foreign policy, and Western interpretations of the conduct of the Stalinist regime suffered accordingly. A continuity of Bolshevik practice in policy formulation was mistakenly assumed. During the postwar years of Stalin's reign, it was generally believed abroad that the higher Party organs, notably the Politburo, remained in command of Soviet policy, and that Stalin was no more than the dominant individual within them, as Lenin had been before him. In America it even became an issue of public discussion in 1948 whether or not Stalin was a "prisoner" of the Politburo. Having served as American Ambassador in Moscow in 1946–49, General Walter Bedell Smith later commented on it as follows: "He is not, for instance, an absolute dictator, on the one hand, nor a prisoner of the Politburo, on the other; his position, I would say, is more that of chairman of the board with the decisive vote."[37]

Nor was scholarly opinion inclined to challenge this erroneous view of the situation. One of the best Western texts of the time on Soviet government affirmed that the *Führerprinzip* was foreign to the politics of Stalin's as well as Lenin's Russia.* A book published in 1951—when, as we now know, the Politburo had virtually ceased to exist—treated contemporary Soviet foreign policy as strictly a policy of "the Politburo."[38] A noted European student of Communist affairs even speculated that the formation of the Cominform in 1947 was an "act of rebellion" against a reluctant Stalin who had lost his majority in the Politburo to an aggressive faction headed by Zhdanov.[39] Surely the wisest judgment of the time was

---

*"Though Stalin's influence is great, all of the members of the Politbureau take part in the consideration of questions before it, and their votes are of equal value. Differences of opinion can and do develop, and Stalin has been outvoted on occasion. But once a decision has been reached by majority vote, the Politbureau acts as a team under Stalin as manager in carrying out the decision. This is a different conception from the *Führerprinzip*." (Julian Towster, *Political Power in the U.S.S.R., 1917–1947* [New York: Oxford University Press, 1948], p. 392.)

the one expressed by Max Beloff: "But the bare fact remains, that we know so little about the foreign policy of the Soviet Union because we are so far as yet from understanding to the full the working of its institutions."[40] Unfortunately, theoretical ignorance was here a matter of incalculably great practical importance: Not having discerned the paranoid autocrat behind the conduct of his regime in foreign affairs, people and governments in the West were unable to foresee that his death would bring changes in the motivation of Soviet foreign policy, or to grasp the meaning of these changes when they began to manifest themselves in the spring of 1953.

IV

The autocracy collapsed upon the death of the autocrat, and in the aftermath "collective leadership" was proclaimed, though without any very clear definition of what it meant, as the highest principle of Soviet government at all levels. At the top level, meanwhile, various factions fought to fill the vacuum of supreme leadership. Khrushchev emerged in early 1955 as the dominant figure in the regime, and in late 1957 as the clear victor in the succession struggle. In early 1958, he consolidated the victory by assuming the office of chairman of the Council of Ministers, thus combining in his person—as Lenin and Stalin had done before him—the leadership of both Party and government.

"Rise and fall of collective leadership" is the formula often used to describe this course of development at the apex of Soviet politics in the first five years after Stalin. It is applicable, but by no means adequate. Collective leadership fell in the sense that supreme political authority, which was divided or shared for a time, was again clearly concentrated in the hands of one man. But this did not mean, and there is no indication that it will mean, the return to autocratic government as practiced by Stalin. Khrushchev came to power in a restored system of oligarchical government, meaning (as suggested above) one in which the supreme leader decides questions of high policy in company with a group of the politically powerful whose consent to his views is won largely by means of persuasion. If Stalin revived the autocratic pattern of Czarism, Khrushchev has done much to revive the oligarchic pattern of Bolshevism. Putting it differently, his rise has been part of a larger political process consisting essentially in the resurgence of the Communist Party, and particularly its higher leadership, as the ascendant force everywhere in the Soviet polity. His personal success is probably to be explained in large part by the energetic and convincing way in which he has espoused the cause of the *Party's* political resurrection.

Khrushchev's bid for supreme leadership of Soviet foreign policy was made by way of asserting the paramount role of the Party and its higher institutions in this field. In the process, he collided with Molotov, who, after Stalin's death, had acquired not only direct charge of the Foreign Ministry, but a degree of authority in foreign policy that he had never previously enjoyed. The issues between them came to a head at the Central Committee plenum of July, 1955, which approved, over Molotov's objections, the effort that Khrushchev had undertaken to achieve a full-scale reconciliation with Marshal Tito. Molotov and the Foreign Ministry were assailed on this occasion for the arrogant behavior of Soviet diplomats in the satellites and other blatantly imperialist practices inherited from the Stalinist period.[41] All this underlay Molotov's statement to the Twentieth Party Congress that "Probably never before in the past has the Central Committee of our Party and its Presidium dealt so actively with problems of foreign policy as in the period just passed," and it suggests the nature of the shortcomings of the Foreign Ministry to which he alluded in this speech.[42] His resignation followed not long afterward. His successor, Shepilov, a career Party official, accompanied him into political oblivion in 1957, after joining the unsuccessful move against Khrushchev. The Soviet Foreign Ministry has since been headed by Andrei Gromyko, who fits the description of Lamsdorff cited above—"a minister of foreign affairs *à la russe,* which is to say that he does not have charge of the foreign policy, but only of the diplomacy of Russia, with the mission of adapting the latter to the former."

It is the Party leadership that now has charge of the foreign policy of Russia. The method of deciding the major foreign policy questions appears to conform to the pattern established in Lenin's time and in the early years after his death. The chief policy-making body is the Party Presidium, which meets regularly and frequently and considers the important foreign-policy issues on the basis of careful preparation and coordination of materials and policy positions at lower levels of the Party and government hierarchy. Decisions are taken either by the Presidium meeting as a body, or by a policy planning board of the Presidium consisting of Khrushchev and several other members most concerned with foreign affairs.[43] Khrushchev and his associates are kept well informed on international developments. As in the past, the Foreign Ministry reports directly to the Presidium and works under its close guidance. Also, the central Party apparatus plays an exceedingly important role in the preparation and implementation of foreign-policy decisions. It has an international department as well as departments for liaison with Communist parties of Soviet-bloc countries and Communist parties of other countries. These and the other executive offices of the Central Committee are supervised by the Secretariat.

The revival of oligarchial government in the post-Stalinist period has also been reflected in the changed position of the Party Central Committee. This assembly of the Soviet power elite has resumed its earlier importance as a regularly convened "superior Party conference" for discussion and ratification of the current Party line in internal and external affairs. On occasion it has been thrust into the role of arbiter of disputes within the Presidium. This occurred at the 1955 plenum mentioned above, and again in June, 1957, when the anti-Khrushchev majority in the Presidium went down to defeat before the Central Committee. On both occasions, foreign-policy issues figured prominently in the Central Committee debate. This appears to have been the case also at the Central Committee plenum of May, 1960, at the time of the U-2 incident, and it seems probable that subsequent changes in Soviet tactics in foreign policy were determined, at least in part, by pressure of Central Committee opinion.

The relation of Khrushchev to Soviet foreign policy did not, then, become that of an autocrat. Although he came to wield very great power in the decision-making process, he did not acquire—or appear to seek—the kind of power *over* the Party and state that Stalin managed to obtain. He was never in a position to dictate his will arbitrarily and without resort to the processes of persuasion within the higher councils of the Party.

When all this has been said, however, it remains to be added that Soviet foreign policy in the post-Stalinist period, and especially after early 1955, reflected in very many ways the personal leadership of Khrushchev. In the first place, this forceful, rough-hewn individual exhibited a style in foreign policy that was manifestly his own. Reviving a tradition that goes back very far into the Russian past, he took upon himself the principal role in the implementation as well as the formulation of policy. He devoted himself assiduously to representing the Soviet Union in world affairs, relegating his foreign minister to a distinctly subordinate position in this field of activity. In the process, he displayed resourcefulness, a frequent impetuosity, a domineering manner, an impatience with diplomatic decorum, showmanship, and love of the limelight. He demonstrated the ability to act as a tough, astute, and agile negotiator, and the propensity to appear before the world in the homely role of a Party agitator expatiating on the superiority of all things Soviet.

But this distinctive style of action does not exhaust Khrushchev's contribution to Soviet foreign policy. Although not basically a man of general ideas, and doubtless more at home in a debate on methods of corn-planting than in a dispute about Marxist fundamentals, he espoused—and on the whole successfully—certain ways of thought that comprise in their entirety a new philosophy of Soviet foreign policy.* Some of the ingredients, such as the doctrine of the noninevitability of general war, are novel to a degree; others are long-established articles of Leninist doctrine. The resulting amalgam is the ideology of competitive coexistence, or the program of a long-range, unremitting, but preferably nonmilitary contest between the Soviet and Western coalitions for predominance on the planet. This ideology expresses the interests of the Soviet ruling class and not simply the personality of a particular supreme leader. Yet it has found a powerful and persuasive protagonist in Khrushchev, and it gave expression to the deepest trait of his political personality—a boundless confidence in the virtue, viability, and world destiny of the Soviet way of life.

* A systematic exposition of the new philosophy is presented in the following chapter.

10 STALINISM AND COLD WAR

I

The story of Soviet foreign policy in the first four post-Stalin years is in some sense epitomized in the biblical adage "Pride goeth before a fall." The high-water mark of pride was set in early 1956, at the time of the Twentieth Party Congress. There Anastas Mikoyan declared: "Striking are the successes of Soviet foreign policy, especially in the past year. Here, too, the directing collective of the Party has injected a fresh new current, pursuing a high-principled, active, and flexible foreign policy, set forth in calm tones and without invective. . . . Certain ossified forms have been cast aside in the work of our diplomacy. . . . Let those swaggering Americans who boast of their wealth of today, of their 'American way of life,' join a contest with us in this field, and they will see where more is done for the good of the people, and whose way of life proves better." This speech, and those of Mikoyan's colleagues, reflected a confident and self-assured mood. Stalin is dead and gone, it seemed to say, and a new administration has taken matters in hand. It has set the wrongs to right, corrected the errors, banished the terror, gone out into the world. It has ended the stagnation and charted a new course big with promise, especially in foreign affairs. Thus, the horizons of possibility seemed wide and beckoning. To paraphrase a Russian proverb, the sea itself looked to the Kremlin no more than knee-deep.

So confident, in fact, was the attitude that it now seemed expedient to set the Congress straight on certain disagreeable facts out of the past, and Khrushchev revealed in closed session a part of the story of Stalin's dark record of evil. This speech was the beginning of the fall. By the year's end, the Soviet Army was sup-

226

pressing a popular revolution in Hungary. Poland was launched on the troubled waters of national Communism. Foreign Communist parties were in deep difficulties. The U.S.S.R. was morally isolated again in Europe and large parts of Asia. And various people around the world were speaking seriously of such things as the dissolution of the Soviet empire and the beginning of the end of Soviet Communism.

My purpose here is to search for some of the deeper forces and factors at work behind this historic sequence of pride and fall. What are the spiritual roots of the predicament in which the Soviet regime clearly finds itself today? Basically, the problem is to deepen our understanding of what Stalinism meant and the way in which Stalin's death caused change in Soviet policy. In one important aspect, the change had to do with the matter of persuasion. The new Soviet foreign policy that Mikoyan spoke of so proudly in early 1956 was, in a distinctly un-Stalinist sense, a diplomacy of persuasion; and it is just this diplomacy of persuasion that later suffered a shattering setback. But how are we to account for the shift in the Soviet orientation toward persuasion? The view to be developed in these pages holds that it was not simply a matter of shifting tactics, but that it had a psychological origin. The crucial fact is that Stalin's death occasioned a psychological revolution in Soviet foreign policy. The meaning of this proposition will be expanded in what follows.

First, let us briefly reconsider the classic period of the cold war. The final chapter in Stalin's life, from the end of World War II to his death in early 1953, was the culminating period of Stalinism in all departments of Soviet life and policy. And in foreign policy, Stalinism means cold war.

Before hostilities ended, Stalin was embarked upon a grandiose endeavor of empire-building in countries coming under the sway of Soviet forces. Contrary to Soviet propaganda, very little in the way of a spontaneous revolutionary process took place there. In fact, Stalin's policy had by now come to frown on spontaneous revolutionary movements, as was shown, for example, by Tito's wartime difficulties with Moscow. What Stalin wanted to do—and succeeded in doing—in most of Middle Europe can best be described by the Nazi term *Gleichschaltung,* which connotes a process of forcibly bringing a foreign area under control and into conformity. Middle Europe, along with North Korea and, later, China and North Vietnam, came to constitute parts of an enormous, expanded Soviet control-sphere with its center in Moscow.

As this process of *Gleichschaltung* developed in 1944 and 1945, stiffening Western reaction and eventual efforts by the United States and Britain to counteract it were met with Soviet intransigence and, increasingly, Soviet hostility. A set pattern of belligerency came to pervade all aspects of Soviet relations with Western and other countries, and especially with the United States.

In Zhdanov's report at the founding meeting of the Cominform in Warsaw in September, 1947, Stalin issued a kind of official declaration of permanent Soviet cold war against the West. From then on until his death, the pattern of belligerency remained rigidly in force. The expressions ran a gamut from hate propaganda and diplomacy of invective to warlike acts such as the Berlin blockade and the systematic shooting down of U.S. aircraft, and finally to outright war by proxy in Korea. International tension increased. The director-general of Soviet belligerency all through this period was Stalin himself. Among the totalitarian despots of this century, he was the supreme practitioner of cold war.

So far as the motivation of Soviet foreign policy during this period is concerned, it is essential to distinguish between its formal and operative aims. A formal aim is the object one declares oneself to be seeking; an operative aim is the object implicit in what one actually does. The two may or may not coincide.

The discrepancy between them has rarely been more glaring than it was in Stalin's foreign policy during the cold war. The "strengthening of peace" was constantly proclaimed as a Soviet aim; but Soviet actions were blatantly inconsistent with the notion of strengthening peace. Another aim frequently if not always unequivocally declared was that of promoting the cause of the world revolution and the liberation of peoples from the "capitalist system of exploitation." Here, too, a discrepancy appeared, although less obviously. Stalin, as already suggested, had grown deeply hostile to spontaneous revolutionary processes of every kind, including social revolutions from below. He still talked revolution, but he showed in many ways that the revolutionist in him had given way to the conservative, enamored of the values of stability, authority, and order. In his essay on linguistics in 1950, he had anathematized the Marxian notion that development always takes place through periodic upheavals or "explosions." The very idea of revolutionary explosions had become profoundly distasteful to him. As for the liberation of peoples from "capitalist exploitation," it is hard to believe that this was Stalin's operative aim, since the Soviet system had taken on the characteristics of a system of state-monopoly capitalism and had become the most exploitative in modern history. Nor could his aim have been simply to replace private capitalism with state capitalism or nationalized economies. Had it been, he would logically have softened the Soviet attitude toward Britain and other European countries that had begun to nationalize their economies after the war. And he would not have feuded as he did with Tito's Yugoslavia, where Soviet principles of economic organization had been carried farther after the war than in most of the satellite states.

The crucial operative aim for Stalin was *control*. This is the conclusion dictated by Stalinist behavior, as distinct from the official Stalinist image of that behavior. The operative aim, implicit in all that Stalin did, was to get control of territory and people and to absolutize that control by every available means, the principal one being police terror. Examination of the whole postwar process of Soviet *Gleichschaltung* of foreign lands bears out this judgment about the operative aim. Critical confirmation is afforded by the Stalin-Tito conflict. The issue was Tito's refusal to permit Yugoslavia to be incorporated into the Soviet command-and-control structure. Tito was among the Communist leaders most antagonistic to private capitalism. It was not any deviation on this score that underlay the break, but rather Tito's resistance to Stalin's claim to absolute Soviet control of Yugoslavia. The consequence was a Soviet "little cold war" against Belgrade for as long as Stalin lived; the moment he died, it began to slacken.

The Stalinist ideology of cold war reflected this operative aim of total control indirectly in its image of international reality. This image dichotomized the globe into two "worlds," called the "Soviet camp of peace, socialism, and democracy" and the "American camp of capitalism, imperialism, and war." The political universe was divided cleanly into the white world of Soviet socialist progress and the black world of American capitalist reaction. Stalin had enunciated such a conception of a polarized political universe, with Russia and America as the two antagonistic poles of power, as early as 1927. Twenty years after, it reappeared as the Soviet working conception of international reality; that is, it was acted out in foreign policy. A Soviet document of 1948 stated: "The struggle of the two camps determines now the fate of the whole world, the fate of mankind. This struggle emerges more and more as the chief moving force of the development of our age toward Communism. Here lies the basic content of the political struggle of our time."[1]

The relation between the two-world image and the drive for total control can be stated very simply: The working criterion of "belongingness" to the one world or the other was the criterion of Soviet control. Consequently, the Stalinist definition of the character of a given country's regime turned essentially on the question: Does it constitute a part of the Soviet control sphere? If so, it was socialist and democratic; if not, capitalist and fascist. The Yugoslav regime, for example, underwent metamorphosis almost overnight in 1948 from a "people's democracy" into a "police regime of the fascist type." Its actual institutional structure had not changed at all; but its relation to the Soviet control structure had, and this was crucial for Stalin.

There was no geographical or political space between the two worlds, no room for neutralism, no possibility of a "third force," no such thing as nonalignment. Political neutrality in the cold war was just a blind. The pretense of neutrality might be tolerated very grudgingly in a marginal case, such as Finland's, but never admitted in principle. The notion of an "uncommitted nation" or "third force" was nothing but a crude political myth devised for devious Western purposes. The Soviet document already quoted said: "The 'third line' or 'third force' concocted by the right-wing socialists is in fact nothing other than a cover for the policy of defense of capitalism and fight against Communism. In our epoch there is not, and cannot be, a 'third force.' . . . Two forces, two camps, exist throughout the world."[2]

One of the most fateful political consequences of the captivity of Stalinist policy to this conception was the attitude taken in the Kremlin toward the new Asia. Next to the cold war itself, the most important historical fact of the period following World War II was the political emergence of Asia from Western tutelage. There was no way to square this fact with the logic of the Stalinist drive for total control and the two-world image associated with it. For this would mean recognizing Asia as a "third force" or a space between the worlds. Consequently, Stalin, and therefore Stalinist policy, denied the fact, legislated it out of existence. This was one of the key issues of the famous Varga controversy in 1947. In a book written before the end of the war, the Soviet economist Eugene Varga had spotted the new trend, the changing relationship of

Europe and Asia. On Stalin's orders, the book was condemned and its author forced to recant what he knew to be absolutely true. The real facts about the new Asia were purged along with Varga. The newly won national independence of India, Burma, the Philippines, and other former Western dependencies was pronounced a "fiction," a cunning imperialist device for continuing to exercise control over these countries without appearing to do so. According to the logic of the drive for control, they could not be considered "liberated" so long as they had not yet been incorporated into the Soviet control sphere. Not having changed worlds in this way, they had to remain integral parts of the black world, *de facto* colonies that the West held on to with the help of "antinational ruling circles," puppets such as Nehru, U Nu, and others.

Thus, Stalinist policy was predicated on an official delusion of continued Asian bondage to the West. There was no essential change in this regard until Stalin died. There is every reason to believe that most of the men around Stalin were quite aware of the delusive character of this image of the new Asia, and the Stalinist image of the external world generally. They could see that it was nothing but an externalized portrait of Soviet-bloc reality, and that the external world was not really like that. Some, it seems, were painfully conscious of the resulting detriment to Soviet Russia's interests as a great power. In effect, the image blocked off the new Asia as a profitable field for Soviet power politics, constraining policy to costly and risky ventures such as the aggression by proxy in Korea. But the men around Stalin could do nothing, or next to nothing, to correct the situation so long as he was alive and in autocratic control. Few situations could illustrate more convincingly the potential importance of personality, and specifically the pathological personality, in foreign policy.

II

This brings us back to the question of persuasion. Foreign policy in the normal course of events is largely an activity of intergovernmental persuasion. Persuasion aims at influencing other governments to do or not to do certain things, such as concluding a treaty, settling a dispute, joining or not joining an alliance. The basis of appeal is mutuality of interest. Recognition of the other government's interest in its own continued existence and security is always necessarily presupposed.

The Stalinist politics of cold war were not politics of persuasion, and the foregoing discussion suggests the reason why. When the operative aim is total control, persuasion is not a fit instrument of policy; one form or another of aggression is necessitated. Save for the marginal case, Soviet diplomacy withered on the vine between 1945 and 1953; the whole range of intergovernmental activities of persuasion by conventional means was excluded.

In the case of Yugoslavia, there was no possibility of negotiating the issue of total Soviet control. The Tito regime might be persuaded to do all sorts of things in the Soviet interest. The one thing it could not be persuaded to do was to part with its independence, but this was precisely Stalin's demand. Following Stalin's death, the Soviet Government began to pursue a policy of persuasion vis-à-vis Belgrade, and it is still doing so. The precondition of this, however, was a drastic scaling-down of Moscow's demand upon Tito, a change of the operative aim from total control to a relationship of influence. A similar change occurred in the motivation of Soviet policy toward other areas of the non-Soviet world, with similar results in the form of efforts to persuade. What underlay this change was a lessening of the felt need for control. This, in turn, was a consequence of the fact that when Stalin died the peculiar needs of his personality ceased to determine the motivation of Soviet foreign policy.

Paradoxically, Stalinist policy in the cold war placed the greatest emphasis on international propaganda. Since propaganda is ordinarily regarded as an instrument *par excellence* of persuasion, how explain the fact that propaganda claimed so much Soviet attention and effort at the very time that policy all but excluded international persuasion in the sense defined? The question is too complex for adequate treatment here. But one important aspect of the answer lies in the two-world fantasy. It saw the black world as inwardly bifurcated, in contrast to the white world, which was monolithic. As the previously quoted ideologist of Stalinism put it, "Two forces, two camps, exist in any capitalist country." The second camp in the black world consisted of all those who belonged—in attitude, in thought, and in deed—to the white world, who regarded themselves as *its* citizens living in a foreign land, and who, therefore, submitted to Soviet control voluntarily.

The Stalinist designation for such persons was "proletarian internationalists." The nucleus of the universal fraternity of spiritual citizens of the Soviet Union was, of course, the membership of foreign Communist parties. But the fraternity was not confined to this circle. *Anybody* could belong. The decisive test of belonging was laid down by Stalin in 1927. "He is an internationalist," said Stalin then, "who unreservedly, unhesitatingly and unconditionally is prepared to defend the U.S.S.R., because the U.S.S.R. is the base of the world revolutionary movement."[3] This reasoning was further elaborated during the period of the cold war. A statement of 1948, for example, refined it as follows: "At the present time, the sole and decisive criterion of proletarian revolutionary internationalism is: *for or against the U.S.S.R., the fatherland of the international proletariat. . . . Only he is a genuine internationalist who carries his sympathy, respect, recognition to the point of practical and maximum aid, support and defense of the U.S.S.R. by every means and in various forms.*"[4]

It is to be noted that the criterion for admission to the white camp in the black world was not intellectual; that is, it was not the acceptance of an idea or set of ideas as such. It was rather an act of total self-identification with the Soviet system. It was the participation in a cult, the cult of the U.S.S.R., regarded by definition as the repository of the socialist idea. The criterion did not say: Believe in socialism, accept the socialist idea. It said: Believe in the U.S.S.R. as the fatherland of socialism, accept whatever it tells you as the sacred truth, and do whatever it bids you, for its sake. This difference is more significant than it may seem. It must be borne in mind in analyzing the traumatic effect of Khrushchev's denunciation of Stalin on thousands of Soviet sympathizers abroad. It also throws light on Stalinism's thinly veiled distrust and contempt for intellectuals. The intellectual is suspect precisely because of his devotion to ideas and principles as such. Every true totalitarianism—whether Stalin's or Hitler's or any of the others—tries to set up complete loyalty and devotion to itself, to the system and the Leader, as the only ultimate principle.

Returning to the question about propaganda, it is not hard to see why so much effort was expended in this field during the very years when so little attempt was being made at international persuasion. The principal function of the international propaganda was to preserve and foster the cult of the U.S.S.R., and for this reason it may be regarded as essentially an extension of Soviet internal propaganda to the foreign field. The purpose was not to persuade the audience through an appeal to the intellectual faculties; it was rather to indoctrinate participants in the cult, to train "internationalists." That is, it presupposed the surrender of the critical faculties, the will to believe, the prior emotional self-identification *in toto* with the object of the cult, the U.S.S.R.

Given such identification, everything might be credible, no lie too big to be swallowed as gospel truth. If Moscow, for example, said that the Americans were waging germ warfare in Korea, this—to the participant in the cult—had to be true because Moscow said so. Hence, the basic task of the international propaganda was to furnish continual new material for the cult, to hold aloft day in and day out the glorious, glowing image of Soviet reality and at the same time to besmirch to the utmost the image of the enemy camp. The inner content of the cold war propaganda can therefore be epitomized in ten words: The Soviet world is white; the American world is black. The vital importance of the Iron Curtain as a protective shield for this two-world fantasy is obvious.

It has been suggested above that the two-world conception was a reflex of the Stalinist drive for total control, which operated at its high point during the period of the cold war. However, the argument now indicates that the relation between these two phenomena was an interactive one. On the one hand, the felt need for absolute control reinforced the image of the world as split in two. But on the other hand, this image, and particularly the projection of the Soviet world as glisteningly white, greatly reinforced the need for control, dictating, for example, all the devices of control summed up in the phrase "Iron Curtain." Thus, one very important contributing motivation for the Stalinist control drive was the urge to make an illusion about Russia seem real.

The actual fact was that Russia had become in the Stalin period a powerful, industrialized country with an enslaved, miserable, poverty-stricken population, with an economy best described as state-monopoly capitalism, and with a political system of führerist police-state variety; and the empire was an extension of all this to captive peoples abroad. In the official illusion, however, the U.S.S.R. appeared as the realization of man's dream of social utopia, a land of progress and prosperity, where all the economic problems were solved or in process of solution, where culture was in flower, where freedom and justice prevailed, where nearly everybody was happy; and the empire was just an extension of all these benefits to grateful peoples on the periphery.

As pointed out in an earlier chapter, this was no mere Potemkin village; it was a Potemkin Russia, fabricated out of words and pictures and mass spectacles in Red Square. Absolute centralized control was necessary in order to make the illusion *appear* to be true. The discrepancy between the Potemkin Russia and the real Russia could be hidden from view so long as the MVD terror machine operated to keep everything under control, to see to it that nobody revolted, that few if any people got in or out, that everyone in Russia and the satellites pretended to be living in the Potemkin world, that no one spoke the truth out loud, and that articles and books and films complied with the dictates of "socialist realism"; that is, that they depicted the illusion.

But from whose view would the discrepancy be hidden by such means? Not, certainly, from the ordinary Soviet citizen's; he realized what kind of Russia he was living in, and that it had nothing in common with the heavenly system portrayed in the propaganda. The Soviet and satellite peoples knew all about the discrepancy, knew much more about it than their well-meaning friends in the West who were trying to enlighten them on the point. The bureaucracy knew about it. Even high up in the Politburo much was known about it. For whom, then, was the great show staged? In part it was staged for the "proletarian internationalists" abroad, to keep them comfortably deluded. But the enormous investment of effort that this enterprise of political stagecraft entailed was undertaken mainly for another reason: the main spectator was Stalin. It was he who imperatively needed the Potemkin Russia. The same force of self-idealization that underlay the Stalin cult also underlay the cult of the U.S.S.R. The latter had become an extension of the former: The idealized Russia was a background panorama for the figure of the idealized Stalin.

For insight into Stalin's need for the Potemkin Russia, we may return to a passage in Khrushchev's secret report that has been cited in an earlier chapter. Khrushchev spoke of the agricultural situation, which was going from bad to worse in Stalin's final years, and went on:

All those who interested themselves even a little in the national situation saw the difficult situation in agriculture, but Stalin never even noted it. Did we tell Stalin about this? Yes, we told him, but he did not support us. Why? Because Stalin never traveled anywhere. . . . He knew the country and agriculture only from films. And these films had dressed up and beautified the existing situation in agriculture. Many films so pictured kolkhoz life that the tables were bend-

ing from the weight of turkeys and geese. Evidently, Stalin thought
that it was actually so.

Clearly, Khrushchev was not a very good psychologist on this
occasion. He said that Stalin remained ignorant of the crisis in
Soviet agriculture because he never traveled anywhere. The point
is true but trivial. For it only raises the question: What kept him
from traveling around or taking other steps to learn the real state
of affairs? The answer is to be found in Stalin's stringent need for
the idealized image of Russia, one aspect of which was the image
of kolkhoz prosperity. Naturally, police terror could not produce
more grain, nor build houses for the workers, nor outstrip the
U.S.A. in technology, nor make the Soviet people happy and con-
tented and the satellite peoples grateful to Russia and Stalin. But it
could make it *seem* as though all this was so, and that was its essential function. The key requisite was total control. Stalinist policy,
internal as well as external, was harnessed to a prodigious effort to
act out for Stalin an official illusion about Russia and the world.
That is why Stalinism rested on Stalin and why his death marked
a decisive turn in Russian history and world politics. It knocked
the psychological prop out of the structure of Stalinist policy. It
removed the motivating source of the politics of megalomania. A
stream of changes followed swiftly.

III

This psychological revolution forms the proper starting point for
an analysis of Soviet policy in the post-Stalin period. In one aspect,
it is a story of official Russia's move to readjust to the real world.
In another, it is a story of the failure to carry through the readjustment, and especially of ignorance or disregard of the full extent
of popular disaffection in Russia and the satellites. The Malenkov
policy, a pale Soviet version of what we have come to call "national Communism," seemed to reflect some awareness of this; but
it fell under the onslaught of Khrushchev, in whom the mentality
of the provincial Party officialdom found its classic expression.

Khrushchev was able and willing to admit that Soviet agriculture
was in a crisis, that the bureaucratic administration was grossly
overcentralized, that Soviet intellectual life was stagnating in its
isolation from the world, that the terror had been terribly costly in
terms of national progress, and so on. But he would not admit, or
could not see, certain other realities, such as the fact that most

Russians are heartily sick of such things as Five-Year Plans, the priority of heavy industry, the sacrifice of the present to a future that never comes, and that they will not cooperate voluntarily with a regime that endeavors to reform in the interests of *its* efficiency rather than *their* welfare.

Readjustment to the realities of the external world was not so inhibited, however. After an interlude of relative quiet under Malenkov, the Soviet regime embarked on a dynamic new policy designed to reshape the international environment. This was no longer a policy of cold war in the classic Stalin sense. The cold war pattern of total belligerency subsided in favor of the slogan of *détente,* the meeting at the summit, and the challenge to peaceful competition of systems. However, the new policy also was fundamentally anti-Western and anti-American from the start. It was addressed in large part to the breaking up of the Western alliance system, which Stalin's cold war had brought into existence and constantly solidified. It was only the shift of motivation, the subsiding of the drive for total control consequent upon Stalin's death, which made it possible for this to become an operative as distinguished from merely a declared aim of Soviet foreign policy. No longer harnessed to the obsession with absolute control, the new policy expressed an expansionism of Soviet influence.

All this was accompanied by a change in the official Soviet image of the world, ratified by the Twentieth Party Congress. The compulsion to dichotomize the image of the world was no longer operative. The two-world conception faded out, giving way to the picture of *one* world in which two rival systems of states, the socialist and the capitalist, compete for a preponderance of world influence. This was no longer a Stalinist world of "capitalist encirclement." On the contrary, territories contiguous to the Soviet orbit were now seen as fields for the penetration of Soviet capital, Soviet know-how, Soviet arms, and Soviet ideas. Moscow gave the new Asia the political recognition that Stalin had withheld. This new world of Soviet foreign policy was a world that did not exclude political neutrality, or third forces, or the notion of an uncommitted nation. For countries outside the Soviet bloc, there were alternate roads to socialism, even a parliamentary road. The rightwing socialists were, after all, rightwing socialists. Tito's Yugoslavia was not a capitalist-fascist degeneration, merely a wayward form of people's democracy.

In short, Stalin's successors reintegrated the political universe.

The world as projected on the new political map was not a stark contrast in black and white. There were various shades of gray in the non-Soviet part of it, and the gray areas were the focus of the new expansionism of influence. A non-Soviet nation unaligned with the Western military system and friendly to the U.S.S.R. was now described as part of a "peace zone." The ambitious new policy envisaged the eventual transformation of the whole of the Eurasian continent into one immense "peace zone," that is, one big zone of preponderant Soviet influence.

When influence is the operative aim, persuasion is a logical means. Hence the new policy placed tremendous emphasis upon the function of persuasion. The revival of diplomacy and trade, the sponsoring of cultural and technical exchange, the encouragement of official contacts at many levels, the drive to normalize relations with many countries, and the participation in previously boycotted international bodies were, from this point of view, ways of persuading countries that they could do business safely and profitably with the U.S.S.R. Many of the major acts of Soviet foreign policy in 1955 were intended primarily as acts of persuasion. From the standpoint of detaching middle nations from dependence upon the Western security system, it was imperative to persuade them that the world was safe for nonalignment. The Soviet motivation in bringing about the Geneva summit conference was closely linked with this ulterior aim of persuasion. Austria was evacuated, and the long-delayed treaty signed, largely in order to make of this country a showcase of Soviet willingness to coexist with small neutrals in its vicinity, the idea being to persuade other countries that they, too, could be Austrias and flourish in peace.

Finally, changes of Soviet policy in Eastern Europe were partly inspired by this aim of persuasion. If independent countries were to be persuaded to disalign themselves from the West and enter into close relationships with the Soviet Union, something had to be done about the satellites; at the very least they had to be made to look less like satellites. One step to be taken was the partial undoing of the *Gleichschaltung*. Another was the creation of the Warsaw treaty system as a NATO-looking device for retention of Soviet military control of the whole area after police control was relaxed. Further, the potential appeal of Titoism to semi-autonomous Soviet dependencies in Eastern Europe had to be neutralized, and this, it seemed, could best be done by making friends with Tito, or at least making it *appear* that friendship was restored. Then

Titoism could cease being a symbol of anti-Sovietism and its disruptive force would be negated.

This was the point at which the new policy of international persuasion began to get ahead of itself. Ironically, the trouble sprang in part from the old habit of blinking the distinction between appearance and reality, in this case between the appearance and reality of a Soviet *entente* with Tito. It was a momentous miscalculation to suppose that a mere façade of *entente* would serve the Soviet purpose adequately. Actually, it contributed to the ripening of the conditions that produced the explosion of popular wrath in Hungary. The whole boldly conceived policy of international persuasion came to grief, at least temporarily, in this explosion. The spectacle of Hungary displayed the Soviet regime to the world as a repressive, imperialist, and antipopular dictatorship. Some countries that had been objects of the new expansionism of influence drew back. Others at least began to have second thoughts about doing much political business with the U.S.S.R. The scheme of transforming Eurasia into a zone of preponderant Soviet influence suffered an extremely serious setback. The great campaign to persuade culminated in a crisis of Soviet persuasion.

11 DIALECTICS OF COEXISTENCE

Whether or not Lenin was the first to use it, the phrase "peaceful coexistence" was established in the Soviet political vocabulary by the mid-1920's. It referred to the at least temporary hostile "existing together" of the revolutionary Soviet republic and the rest of the world, the absence of war between them. Since coexistence in this sense was a fact after the Civil War period and the beginnings, at Genoa and Rapallo, of Soviet Russia's entry into the international system, it is not surprising that the Soviet leaders began to use language descriptive of the fact. "What we at one time regarded as a brief respite after the war has become a whole period of respite," said Stalin, in a speech of 1925. "Hence a certain equilibrium of forces and a certain period of 'peaceful coexistence' between the bourgeois world and the proletarian world."[1]

During the ensuing years of the Stalin period, the concept of coexistence took on a certain programmatic aspect and was elaborated as one part of a comprehensive Soviet teaching on international relations and foreign policy in what was called the "imperialist epoch of wars and proletarian revolutions." Stalin himself was the foremost exponent of this orthodox Communist doctrine of coexistence. After his death, it underwent substantial renovation and development at the hands of a group of Soviet political leaders and ideologists led by Khrushchev.

Khrushchev's report to the Twentieth Party Congress outlined the fundamentals of the new coexistence doctrine, one which has been dubbed "revisionist" or "modern revisionist" by its opponents within the Communist camp. It has since been further elaborated, particularly in Soviet writings and pronouncements of the early 1960's. Moreover, this doctrine of "competitive coexistence," as it may be called, has been incorporated into the official Soviet Party Program adopted by the Twenty-second Party Congress in October, 1961. However, the adoption did not take place without considerable intra-Party debate and conflict, echoes of which were recorded in the public proceedings of the Twenty-second Congress.

Still more formidable resistance was met in foreign Communist quarters. Efforts by Soviet Communists to secure adoption of the "Twentieth-Congress line" as the general line of the world Communist movement were opposed by conservative elements in various Communist governments and parties, most notably those of China and Albania. Dominant groups in these two Communist countries championed the orthodox or Stalinist point of view, which was stigmatized as "dogmatist" by the proponents of the new position. So emerged the great new conflict in international Communism that has come to be widely known as the "Sino-Soviet dispute." To a very important extent it has revolved around the clash between the old and the new approaches to coexistence.

It must be emphasized that we deal here with a division within the Communist mind as well as a geographical division within the Communist world. The coexistence controversy is far more than a "Sino-Soviet dispute" or, as has also been suggested, a disagreement between Communist "have" and "have-not" countries. The quarrel between the orthodox and revisionist conceptions of coexistence, and the conflicting policy orientations associated with them, has gone on and continues to take place within as well as between Communist parties. The conflicting positions are essentially positions men take as Communists even though, in doing so, they are inevitably influenced by national attitudes, interests, and biases. Thus the coexistence controversy has gone on among Soviet Communists too.

This fact was reflected in the Twenty-second Party Congress. There Khrushchev, Mikoyan, and their close followers violently assailed Molotov as an opponent of the revised coexistence doctrine. Molotov reportedly dispatched a lengthy letter from Vienna to the Party Central Committee in Moscow on the eve of the Congress criticizing the published draft of the new Party Program for "revisionism" and "pacifism" in international policy. The letter contended that the new philosophy of Communist victory through peaceful competition was "antirevolutionary" in spirit and contrary to the teachings of Lenin, who, Molotov alleged, had never used the phrase "peaceful coexistence" and certainly had never viewed coexistence as the general line of Communist international policy.[2] In refutation, the proponents of the revised doctrine maintained that Lenin had at any rate spoken of "peaceful cohabitation," had asserted that "socialism has the force of example," and had even suggested that the Soviet Union would mainly influence international development "by its economic policy." They denounced Molotov as an unregenerate cold warrior who, in Mikoyan's words, "rejects the line of peaceful coexistence, reducing this concept merely to a state of peace or rather to the absence of war at the given moment and to the denial of the possibility of averting a world war." Mikoyan went on: "In essence, such a view fits in with that of foreign opponents of peaceful coexistence who interpret it as a form of 'cold war,' as a state of 'armed peace.'"[3] Molotov was undoubtedly not the sole target of these polemics. Their intensity was a recognition of the persistence within the Soviet ruling elite of a current of Stalinist thought and feeling articulated in the Molotov letter.

Since it is one of the basic conventions of Soviet and generally of Communist politics that a doctrine or a policy can only be valid if it is authentically Leninist, it is not surprising that the debate about coexistence has revolved to such an extent around the issue of what Lenin said and thought on this subject. On the one hand, we have Molotov's (and Stalin's and Mao's) Lenin, who always preserved a stance of uncompromising revolutionary belligerence toward the hostile capitalist world and considered coexistence merely a temporary strategem. On the other side stands Khrushchev's Lenin, who was realistically ready to make compromises and concessions on occasion (but only if reciprocated), who built Soviet foreign policy on the foundation of the idea of coexistence, dreamed of expunging war from the life of human society, and looked to victory in economic competition as the highroad of Communism's final triumph on a world scale. Neither of these is the real, historical Lenin, though both contain elements of his variegated legacy. Each is a political artifact representing a certain orientation in the contemporary Communist mind. But if so, there is no particular reason—other than historical interest—for devoting much attention to this aspect of the controversy, as though we could impugn the seriousness of either position by disproving the interpretation of Lenin in terms of which it is argued.

Here it should be added that the adherents of the revised Soviet coexistence doctrine, while contending that their position is authentically Leninist, do nevertheless admit that it contains some novel elements, such as the revision of Lenin's thesis on the inevitability of war in the age of imperialism. Defending the innovations against charges by the orthodox Communists that they have betrayed "revolutionary Marxism-Leninism," Khrushchev and his allies have claimed to stand for a "creative Marxism-Leninism" that adapts Communist teachings to the changed conditions of the modern world. These conditions differ greatly from those of Lenin's time, Khrushchev has said, and so "one cannot mechanically repeat now what Vladimir Ilyich Lenin said many decades ago regarding imperialism, or continue asserting that imperialist wars are inevitable until socialism triumphs throughout the world."[4] On a later occasion he frankly acknowledged that the concept of coexistence has undergone a change of content. At one time, he said, the policy of coexistence had been aimed simply at winning time and a breathing spell for an isolated Soviet state, whereas "Now, in connection with the change in the character of war and the new balance of power in the world arena in favor of the forces of peace and socialism, the policy of peaceful coexistence has far more meaningful aims and tasks, in effect is *filled with new content*. Its final aim is to secure the most favorable conditions for the victory of socialism over capitalism in peaceful economic competition." (Italics added.)[5]

II

It may be helpful to start my analysis of the "new content" by pointing out three changes that the concept of coexistence has undergone in the transition from the orthodox to the revised doctrine. First, the concept has been greatly enlarged, as reflected in the thesis that coexistence has now become the "general line" of Soviet international policy. It may, in fact, be said that whereas the orthodox coexistence doctrine was merely one part of a more comprehensive body of teachings on international relations and foreign policy in the age of the world Communist revolution, now the theory of international relations and foreign policy in the present age have been incorporated within a broad concept of competitive coexistence as a dynamic system of international relations. Second, peaceful coexistence has ceased under the revised doctrine to be viewed as a mere interlude between periodic outbreaks of war. The revised doctrine, in other words, envisages the possibility that the postulated world-wide Communist revolution will be continued and completed under conditions of coexistence: *"There is now a prospect of achieving peaceful coexistence for the entire period in which the social and political problems now dividing the world will have to be solved.* The indications are that it may actually be feasible to banish world war from the life of society even before the complete triumph of socialism on earth, with capitalism surviving in part of the world."[6] And thirdly, a highly significant change has taken place in the image of coexistence as a process.

The orthodox Communist coexistence doctrine characteristically viewed (and views) the process of coexistence as a special form of conflict or international class struggle between states representing the opposing "socialist" and "capitalist" socio-economic formations. The coexisting states are assumed to be engaged in a conflict that they wage in the political, diplomatic, ideological, economic, cultural, and other spheres. The coexistence process is "peaceful" only in the sense that it falls short of major war between the antagonists, although episodes of armed violence or local armed conflicts, as in Korea, may be an organic part of it. Accordingly, the orthodox doctrine projects coexistence as "hostile coexistence" or "cold war." It is noteworthy that the contemporary Chinese Communist defenders of the orthodox position have suggested that "cold war" is a fair description of the coexistence process in their image of it.[7]

The revised doctrine does not by any means deny that conflict belongs to the essence of coexistence as a system of international relations. It emphatically repeats that coexistence is a special form of international class struggle between states of the opposed systems. As Khrushchev himself clearly expressed it in a speech of 1959: "Coexistence is the continuation of the struggle of the two social systems, but by peaceful means, without war, without interference of one state in the internal affairs of another state. . . . We consider that it is an economic, political, and ideological struggle, but not a military one. It will be a competition of the two systems on a world scale."[8] In the changed image of coexistence as a process, conflict of systems has not been expunged or minimized, but the process is no longer envisaged exclusively in terms of conflict. The relationship has come to be envisaged as a "dialectical" one in the sense that it embraces *both conflict and cooperation.* In the words of N. Inozemtsev, one of the leading exponents of the revised doctrine, "Peaceful coexistence is a dialectical process combining organically the sharpest class struggle between socialism and capitalism and cooperation of states of the two opposite systems for the sake of maintaining peace."[9] Another Soviet thinker in like manner defines coexistence as "a complex, many-sided, and contradictory process" in which conflict (*bor'ba*) is interwoven with "businesslike cooperation."[10]

What is distinctively new in this "dialectical" approach is the idea that elements of cooperation between adversaries have a legitimate and indeed an integral place in the total process of coexistence. This transcends the often-reiterated idea that peaceful coexistence entails mutual renunciation of the resort to war as a means of resolving disputes between states. For that is a matter of *not* doing something, whereas cooperation between the antagonists for avoidance of war involves positive action. This theme emerged at the Twentieth Party Congress, where Khrushchev said: "We believe that countries with differing social systems can do more than exist side by side. It is necessary to proceed further, to improve relations, to strengthen confidence among countries and cooperate."[11] Soviet theorists proceeded on this foundation to elaborate the "dialectical" approach. Moreover, it was reaffirmed at both the Twenty-first and Twenty-second Party Congresses and in the new Party Program. The Program speaks of coexistence as "a specific form of class struggle," but also specifies that coexistence involves the renunciation of war as a means of settling disputes between states, the negotiated settlement of such disputes, the development of mutual understanding and trust between states, and the "taking of each other's interests into account."[12]

It is particularly at this point that the doctrine of competitive coexistence is vulnerable to the charge of "revisionism" that Molotov and other Communist conservatives have leveled against it. "The dogmatists," writes a Soviet theorist, "are distrustful of cooperation for it strikes them as an abandonment of conflict, a reconciliation of class interests. It is not so in reality. Conflict is just as indivisible an aspect of peaceful coexistence as is cooperation."[13] But no amount of insistence on this latter point can alter the fact that the "dialectical" approach subtly breaks with Communist tradition by setting up intersystem cooperation as an integral and coordinate part of the coexistence process, and by taking the position that in the nuclear age the adversaries, while remaining deeply divided in very many ways, have in common at least a basic interest in the prevention of major war.

Classic Communist coexistence doctrine has never been "dialectical" in the pecular sense just mentioned. It has never viewed coexistence as a contradictory dual process of conflict-*cum*-cooperation. It has always been a "conflict doctrine," an interpretation of coexistence as a system of relationships made up of "contradictions" and "struggles" and the complex interweaving of these, with no real provision being made for collaboration between the two sides. Negotiation and the reaching of specific agreements have never been ruled out, but diplomacy between states representing the opposing systems has always been regarded as a form of political combat, a tactical weapon in the struggle. The underlying assumption has been that the adversaries have no basic common interests, that the enemy must never be regarded as anything but an enemy and can never in any meaningful sense be a partner. Mao Tse-tung has vividly summed up this classic Communist outlook toward the antagonist in his dictum that Communists should "snub the enemy strategically and take full account of him tactically."[14] Dealings with the enemy are thus never to be seen as ways of establishing a *modus vivendi* or stabilized relationship with him.

The shift of outlook that has occurred in the transition from the orthodox to the revised Soviet coexistence doctrine is reflected, significantly, in a new tendency of Soviet writers to draw a distinction between the concepts of "coexistence" and "cold war." They object, for example, to statements by some Western students of Soviet affairs to the effect that "coexistence" to the Soviet mind is just another term for "cold war," and in this connection they have suggested some definitions of the latter concept. One of them writes: " 'Cold war' means the worsening of relations between states along all lines."[15] Others variously define cold war as a policy of increasing international tension to the verge of armed conflict[16] and as a policy of using all means, propaganda included, to prepare and ignite a "hot war."[17] What all their formulations have in common is the idea that "cold war" signifies a state of unrestrained political hostilities, rising tension, and drift toward war, whereas "coexistence" signifies a system of international relationships in which an intense competitive struggle is kept within certain bounds and stabilized short of war by deliberate cooperative efforts on the part of the competitors themselves.

Soviet theorists have contrasted this "dialectical" model of the coexistence process with a "metaphysical" way of thinking that is said to be characteristic of the "bourgeois ideologues." The former sees *both* conflict *and* cooperation as belonging to coexistence, while the "metaphysical" mind thinks in terms of "either/or": "Either conflict or cooperation—this, in their view, is how the question of the interrelations of the two social systems must be resolved."[18] Hence one group of bourgeois writers constructs a model of coexistence as cold war, as conflict without cooperation, whereas another calls for cooperation without conflict, wrongly supposing that it is possible to reconcile the conflicting ideologies.

This Soviet critique of Western images of coexistence should not mislead us into thinking that their "both/and" approach actually does derive from the mental world of Marxist dialectics. As already noted, the orthodox Communist mind has never taken this view of it. Moreover, it could be argued that the classic Leninist-Stalinist picture of the relations between the opposing systems as a sphere of "contradictions" only, with no meaningful admixture of cooperation, is dialectical in the meaning given to dialectics by Lenin: "Dialectics in the proper sense is the study of contradiction in the very essence of objects."[19] But however that may be, one point must be emphasized here: There is nothing peculiarly Marxist in the conception of coexistence as a contradictory unity of conflict and cooperation. For this is a way of thought and a pattern of behavior that is found in various contexts, capitalist ones included.

We meet with it, for example, in "oligopoly" or "oligopolistic competition," where a small number of giant firms dominate an industry. Significantly, the pattern of intercorporate relationships that tends to emerge in an oligopolistic industry is described by a Western economist as "peaceful" or "collaborative coexistence."[20] He explains that this is a pattern characterized by the development of cooperative relations among leading "powers" that continue energetic competition (especially "technological" or "product" competition as opposed to the more "warlike" price competition). The cooperative relations grow out of a sense of interdependence. In effect, competitive rivalry is accompanied and to some extent curbed by collaborative action to stabilize the market environment in the security interests of the major units involved. A system of relationships emerges in which there are simultaneous processes of competition and cooperation.

The analogy with international competitive coexistence in the new Soviet "dialectical" model of it is at best a crude and imperfect one. Yet it has a certain heuristic value. And it suggests that the appeal to dialectics represents here a way of providing ideological rationalization for a thought pattern that grows out of practical Soviet concerns and interests.

III

Soviet discussion of the cooperative element in the coexistence process is pervaded by the theme that the two sides must collaborate to guard against the outbreak of a new world war. Inozemtsev, for example, writes that the "platform" for political cooperation between states of the two systems is "the mutual interest of all states, all people, in averting a world thermonuclear war."[21] The purpose of such cooperation is not to eliminate the competitive struggle, but to make the world safe for its continuation. As an editorial in the *Kommunist* put it, "the Soviet Union proceeds from the assumption that it is possible to prevent the escalation [*pererastanie*] of this struggle into armed conflicts between states and that it can be guided into channels that would not threaten civilization with catastrophic wars, channels that would best fit the needs and interests of humanity."[22]

This is the context of thought in which it has seemed imperative to revise the classic Leninist-Stalinist thesis on the inevitability of wars under imperialism. The central issue in the Communist debate over the inevitability or noninevitability of wars in the present age is not, as might seem, the question of whether or not wars will occur. It is, rather, the division between the two Communist images of the process of coexistence in conditions short of major wars. The doctrine that wars have ceased to be inevitable in our time is an ideological correlate of the orientation toward competitive coexistence, whereas the older view that wars are inevitable so long as the imperialist system exists is part of the logic of the cold-war orientation in Communist international policy. Let us see how this is so.

Lenin's argument in *Imperialism: The Highest Stage of Capitalism* was that the age of imperialism necessarily witnesses periodic wars between unevenly developing imperialist powers for redivision of the world, especially the colonial part of it. In its post-1917 development, this theory was amended to read that future interimperialist wars would inevitably show a tendency toward transformation into coalition wars of imperialist powers against the socialist camp. In short, they would tend to become world wars. Thus when Communist doctrine speaks of the inevitability of wars under imperialism, the reference is not solely to interimperialist wars but to wars in general.

From the standpoint of those Communists who see coexistence solely as protracted conflict and reject all idea of cooperating with the "enemy" to minimize the danger of war, it is imperative to hold fast to this traditional ideological position. For if it is the very nature of imperialism that breeds various kinds of wars, and if wars will therefore necessarily go on occurring or tending to occur so long as imperialism survives on any significant scale, then it is quite futile to suppose that the war danger could be substantially affected by cooperative efforts to reduce East-West tensions, encouragement of a movement for peace, and so on. And by the same token, the only possible way in which Communists can effectively work for peace is to *intensify the cold war*, to carry on the conflict against the imperialist enemy relentlessly, to redouble their efforts in the revolutionary struggle to wrest the world, area by area, out of the enemy's control and thus to destroy the imperialist system together with its accompaniment—war. As Stalin summed it up in *Economic Problems of Socialism in the U.S.S.R.,* "To eliminate the inevitability of war, it is necessary to abolish imperialism."[23] This conclusion was part and parcel of the argument in his final work for the permanency of cold war in future East-West relations.*

Just as the inevitability thesis forms the ideological correlate of the cold-war orientation in Communist policy, so the contrary position logically belongs to, and has become a way of arguing, the "dialectical" approach to coexistence. For the noninevitability of wars is a necessary presupposition of a deliberate effort to reduce their likelihood. A politics of *détente* and a diplomacy of peacekeeping in East-West relations make no sense unless it is assumed that wars nowadays are, within limits, a controllable phenomenon, that there is some correlation between the relative likelihood of wars and what political leaders on both sides do or fail to do to prevent them. Given this assumption, the attainment of a *relatively* warless world no longer necessarily depends upon the prior liquidation of what remains of the "imperialist system." It is something toward which Communist and non-Communist leaders can work

* See pp. 99–101 above for an analysis of the argument.

now, while the world is still divided between their opposing systems, by taking certain precautions, by instituting certain reciprocal restraints, by keeping in close contact (for example, via the new Washington-Moscow communications line), and by making it their deliberate policy to resolve disputes without resorting to armed force. The noninevitabilty thesis therefore appears as the premise in a political syllogism that a Soviet writer formulates as follows: "Communist and worker parties proceed from the assumption that socialism can win final victory over imperialism without a world war. *From this it follows* that it is necessary to pursue a policy ensuring the prevention of war." (Italics added.)[24] In actuality, the premise on the noninevitability of war has been generated by the policy prescription.

Although this premise was first publicly unveiled at the Twentieth Congress, certain elements in the Soviet leadership had already been arguing it in private in Stalin's last years.* Stalin's death removed a decisively important obstacle to its adoption as official doctrine in the Soviet Union. Stalin was not, however, the only obstacle to the revision, for Stalinist habits of mind have remained a formidable force in the Soviet and other Communist parties. Thus the revision of the inevitability thesis by the Twentieth Congress was not a sudden maneuver; it represented the outcome of a long hard fight over this issue. Nor did the battle end then. Stalin's argument in the final work has been carried forward by the orthodox wing of the Communist movement led by the Maoist group in Communist China. The position that Mao has been upholding in the Communist coexistence controversy is not Maoism but Stalinism. It is the Stalinist theory of permanent cold war between Communism and the West. The great dispute between Moscow and Peking is thus, in its way, a dispute across time as well as across space. It is a clash between the Stalinist and the post-Stalinist orientations in international policy. As such it dramatizes the reality and deep significance of the change that has taken place in the mind of *Soviet* foreign policy from Stalin to Khrushchev.

From the standpoint of the latter-day Stalinists, the idea that

* In *Economic Problems of Socialism in the U.S.S.R.*, Stalin attributed to "some comrades" the view that wars between capitalist countries were no longer inevitable, and also that it might now be possible to prevent a third world war: "It is said that Lenin's thesis that imperialism inevitably generates war must now be regarded as obsolete, since powerful forces have come forward today in defense of peace and against world war. That is not true." (*Economic Problems of Socialism*, p. 30.)

cooperation with the enemy belongs integrally to the coexistence process is anathema. As the Chinese Communist Central Committee stated in its letter of June 14, 1963, to the Soviet Central Committee, "In the application of the policy of peaceful coexistence, struggles between the socialist and imperialist countries are unavoidable in the political, economic, and ideological spheres, and it is absolutely impossible to have 'all-around cooperation.' "* What makes the concept of cooperation with "the imperialists" to preserve peace so disturbing to the mind of the orthodox Communists is the possibility that it could lead by gradual steps to a substantial Soviet-Western accommodation and, with it, a stabilization of the world situation. To borrow an applicable term from recent American public discussion, they see in it the seeds of a "no-win" policy of settling down to live with the other side, as opposed to a policy of pressing forward in an unremitting offensive. So they have tenaciously held on to the Stalinist argument that there is no liquidating wars without first liquidating imperialism, whose inner tendency to generate periodic armed conflicts cannot be curbed by diplomatic means. They have contended furthermore that the most that can possibly be done directly by the Communist side to avert a major new war (which they profess not to want) is to be so formidably strong and *so demonstratively unafraid of a war* that the other side will be deterred from starting it. To suppose that cooperation with the enemy can achieve this end—their argument goes on—is to give way to the illusion that imperialism has undergone, or can undergo, a change of nature, that it can cease breeding wars, that the imperialist tiger can change its stripes. To imagine that it is possible to come to terms with the other side strategically, if only on the question of steps to ensure cosurvival, is to misunderstand the changeless nature of the enemy.

Soviet supporters of the revised coexistence doctrine have denied the charge that they believe that the nature of imperialism has changed. What has changed, they say, is not the nature of *imperialism* but the nature of the *world situation,* one vitally important feature of which is the existence of thermonuclear weapons and the means of their delivery by both sides—factors that would make a third world war incredibly and unbearably catastrophic. In these

* An even more sinister appraisal of the theme of cooperation has been given by the Albanian Communist press, which speaks of "a great conspiracy that aims at establishing and broadening links of collaboration between imperialists and modern revisionists." (*Zeri i Popullit,* June 23, 1963.)

unprecedented new circumstances, total war would mean total destruction for those who initiated it, and this gives ground for belief—so runs the Soviet counterargument—that an instinct of self-preservation will restrain the imperialist tiger from attacking. "The tiger is a beast of prey and will remain one as long as it lives," Khrushchev said, "but everyone knows that a tiger will never attack an elephant. . . . To continue the simile, it must be said that the Soviet Union, the countries of the socialist world, are today a much tougher proposition for the imperialists than the elephant is for the tiger."[25]

Advocates of the revised coexistence doctrine have a second line of defense against the charge of deviation from Lenin's analysis of imperialism. It turns on the seemingly abstract ideological question of the "nature of the epoch." Classic Leninist-Stalinist ideology defines the present age as an "imperialist epoch" whose essential characteristic is that historical development proceeds through periodic interimperialist wars that tend to turn into world wars and give rise, as in Russia in 1917, to revolutions and the spread of Communism. Now the revised Soviet coexistence doctrine has proclaimed the need to redefine the character of the epoch in view of such historic postwar changes as the formation of a "world system of socialist states," the growth of the "peace zone" around it, and the emancipation of the greater part of the former colonial world from imperialist control. The argument is that under these changed historical circumstances, imperialism has ceased to be the *dominant determinant* of the world's development, that its dynamics no longer necessarily dictate the pattern of events but are at most one important influence. Hence this is no longer an "imperialist epoch," but rather one of transition from the era of imperialist dominance that lasted until World War II to a dawning postimperialist era. And not being an "imperialist epoch" in the strict sense any longer, it is no longer an epoch in which wars are an unavoidable phenomenon. Lenin's analysis remains completely valid, then, but only as an analysis of an era that has now passed, or is now passing, in world history. In this way, the new Soviet doctrine proclaims its fidelity to Lenin in the very act of revising his conclusions.

IV

But the question arises whether the postulated objective changes in the world situation have been subjectively recognized and accepted by the "imperialists," whether the men in power on the other side have perceived and made adjustment to the new realities of the present age. The revised Soviet coexistence doctrine replies with a "yes-and-no" in the form of a theory of "two tendencies" in the mind and policy of the Western leadership. "In the politics of the capitalist camp in relation to the socialist countries," according to Khrushchev, "two tendencies make themselves felt: a bellicose-aggressive one and a moderately sober one."[26]

The antecedents of this idea go back to Lenin. But only in the post-Stalin period has this conception come into prominence and assumed a central place in Soviet doctrine. And it represents a significant departure from the Stalinist thought pattern. To the orthodox Stalinist mind, the men in power on the other side tend to appear as a more or less homogeneously hostile group, any seeming conciliatoriness from that quarter being in the nature of a ruse. In contrast, the advocates of the revised coexistence doctrine see an inwardly divided group within which one element remains implacably hostile and unamenable to a cooperative relationship with the U.S.S.R., while another, impeccably anti-Communist in its ideology, realistically appreciates the realities of the nuclear age, sees the need to coexist if at all possible, and will, especially if given real encouragement, act accordingly.* It is noteworthy that the Soviet mind here manifests a certain "psychologism" in the sense that it ignores Marxist notions of economic determinism, etc., and stresses the great importance of subjective phenomena, of states of mind in politically influential persons. This is illustrated in an assessment of the American policy mind offered in a speech by Gromyko: "On the U.S. political scene, in the Administration and Congress and also behind the scenes of the American machine of state, there are forces in action that *evaluate* the international

---

* The contrast between these two Communist images of the adversary is well reflected in the Twenty-second Congress speech of A. Adzhubei, editor of *Izvestia* and close associate of Khrushchev. Of Molotov he said: "From the height of his 'orthodox' immaculateness, Molotov warns: 'Look out, steer clear of contracts, they're dangerous, don't make concessions to the capitalist world.' " Then referring to Khrushchev's 1959 dinner at the Waldorf with 2,000 U.S. businessmen, he went on: "Contacts with people of this kind are a seditious thing from the standpoint of orthodox immaculateness. But these people stand at the head of the biggest capitalist state in the world; it is necessary to talk with them; they have to be dealt with. Some of these gentlemen have cold eyes, some have furious eyes, but some have attentive eyes, because over there, too, some people realize that we live on one planet." (*XXII S"ezd KPSS,* II, 469–70, 471.)

situation *differently* and have *different approaches* to the development of Soviet-American relations." (Italics added.)[27]

In a way, what the theory of the "two tendencies" is saying is that the division between Stalinist and post-Stalinist orientations to coexistence within the Communist ruling elite has its direct counterpart on the non-Communist side. Over there, too, it implies, there are the Cold Warriors who see the future of East-West relations only in terms of protracted conflict, and, on the other hand, there are those who would prefer to work together with the other side to keep the competition peaceful. And over there, too, the behind-the-scenes foreign-policy process is a continuing debate in which the conflicting orientations vie for ascendancy, with the result that policy moves in a zigzag pattern as one or the other of the two tendencies prevails.*

This Soviet picture of a conflict-ridden Western or American policy in East-West relations no doubt contains some elements of truth as well as a distorting admixture of projections based on Soviet experience. In other words, it reveals a great deal about the inner dynamics of the foreign-policy process that has been going on behind the scenes of the *Soviet* "machine of state." But for purposes of the present discussion, the important thing to note is the policy inference, which is that a working relationship for peace-keeping purposes is a realistic possibility insofar as the "moderately sober" tendency prevails in the ceaseless struggle going on, as the Soviet mind sees it, within the Western ruling groups.

Soviet writings so far offer no detailed prospectus of the process of cooperation as envisaged under the revised doctrine, but certain general themes can be noted. Cooperative relations between states of the two systems are said to be possible and desirable in the political, economic, cultural, scientific and technical areas but not in the realm of ideology, where there can be no coexistence but only an "irreconcilable struggle." Not surprisingly, in view of the concern with the issue of war and peace, political cooperation is rather strongly stressed. Even when discussing cooperation in the economic and cultural fields, Soviet leaders are inclined to note the political implications. Khrushchev gave a homely expression of this outlook when he discussed Soviet-American trade relations with American newspapermen in 1962. Saying that the absence

* Such, for example, is the picture of the American foreign-policy process given by Foreign Minister Gromyko in the above-quoted address to the Supreme Soviet of December 12, 1962.

of trade between the two countries was regrettable mainly for political rather than economic reasons, he added: "Since ancient times it has been accepted that if states trade with one another and try to develop commerce, they do not fight but live in peace. For this very reason the cessation of trade has always been a sign of worsening of relations between countries."[28] The same idea is reflected in such Soviet statements on cultural exchange relations as the following: "Cooperation in this sphere helps the peoples of different countries to know each other better, promotes mutual understanding, *creates a good basis for political negotiations."* (Italics added.)[29]

Soviet doctrine on the cooperative process in the political field emphasizes the special role of the great powers, the desirability of working contact between political leaders on both sides, the basic importance of acceptance by all concerned of the principle of pacific settlement of disputes, and, finally, the need for reciprocal concessions in the process of conflict resolution. On the first of these points, the view is often stated that the U.S.S.R. and U.S.A. bear "special responsibility" for peace and so have a natural leadership role in relations between the opposing systems. The fullest and clearest exposition of this position has been given by Gromyko in his speech in the aftermath of the 1962 Cuban crisis:

History has so developed that without mutual understanding between the U.S.S.R. and U.S.A., it is impossible to resolve a single serious international conflict, impossible to reach agreement on a single important international problem. . . . Even when the interests of these two powers are not directly involved in this or that region, the development of events there is not unaffected by the way in which Soviet-American relations take shape. If the U.S.S.R. and U.S.A. unite their efforts for the purpose of settling the conflicts and complications that arise in these regions, the thrusting flame of war dies out and tension goes down. Laos is an example.[30]

Political cooperation between the opposing camps is thus projected in the frame of a Soviet-American working relationship for peace-keeping purposes. What is envisaged, if Soviet public utterances may provide a basis for judgment, is not a formal alliance, and not a division of the world into spheres of interest, but rather a reasonably stable working relationship under which the political leaders of the two states would cooperate to prevent conflict-situations in various parts of the world from getting out of hand

and "escalating" into major wars. Nothing is said, however, to suggest that the Soviet-American relationship should be an exclusive one or that the two governments should not coordinate their views and positions on all important matters with those of their allies.

V

In expounding the "dialectical" understanding of coexistence, Soviet thinkers maintain that conflict and cooperation "interpenetrate" in the process. It is not as though conflict went on along certain lines while cooperative relations were maintained along others. They do not form two separate parallel processes. Rather, coexistence is treated as a contradictory "unity" under which conflict may have a cooperative aspect (save in the ideological field) and cooperation always has a competitive aspect. "Cooperation and conflict are indivisible in the process of peaceful coexistence," writes I. Krasin. "Economic cooperation is at the same time economic competition. Political cooperation is at the same time political struggle by peaceful means. Cultural exchange is at the same time a struggle of the ideological principles underlying each of the cultures, etc."[31]

To this way of thinking, trade, for example, is a field both of cooperation and conflict of systems. It is cooperation insofar as it involves agreement and peaceful intercourse and also insofar as it promotes a more peaceful international atmosphere. But it is conflict insofar as the trading partners engage in hard bargaining for the best possible terms under trade agreements and insofar as the trading relationship brings greater or lesser benefits to the competing economies and politics. So, too, with cultural relations, scientific intercourse, educational exchange, and so on. In all these fields, competition goes on intensely within a framework of cooperation.

Soviet thinkers discern the same pattern of duality in the sphere of political relations between states of the opposing systems. Here cooperation is understood as a joint arrangement under which the major powers on both sides undertake to promote peaceful resolution of conflicts in various places, to guide the development of international relations into nonviolent channels. It must now be added that from the "dialectical" point of view expressed by Soviet thinkers, this diplomacy of conflict resolution and conflict control is, simultaneously, a field of political rivalry. Soviet minds presuppose that both sides will seek to promote the competitive political interests of their respective systems in the very activity of working together to guard against the outbreak of war. Not peace as such, but *peace on terms most favorable to my country and my camp* is presumed to be the concern of the negotiators when they seek solutions of vexing international problems.

For example, in seeking to negotiate for the "defusing" of the situation in Berlin—which would represent an act of political cooperation for the prevention of war—East and West would both strive for competitive political advantage. The Soviet Union would press, as indeed it has done, for a set of defusing arrangements that would be best calculated to advance the interests of the Soviet Union by consolidating the East German Communist state and the entire East European structure of Soviet domination. The West for its part would strive, as it has in fact done, to minimize such consolidation and maintain the strongest possible footing in Berlin. A settlement, if achieved, would represent a mutually acceptable compromise at some point between the maximum and minimum positions of both sides. Such is the logic of coexistence in the "dialectical" view.* It would apply to all efforts of East and West to resolve international issues. Arms control and disarmament, for example, would represent at once a field of cooperation and an arena of struggle. An arms reduction agreement, if negotiated, would represent an example of intersystem cooperation to reduce world tension and the danger of war. But it would also be a competitive fact inasmuch as both parties would strive to negotiate it in such a way as to maintain or improve their relative military position. Furthermore, it would represent, from the Soviet point of view, a possible benefit in the long-range economic competition of the systems.

Against this background it is not hard to explain why the re-

---

* The analogy mentioned earlier between the "dialectical" approach and the pattern of coexistence of firms under oligopoly is very striking in this respect. We read the following, for example, concerning the negotiating process among major firms in the oligopolistic chemical industry: "They reach their decisions by driving hardheaded bargains. Each party tries to obtain the best terms for itself. Thus these decisions reflect the relative bargaining power of the parties involved. . . . In the final analysis, the issue turns on the comparative readiness of the several parties for a competitive 'war' if negotiations break down." (George W. Stocking and Myron W. Watkins, *Cartels in Action: Case Studies in International Business Diplomacy*. New York: The Twentieth Century Fund, 1947, p. 420.)

vised Soviet coexistence doctrine continues to attach small importance to the U.N. and associated organizations, including the World Court. In the Soviet view, the diplomacy of peacekeeping should be carried out by the major powers themselves, acting through bilateral channels, summit conferences, and so on. A well-known Soviet international-law theorist argues the superiority of such procedures over measures of diplomatic influence applied by international organizations on the ground that the former "are free of the formal limitations of method and result of the settlement of a disputed issue that are inherent in conciliation procedure, and . . . exclude the danger of pressure upon the disputants from third states aimed at utilizing the dispute in their own interests—a danger that cannot be avoided in mediation." As for international arbitration and judicial procedures, he continues, these can only be applied to "legal disputes" and not to cases involving serious political disagreements.[32] These are formal arguments. Underlying them is the point of view summarized above, the notion that the diplomacy of international conflict control is a *political* affair through and through in which both sides strenuously promote their competitive interests in the process of working together to reduce threats of war. From this point of view, the procedures of "old-fashioned diplomacy" must seem superior to all others.

We now come to a further instance of the indivisibility of conflict and cooperation in the revised coexistence doctrine. The world of the new coexistence theory is essentially tripartite. In addition to the Communist countries ("world system of socialist states") it includes, on the one hand, the developed "capitalist" states of the West and, on the other, the non-Communist new states of Asia, Africa, and Latin America, many of them politically unaligned and nearly all economically underdeveloped. This vast "third world" is envisaged as the decisive arena of the long-range contest of systems. The Soviet doctrine holds that the states composing it will develop either along Western "capitalist" lines or Soviet "socialist" lines depending, in part, upon the comparative performance of the Communist countries and the West in all departments of life, but above all in the economic field. Internal policy thus becomes foreign policy in the Soviet philosophy of competitive coexistence. The contest with the West for eventual predominance on the planet may and must be carried on through internal improvement and development, particularly by demonstrating that Soviet society is better able to create for its citizens a life of secure employment and material abundance. Needless to say, this part of the doctrine has, for Soviet politicians, the added attraction of providing an ideological rationalization for a policy of investing a greater share of Soviet resources in *Soviet* economic progress and correspondingly less in economic aid to other Communist states.

But if internal policy is foreign policy, foreign policy is not wholly internal. The Soviet doctrine calls for direct cooperative relations between Communist countries and those of the third world as a means of influencing the policy of the latter in a pro-Communist direction and of promoting their internal development along what is termed the "noncapitalist path." Economic assistance for developmental purposes, the provision of military equipment, and diplomatic support in international issues are prominent among the means employed by the U.S.S.R. in effecting this line of policy. Here, then, is a further expression of "dialectics" in the coexistence process: *cooperative* relations of the Soviet bloc with countries of the third world in the economic, diplomatic, and military spheres are simultaneously methods of waging the *competitive* struggle against the West. As a Soviet theorist expresses it: "The economic collaboration of these countries with the camp of socialism delivers them from economic subjection to the imperialists."[33] In order, we may add, to draw them into the Communist orbit of influence, which in turn is seen as a way station on their journey into the Communist world itself. In ideological terminology, this is called a movement via the stage of "national democracy" to that of "people's democracy."

In one fundamental respect, then, the revised Soviet coexistence doctrine is ideologically orthodox. It projects final Communist victory in the long-range contest of systems. It postulates the eventual end of the coexistence of systems as a result of the spread of the Communist form of society throughout the world. It holds, however, that the further progress of world Communist revolution can and will take place through the operation of forces indigenous to the societies concerned and that the proper function of Communist international policy is not to push through this process by "export of revolution" (i.e., the use of force from without to bring Communism to power), but to aid and abet it by methods that conform to the rules of international law and principles of competitive coexistence. In addition to the methods already discussed, mention should be made here of a vital supporting role that is allotted in this connection to Soviet military power. Its function, according to the revised coexistence doctrine, is not to help bring Communist governments to power but to deter what is called "export of counterrevolution," i.e., outside intervention to suppress by force a Communist government that has come to power in a given country by its own devices. Not the *use* of Soviet armed force to engineer Communist revolutions but the *threat* of it to help ensure them an opportunity to survive in power is, then, the prescription of the revised coexistence doctrine. It is logical in this light that the development of the revised doctrine since 1955 has gone along with a rising stress on the role of nuclear weapons in modern war; for these are the weapons that all contemporary theories of deterrence generally have most in view.

If external armed intervention either to install or remove Communist regimes is ruled out under the Soviet doctrine, there is still the question of the place of civil wars in the hypothetical future cases of Communism coming to power through operation of indigenous forces. This is a difficult question from the Soviet standpoint because, as shown above, the revised coexistence doctrine calls for the minimizing of the place of war in world affairs, and civil wars too are, after all, a form of war. A somewhat equivocal solution was first propounded at the Twentieth Congress. Altering the orthodox Communist view of the process whereby a Communist Party comes to power, it holds that civil war, while fully legitimate and possibly still necessary in individual cases, is not the only way. A "peaceful path" to power has become both possible and preferable in present-day conditions. By this it is meant that Communist parties may be able to achieve power in various countries by winning political victory without the use of armed violence. This theory of the "peaceful path" represents an effort to reconcile that part of the doctrine that concerns Communist revolutions with the part that concerns wars and the desirability of averting them. It has been attacked by the forces of orthodoxy in the Communist movement on the ground that there are no instances in which Communism has come to power by such a "peaceful path."

There remains the question of the Soviet position on "national-liberation wars," of which the Algerian conflict is the example most often cited in the Soviet literature. These are defined as popular armed struggles for independence in colonies or dependencies. They are not only endorsed as legitimate, but pronounced to be deserving of international moral and material support. Inconsistently, the Soviet doctrine argues at the same time that "local wars" involving forces of different nations should be avoided because they have a tendency to escalate into global wars. For may not international support cause a "national-liberation war" to escalate into a "local" one? Soviet leaders, it must be said, appear to be aware of this inconsistency in their position. One of their responses has been to espouse proposals for international action under the U.N. to effect the peaceful emancipation of all remaining colonies and dependencies. More important, they have apparently expressed views in private that diverge from the public endorsement of national-liberation wars. Referring to closed talks with Soviet leaders in 1959, a recently published Chinese Communist document says of them: "Although they occasionally spoke of the necessity of supporting national liberation wars and people's revolutionary wars, they repeatedly stressed that 'a war under contemporary conditions would inevitably become a world war,' that 'even a tiny spark can cause a world conflagration,' and that it was necessary to 'oppose all kinds of wars.' "[34]

One final aspect of the "dialectics" of coexistence merits mention. The revised doctrine holds that the less international tension exists, the better it will be for Communism. This is argued on the ground that the postulated internal processes leading individual countries toward Communism will be most fully liberated to do their work if relatively more peaceful international conditions prevail. Hence the Soviet Union can indirectly promote Communist victory in the long-range competitive struggle by its very activity of cooperating with amenable Western leaders to decrease tensions and the danger of war. The dialectical indivisibility of conflict and cooperation in the coexistence process here finds one more illustration. According to this reasoning, a state of international cold war tends both to unify the non-Communist world and to freeze its internal *status quo,* whereas a more relaxed international situation will provide the most favorable climate for success of the internal forces for social and political change in non-Communist societies. The argument is an interesting one. The question that I would like to raise in conclusion is whether it may not have greater applicability to Communist countries than to others. The dialectics of coexistence may work more favorably for democratic evolution in Communist society than for Communist revolution in democratic society.

12 RUSSIA, THE WEST, AND WORLD ORDER

There is a feeling abroad today that Western civilization is on trial before history. One of the clearest signs of it is the frequency with which we hear the word "challenge" in connection with the policies and progress of Soviet Russia and the Communist world at large. The challenge of the sputniks, of Soviet science and education, of Soviet economic development—these phrases, and variations on them, have recently grown familiar in America and Europe. We realize, of course, that the situation is not wholly a dark one for the West, that our Communist adversaries have serious internal problems of their own to contend with, that they too face some challenges. Still, nowadays few in the West find grounds for complacency in that fact.

In the following pages, attention will be directed to a generally neglected aspect of this large problem—the thinking on both sides about what is happening in the world in the twentieth century. The topic of this chapter is the Soviet challenge to the West in the field of theory. The term "theory" is used here in a quite specific sense. It refers not to theoretical ideas in general, and not to science, but specifically to comprehensive conceptions of the historical process of our time, conceptions of the direction or directions in which events are tending on a world scale. The thesis to be defended is that Soviet Russia does present a most serious challenge to the West in this particular sphere, albeit a challenge of which people in the West are not generally aware. One of the reasons why it is so serious is that "theory" in the particular meaning just specified is intimately related to policy-making, and the latter, in turn, influences or may influence the actual world trend of development.

Notoriously, we in the West tend to minimize the need for theory (and theorists) in the policy-making function, whereas the Soviet policy-makers attach considerable importance to it. In this respect they continue a tradition that goes far back into the past, and most notably to Lenin's important work of 1902, *What Is To Be Done?*, in which he contended that "Without a revolutionary theory there can be no revolutionary movement." Lenin here went far beyond his master, Marx, whose position was just the reverse of this; for Marx the correct formulation would be that without a revolutionary movement there can be no revolutionary theory.* The Russian Communist mind has changed considerably since Lenin's time, but theory in the above-mentioned sense of the word still shapes its thinking to an important degree. It is a measure of the persistence of this theoretical bias that Khrushchev, who is exceedingly theory-oriented compared with leading statesmen in most Western countries, has been criticized by certain elements within the Soviet Communist Party for being insufficiently so. He has rejected their charge of "practicalism."

The contrast between this outlook in policy-making and the characteristic Western one scarcely requires documenting. A pragmatic or instrumentalist approach to world problems typifies the Western policy-maker. Not theoretical conceptions enabling him to relate policy to the general trends of events, but know-*how* in the face of concrete problem-situations is what he typically emphasizes. He wants to "solve" the immediate, given concrete problem that is causing "trouble," and be done with it. Accordingly, diplomatic experience—always of great importance, of course—is exalted as the supreme qualification for leadership in foreign policy. For experience is the royal road to know-how. It teaches the statesman how to negotiate with the Russians, how to coordinate policy with the allies, how to respond to emergencies, and so on.

In facing foreign-policy problems it is not the Western habit to attempt first of all to form a valid general picture of the world-setting of events in which the problems have arisen. The tendency is rather to isolate the given problem-situation from the larger

* See, for example, Marx's statement that "The existence of revolutionary ideas in a particular period presupposes the existence of a revolutionary class." (K. Marx and F. Engels, *The German Ideology* [New York, 1939], p. 40.)

movement of history and ask: What can and should we *do* about it? And, characteristically, even when one of the West's foremost thinkers, George Kennan, seeks to *rethink* our foreign policy, as in his 1957 Reith lectures in England, he begins not by asking what is broadly happening in the twentieth-century world, but by pointing to the German situation as the crucial knot in the tangle of East-West relations and suggesting a new, practical approach to it.

So strong is the instrumentalist bias in our foreign-policy thinking that we cannot easily perceive the existence of a Soviet challenge to the West in the area of theory. We can readily see that the Russians challenge us in science, education, military power, economic growth, missiles—everything, in fact, about which we can straightway *do* something without becoming involved in the work of theorizing. On the other hand, some of our Asian friends take a very different view. A Ceylonese scholar visiting in the United States suggests that a technological bias is unfortunate in Western relations with contemporary Asia. The Western democracies, he writes, appear to be hamstrung vis-à-vis Asia, and will have to learn that "support of freedom alone as an essential for the life of Asia is not enough." And, referring to the Soviet bloc, he goes on to say: "The strength of the Marxist group stems from the fact that they provide theory or ideology which is relevant to the clamant needs of the peoples. *Tools alone are not enough.* This is what aid under the Colombo plan reveals." (Italics added.)[1] I believe that we would do well to reflect seriously on this criticism of the Western approach to the problems of Asia and note that the deficiency to which it calls attention is a deficiency of "theory."

However, our image of a pragmatic, technique-minded West versus a theory-conscious Soviet Russia requires some modification. For the foreign policy of the Western coalition has a certain grand design that is not devoid of doctrinal foundation. Curiously, though, this underlying philosophy of the Western position derives from a single source—a rather brief essay by George Kennan entitled "The Sources of Soviet Conduct," published in *Foreign Affairs* in 1947. Here Kennan explored the motivation of the Soviet expansionism that, as he correctly foresaw, would confront the West for years or decades ahead with a profoundly serious challenge. And he formulated the concept of "containment" of Soviet expansionism that still serves as the theoretical base of the entire structure of Western policy in the present world situation. Ironically, it was Kennanism in this form that rose to do battle with

Kennan when, in his Reith lectures, he embarked upon the search for a new perspective.

The philosophy of containment played a great and positive role during the years following World War II. But, beginning in 1953, the year of Stalin's death and the Soviet explosion of a thermonuclear device, the development of events has revealed signs of its inadequacy. And looking back now upon the essay in which this philosophy was stated, I think that its essential deficiency can be stated as follows: the reasoning relates only to *Russia*. This is not said in criticism of Kennan, who had every right to confine himself to his announced subject—the sources of Soviet conduct. It is a criticism of the essay only in its acquired historical role as the theoretical underpinning of Western policy in the contemporary world.

The essay examined the powerful expansionist drive that was manifest in the actions of the Stalin regime in the war's aftermath, but it did so in abstraction from the over-all world setting. It did not construct a broad frame of reference, did not visualize the Russian developments in relation to the general pattern of events of our time in the world at large. The global situation and tendencies in the twentieth century lay outside its scope. The horizon of thinking was a Russian and not a world horizon. And this basic limitation entered into the structure of Western policy as it took firm shape in the late 1940's.

Here, I suggest, we touch upon a fundamental flaw in the Western position and a source of some of the troubles that the West is experiencing. Here too is one of the explanations for the uneasiness that many thoughtful people in the West feel nowadays about the established ways of thinking and acting in foreign affairs. Our response to the global situation is an inadequate one. Lacking a world horizon in its thinking, the Western coalition lacks an affirmative policy for the world. To state it otherwise: The West, instead of dealing with Russia in terms of a world policy, persists in the attempt to deal with the world in terms of a Russian policy, this being in essence the policy of containing Russia all over the world. The underlying orientation is faulty.

Here is the context in which the Soviet challenge to the West in the field of theory takes shape. For Soviet thinking and policy do not suffer from the deficiency just pointed out. Of Soviet Russia it cannot be said that, instead of dealing with America in terms of a world policy, it deals with the world in terms of an American policy. Whatever its own peculiar deficiencies may be—and these will be mentioned below—the Soviet philosophy of foreign policy has a world horizon. That is, Soviet foreign policy and, more generally, the policy of the Communist bloc are predicated upon a certain theory of contemporary history, a broad conception of what is transpiring in the twentieth century. What is this conception, and what light if any does it shed upon the realities of world history in our time?

II

The answer to the first part of this question is a great deal more complicated and obscure than one might offhand suppose. The theory of history to which the Soviet leaders officially give their allegiance is Marx's, as elaborated in the *Communist Manifesto.* According to Marx, all modern capitalist societies are arenas of civil war between the classes of property-owning exploiters and exploited working masses; and the civil wars are approaching violent *dénouements* in social revolutions that collectively will mark the transition to the universal Communist society wherein man realizes his human nature and history comes to rest.

While this is the doctrine of history to which the Soviet leaders pledge their allegiance, it is by no means the full story of what they think. In fact, it has long since receded into the background of the Russian Communist mind and become a kind of formal first premise for a working theory of history that reflects events of our time and is not to be found in the annals of nineteenth-century Marxism. The working theory not only goes beyond anything that Marx ever thought or wrote. It is in some important respects *inconsistent* with his view of history. Whereas Marx, for example, visualized the world revolution as a simultaneous act of the rebellious proletarian classes of the most advanced capitalist countries of Europe (specifically England, France, and Germany), the Soviet working theory sees it as a long-drawn-out historical process beginning in Russia and having its center of gravity in the East.

This working theory of contemporary history has come to be known as the theory of the "general crisis of capitalism." It evolved gradually during the 1920's, as the Russian Communists sought to work out a scheme of ideas that would, as it were, "save" Marxism, but at the same time reflect what had actually happened in Russia and anticipate what was yet to happen elsewhere in the future. The one constant in their thinking—still operative today—

was the postulate that the October Revolution was not a mere national event, not simply a momentous incident in the history of Russia, but the beginning of a larger process, a general movement in world affairs. Without this postulate, of course, the Russian Communists could not have maintained the affiliation with Marxism, which rests on the notion of "world history."

What underwent change as the Soviet working theory evolved was the concrete image of the larger process of which the Russian Revolution was taken to be a part. In the immediate post-Revolutionary period, Lenin and others clung to the idea that October was the somewhat fortuitous first step of a world revolutionary process whose epicenter lay in Western Europe. They looked particularly to revolution in advanced Germany as the salvation of backward Red Russia. But when revolution failed to materialize in Europe and Soviet power consolidated itself in Russia, a vast orientation of thinking began in Moscow. The larger world process initiated by the Russian Revolution came to be seen and felt as a process with its epicenter in the awakening Asian hinterlands of Europe. The postulated division of the world between capitalist and Communist camps took concrete shape in Russian Communist thinking as a division between what Lenin, in one of his last writings, called "the counterrevolutionary imperialist West" and the "revolutionary and nationalist East."[2]

World War I, Lenin said, had dislodged the Eastern countries, including India and China, from their groove and drawn them into "a process of development that cannot but lead to a crisis in the whole of world capitalism" (here we have the origin of the phrase "general crisis of capitalism"). And he went on to add: "In the last analysis, the upshot of the struggle will be determined by the fact that Russia, India, China, etc., account for the overwhelming majority of the population of the globe. And it is precisely this majority that, during the past few years, has been drawn into the struggle for emancipation with extraordinary rapidity, so that in this respect there cannot be the slightest shadow of doubt what the final outcome of the world struggle will be."[3]

What was reflected in Lenin's statement, which has since become one of the most quoted in Communist literature, was the growth of what might be called an "Eastern orientation" in the Russian Communist mind. Briefly, the epicenter of world revolutionary development was transferred from the industrialized West, where Marx himself had placed it, to the backward, agrarian, colonial, but in-

creasingly rebellious East. The world revolutionary process came
to be conceived of not as an all-European proletarian revolution
on Marx's model, but as a long-drawn-out revolt of the colonial
East against European hegemony on the model of the revolution
in semi-Asiatic peasant Russia. Now all this was quite un-Marxian.
But it was and is related to certain real and profoundly important
world developments of the twentieth century.

The Leninist phrase "general crisis of capitalism" is an inaccurate description of these developments, because it places prime
emphasis on the economic factor, not on the political aspect, where
it belongs. It is quite true that the world-wide economy of exchange
that was brought into being in the nineteenth century has suffered
great disruption in the twentieth, and that World War I and the
Russian Revolution inaugurated this process. But the supremely
significant historical fact marked by these events was the breakdown of an international political order characterized by the world
hegemony of Europe.

True, the international order of the nineteenth century never institutionalized itself as a world-wide political system; it was not an
organized system of international order. It was, however, such a
system in embryo. The core was the European political system
created by the Vienna settlement in 1815, a system whose mechanism of balance of power maintained what has been called the
"hundred years' peace"; it kept wars of world-wide scope from
occurring for a century. What gave this intra-European political
order global significance was the fact that Europe in the nineteenth
century, together with the United States, brought most of the rest
of the world within its political and economic orbit of control or
influence.

The basic fact of contemporary history to which the new "Eastern orientation" in the Russian Communist mind and the new post-
Marxian working theory corresponded was the collapse of the
Europe-centered international order in and after World War I. As
this working theory saw from the beginning, the defection of Soviet
Russia from the European system signalized most dramatically and
consequentially the collapse of the old order. And instead of
treating this initial great defection as a fluke or reparable accident,
the theory construed it to be the momentous beginning of a long
process of further decline and eventual total fall of the Europe-
centered order in the world. It projected the departure of Russia

from the European system in 1917 as an augury of the shape of things to come.

Russia had been a great European power from the time of Peter two centuries earlier, and in the nineteenth century became one of the five European powers on which the balance-of-power system rested. As one historian writes of the imperial Russian government, "If there was any constant element in her policy, it was her devotion to the idea of a European system, to be maintained, developed, and defended against every threat."[4] Seen, then, in the perspective of history, the outstanding significance of the October upheaval is that Russia as a consequence retired into the isolation from Europe of the state of Muscovy before Peter's time, reverting to the historic Muscovite anti-European posture. Some perceived this at a very early stage. For example, a group of Russian *émigrés* who called themselves "Eurasians" published a volume in Sofia in 1921 called *Outlet to the East,* which described revolutionary Russia as "a former European province" now in revolt against Europe.[5] Lenin, as a Marxist with a high regard for certain aspects of European civilization, could not have agreed that this accurately summed up the essential historical meaning of Russia's October Revolution. But a dim cognizance of it was surely reflected in his words of 1923 quoted above, and entered into Moscow's working theory of the world situation as elaborated in subsequent years.

This Moscow of the Third International reverted in its outlook to the earlier Moscow that had proclaimed itself the Third Rome. It saw itself as the embodiment of the ascendant principle as against a decadent Western world, and the new Russia as the *nucleus* around which other "former European provinces" in revolt against Europe would cluster as the world movement proceeded further. Stalin, himself a man of the East, found this ideology very congenial. He had significantly entitled one of his articles of the revolutionary period "Light Comes from the East." As early as April, 1917, he had propounded the idea that "Russia may be the country that points the way to socialism." And the concept of Russia as the nucleus of the world-revolutionary process was given its classic formulation by him in an interview with a delegation of American workers in 1927:

In the further progress of development of the international revolution, two centers will be formed: the socialist center, attracting to itself all the countries gravitating towards socialism, and the capitalist center, attracting to itself all the countries gravitating towards capitalism. The fight between these two centers for the conquest of world economy will decide the fate of capitalism and communism throughout the whole world, for the final defeat of world capitalism means the victory of socialism in the arena of world economy.[6]

As his later writings showed, the two opposing hegemonic centers around which the world was destined to be polarized were Russia and America. Stalin's statement of 1927 was constantly quoted in Soviet writings after World War II to show that he had foreseen the cold war. However, it was quoted in an edited form.

In the original form, just cited, economics was called the decisive arena of world conflict. The fight between the two world "centers" would be primarily a fight for "conquest of world economy." Now, in the background of this idea lay another important element of the working theory that was originated by Nikolai Bukharin. In his book *Economics of the Transition Period,* published in Moscow in 1920, Bukharin had pictured the growth of the world revolution as a gradual historical process in which industrialized "socialist" countries would draw other former colonies into their orbit by force of *economic attraction.* The process would work itself out as follows:

> Former colonies and backward agrarian countries, where there is no proletarian dictatorship, nevertheless enter into economic relations with the industrial socialist republics. Little by little, they are drawn into the socialist system, approximately in the same way that peasant agriculture is drawn into it in individual socialist countries. Thus does the world dictatorship of the proletariat grow little by little. As it grows, the resistance of the bourgeoisie weakens, and toward the end, the remaining bourgeois complexes will in all probability surrender with all their organizations intact.[7]

It was this Bukharinist image of future world development that underlay Stalin's reference in 1927 to the "victory of socialism in the arena of world economy."

However, the concept of Soviet expansion through "conquest of world economy" was destined to be laid aside for many years—in fact, until the 1950's, when Khrushchev resuscitated it. It faded out of Stalinist thinking in the period before and after World War II. An interesting historical reflection of this is the fact that when Stalin re-edited his earlier writings after the war, for inclusion in his collected works, he *deleted the phrases* "conquest of world economy" and "in the arena of world economy" from his 1927 statement on the future emergence of two antagonistic world centers. Doubtless what moved him to do so was the inconsistency between this bloodless picture of a world-wide revolutionary development that was economically determined, and his own gradually evolved image of the cold war as a politico-military duel between the U.S.S.R. and the United States for world empire.

Already in the early 1930's, he had gravitated toward the idea that the advancement of the world-revolutionary process would take place by the very same means as that by which it was initiated: a world war. In 1934, he stated that a new war "will certainly unleash a revolution and will place in question the very existence of capitalism in a number of countries, as happened during the first imperialist war." "Let not Messrs. the bourgeoisie blame us," he went on, "if on the morrow of such a war certain governments close to their hearts, now ruling safely 'by the grace of God,' turn up missing."[8] The war came, and he undertook in the aftermath to compel history, against the will of the Eastern European peoples, to fulfill his earlier prediction. He took the path of imperialist expansion that led to the creation of the system of satellite states. As a consequence of this, and of the Communist revolution in China, the great Sino-Soviet sphere came into being more or less as it exists today—a conglomeration of states covering a quarter of the earth's territory, possessing a total population of more than a billion, and accounting for perhaps about a third of the world's industrial production.

III

While the Communist sphere was being expanded in the postwar years, the official Soviet theory of the world situation was being reformulated in Moscow in the light of the new developments and under Stalin's personal guidance. There was much doctrinal discussion of the "general crisis of capitalism" and its further development during and after World War II. Finally, Stalin made an authoritative pronouncement on it in his *Economic Problems of Socialism in the U.S.S.R.*

He stated there that the general crisis had entered upon a second stage. The first stage began during World War I, especially as a result of the secession of Soviet Russia from the world capitalist system, which split the world in two. The second stage developed during World War II, especially after the secession of China and the other "people's democracies" from what remained of the world capitalist system. These were successive stages in the development of a single, pervasive, over-all crisis of the former world capitalist system. The crisis was to be seen as a historical process embracing both economy and politics on a global scale. The second stage witnessed a deep aggravation of the crisis. No longer was Soviet Russia pitted all alone against the world from which it had defected in 1917. The picture now was rather one of two *worlds* in opposition—reflected, for example, in the emergence of a "parallel world market" in the Soviet East. Stalin, in short, saw the present situation as a realization of his prophecy of 1927 about the future polarization of the globe around two antagonistic world centers. However, as his earlier deletion of the reference to *economic* competition indicated, he visualized the continuing contest between them for global hegemony in the military-political terms of the cold war against the West, as he had been waging it since 1947.

It was suggested earlier that the Soviet working theory of the world situation corresponded broadly to certain real developments of this century connected with the breakdown of the old Europe-centered international order. Regarded from this point of view, Stalin's postwar reformulation of the doctrine of the general crisis erred on the side of conservatism. It recognized that the crisis of international order entered a new and aggravated stage during and after World War II. But it failed to take adequate measure of the deepening of the crisis, the extent to which the old international order has further crumbled in our time. Stalin saw this development solely or primarily in terms of the rise of the Sino-Soviet empire in opposition to the erstwhile dominant West. But that is only one major component of the process of dissolution of the old order.

The other major component is the departure of the Afro-Asian-Arab nations from colonial dependency and the tutelage of the West. It is the breakdown of the structure of Western dominion in the non-European parts of the world, the disappearance of most of what remained in the interwar period of the great European colonial empires. And the fact that many of the newly independent countries are now called "uncommitted nations" shows that independence has tended in numerous instances to mean departure from the Western order of things. Viewed as a whole, this process marks a radical shift in world affairs. In an important sense it could be said that the nineteenth century finally came to an end in the after-

math of World War II. The downfall of the old international order
is now nearly complete. The Europe that once controlled the world
has become a truncated peninsula of Asia holding a few outposts
here and there, and even in its African hinterland the dissolution
of the old order is swiftly proceeding.

This trend of development was seen and understood by students
of international affairs in Moscow. The economist Eugene Varga,
for example, foresaw the postwar line of development in Asia and
cautiously called attention to it in a book written at the war's end.
Stalin, however, resisted and overruled this appraisal. He compelled
the professional theorists to deny the facts and contradict what
they knew to be true. He refused to recognize the revolutionary
implications of such developments as the granting of independence
to India, Burma, the Philippines, and other former dependencies
of the West. He insisted that no meaningful change had taken
place, that the independence of these newly independent nations
was merely a cunning fiction by which the colonialists and their
local agents—such as Nehru—were trying to conceal the continuing reality of colonial dependence upon the West.

For psychological reasons explored in the preceding chapter, he
considered that there was simply no such thing as a neutral or
"uncommitted" country, no space between the two antagonistic
worlds. Any territory necessarily remained an Anglo-American
preserve until such time as it changed worlds and became a part
of the Soviet empire. This, as we have seen, was the logic underlying the Stalinist theory of cold war. It also underlay the Stalinist
practice of cold war, with its emphasis on territorial conquest,
which found supreme expression in the Korean War. Stalin, right
up until the end in March, 1953, appears to have overruled any
idea of a Korean armistice. His death was the crucial factor behind
the cessation of hostilities in Korea as well as the broader reorientation of Soviet foreign policy that took place in the following period.

The reorientation made possible by Stalin's death, and by the re-
lease of Soviet policy from the autocrat's personal psychology, has
theoretical as well as practical aspects. Among the former, first
place goes to the recognition of the realities of postwar political
development outside the Communist sphere, which Stalin had
forced the theorists to deny. This change, however, has taken place
within the framework of a basic continuity of doctrine. The conception of contemporary world history as a reflection of a "general
crisis of capitalism" remains fully in force under Khrushchev. The

division of the world between what is now called the "world system
of socialist states"—that is, the Communist bloc—and all other
countries is taken to be the central fact of the general crisis and the
international situation. The general crisis is still seen as a developmental process on a world scale, and Soviet doctrine holds to Stalin's tenet that during and after World War II it entered a second
and greatly aggravated stage.

But the official assessment of the crisis in its present stage no
longer errs on the side of conservatism. Stalin's refusal to recognize
the postwar collapse of Western hegemony over vast tracts of the
non-Western world is now a thing of the past. Indeed, "breakdown
of the colonial system of imperialism" is taken by Soviet theorists
not only as largely a *fait accompli* of history, but also as a principal
expression of the *deepening* of the general crisis in the present
"third" stage. They affirm that countries with an aggregate population of more than 1.3 billion have, since the war, ceased to be
colonies or dependencies of the West, whereas before the war the
population of colonies and dependencies was 1.5 billion.

A Soviet monograph of 1958 divides the former colonies and
dependencies into three big groups: (1) the Asian Communist
states of China, North Korea, and North Vietnam, where the breakdown of colonialism is said to appear in its "most mature form";
(2) countries such as India, Egypt, Indonesia, and Burma, which
have won political independence under the leadership of a "national bourgeoisie" and remain capitalist in economic structure although they have set out to attain economic independence by industrialization and have made some inroads on foreign property
holdings (as in the incident of Egypt's nationalization of the Suez
Canal Company); and (3) countries such as the Sudan, Morocco,
Tunisia, and Libya, which have likewise won political independence
but have yet to consolidate their national sovereignty and embark
on national economic development. The monograph also refers to
a fourth group of countries, those still in the position of colonies
and dependencies, but points out that forces are in motion that
will eventually bring them, too, from colonial status to independence.[9]

Thus in one important respect, a drastic change has taken place
since Stalin's death in the Soviet doctrine of the world situation.
The departure of non-Communist as well as Communist countries
from the Europe-centered international order of the nineteenth
century has been recognized as a fact. Further, it has been evalu-

ated as a positive and progressive development in history, a movement that deepens the "general crisis" and whose support thus is in the Soviet interest. The above-mentioned monograph, for example, reasons as follows: The tendency in the newly independent countries is toward "a new form of state capitalism," whose main feature is the promotion of the development of the national economy. Not only does such development in turn strengthen the newly won political independence from the West; it also creates big native enterprises that can compete with foreign (i.e., Western) concerns, even in world markets. It strengthens the local economy against Western economic penetration and influence. It constricts Western markets, as, for example, in India, where the development of a textile industry has reduced the market for British textiles and so has helped keep the British textile industry in its state of chronic crisis. It intensifies internal class conflict in the Western countries by forcing manufacturers to cut labor costs in the effort to meet increased foreign competition. And it increases tensions between the Western powers themselves.[10]

The monograph goes on to say that the decline and fall of the old colonial order are of "special" importance in that they make possible a *rapprochement* between the Soviet bloc and a whole series of countries that used to constitute the "reserve of imperialism." The majority of these countries pursue an independent policy, are friendly to the "socialist" states, refuse to participate in anti-Soviet blocs and alliances, and enter into what is called a "peace zone." This phrase was introduced into official Soviet doctrine by Khrushchev in his public report to the Twentieth Party Congress. He declared that an immense "peace zone" was taking shape in the world, including "socialist" and "nonsocialist" states and embracing territories in which live nearly 1.5 billion people, a majority of the world's population. In this same report Khrushchev said that the period of world history foretold by Lenin, when the peoples of the East would become a primary determining factor in the destinies of the world, had now come to pass.

M. S. Dragilev, the writer of the 1958 monograph already cited, uses the phrase "anti-imperialist bloc" as an alternative to "peace zone." He writes that the postwar formation of the "world system of socialist states," combined with the breakdown of the colonial system, has brought the bloc into being. The "anti-imperialist bloc" includes (1) the "socialist" countries—i.e., the Soviet bloc: (2) former colonial countries that have won their independence; and

(3) the colonies. This is a heterogeneous collection, he points out, but is cemented by the presence of a common enemy—"imperialism."[11] By "imperialism" he obviously means the Western powers, headed by the United States. The choice of the phrase "anti-imperialist bloc" in place of the relatively toothless term "peace zone" is most interesting and significant as an indication of Soviet thinking. It shows clearly that the alliance of the Soviet bloc with the non-Communist or not-yet-Communist "former provinces of Europe" in Asia, the Near East, Africa, etc., is envisaged as a distinctly anti-Western grouping of the great majority of nations and peoples. Thus, a specifically anti-Western and pro-Soviet neutralism, and not a genuine neutralism, is projected as the proper stance for a non-Communist nation in the "peace zone" or "anti-imperialist bloc." In short, the underlying theoretical postulate of the Soviet thinkers is that what was formerly a huge "reserve of imperialism" —the Eastern hinterlands of Europe—shall in time become a reserve of sovietism, that a partnership shall take shape between the Soviet bloc and the remainder of the non-Western world *against* the West, that the great Afro-Asian-Arab zone will become increasingly oriented toward the Soviet bloc as it is emptied of what remains of Western influence. Nor, in this thinking, does the anti-Western bloc exclude certain states that geographically belong to the "West," such as the Latin American countries.

Here is the theoretical background of Khrushchev's doctrine of long-range economic competition between the Soviet bloc and the West. This doctrine has evolved in the post-Stalinist period along with the practical Soviet program of aid-and-trade, under which large sums have been granted to non-Communist countries in the form of credits for arms and economic development. The political rationale of the new policy is directly related to the broad theoretical conceptions just outlined. The concrete economic assistance is regarded as having a political purpose of prime importance: to help along the ongoing process of self-detachment of non-Communist countries in the "anti-imperialist bloc" from economic dependence upon the West and Western political influence. Beyond this, however, Soviet writers now frankly acknowledge that the policy has the further positive goal of attracting these countries into more and more intimate relations with the Soviet bloc and encouraging them to adopt Soviet patterns of economic organization and society. Dragilev, for example, states:

As the former colonies win political independence, they enter an ever closer *rapprochement* with the socialist countries, which extend to them all-round economic and political assistance on a basis of equality to strengthen their independence. Already at this time there is much interest being shown within India, Egypt, and Indonesia in the methods of economic construction employed in the socialist countries.[12]

As noted earlier, Bukharin in 1920 envisaged economics as the decisive field of battle between the world revolutionary forces embodied in Soviet Russia and the bourgeois powers of the West. Industrialized Soviet republics, he prophesied, would exert an increasing power of attraction upon former colonies and backward agrarian countries, drawing them "little by little" into the Soviet orbit of political influence. Stalin initially endorsed this economic emphasis in Communist theory, but subsequently abandoned it in his obsession with the cold war as a politico-military duel between the two superpowers. Viewed against this background, the doctrinal innovations of the Khrushchev period appear as largely a revival of some older Russian Communist ways of thought. The fundamental identity of Khrushchev's conception, as formulated by Dragilev in the passage just cited, with that which Bukharin sketched thirty years ago is easily discernible. The language is now more cautious, but it is clearly the old idea that is being expressed. The basic political conception that underlies Khrushchev's doctrine of long-range economic competition between the Soviet bloc and the West is a novelty only in relation to later Stalinism—the Stalinism that deleted "conquest of world economy" from Stalin's own earlier writings. But it has a doctrinal ancestry going back to the Lenin period. The great difference is a practical one: Soviet Russia today has the economic potential to act on an idea that, at the time Bukharin first formulated it, could be little more than a prophecy.

Together with many of his other policies, Khrushchev's effort to revive the theory and develop the practice of Soviet economic competition with the West in the underdeveloped countries has met some resistance. Certain highly conservative elements within the leadership of the Soviet Communist Party have opposed the policy of extending credits for economic development to non-Communist countries such as India, Egypt, and Indonesia. Specifically, some members of the now ousted conservative opposition, who vainly attempted to unseat Khrushchev in mid-1957, appear to have fought Khrushchev on the issue of "foreign aid" as well as on numerous other external and internal questions.*

The controversy has since come into the open as one of the major issues of the Sino-Soviet conflict. Soviet published materials of mid-1958 remain of interest, however, as a reflection of the manner in which the policy debate was being conducted inside the Soviet Party. Dragilev, for example, formulates—for purposes of refutation—the anti-Khrushchev position on Soviet economic assistance to non-Communist countries. Does not the process of self-detachment of former colonial countries from colonialism signify, he inquires, an enlargement of the capitalist sphere of the world? And do not the "socialist" countries therefore encourage the expansion of *capitalism* by supporting this process with economic aid? If this, as seems quite probable, is a reflection of the actual line of argument used by the anti-Khrushchev opposition, the burden of the argument would be that Soviet economic assistance to newly independent but non-Communist countries is calculated to strengthen their position as non-Communist, so why extend such assistance? The steel mill we are building at Bhilai, one can hear the opposition saying, is costing us a lot, and at the same time will help to consolidate India's independent economic position as a non-Communist country; it will inhibit rather than promote a Communist revolution in India.

To this line of argument the Khrushchev school of thought replies that Soviet economic assistance will not *in the long run* promote "capitalist" prospects in non-Communist Asia or elsewhere. Writing in *Pravda* in July, 1958, Academician Arzumanian contended that the newly independent countries cannot solve their problems of industrialization by developing "along ordinary capitalist lines." He then added, rather imperiously and without supporting arguments: "The peoples of these countries will become more and more convinced that socialism, not capitalism, is their immediate future."[13] Dragilev reasons similarly in reply to the opposition, but places main emphasis upon a further point. The question of the development of capitalism in former colonial countries, he writes, has to be approached from the standpoint of the "relationship of world forces." Present developments in these countries are undermining the positions of the "monopolies" (i.e., the West),

---

* See particularly Maxim Saburov's speech of recantation at the Twenty-first Party Congress, in which he stated that the "anti-Party group" opposed Soviet "assistance to underdeveloped countries."

and "Everything injurious to the monopolies alters the relationship of forces in favor of socialism" (i.e., whatever hurts the West helps us).[14]

Behind this reasoning lurk not only the interests of the Soviet state, but also the Soviet working theory of history as outlined earlier. The argument is that Soviet economic assistance to non-Communist, former colonial countries must be viewed primarily in terms of its *political* effect. While it may temporarily strengthen the economic position of the recipient as a non-Communist country, it likewise reinforces the new political status of non-attachment to the West. And whatever accelerates the movement of the newly independent countries *away* from the Western political order and Western influence thereby alters the balance of world power in favor of the Soviet camp and indirectly promotes the eventual expansion of Communism within the new "anti-imperialist bloc." In short, the foreign economic assistance program is advocated by the Khrushchev school in Soviet policy as an instrument for accelerating a deep, ongoing, historical process of secession of "former European provinces" from the old order. Beyond this, the Khrushchev school confidently predicts that the beneficiary of this whole process will be the Soviet-led "world system of socialist states." The newly independent countries are frankly visualized as gravitating into the Soviet orbit little by little. It was no doubt with this prospect in view that Soviet doctrine was amended in 1956 to provide for a "peaceful" mode of "transition to socialism." In his report to the Twentieth Party Congress, Khrushchev particularly singled out countries where capitalism is weak and relatively undeveloped as the most likely places for the "peaceful" mode of transition. Soviet theorists since then have emphasized, by the way, that "peaceful" does not imply absence of coercion. All that is meant, they indicate, is that Communism may come to power without civil war, widespread armed violence, or military intervention by the Soviet bloc.

IV

This chapter has traced the evolution in Soviet thought of a working theory of contemporary world history not contained in original Marxism. What claim the theory has to validity derives from its departure from Marx's false prophecy of an all-European proletarian revolution—a departure carried out in order to relate what happened in Russia in October, 1917, to an actual world trend of development. The postulate of the theory all along has been that the October Revolution was more than a national Russian occurrence, that it betokened a movement of things, a tide in human affairs, not localized in Russia. The revolution came to be seen—or felt—as Russia's mighty act of secession from the Europe-centered world order of the nineteenth century, and as a beginning and major part of a general movement of secession of nations from that order, a movement having its epicenter in the awakening colonial East.

In the doctrine of the "general crisis of capitalism," as evolved in the 1920's and amended in the 1940's and 1950's, the disintegration of the old world-embracing order is viewed as proceeding in two great stages connected with the two world wars of the twentieth century. The doctrine, moreover, sees the seceding nations as forming an embryonic and expanding *new* world order, with Soviet Russia or the "socialist world system" as the hub of power and fountainhead of world-wide political and ideological influence, corresponding to Europe in the nineteenth century. Since Stalin's death, the concept of seceding nations has been greatly broadened to include not only nations that already form a part of the Soviet bloc, but also former dependencies of the West that, while as yet "uncommitted" and non-Communist in political regime, nevertheless cohere with the Communist countries in a huge "peace zone" or "anti-imperialist bloc" whose essential defining characteristic is anti-Westernism. Soviet theorists predict the further widening of the "anti-imperialist bloc" via the secession of remaining colonial areas from dependence upon the West. And within this wider non-Western or anti-Western grouping in the world, they foresee the gradual but consecutive spread of regimes of the Communist type, with Soviet economic foreign policy as one of the chief instrumentalities of this process. Ultimately, they envision the new Russia-centered international order as world-wide in scope.

This, in brief, is the Soviet working theory of contemporary history. Having suggested at the outset that it poses a serious challenge to the West, and to the United States particularly as the principal Western power, I should like, in conclusion, to reformulate this thesis in more concrete terms. What, precisely, is the Soviet challenge to us in the field of theory? The answer, it seems to me, is that the Soviet working doctrine of history recognizes a basic fact of world development in the twentieth century, or reflects such recognition, whereas Western policy thinking has not hitherto clearly recognized this fact *as* a basic fact and Western grand policy itself suffers as a consequence. The fact in question is the progressive disintegration and breakdown of the world-wide Europe-centered order of the nineteenth century.

Western thinking does increasingly reflect an uneasy awareness that the rise and spread of Russian Communism are not the whole story of what is happening in the world in the present century, and that a policy predicated on the one idea of "containment" of Communism scarcely suffices as the Western response to the world situation. The efforts to fix upon these larger contours of the problem have not, however, been very successful. Western thinking is typified by phrases such as "revolution of rising expectations" or "rising tide of nationalism in the world" or even "anticolonial revolution." They do have the merit of suggesting that something very consequential is happening that is not exactly Soviet-inspired, even though Moscow tries to encourage it and to capitalize upon it, and that Western policy consequently errs insofar as it focuses *exclusive* concern on the containment of the Soviet Union and Communism. But they fail to go to the root of the matter—to the fact that an erstwhile world scheme of things is today in a very advanced stage of decomposition. And while they suggest that the West badly requires a *world* policy as distinguished from a policy of containing Soviet Russia all over the world, they do not yield ideas as to what an effective, or at least relevant, Western response to the present situation might be.

If we take the disintegration of international order as the fundamental fact and trend of the twentieth century—a trend not yet really checked or altered by the two great experiments in world organization undertaken during this century—the challenge to Western thinking becomes a challenge to frame a new world policy in the light of what has happened. If, further, we take international order as something supremely desirable, especially in the nuclear age and dawning space age, then it may appear that the rebuilding of order into the affairs of nations should become the master concept in the world policy of the Western coalition.

Of course, the reconstitution of international order as the goal and guiding principle for Western policy does not mean the restoration of the world of 1914. The nineteenth century is beyond resurrection. The contemporary West can hope that certain values of its civilization will take root and flourish in former dependencies that have now become or are on their way to becoming independent nations. It can work by certain methods to achieve this, not least by the force of example, by a conscious effort to show how successful the open society can be in solving its serious problems and how exciting and satisfying to live in. It can strive to cultivate close and productive relations with these nations in commerce and culture and many other fields. But they cannot be resubordinated to Western political influence or control.

The issue then is whether or not the Western mind and spirit are capable of one more supreme historic impulse of political initiative, whether the West can proceed, first in its thinking and then in the action that flows from thought, beyond the nationalist principle to a concept of international order not predicated upon the hegemony of any one great power or group of powers, or upon the universalization of any one form of internal social-economic system. To make international order in this historically new sense the conscious goal of national policy would evidently mean placing ever-greater emphasis upon the existing machinery of world community, particularly the United Nations and its associated agencies, such as the World Court. But the positive content of such a new internationalism would by no means be confined to that. International order and international organization are related yet distinguishable concepts. Given the existence of several dozen national sovereignties in the present world, international order essentially means the establishment of certain operative norms of orderly behavior of national states in their relations both with each other and with their own peoples. It is open to the Western countries, and above all to the United States, to take the initiative toward the growth of international order so conceived.

NOTES

Chapter 1. On Revolutionary Mass-Movement Regimes

1. Daniel Bell, "Ten Theories in Search of Reality: The Prediction of Soviet Behavior in the Social Sciences," *World Politics,* April, 1958. The article is reprinted in Alexander Dallin (ed.), *Soviet Conduct in World Affairs* (New York: Columbia University Press, 1960), and will be quoted from the latter source.
2. Dallin, *op. cit.,* pp. 3, 5.
3. Carl J. Friedrich (ed.), *Totalitarianism* (Cambridge, Mass.: Harvard University Press, 1954), pp. 335–36.
4. Arendt, *op. cit.,* p. 312.
5. Friedrich and Brzezinski, *op. cit.,* p. 295.
6. V. I. Lenin, "What Is To Be Done?," in *Selected Works* (Moscow, 1946), I, 165.
7. Hans E. Tütsch, "Bourguiba's Tunisia—I," *The New Leader,* February 29, 1960, p. 7.
8. "New Mood Found in Nasser's Egypt," by Dana Adams Schmidt, *New York Times,* December 29, 1959, p. 2. The Pakistani experiment is reported by Paul Grimes in "Pakistanis Study Government by Practice on Local Problems," *ibid.,* June 29, 1960, p. 14.
9. Hans Kohn, *Nationalism: Its Meaning and History* (Princeton, N.J.: D. Van Nostrand Company, 1955), p. 79.
10. The statement was quoted by Khrushchev in his secret report to the Twentieth Party Congress in 1956, and appears in N. S. Khrushchev, *The Crimes of the Stalin Era: Special Report to the 20th Congress of the Communist Party of the Soviet Union* (published as Section Two of *The New Leader,* July 16, 1956, p. S 48).
11. "The Durability of Soviet Despotism," in Dallin, *op. cit.,* p. 268.

Chapter 2. The Dictator and Totalitarianism

1. See, for example, G. M. Gilbert, *The Psychology of Dictatorship* (New York: Ronald Press, 1950); Sigmund Neumann, *Permanent Revolution* (New York: Harper & Brothers, 1942); chap. 2; C. J. Friedrich and Z. Brzezinski, *Totalitarian Dictatorship and Autocracy* (Cambridge, Mass.: Harvard University Press, 1956), chap. 2; and A. Inkeles, "The Totalitarian Mystique," in C. J. Friedrich (ed.), *Totalitarianism* (Cambridge, Mass.: Harvard University Press, 1954).

2. The important earlier contributions include Sigmund Neumann, *Permanent Revolution;* Emil Lederer, *State of the Masses* (New York: W. W. Norton, 1940); Franz Neumann, *Behemoth* (New York: Oxford University Press, 1942; and Hannah Arendt, *The Origins of Totalitarianism* (New York: Harcourt, Brace, 1951).
3. *The Origins of Totalitarianism,* p. 391.
4. *Hitler: A Study in Tyranny,* rev. ed. (New York: Harper & Brothers, 1962), p. 375.
5. *Psychopathology and Politics* (New York: Viking Press, 1960), pp. 173, 186.
6. See, in particular, Merle Fainsod, *How Russia Is Ruled* (Cambridge, Mass.: Harvard University Press, 1953); Z. Brzezinski, *The Permanent Purge* (Cambridge, Mass.: Harvard University Press, 1956); Friedrich, *Totalitarianism;* and Friedrich and Brzezinski, *Totalitarian Dictatorship and Autocracy.*
7. *State of the Masses,* p. 45. See also Arendt, *The Origins of Totalitarianism,* chap. 10, and William Kornhauser, The Politics of Mass Society (Glencoe): The Free Press, 1959). Franz Neumann, while agreeing that the transformation of men into "mass-men" is completed under totalitarianism, disagreed with the position of Lederer according to which the totalitarian state is a state *of* the masses. On this point, see *Behemoth,* pp. 365–67.
8. Friedrich and Brzezinski, *Totalitarian Dictatorship and Autocracy,* 19.
9. *The Origins of Totalitarianism,* p. 245. For Franz Neumann's view, see *Behemoth,* pp. 372–73. He writes there that "National Socialism must carry to an extreme the one process that characterizes the structure of modern society, bureaucratization." The thesis about the "radical efficiency" of totalitarian as distinguished from traditional bureaucracy appears to have been conclusively disproved in the light of what is now known about both the Nazi and the Stalinist bureaucracies. Bullock's investigations have led him to the conclusion, for example, that "The boasted totalitarian organization of the National Socialist State was in practice riddled with corruption and inefficiency under the patronage of the Nazi bosses. . . . At every level there were conflicts of authority, a fight for power and loot, and the familiar accompaniments of gangster rule, 'protection,' graft, and the 'rake-off' " (*Hitler: A Study in Tyranny,* p. 676). In *The German Occupation of Russia* (New York: St. Martin's Press, 1957), Alexander Dallin reaches a similar conclusion with regard to Nazi administration of the occupied territories. The speeches of Nikita Khrushchev and other official Soviet sources of the post-Stalin period provide a mass of illuminating detail on the inefficiency of the Stalinist totalitarian bureaucracy.
10. *The Origins of Totalitarianism,* pp. 315, 335. This distinction appears to be of use in explaining why Mussolini's Italy was only marginally a totalitarian state: the terror was of the "dictatorial" rather than of the "totalitarian" variety.
11. Brzezinski, *The Permanent Purge,* p. 27. Brzezinski adds, in support of a view expressed by Arendt, that "terror within the totalitarian system actually must increase both in scope and in brutality with the growing stability of the regime," and further: "It is also a constant and pervading process of mass coercion, a continuum which persists throughout

the totaliarian era" (*ibid.*).

12. Fainsod, *How Russia Is Ruled,* 1st ed., p. 354.
13. Friedrich and Brzezinski, *Totalitarian Dictatorship and Autocracy,* p. 132. They add: "The total scope and the pervasive and sustained character of totalitarian terror are . . . its unique qualities (*ibid.,* p. 137).
14. *The Permanent Purge,* pp. 30, 36. Brzezinski's argument here appears to be, in part, an elaboration of the suggestion by Arendt that the Stalinist purge, as distinguished from earlier Bolshevik purges, was a means of maintaining a "permanent instability" in Soviet society, such instability being interpreted in turn as a functional requisite of totalitarianism as a system (*The Origins of Totalitarianism,* p. 376n.).
15. *Totalitarianism,* p. 55.
16. *The Origins of Totalitarianism,* pp. 431–32.
17. Friedrich, ed., *Totalitarianism,* pp. 88, 91, 95–96. It may be noted that Inkeles views the "mystique" as a way of characterizing the totalitarian leader as a "psychological type." However, he seems to mean by "totalitarian leader" not solely the dictator but the whole higher leadership or ruling elite. And he explicitly discounts the need to penetrate beyond the ideological "mystique" into the psychology of the dictator as an individual. Indeed, he describes any attempt to trace the dictator's actions "to caprice, to paranoia, or some similar deviant personality manifestation" as a "residual category" type of explanation that can and should be avoided, e.g., by the "mystique" hypothesis (*ibid.,* p. 93).
18. *Totalitarian Dictatorship and Autocracy,* pp. 132, 137.
19. *Behemoth,* pp. 366, 469.
20. In "Notes on the Theory of Dictatorship," Franz Neumann found five essential factors in the modern totalitarian dictatorship: a police state, concentration of power, a monopolistic state party, totalitarian social controls, and reliance upon terror (*The Democratic and Authoritarian State* [Glencoe: The Free Press, 1957], pp. 244–45). In 1953 C. J. Friedrich proposed the following five features: an official ideology, a single mass party ("usually under a single leader"), a near-complete monopoly of control of all means of effective armed combat, similar control of all means of mass communication, and a system of terroristic police control (*Totalitarianism,* pp. 52–53). In *Totalitarian Dictatorship and Autocracy* (pp. 9–10) a sixth feature—central control and direction of the economy—was added to the "syndrome."
21. *Totalitarian Dictatorship and Autocracy,* pp. 17, 18, 26.
22. *Permanent Revolution,* p. 43; *The Origins of Totalitarianism,* pp. 361, 392.
23. *Ibid.,* p. 374. She writes further that "the Leader is irreplaceable because the whole complicated structure of the movement would lose its *raison d'être* without his commands" (*ibid.,* p. 362).
24. For the concept of a "rationalist totalitarianism," see Z. Brzezinski, "Totalitarianism and Rationality," *American Political Science Review,* L (September, 1956), 751–63. Examples of recent criticisms of the concept of totalitarianism are A. J. Groth, "The 'Isms' in Totalitarianism," *ibid.,* LVIII (December, 1964), 888–901; and this writer's "Towards a Comparative Politics of Movement-Regimes," *ibid.,* LV (June, 1961), 281–89.
25. Bullock, *Hitler: A Study in Tyranny,* p. 703. On Hitler's hysterical

outburst on the eve of the war about annihilating his enemies, see Birger Dahlerus, *The Last Attempt* (London: Hutchison, p. 1948), chap. 6; also Gilbert, *The Psychology of Dictatorship*, p. 301. For a full account of Hitler's actions and reactions during the entire crucial period of the war's beginning, see Bullock, chap. 9, esp. pp. 536–59. Also of interest in this general connection is Ivone Kirkpatrick's account of the psychological motivations underlying Mussolini's decision to embark upon the Abyssinian war (*Mussolini: A Study in Power* [New York: Hawthorn Books, 1964], p. 320).

26. N. S. Khrushchev, *The Crimes of the Stalin Era: Special Report to the 20th Congress of the Communist Party of the Soviet Union* (published as Section Two of *The New Leader*, July 16, 1956), p. S48.

27. The menace of the paranoid in the nuclear age has been strongly emphasized by Lasswell. Pointing out that "All mankind might be destroyed by a single paranoid in a position of power who could imagine no grander exit than using the globe as a gigantic funeral pyre," he goes on: "Even a modicum of security under present-day conditions calls for the discovery, neutralization and eventual prevention of the paranoid. And this calls for the overhauling of our whole inheritance of social institutions for the purpose of disclosing and eliminating the social factors that create these destructive types" (*Power and Personality* [New York: W. W. Norton, 1948], p 184). My own remarks above are meant to suggest that, pending the requisite systematic attack upon the problem, it may be possible to devise interim means of dealing with developing situations of this kind before it is too late.

28. *Ideology and Power in Soviet Politics* (New York: Frederick A. Praeger, 1962), pp. 80, 88–89. Fainsod, who in the 1953 first edition of his study of Soviet government had called terror the "linchpin of modern totalitarianism," in the 1963 edition revises this sentence to read: "Every totalitarian regime makes some place for terror in its system of controls' (*How Russia Is Ruled*, 2nd edn., p. 421). See also Allen Kassof, "The Administered Society: Totalitarianism Without Terror," *World Politics*, xvi (July, 1964), pp. 558–75.

29. See, for example, "Was Stalin Really Necessary?" in Alec Nove, *Economic Rationality and Soviet Politics*, or *Was Stalin Really Necessary?*, Frederick A. Praeger (New York, 1964). Soviet second thoughts have been expressed, albeit very cautiously, in the form of criticism of unnecessary "excesses' in the implementation of the collectivization policy by Stalin.

30. Leonard Schapiro, *The Communist Party of the Soviet Union* (New York: Random House, 1959), pp. 428–29. Marshall D. Shulman goes farther and questions "how far 'the system' can be absolved of responsibility for Stalinism, whatever may have been the condition of Stalin himself." He continues: "Perhaps 'the system' bore the main brunt of policy formation. It is reasonable to suppose that, even in a dictatorial society, much of what is done in the name of a leader is necessarily the product of a bureaucracy, and may imply any degree of responsibility from his active guidance to his inattention" (*Stalin's Foreign Policy Reappraised* [Cambridge, Mass: Harvard University Press, 1963], p. 261). This is to disregard the factual evidence from post-Stalin Soviet sources, including Khrushchev's secret report, on the

actualities of decision-making in Stalin's final years. The evidence may, of course, be incomplete and faulty, but it cannot simply be dismissed.

31. Sidney Verba, "Assumptions of Rationality and Non-Rationality in Models of the International System," *World Politics*, XVI (October, 1961), 105. "Non-logical explanations" are here defined as those referring to unconscious psychological pressures in the decision-making individuals.

32. Morton A. Kaplan, "Old Realities and New Myths," *World Politics*, XVII (January, 1965), 359.

33. This is one of the themes, for example, of Arnold Rogow's important study of the career of James Forrestal as an instance of an emotionally disturbed personality rising close to the pinnacle of power. Rogow writes that beyond a certain point counterpressures were generated inside the military establishment that Forrestal headed: "As Forrestal's behavior became more and more tense, he was consulted less by his associates and involved less in decisions." As part of the explanation for this, Rogow states: "Bureaucracies, whether governmental, corporate, or academic, do not welcome in their ranks those who are odd, deviant, or excessively nonconformist in behavior, and the military bureaucracy was no exception" (*James Forrestal: A Study of Personality, Politics, and Policy* [New York: The Macmillan Company, 1963], p. 350).

34. "Political Constitution and Character," *Psychoanalysis and the Psychoanalytic Review*, XLVI, No. 4 (Winter, 1960), 16.

35. "The Selective Effect of Personality on Political Participation," in R. Christie and M. Jahoda, eds., *Studies in the Scope and Method of "The Authoritarian Personality"* (Glencoe: The Free Press, 1964), p. 223. See also in this volume the essay by E. A. Shils, who argues that American "nativist leaders," generally characterized by "strong paranoid tendencies," are unable to develop "the flexible self-control required to build the administrative machinery in their organizations" and for this and other personality-associated reasons have had a "hard row to hoe" (*ibid.*, p. 46).

36. The official handbook of the American Psychiatric Association describes paranoia as "characterized by an intricate, complex, and slowly developing paranoid system, often logically elaborated after a false interpretation of an actual occurrence," and adds: "The paranoid system is particularly isolated from much of the normal stream of consciousness, without hallucinations and with relative intactness and preservation of the remainder of the personality, in spite of a chronic and prolonged course" (*Mental Disorders* [Washington, D. C., 1952], p. 28).

37. For a public formulation of reasoning to this effect, see, in particular, the beginning of Malenkov's address of November 6, 1949 (*Pravda*, November 7, 1949).

38. *Hitler: A Study in Tyranny*, p. 548. A similar view is presented by H. R. Trevor-Roper, who writes also that Nazi Germany's leading politicians "were not a government but a court—a court as negligible in its power of ruling, as incalculable in its capacity for intrigue, as any oriental sultanate" (*The Last Days of Hitler* [New York: The Macmillan Company, 1947], p. 1).

39. This description of the situation under Stalin is based on Khrushchev, *Crimes of of the Stalin Era*, S61–S62. See also the note by Boris Nicolaevsky, *ibid.*, S61.

Chapter 3.   STALIN, BUKHARIN, AND HISTORY AS CONSPIRACY

1. See in particular W. G. Krivitsky: *In Stalin's Secret Service* (New York: Harper & Brothers, 1939) and Alexander Orlov: *The Secret History of Stalin's Crimes* (New York: Random House, 1953).
2. *Memoirs: 1921–1941*, translated by T. Shebunina in collaboration with Y. Kapp (Cleveland and New York: World Publising Co., 1963), pp. 426–27.
3. *Documents of the Twenty-second Congress of the CPSU* (New York: Crosscurrents Press, 1961), I, 228.
4. This and all further references to Khrushchev's secret report are based on the text as originally printed in *The New York Times* for June 5, 1956 and reprinted in *The Crimes of the Stalin Era* (New York: *The New Leader*, 1956), with annotations by Boris I. Nicolaevsky.
5. Joseph Stalin: *Mastering Bolshevism* (New York: New Century Publishers, 1946), p. 45.
6. J. V. Stalin: *Works* (Moscow: Foreign Language Publishing House, 1954), XI, 57.
7. *Mastering Bolshevism*, pp. 26–27.
8. For an account of the Right Opposition see Robert V. Daniels: *The Conscience of the Revolution: Communist Opposition in Soviet Russia* (Cambridge: Harvard University Press, 1960), Chapter 13. A full-scale treatment of the development of the views of the right-wing group in the 1920's will be presented in a forthcoming study by Stephen F. Cohen: *Bukharin and Russian Bolshevism.*
9. Boris Souvarine, *Stalin: A Critical Survey of Bolshevism* (New York: Alliance Book Corporation, 1939), pp. 482–85.
10. For an account of this meeting, see Leonard Schapiro: *The Communist Party of the Soviet Union.* (New York: Random House, 1959), p. 373.
11. There was no official announcement of this meeting. An account appears in Uralov (pseudonym of Abdurakhman Avtorkhanov, a Party official and historian then living in the U.S.S.R.): *The Reign of Stalin* (London: Bodley Head, 1953), pp. 43–47. Many Western specialists accept this account as on the whole trustworthy, although there is some dispute about the particulars, e.g., whether the reported meeting was a full plenary session as reported by Avtorkhanov or a more informal meeting of high-ranking persons within the Central Committee.
12. Norman Cameron: "Paranoid Conditions and Paranoia," in *American Handbook of Psychiatry* (New York: Basic Books, 1959), p. 519. Dr. Cameron adds that the malevolent pseudo-community may be conceived as a gang of international spies, a secret police force, or a racial or religious group. The official handbook of the American Psychiatric Association describes paranoia as "characterized by an intricate, complex, and slowly developing paranoid system, often logically elaborated after a false interpretation of an actual occurrence," and adds: "The paranoid system is particularly isolated from much of the

normal stream of consciousness, without hallucinations and with relative intactness and preservation of the remainder of the personality, in spite of a chronic and prolonged course" (*Mental Disorders* [Washington, D. C.: American Psychiatric Association, 1952], p. 28).

13. On this point Isaac Deutscher writes: "Among all the documents of the Nuremberg trial of the Nazi leaders not a single one contains as much as a hint at the alleged Nazi fifth column in the Soviet Government and army. Could there be a more eloquent refutation of the purge trials than that amazing gap in the otherwise abundant evidence of Hitler's preparations for the war?" (*Stalin: A Political Biography* [New York: Vintage Books, 1960], p. 379 n.). Deutscher does suggest, however, that Marshal Tukhachevsky and his military associates were planning a *coup d'état* against Stalin, entirely on their own. It must be said that no evidence has appeared to support this hypothesis.

14. *Vsesoiuznoe soveshchanie o merakh uluchsheniia podgotovki nauchnopedagogicheskikh kadrov po istoricheskim naukam* (Moscow, 1964), p. 298.

15. *Op. cit.,* p. 426.

16. F. Beck and W. Godin: *Russian Purge and the Extraction of Confession* (New York: Viking Press, 1951), p. 215.

17. *The Origins of Totalitarianism* (New York: Harcourt, Brace, 1951), p. 376 n. For an elaborated interpretation of the Stalinist purge in terms of postulated functional needs of the Soviet system, see Zbigniew K. Brzezinski: *The Permanent Purge: Politics in Soviet Totalitarianism* (Cambridge, Mass.: Harvard University Press, 1956), esp. Chapters 5 and 10.

18. For the computations underlying the estimate of nine million, see Alexander Weissberg *The Accused* (New York: Simon and Schuster, 1951), pp. 318–25. Boris Nicolaevsky has estimated that from five to eight million persons were victims of the Great Purge. The number of those who were executed at the time has been estimated by a high Yugoslav Communist source at three million (V. Dedijer: *Tito* [New York: Simon and Schuster, 1953], p. 106).

19. Speaking of paranoid delusions, Dr. Otto Fenichel writes that "the hatred is never projected at random but is felt usually in connection with something that has a basis in reality. Patients with persecutory ideas are extremely sensitive to criticism and use the awareness of actual insignificant criticisms as the reality basis for their delusions. This basis has, of course, to be extremely exaggerated and distorted in order to be made available for this purpose. Just as the 'monsters' in a dream may represent an 'amoeba' from daily life, so the monster of a paranoid delusion may be a misapprehended real microbe" (*The Psychoanalytic Theory of Neurosis* [New York, Norton, 1945], p. 428). Elsewhere we read that the paranoid individual "is constantly looking for hidden meanings in the statements and activities of those about him" (R. M. Dorcus and G. W. Schaffer: *Textbook of Abnormal Psychology* [Baltimore: Williams and Wilkins, 1950], p. 438).

20. N. Leites and E. Bernaut: *Ritual of Liquidation: The Case of the Moscow Trials* (Glencoe: The Free Press, 1954), p. 111. These writers express here the view that the defendants "accepted" these rules of translation because (1) they shared a contemptuous belief that the

masses can only understand a simple and extreme story, and (2) they had come to feel that the fables they agreed to tell were in some special sense true. I believe, on the contrary, that their acceptance of the rules of translation was strictly a forced acceptance, and that they did not consider the fables true even in some special sense.

21. *The Case of the Anti-Soviet Trotskyite Center* (Moscow: People's Commissariat of Justice of the U.S.S.R., 1937), pp. 188–89. Vyshinsky replied at this point: "I know what you mean by algebra, but I must now deal not with algebra but with facts." Apropos this exchange, George F. Kennan, then Second Secretary of the American Embassy in Moscow, who attended the Piatakov trial as an official U.S. observer, commented as follows in a memorandum to the State Department dated February 13, 1937: "Those who attended the sessions and watched the bearing and the faces of the State's Attorney and the defendants had the distinct impression that they were talking in symbols, — that many of the expressions which they used repeatedly throughout the proceedings had different meanings in their minds than in the minds of the spectators, — that these expressions, in other words, were algebraic equivalents, behind which the real values were concealed. It seems almost certain, for example, that the phrase "terrorism," which was used so frequently throughout the proceedings, was understood by all the participants in the spectacle to mean simply illegal opposition activity." (United States Department of State, *Foreign Relations of the United States. Diplomatic Papers. The Soviet Union 1933–1939* [Washington: U.S. Government Printing Office, 1952], pp. 363–64.)

22. *Stalin: A Political Biography*, pp. 377–78.

23. *XVII S'ezd vsesoiuznoi kommunisticheskoi partii (b). Stenograficheskii otchet* (Moscow, 1934), pp. 128–29.

24. *Ibid.*, pp. 13–14.

25. *In Stalin's Secret Service*, pp. 1–4. For a detailed and convincing argument that the Soviet leadership until the Great Purge was divided over the main lines of its foreign policy, with Stalin and Bukharin as exponents of the two main opposing positions, see Robert M. Slusser: "The Role of the Foreign Ministry," in Ivo J. Lederer, (ed.): *Russian Foreign Policy: Essays in Historical Perspective* (New Haven: Yale University Press, 1962).

26. "We even met prisoners who had been prophesying the Hitler pact since 1938, simply on the basis of the categories that had been arrested" (Beck and Godin: *op. cit.,* p. 234).

27. The Aesopian message was very probably intended for the Western world as well as for Soviet and foreign communist circles. In this connection we have Bukharin's own word for it that he consciously endeavored to communicate messages to the outside world by the use of veiled language in press articles. In one of his meetings with Boris Nicolaevsky in Paris in early 1936, Bukharin said that his unsigned editorial articles in *Izvestia* written after the murder of Kirov had contained various passages in which he had tried to reveal by indirection the substance of issues then under debate behind the scenes in higher Party circles. I am indebted to Mr. Nicolaevsky for his permission to reveal this here.

28. To say that the Western world failed to decipher Bukharin's messages and grasp the meaning of developments afoot in Russia at that time would be putting it kindly. Hugo Dewar describes, for example, as follows the reaction of *The Times* of London in 1936 and 1937: "The trials, it thought, reflected the triumph of Stalin's 'nationalist' policy over that of the revolutionary diehards. The conservative forces, with the overwhelming support of the nation, had now demonstrably gained the day" ("How They Saw the Moscow Trials," *Survey*, April, 1962, p. 94).

29. Orlov: *The Secret History of Stalin's Crimes*, pp. 280–81. I am again indebted to Mr. Nicolaevsky for pointing out to me in this connection that the three principal defendants in the 1938 trial, Bukharin, Rykov, and Krestinsky, all had children with whom they were very close, whereas Yenukidze and Karkhan, both of whom would have been in Stalin's eyes logical candidates for major roles as defendants in this trial, did not. These two men were executed in 1937 without public trial.

31. *Escape to Adventure* (Boston: Little, Brown, 1950), p. 74.

32. An important rule to bear in mind in translating Bukharin's Aesopian language in the trial is that a certain spacing is necessarily involved. He cannot, without being too obvious, present a whole sequence of his own points in any one passage, but must confine himself to saying one thing. So we must look for the sequence of his argument in a series of separate passages each of which contains some one component of it. A telltale sign of the presence of an Aesopian point in a given passage is a certain suggestion of incoherence or lack of full coherence at this place. A further presupposition of his mode of communicating is that symbols have multiple meanings. In one of its meanings a given symbol may belong to the logic of the show trial; in another, to that of the anti-trial. Thus "Trotsky" may, as in an instance mentioned above, mean "counter-revolutionary" in terms of the show trial and "person living abroad" in terms of the anti-trial. Bukharin refers in one place to "my terminology" in order to convey that he is using words in special ways of his own.

Chapter 4. THE STALIN HERITAGE IN SOVIET POLICY

1. Vladimir Dedijer, *Tito* (New York: Simon and Schuster, 1953), p. 296.
2. *Pravda,* February 10, 1946.
3. *Ibid.*
4. *Ibid.,* June 20, 1950.
5. *Ibid.,* June 27, 1951.
6. Joseph Stalin, *Economic Problems of Socialism in the U.S.S.R.* (New York; International Publishers, 1952), pp. 21–22.
7. *Bol'shevik,* No. 16, 1951, p. 61.
8. *Pravda,* November 7, 1949.
9. *Bol'shevik,* No. 16, 1951, p. 61.
10. *Kommunist,* No. 2, 1953, p. 19.
11. *Pravda,* February 6, 1953.
12. N. S. Khrushchev, *Crimes of the Stalin Era*, p. S49.

13. *Kommunist,* No. 2, 1953, p. 22.
14. *Ibid.*
15. Stalin, *op. cit.,* p. 30.
16. *Kommunist,* No. 12, 1953, p. 27.
17. Stalin, *op. cit.,* p. 28.

Chapter 5. SEVERAL STALINS

1. Zhores A. Medvedev, *The Rise and Fall of T. D. Lysenko* (New York: Columbia University Press, 1969).
2. Nadezhda Mandelstam, *Hope Against Hope: A Memoir* (New York: Atheneum, 1970).
3. L. Trotsky, *My Life* (New York: Grosset and Dunlap, 1960), pp. 481, 506, 512–13.
4. Alexander Solzhenitsyn, *The First Circle,* trans. Thomas P. Whitney (New York: Harper & Row, 1968), pp. 101–102.
5. E. H. Carr, *Socialism in One Country* (New York: The Macmillan Company, 1958), I, 174–86.
6. Isaac Deutscher, *Stalin: A Political Biography* (New York: Oxford University Press, 1949), pp. 273, 295, 318, 322, 326.
7. G. F. Kennan, *Russia and the West under Lenin and Stalin* (Boston: Little, Brown, 1960), p. 248. For Djilas' observations see *Conversations with Stalin* (New York: Harcourt Brace and World, 1962), *passim.* See also Kennan's later statement: "Stalin's greatness as a dissimulator was an integral part of his greatness as a statesman" (*Memoirs: 1925–1950.* [Boston: Little, Brown, 1967], p. 279).
8. Boris Souvarine, Stalin: *A Critical Survey of Bolshevism* (London: Secker and Warburg, n.d.), p. 134; and Francis B. Randall, *Stalin's Russia; An Historical Reconsideration* (New York: The Free Press, 1965), p. 34.
9. On this conflict, see Richard Pipes, *The Formation of the Soviet Union* (2nd ed., New York: Atheneum, 1968), pp. 270–89; and Moshe Lewin, *Lenin's Last Struggle* (New York: Pantheon Books, 1968), chap. 7.
10. See especially Moshe Lewin, *Russian Peasants and Soviet Power* (Evanston: Northwestern University Press, 1968); and Alec Nove, *An Economic History of the U.S.S.R.* (London: The Penguin Press, 1969). Also, Stephen F. Cohen's forthcoming study on *Bukharin and Russian Bolshevism.*
11. Sidney Hook, *The Hero in History* (Boston: Beacon Press, 1943), pp. 166–70.
12. Svetlana Alliluyeva, *Twenty Letters to a Friend* (New York: Harper & Row, 1967), p. 197. In her later book, Alliluyeva takes issue with the idea that her father's behavior might be attributed to "madness" (*Tol'ko odin god* [New York: Harper & Row, 1969], p. 311). What are of concern here, however, are her direct observations. For an evaluation of her testimony on Stalin, see the present writer's "Svetlana Alliluyeva as Witness of Stalin," *Slavic Review* (June, 1968).
13. *Memoirs: 1925–1950,* p. 279.
14. Charles Bohlen, *The Transformation of American Foreign Policy* (New York: W. W. Norton, 1969), p. 23. Bohlen interprets Stalin's outburst

as a tactical device to express irritation and concern at Churchill's reluctance to fix a definite date for the overseas invasion.

15. Leonard Schapiro, *The Communist Party of the Soviet Union* (New York: Random House, 1959), p. 428.
16. Emile Kraepelin, *Clinical Psychiatry* (New York: The Macmillan Co., 1902), p. 316.
17. *Khrushchev Remembers* (Boston: Little, Brown, 1970), p. 307. This description of Stalin's inner mechanism of distrust is remarkably akin to that of Svetlana Alliluyeva. See her *Twenty Letters to a Friend* (New York: Harper & Row, 1967), esp. p. 78.
18. *Khrushchev Remembers*, pp. 259–61, 309.
19. *Ibid.*, p. 246.

Chapter 6. THE IMAGE OF DUAL RUSSIA

1. L. Barrive, *Osvoboditel'noe dvizhenie v tsarstvovanie Aleksandra Vtorogo. Istoricheskie ocherki* (1909), p. 11.
2. P. N. Miliukov, *Russia Today and Tomorrow* (1922), p. 10.
3. Miliukov, *Ocherki po istorii Russkoi kul'tury* (1904), I, 206.
4. V. O. Kliuchevsky, *Kurs Russkoi istorii* (1937), III, 11.
5. A. I. Herzen, *Izbrannie filosofskie proizvedeniia* (1946), II, 253.
6. Herzen, *Dvizhenie obshchestvennoi mysli v Rossii* (1907), p. 181.
7. Donald MacKenzie Wallace, *Russia* (1912), p. 379.
8. Michael Karpovich, "Russia's Revolution in Focus," *The New Leader* (November 4, 1957), p. 15.
9. Herzen, *Dvizhenie obshchestvennoi mysli*, p. 170.
10. N. L. Brodsky, *Rannie slavianofily* (1910), p. 89.
11. *Ibid.*, pp. 98–99.
12. Herzen, *Dvizhenie obshchestvennoi mysli*, p. 137.
13. Quoted by Alexander Kornilov, *Modern Russian History* (1943), II, 208.
14. Miliukov, *Russia Today and Tomorrow*, p. 11.
15. R. V. Ivanov-Razumnik, *Istoriia russkoi obshchestvennoi mysli* (1914), II, 109.
16. Lenin, *Selected Works* (1947), II, 181, 221.
17. Quoted by Martin Buber, *Paths in Utopia* (1949), p. 104.
18. *Kommunisticheskaia partiia v rezoliutsiiakh i resheniiakh s"ezdov, konferentsii i plenumov Ts.K.* (1954), II, 555.
19. G. M. Malenkov, *O zadachakh partiinykh organizatsii v oblasti pro-myshlennosti i transporta* (1941), p. 39.
20. *Pravda*, June 20, 1950.
21. Vladimir Dudintsev, *Ne khlebom edinym* (*Not By Bread Alone*) (1957), p. 196.
22. M. E. Aliger (ed.), *Literaturnaia Moskva. Literaturno-khudozhest-vennyi sbornik II* (1956), pp. 510, 513.

Chapter 7. STALIN AND THE USES OF PSYCHOLOGY

1. *The Situation in Biological Science. Proceedings of the Lenin Academy*

of Agricultural Sciences of the U.S.S.R. Session: July 31–August 7, 1948. Verbatim Report (1949), p. 274.
2. *Ibid.*, p. 37.
3. Nathan Leites, *A Study of Bolshevism* (1953), pp. 67, 84.
4. *The Situation in Biological Science*, pp. 614–15.
5. *Ibid.*, p. 615.
6. "Ekonomicheskie problemy sotsializma v SSSR," *Voprosy filosofii*, No. 5, 1952, pp. 6, 8, 47.
7. B. M. Kedrov, "O materialisticheskom ponimanii zakonov prirody," *Voprosy filosofii*, No. 6, 1952, pp. 69, 71.
8. *History of the Communist Party of the Soviet Union (Bolshevik): Short Course* (1945), pp. 114–15.
9. *Pravda*, April 19, 1952.
10. *Ibid.*, September 23, 1949.
11. *Ibid.*, September 27, 1949.
12. *Ibid.*, July 1, 1950.
13. *Ibid.*, July 2, 1950.
14. B. M. Teplov, *Sovetskaia psikhologicheskaia nauka za 30 let* (1947), p. 14.
15. N. P. Antonov, "Dialekticheskii materializm—teoreticheskaia osnova psikhologii," *Voprosy filosofii*, No. 1, 1953, p. 195.
16. A. V. Petrovsky, "K itogam soveshchaniia po psikhologii," *Voprosy filosofii*, No. 5, 1953, p. 261.
17. A. A. Smirnov, "Sostoianie psikhologii i ee perestroika na osnove ucheniia I. P. Pavlova," *Sovetskaia pedagogika*, No. 8, 1952, p. 76.
18. In this brief summary of earlier trends, I have followed the interpretation set forth by Raymond A. Bauer in his important study *The New Man in Soviet Psychology* (1952).

Chapter 8.   THE POLITICS OF SOVIET DE-STALINIZATION

1. S. M. Dubrovsky, "Protiv idealizatsii deiatel'nosti Ivana IV," *Voprosy istorii*, No. 8, 1956, p. 128.
2. All following citations of the report are taken from Khrushchev, *Crimes of the Stalin Era.*
3. Alexander Orlov, *The Secret History of Stalin's Crimes* (New York, 1953), p. 206.
4. Dubrovsky, *loc. cit.*
5. *Ibid.*
6. *Pravda*, February 10, 1946.
7. V. N. Sheviakov, "K voprosu ob oprichnine pri Ivane IV," *Voprosy istorii*, No. 9, 1956, p. 77.
8. *Pravda*, July 2, 1956.
9. *Ibid.*
10. Seweryn Bialer, "I Chose Truth," *News from Behind the Iron Curtain*, No. 10, October, 1956, pp. 9–15.
11. *Pravda*, October 29, 1961.

Chapter 9. RULING PERSONALITIES IN FOREIGN POLICY

1. Karl Marx and Friedrich Engels, *The Russian Menace to Europe,* Paul W. Blackstock and Bert F. Hoselitz, eds. (Chicago: The Free Press of Glencoe, 1952), pp. 26, 27.
2. Nikolai Turgenev, *Rossiia i russkie* (Moscow, 1907–8), Part III, p. 155. This book was originally published outside of Russia, where the author was living in political exile.
3. *Ibid.,* p. 160.
4. R. Wipper, *Ivan Grozny* (Moscow, 1947), pp. 171–72.
5. *Ibid.,* p. 172.
6. Michael T. Florinsky, *Russia: A History and an Interpretation* (New York: The Macmillan Company, 1955), I, 335.
7. Marc Raeff, *Michael Speransky: Statesman of Imperial Russia* (The Hague, 1957), p. 30.
8. G. H. Bolsover, "Aspects of Russian Foreign Policy, 1815–1914," in R. Pares and A. J. P. Taylor, eds., *Essays Presented to Sir Lewis Namier* (New York: St. Martin's Press, 1956), p. 324.
9. Andrei A. Lobanov-Rostovsky, *Russia and Asia* (Ann Arbor, Mich.: George Wahr Publishing Co., 1951), pp. 137–38, 141.
10. Bolsover, *op. cit.,* p. 325.
11. A. E. Presniakov, *Apogei samoderzhaviia. Nikolai I* (1925), p. 61.
12. Bolsover, *op. cit.,* pp. 323, 325.
13. Florinsky, *op. cit.,* II, 826.
14. Gregor Alexinsky, *Modern Russia* (London, 1913), p. 175.
15. Louis Fischer, *The Soviets in World Affairs* (New York: Alfred A. Knopf, 1960), p. 40.
16. Cited by E. H. Carr, *The Bolshevik Revolution, 1917–1923* (New York: The Macmillan Company, 1951), I, 220.
17. V. I. Lenin, *Selected Works,* II, 840.
18. *Ibid.,* p. 850.
19. *Izvestiia,* January 30, 1924.
20. Some interesting documentary materials on Lenin's part in organizing Narkomindel are cited in a recent Soviet source, S. Iu. Vygodskii, *V. I. Lenin—rukovoditel' vneshnei politiki sovetskogo gosudarstva 1917–1923* (Leningrad, 1960), chap. ii. However, omission of all reference to Trotsky's role detracts from the scholarly value of this work.
21. Cited by P. N. Miliukov, in *Rossiia na perelome* (Paris, 1927), I, 317.
22. *Izvestiia,* January 30, 1924.
23. *Ibid.*
24. Khrushchev, *Crimes of the Stalin Era,* p. 21.
25. Alexander Barmine, *One Who Survived* (New York, 1945), p. 213.
26. Merle Fainsod, *How Russia Is Ruled* (Cambridge, Mass.: Harvard University Press, 1953), p. 213. Fainsod attributes this information to an unnamed "highly placed informant familiar with the Commissariat of Foreign Affairs under Litvinov in the late thirties."
27. Khrushchev, *op. cit.,* p. 62.
28. *Ibid.,* pp. 61, 62.
29. *Ibid.,* p. 61, footnote by Boris E. Nicolaevsky.
30. Captain N. Ruslanov, "Voskhozhdenie Malenkova," *Sotsialisticheskii Vestnik,* Nos. 7–8, July–August 1953, pp. 128–29. Captain Ruslanov is

described in an editorial footnote as a recent *émigré* who came to the West in 1949.

31. For evidence bearing on this point, see W. G. Krivitsky, *In Stalin's Secret Service* (New York, 1939), esp. chap. 1; also Isaac Deutscher, *Stalin: A Political Biography* (New York: Alfred A. Knopf, 1960), p. 421 n. For Stalin's role in initiating the pact with Hitler, see R. J. Sontag and J. S. Beddie (eds.), *Nazi-Soviet Relations, 1939–1941* (New York, 1948), esp. p. 76: "Herr Molotov raised his glass to Stalin, remarking that it had been Stalin who—through his speech of March of this year, which had been well understood in Germany—had brought about the reversal in political relations."

32. *Pravda*, September 3, 1945.
33. *Ibid.*, May 25, 1945.
34. Khrushchev, *op. cit.*, p. 46.
35. *Ibid.*, p. 48.
36. *Ibid.*, pp. 48, 60.
37. Walter Bedell Smith, *My Three Years in Moscow* (Philadelphia and New York: J. B. Lippincott Company, 1950), p. 55.
38. Nathan Leites, *The Operational Code of the Politburo* (New York: McGraw-Hill Book Company, 1951).
39. Franz Borkenau, *European Communism* (New York: Harper & Brothers, 1953), pp. 521, 524.
40. Max Beloff, *The Foreign Policy of Soviet Russia* (London and New York: Oxford University Press, 1949), II, 388.
41. Seweryn Bialer, "I Chose Truth," in *News From Behind the Iron Curtain*, V, No. 10 (October, 1956), pp. 9–15.
42. *Izvestiia*, February 21, 1956.
43. U.S. Congress, Senate Committee on Government Operations, *National Policy Machinery in the Soviet Union* (Washington, D.C.: Government Printing Office, 1960), p. 21.

Chapter 10. STALINISM AND COLD WAR

1. Ts. A. Stepanian, "Neodolimoe dvizheniie k kommunizmu," *Voprosy filosofii*, No. 2, 1948, p. 87.
2. *Ibid.*, p. 86.
3. Stalin, *Sochineniia* (1948), X 51.
4. Stepanian, *op. cit.*, p. 86.
5. Speech to the Sixth Congress of the Socialist Unity Party of Germany, *Izvestia*, January 17, 1963.
6. Speech of Khrushchev to the Twenty-Second Party Congress, *XXII S"ezd*, I, 50. See also the Resolution of the Twenty-First Party Congress in 1959, according to which "even before the complete triumph of socialism on earth, while capitalism still exists on a part of the globe, a

Chapter 11. DIALECTICS OF COEXISTENCE

1. Joseph Stalin, *Works* (Moscow, 1954), VII, 268.

2. *XXII S"ezd Kommunisticheskoi Partii Sovetskogo Soiuza. Stenografiicheskii otchet* (Moscow, 1962), II, 353–54 (hereinafter cited as *XXII S"ezd*).
3. *Ibid.*; I, 447–48.
4. N. S. Khrushchev, *Rech' na III S"ezde Rumynskoi Rabochei Partii* (Moscow, 1960), p. 31.
5. Speech to the Sixth Congress of the Socialist Unity Party of Germany, *Izvestia*, January 17, 1963.
6. Speech of Khrushchev to the Twenty-Second Party Congress, *XXII S"ezd*, I, 50. See also the Resolution of the Twenty-First Party Congress in 1959, according to which "even before the complete triumph of socialism on earth, while capitalism still exists on a part of the globe, a genuine possibility will arise of excluding world war from the life of human society (Leo Gruliow [ed.], *Current Soviet Policies* [New York: Columbia University Press, 1960], III, 214).
7. G. F. Hudson, *et al, The Sino-Soviet Dispute* (New York: Frederick A. Praeger, 1962), p. 226.
8. *Pravda*, October 14, 1959.
9. *Ibid.*, January 17, 1962.
10. I. A. Krasin, "V. I. Lenin i problema mirnogo sosushchestvovaniia," *Voprosy filosofii*, No. 9, 1960, pp. 18, 19.
11. Gruliow, *Current Soviet Policies* (New York: Frederick A. Praeger, 1957), II, 37.
12. *XXII S"ezd*, III, 272.
13. Krasin, *op. cit.*, p. 20.
14. For a full discussion of the formula, see "Revolutionary Dialectics and How to Appraise Imperialism," in *Red Flag*, No. 1, January, 1963.
15. G. Starushenko, "Mirnoe sosushchestvovanie i revoliutsiia," *Kommunist*, 1962, No. 2, p. 84.
16. V. Korolov, "Mifotvorchestvo Professora Meissnera," *Politicheskoe samoobrazovanie*, 1963, No. 3, p. 142.
17. "Mirnoe sosushchestvovanie i ideologicheskaia bor'ba," *Kommunist*, 1959, No. 16, p. 11.
18. Krasin, *op. cit.*, p. 21.
19. V. I. Lenin, *Works* (Moscow, 1961), XXXVIII, 253–54.
20. A. E. Kahn, "The Chemical Industry," in Walter Adams (ed.), *The Structure of American Industry: Some Case Studies* (3d ed.; New York: The Macmillan Company, 1961), p. 247. I am indebted to Professor Kahn for advice and suggestions for further reading on this subject.
21. *Pravda*, January 17, 1962.
22. "Mirnoe sosushchestvovanie i ideologicheskaia bor'ba," *Kommunist*, 1959, No. 16, p. 8. Krasin uses a similar but briefer formula, saying that the need is "to direct the struggle of the two classes heading the two world systems into such channels as would not lead to wars." (*Voprosy filosofii*, No. 9, 1960, p. 20.)
23. Stalin, *Economic Problems of Socialism in the U.S.S.R.*, p. 30.
24. A. Arzumanian, "O kharaktere sovremennoi epokhi," in *Nekotorye problemy teorii i praktiki stroitel'stva kommunizma* (Moscow, 1961), p. 191.
25. Speech to the Twenty-second Party Congress, *XXII S"ezd*, II, 576.

26. *Pravda,* January 25, 1961.
27. *Izvestia,* December 14, 1962.
28. *Pravda,* July 18, 1962.
29. Krasin, *op. cit.,* p. 19. For another reflection of the same idea, see the Resolution of the Twenty-first Party Congress, according to which "Extensive development of world trade, cultural exchange and other forms of intercourse among peoples must play an important role in relieving international tension and strengthening mutual trust." (Gruliow, *op. cit.,* III, 214.)
30. *Izvestia,* December 14, 1962.
31. Krasin, *op. cit.,* pp. 20–21.
32. D. B. Levin, "Problema obespecheniia mira i osnovnye nachala mezhdunarodnogo prava," *Sovetskoe gosudarstvo i pravo,* 1958, No. 6, p. 36.
33. Krasin, *op. cit.,* p. 21.
34. "Whence the Differences? A Reply to Comrade Thorez and Other Comrades," *The People's Daily,* February 27, 1963.

Chapter 12. RUSSIA, THE WEST, AND WORLD ORDER

1. *The New York Times,* November 7, 1958.
2. Lenin, *Selected Works,* II, 854.
3. *Ibid.,* pp. 853, 854.
4. Wladimir Weidlé, *Russia: Absent and Present* (New York: The John Day Company, 1952), p. 44.
5. E. H. Carr, *Socialism in One Country, 1924–1926* (New York: The Macmillan Company, 1958), p. 60.
6. Lenin, *op. cit.,* p. 44.
7. Nikolai Bukharin, *Ekonomika perekhodnogo perioda* (Moscow, 1920), p. 153.
8. I. V. Stalin, *Voprosy leninizma* (Moscow, 1947), pp. 431, 432–33.
9. *Materialy vsesoiuznogo soveshchaniia zaveduiushchikh kafedrami obshchestvennykh nauk* (Moscow, 1958), pp. 184–85.
10. *Ibid.,* pp. 188–90.
11. *Ibid.,* pp. 190–91.
12. *Ibid.,* p. 192.
13. *Pravda,* July 9, 1958.
14. *Materialy vsesoiuznogo soveshchaniia . . . ,* p. 192.

INDEX

Adorno, T. W., 23
Adzhubei, Alexei, 253
Aksakov, Konstantin, 126–128
Alexander I, Czar, 208, 209
Alexander II, Czar, 126, 208, 209, 210
Alexander III, Czar, 208, 209, 210
Alliluyeva, Svetlana, 104, 105, 115
Anarchism or Socialism? (Stalin), 109
Anti-Party group, 197–198, 278
Anti-Semitism, 110, 188
Anti-Soviet Bloc of Rights and Trotskyites, 51–54, 63, 71
Antonov, N. P., 160
Arendt, Hannah, 5, 21, 25–27, 28, 34, 66
Arms control, 257
Arzumanian, 278
Austrian peace treaty (1955), 238
Authoritarian Personality, The (Adorno), 23
Autocracy, 178, 206–207, 212, 216, 222
Ayub Khan, Mohammed, 11

Bakunin, Mikhail, 127
Beck, 65
Behemoth (Neumann), 25
Bell, Daniel, 4
Beloff, Max, 222
Beria, Lavrenti P., 190, 192, 195, 197, 199, 200
Berlin, 257
Bessonov, 77
Bohlen, Charles, 115
Bohr, Niels, 150
Bolshevik Party, *see* Communist Party
Bolshevism, 5, 135, 146–147, 222
Bolsover, G. H., 206
Borodin, Mikhail, 10
Bourguiba, Habib, 6, 10
Brest-Litovsk, Treaty of, 56, 60, 62, 72, 212
Brodsky, N. L., 127

Brzezinski, Zbigniew, 5, 26, 27, 35
Bukharin, Nikolai I., 35–36, 49, 51, 52, 56–65, 73–86, 109, 134, 213, 214, 270, 277
Bulganin, Nikolai, 53, 60, 61
Bullock, Alan, 21, 44
Burdzhalov, 104
Bykov, K. M., 153, 154–156, 163, 164, 166, 167

Capitalist encirclement, 94–96
Carr, E. H., 108, 109, 110, 111
Catherine II (the Great), Czarina, 207, 208
Chernov, 61
Chernyshevsky, N. G., 131, 132, 135
Chesnokov, D. I., 97–98
Chiang Kai-shek, 6, 10
Chicherin, G. V., 213, 214, 215
China, 90, 185, 241, 250, 272, 275, 278
Churchill, Sir Winston, 115, 133, 137, 182
Civil War, 104, 113
Clemenceau, Georges, 215
Coexistence, doctrines of, 225, 241–261 *passim*
Cold War, 42, 88, 95, 277
    and coexistence, 241–261
    ideology of, 229
    propaganda of, 234
    Soviet definitions of, 246
    Stalinist theory of, 250
Collective leadership, 191, 222
Collectivization program, 21, 35, 36, 57, 58, 59, 62, 104, 111, 113
Cominform, 87
Communist International, 51
Communist Manifesto (Marx), 266
Communist Party, 6, 29, 134, 175–176, 178–179, 216, 223
    factionalism in, 197–202
    See also names of Party congresses

299